MW01233525

*Nursing & Empire*

# Nursing & Empire

GENDERED LABOR AND MIGRATION

FROM INDIA TO THE UNITED STATES

Sujani K. Reddy

*The University of North Carolina Press    Chapel Hill*

© 2015 The University of North Carolina Press
All rights reserved
Manufactured in the United States of America
Set in Miller by Westchester Publishing Services
The paper in this book meets the guidelines for permanence and durability
of the Committee on Production Guidelines for Book Longevity of the Council
on Library Resources. The University of North Carolina Press has been a
member of the Green Press Initiative since 2003.

Cover illustrations: Vintage template (background), depositphotos.com, © maxim;
caduceus, depositphotos.com, © okumer

Library of Congress Cataloging-in-Publication Data
Reddy, Sujani K., author.
    Nursing & empire : gendered labor and migration from India to the United States /
Sujani K. Reddy.
        p. ; cm.
    Includes bibliographical references and index.
    ISBN 978-1-4696-2507-2 (pbk : alk. paper)—ISBN 978-1-4696-2508-9 (ebook)
    I. Title.
    [DNLM:   1. Nurses, International—history—India.   2. Nurses, International—
history—United States.   3. Nursing—manpower—India.   4. Nursing—manpower—
United States.   5. Emigration and Immigration—history—India.   6. Emigration and
Immigration—history—United States.   7. History of Nursing—India.   8. History of
Nursing—United States.   9. History, 20th Century—India.   10. History, 20th Century—
United States.   11. Women, Working—history—India.   12. Women, Working—history—
United States. WY 11 JI4]
    RT86.73
    610.73—dc23
                                                                                                2015010516

THIS BOOK WAS DIGITALLY PRINTED.

*To the women,*

*both kin and kindred spirits,*

*who pass their strength,*

*courage, wisdom, and (her)stories*

*through me*

# Contents

# Acknowledgments

This book has been such a long journey, and along the way, I have benefited from the invaluable assistance, unconditional support, and sustaining inspiration of too many people to mention in one note. Forgive me for my oversights. I must begin by giving thanks to all of the nurses who shared their stories with me. I am especially grateful to Aleyamma George, Aleyamma Eapen, and Satwant Malhotra, who led me to more contacts and information that was essential. And truly, this project would not be the same without the friendship and guidance of Vasantha Daniel, whose influence is woven throughout the book in ways both named and unnamed.

I am thankful for the staff at the Rockefeller Archive Center, the Kerala State Archives, the Schleisinger Library at Radcliffe, the New York Academy of Medicine, the New York Public Library, Columbia University libraries, the National Library of Medicine, the Bobst Library at NYU, the Yale Divinity School Library, and the Frost Library at Amherst College.

At UNC Press, I have had the great fortune to work with Mark Simpson-Vos, an editor whose sharp questions, generous replies, and genuinely collaborative spirit have made writing this book an exciting endeavor. I am also thankful for the assistance of Lucas Church. I was buoyed by the enthusiasm and insight of Jennifer Guglielmo and Sharmila Rudrappa. Thank you for your careful and critical readings.

Portions of this work have appeared previously in *The Sun Never Sets: South Asian Migrants in an Age of U.S. Power* and are reprinted here with permission from NYU Press.

This project had its beginnings at New York University, where I had the honor of working with a group of academic mentors who continue to inspire me professionally, politically, and personally. Truly, I know I would not have made it this far without the patient and persistent support of Andrew Ross. He is an advisor extraordinaire. I am also forever thankful to Lisa Duggan, who saw me through from beginning to end. I remain deeply indebted to Robin D. G. Kelley, Vijay Prashad, Manu Goswami, Gary Okihiro, Nikhil Pal Singh, and Walter Johnson. I was fortunate to have the support of Alyssa Burke and Madala Hilaire; to have the chance to work with Philip Brian Harper, Juan Flores, Gayatri Gopinath, Arlene Davila, and Jack Tchen; and to learn from and alongside Alyosha Goldstein, Mariel Rose, Richard Kim, Jerry Philogene, Adria Imada, Eric Tang, Kimani Paul-Emil, Miabi Chatterji, Samera Esmeir, and Carlos Decena.

I completed this book while working as a Five College Assistant Professor at Amherst College. I am grateful to my colleagues and coworkers in the American Studies Department as well as at Five Colleges, Inc., the Five College Asian/Pacific/American Studies Certificate Program, and the Five College Inter-Asia working group. My time here has been enriched by the support of Floyd Cheung, Kim Chang, Lili Kim, Donald Tomascovic-Devey, Jeffrey Ferguson, Joshua Roth, Ronald Lembo, Margaret Cerullo, Christopher Dole, Amrita Basu, Karen Sanchez-Eppler, Frank Couvares, Gregory Call, Karen Graves, and Lisa Ballou. It has been exciting also to find friendship and intellectual camaraderie with Asha Nadkarni, Iyko Day, David Hernandez, Wilson Valentin-Escobar, Dayo Gore, Falguni Sheth, Krupa Shandilya, Karen Cardozo, and Banu Subramaniam (who I owe a special thanks to for the last-minute Tamil translation). Finally, as I send this to press, I am also preparing to begin work in the American Studies department at SUNY, the College at Old Westbury. To my new colleagues, I thank you for new opportunities.

Teaching is not just part of my job; it is a true laboratory for learning. To the students I've had the honor of working with: thank you for helping me sort out ideas and for being the ones who most consistently remind me of why and how this work matters.

My scholarship is also, undeniably, influenced by my political commitments. Here I have had the honor of working with, and learning from, Chandana Mathur, Andrew Hsiao, Aniruddha Das, Biju Mathew, Anannya Bhattacharjee, Mir Ali Raza, the Asia Pacific Forum radio collective, the SAMAR magazine collective, the India Resource Center, the International Campaign for Justice in Bhopal, CAAAV Organizing Asian Communities, Youth Solidarity Summer, the Fortune Society's Education Program (John Gordon, Eric Appleton, John Kefalas, and Miriam Garcia), Just Communities, and Justice for Charles. I thank them all for teaching me how to sustain the relationship between thought and action.

In addition to the above, over the years, I have been blessed by friends who have sustained me: Lisa Armstrong, Diana Coryat, Jennifer Guglielmo, Lois Ahrens, Vivek Bald, Manu Vimalassery, Julie Sze, Christina Handhardt, Ifenoa Fulani, Cleo Godsey, Yuko Miki, Jonathan Bogarin, Noah Fischer, Dagan Bayliss, Melissa Myambo, Diana Pei Wu, Aleyamma Mathew, Anandaroop Roy, Pushkala Prasad, Naeem Mohaiemen, Revan Schendler, Elizabeth Kolsky, Beau Shaw, Leyla Mei, Tomio

Geron, Kate Reuther, Scott Blumenthal, Craig Canapari, Swati Sharma, Amina Steinfels, Tariq Jaffer, Uditi Sen, Subhash Kateel, Sahar Sadjadi, Khary Polk, Kara Lynch, Adrienne Fricke, Sylvia Maria Gross, Marcelo Montes-Penha, Shanna Lorenz, Gaiutra Bahadur, and Anna DePold Hohler.

For their unfailing love and support, I do not have thanks enough to give to my family: Nirmala Reddy, Narasimha Reddy, Sumathi Reddy, and Jonathan Rockoff. And for pure joy and light: Nikhil Reddy Rockoff and Priya Reddy Rockoff.

Finally, in memoriam: To my cousin Vinod Reddy and to my friend and our guardian angel, Natalie Sullivan Bimel.

# Abbreviations

| | |
|---|---|
| AIIHPH | All India Institute of Hygiene and Public Health |
| ANA | American Nurses Association |
| CON-D | College of Nursing, Delhi |
| Congress | Indian National Congress Party |
| EVP | Exchange Visitor Program |
| FNG | foreign nurse graduate |
| GEB | General Education Board (of the RF) |
| GOI | government of India |
| Hart-Celler | 1965 Immigration and Nationality Act Amendments |
| ICN | International Council of Nurses |
| IHB | International Health Commission Board of the Rockefeller Foundation |
| IHC | International Health Commission of the Rockefeller Foundation |
| IHD | International Health Division |
| JHU | Johns Hopkins University |
| LPN | licensed practical nurse |
| NACGN | National Association of Colored Graduate Nurses |
| RF | Rockefeller Foundation |
| RSC | Rockefeller Sanitary Commission |
| SBTPE | State Board Test Pool Examination |
| TNAI | Trained Nurses Association of India |
| Vellore | Vellore Christian Medical College |
| WHO | World Health Organization |
| WMC | Women's Medical College, Philadelphia |

*Nursing & Empire*

# Nursing and Empire

If seeing is believing, then as a child, Thankam Vellaringattu's eldest daughter had every reason to believe that her mother was a full-time homemaker. In the morning when she woke up, her mother was there to greet her. At night when she went to bed, her mother was there to tuck her in. Whenever she needed a ride to or from an extracurricular activity, her mother was there to provide it along with all of the other "soccer moms." Little did her daughter know that Thankam was also—at the same time—the family's primary income earner.

Thankam Vellaringattu worked the night shift as a registered nurse (RN) in the coronary care unit (CCU) at a hospital in Long Island, New York. Both the time of the day and the intensity of the unit are not unusual for a foreign nurse graduate (FNG). Indeed, the preponderance of FNGs on the night shift was what prompted Vellaringattu's inclusion in the article, "Clocking in Past Midnight," published in 1998 by *Little India*, a news and features magazine aimed at Indian im/migrant communities in the New York metropolitan area.[1] The piece brings to light the range of locations that Indian im/migrants occupy in the after-dark economy: as medical residents, on-call physicians, nurses, transit workers, convenience store managers, gas station attendants, restaurant workers, and taxi drivers. For some, such as the medical resident turned Harvard professor, the night shift was primarily a rigor to be suffered on the way up the career ladder.[2] For others not as well placed within the labor market, the night shift is a reality that they must endure without an easy or inevitable end in sight. While almost all of those interviewed preferred jobs that would allow them to get a good night's rest, for most, mobility into the daylight hours was much more of a distant dream than a forthcoming reality.

Within the context of the article, Vellaringattu stands out. The only woman interviewed, her story highlights the night shift as a solution, not a (real or perceived) segue. It was part of a family strategy she devised with her husband, Tom. In the article, she describes how "Tom and I worked together—he would give baths to the children, cook the meals and clean up after dinner." Her husband adds, "This is our solution to the child care problem. During the day my wife even manages PTA [Parent Teacher Association] meetings and household errands."[3] This was how the couple managed to raise both of their daughters with round-the-clock parental care. It was also how their family maintained the means and appearance of a stereotypical middle-class lifestyle, because the night shift allowed Thankam to earn more than she would have during the day.[4]

The story of Tom and Thankam Vellaringattu is a story of true love, or, as she described to me in our interview, theirs is a relationship fueled by *"kuch kuch hota hai."*[5] This came across clearly throughout our interview, culminating in her summary statement that "the best thing that ever happened to me is getting to know him [Tom]. You know, getting married. And we are happy."[6] Their mutuality certainly provided a good part of the background to the strategy for how they handled their dual responsibility of raising and maintaining a family. At the same time, the story of how they used the night shift to their advantage takes us beyond the "thick-and-thin" adventure that their life together has been. Most immediately, it signals the kind of negotiations that Indian nurses, their families, and their communities have had to make in order to find some kind of fit with the heteropatriarchal version of the "American Dream" as encoded in dominant images of post–World War II Indian immigrant success. *Nursing and Empire* expands the lens to uncover a global field where the combination of Indian nurses' productive and reproductive labor has been a consistent source of anxiety across the circuits of Anglo-American capitalist imperialism—circuits that have connected that labor to processes of U.S. social formation since the nineteenth century.

In 1869, the Woman's Foreign Missionary Society of the Methodist Episcopal Church deputed Dr. Clara Swain to work in Bareilly, India. It was a moment loaded with firsts.[7] Dr. Swain was among the first female medical graduates in the United States. She has also been recorded as the first female medical missionary in U.S. history as well as the first fully qualified female doctor (according to colonial standards) to work in India. Her arrival on the subcontinent marked the beginning of a pattern of female medical missionary migration that enabled a degree of professional mobility, autonomy, and authority that was as of yet unavailable in metropolitan markets. Single female medical missionaries, and later colonial nurses, were at the vanguard of a movement that positioned Protestant missions as the primary institutions to employ India's first pool of Indian nursing labor.[8] At the same time, their status as *single* was necessary—both for their own upward mobility and their service to a Christian "civilizing" mission that relied on the ideal of a heteropatriarchal nuclear family.[9] At the time, if these women workers wished to marry, they had to give up their wages. Nearly a century later and continents apart, the invisibility of Thankam's career thus serves as a strange sort of mirror, refracting questions about women workers, historically gendered forms of "woman's work," the locations and workings of U.S. imperial expansion, and the latter's relationship to the settlement of Indian nurses within the imperial nation.

By "imperial nation," I mean, of course, the United States, but it is important to be clear here, for I chose my language with care and intent. Understanding the United States as an imperial nation means recognizing its dual and simultaneous status as an imperial power on the global stage and a settler colony "at home." Relegation of this second fact to a distant, settled past is part of ongoing attempts to neutralize continued opposition to white settler colonization. The tenacity of contemporary struggles around im/migration, mass criminalization, and indigenous sovereignty (to name but a few prominent examples) underscores colonization and contestation as the continuous conditions for what began as an offshoot of the British Empire. That the United States has its roots in this imperial project is worth remembering, as it is the origin for my use of the phrase "Anglo-American capitalist imperialism," a shorthand for indexing what continues to be an evolving relationship as the United States has moved from being a part of British imperial expansion to a junior partner, a rival, and ultimately an inheritor with the onset of the Cold War.[10]

Nurses formed part of the mass transfer of labor from India to the United States during the Cold War. They arrived alongside the physicians, scientists, and engineers, who were the stock-in-trade of "brain drain" scares emanating from the Third World[11] and "model minority" adulation propagating in the United States. Amid the global shuffle, nurses' participation was all but lost from view. They were marginalized in the archives, in statistics, and in representations. Their general invisibility reflected the material and ideological devaluation of their labor—both productive (waged) and reproductive (unwaged). Indeed, it is difficult, when writing about a group of primarily women workers whose wage work centers on historically gendered forms of woman's work, to maintain a clear and consistent separation between productive and reproductive labor. In the case of nursing, the two are necessarily overlapping, regardless of whether the nurse in question is also a mother—or even, ultimately, whether said nurse is male or female. In *Nursing and Empire*, I work through this tangled web, separating out forms of labor and laborers when there is a need for such clarity and collapsing them when the distinctions are less the point than the totality of socially relevant labor, as it has been redefined by feminist intellectuals and activists.[12] The need to account for this full range is amply evident when we turn to one of the primary ways in which nurses have appeared in the historical record: through the stigmatization of their labor as both workers and (potential) wives.

## From "Women on the Loose" to "Women in the Lead"

Accounts of nursing in India repeatedly remark on the historically low status afforded this group of workers. With few exceptions, explanations for this privilege the norms of brahmanical patriarchy.[13] According to this system, nursing crosses the lines of ritual purity and pollution that regulate the caste system. The interaction with men outside of the family required in sick nursing also poses a perceived challenge to the strict rules around endogamy that are critical to the reproduction of caste. In this logic, historically, no "good girl" could be a nurse because she would not circulate in public, unregulated, tending to men not in her family and, worse even, dealing with their most "untouchable" parts. Only families desperate for money would allow "their" women to do such deeds, adding nursing to the shaming effects of poverty, lack of male economic authority, and a concomitant drop in marriageability. This was how nurses came to be associated with a certain kind of prostitution—of poor women who do "dirty work" for others, especially other men. Nursing thus became a focal point for anxieties over what might happen when women are on the "loose," outside the hold of the joint family and its caste, class, sexual, and gender norms.

In *Nursing and Empire,* I reevaluate the production of "women on the loose" through an examination of the institutional and ideological context for the development of India's first pool of Indian nursing labor.[14] Protestant medical missionaries primarily recruited and employed Indian Christian converts as nurses. In most cases, these women (and men) were from the oppressed castes and classes. The one major exception was in the region of what is today Kerala, where Christian communities had existed since the first century A.D. The particularities of region, religion, caste, and class are thus central in understanding the evolution of India's first pool of Indian nursing labor, yet they are insufficient on their own. The overwhelming majority of Indians employed in colonial nursing worked for Protestant missionaries, and their castigation was also absolutely a product of the poor working conditions and poor pay at mission institutions as these compounded the racialized hierarchies of colonization and intersected with the norms of brahmanical patriarchy.

Up through the mid-twentieth century, the vast majority of nurses in India labored in what remained an overwhelmingly ill-regarded and ill-paid *occupation*. When these same workers immigrated to the United States, they entered a market where registered nursing was a widely recognized *profession*. For Indian nurses, immigration thus promised professionalization in a manner distinct from others within their much vaunted immigrant cohort. It also often distinguished them within their own families and communities. Because nursing generally drew from India's lower middle classes, few other members of nurse migrants' families had skills that easily translated into upward mobility on the international labor market. Nurses not only led migration out of their communities; they also often remained the primary income earners in their immigrant families. Immigration to the United States transformed Indian nurses from "women on the loose" to "women in the lead."

As "women in the lead," they present a Janus-faced figure. One face symbolizes the economic opportunities and institutional access promised by immigration to the United States. The other confronts the stigmatization that the female dominance characterizing their immigration pattern has cast on Indian nurses, their families, and their communities in the United States. The stereotypical nurse family did not find fit with the gentile image of the Indian American bourgeoisie composed of "properly" heteropatriarchal nuclear families—families where both women workers and woman's work remained necessarily hidden from view. Instead, nurses headed "backwards" families composed of emasculated men and overpowering women. This stereotype offers another context for reading Thankam and Tom Vellaringattu's use of the night shift, as a solution to the persistent "problem" presented by "women on the loose" even as they transform into "women in the lead."

In her ethnographic study of a group of Kerala Christian nurse immigrants and their families settled in the United States, Sheba Mariam George details the stigmatization of nurses, their husbands, and their families by nonnursing families within a larger Indian immigrant community. George traces this back to nursing's low status in India and its reproduction through temporally bound transnational circuits (here, products of the late twentieth-century communications technology). These circuits are only legible to and through Indians and are otherwise immune from the context of the United States, where nurses have professional status and professional managerial Indian immigrants enjoy general approbation.[15] The stigmatization of Indian nurses, however transnational, here remains a resolutely Indian phenomenon in much the same way that its counterpart caste is often understood.

George's work shares in general analyses of skilled Indian labor migration that have—regardless of their particular subject or argument—remained bound to a chronology and geography dictated by a domesticated U.S. social formation, understood as distinct from that of postcolonial India. The critical lever in her account, and those it takes its lead from, is passage of the 1965 Immigration and Nationality Act (Hart-Celler). Hart-Celler's centrality is due to the fact that it completed removal of the race-based exclusion that had targeted Asians while also introducing a series of occupational preference quotas that focused on professionalized workers. The explanatory emphasis on U.S. immigration law alone, however, is tantamount to taking the redrawn boundaries of the nation as the boundaries for one's own analysis. It erases the role played by the U.S. nation-state and U.S.-based interests in global histories of capitalist imperialism, leaves no room for considering the role that this played in fostering global labor migration, and offers no framework for synthesizing the complexities of migrants' decisions alongside their negotiation with this global system. Instead, immigration to the United States begins when migrants are allowed to legally land on U.S. shores, and their decision to do so is implicitly based on economic considerations that coincide with the ideological premise of the American Dream. Ultimately, such a formulation plays into the paradigm of American exceptionalism: the view that the United States is a nation-in-isolation that stands apart from, even as it is a beacon for, the rest of the world. What is more, it does so in order to describe a historical period when American exceptionalism renewed itself in full force on the global stage.

In *Nursing and Empire*, I jettison this framework not as a theoretical gesture but as a practical necessity. From the moment that Florence Nightingale had her epiphany in the war-torn fields of Crimea, nursing's professionalization has proceeded through processes of colonization, decolonization, and recolonization—in India *and* the United States. Analyzing this requires a global map, one that is historically grounded and can move beyond interpretations limited to our contemporary conjuncture. All too often, the latter end up framing immigrants themselves as the bearers of the "transnational" in a way that renders invisible their negotiations with capitalist imperialism (or transnational capitalism, as one would have it) and its attendant state forms. This book endeavors to undo this invisibility and to make clear the ways in which immigration law was but one tool in the expansion of the imperial nation.

*Open Door Nursing*

Analyzing Indian nursing labor within the context of capitalist imperialism takes up the challenge posed by Sucheta Mazumdar's cutting-edge theorization of the gendered dimensions of Indian[16] labor migration to North America prior to World War II. Mazumdar dismisses standardized explanations for the near absence of Chinese and Indian women migrants at this time for their reliance on Orientalism (women didn't migrate because of the prohibitions of "essentially" patriarchal societies) or Asian exclusion in the United States (laws that targeted women as de facto sex workers and were effective enough to prohibit their entry into what would otherwise be a desirable location).[17] She offers instead an explanation of the ways in which capitalist imperialism shifted the local economies in particular regions of India and China to create male out-migration. In response to the question "what happened to the women?," Mazumdar emphasizes that they were not "left behind" to wallow in their sorrows but were instead busy maintaining the farm and/or the family through various forms of productive and reproductive labor. Changes to the scope and content of their work reflected an international division of labor *on the level of the family* in what remained interconnected kinship and communal networks.

The seeming inability to account for these families functioning across continents has much to do with the normalization of the heteropatriarchal, nuclear family within unidirectional analyses of immigration. That the absence of "proper" families came to characterize Asian im/migration in particular speaks to the racialization of that normative *ideal*. The emphasis on "ideal" is necessary for underscoring that the heteropatriarchal nuclear family was a minority form even among whites in the United States, let alone marginally white im/migrants and/or people of color. The relationship between some white women's ability to remain out of the paid workforce was in fact reliant on these "other" women who had to labor outside of their own homes while simultaneously struggling to maintain forms of family, kinship, and control over their reproductive capacities in the face of the genocide, enslavement, colonization, indenture, and illegalization.

Beginning with the feminization and medicalization of the Christian civilizing mission allows for a consideration of the reciprocal role that this normative family ideal had in India. When female medical missionaries migrated across empire to found practices in India, they did so under the banner of "woman's work for woman." The strength of this call drew directly from widespread, popular, Orientalized images of "heathen" Indian women locked away in the *zenana*, the woman's quarters of the colonial phantasmagoria. Such stock images had long served as justification for colonization, as the status of "woman" became an index for the status of society as a whole. The locked away and languishing Indian woman thus provided the cue for colonists who sought to rescue her and, in the process, civilize the society that she symbolized. Single female medical missionaries reworked this script, arguing that only women could rescue women and that only women doctors could intervene during childbirth, that most critical moment of biological and social reproduction. This was how "woman's work for woman" met the "woman question" and revivified a Christian civilizing mission in what was poised to be something akin to a woman's world—but for the disciplinary design of the model mission family.

The mission family—with its male breadwinner and female bread baker—was a civilizing model for Indian Christian converts. As such, it served to discipline the desires of all those within its purview—women and men, Indian and white—in a hierarchically related manner. For white men, it meant the necessity of a "head of household" wage. For white women, it meant the choice between wage work and nonwaged re/productive labor. For the majority of Indian Christians, who were generally not of the elite classes, it meant that the reality of their lives as workers and/with wives rendered them forever less "civilized" even if they converted. Their conversion, however, was not the ultimate goal of "woman's work for woman," which focused instead on accessing, specifically, privileged class and caste Indian women and, thereby, privileged caste and class Indian men. These were the Indians whose coveted conversion fueled the movement that would, in the end, do more to employ oppressed caste and class women in mission hospitals than convert women purportedly locked away from Christian influence. And it was the workers whose continued institutional and ideological subordination enabled the upward mobility of single female medical missionaries and colonial nurses.

The medicalization of "the woman question" reached new ideological heights with the 1927 publication of *Mother India*. Written by U.S. journalist Katherine Mayo, the book revivified images of the degraded and degrading state of Hindu (in particular) womanhood in what Mayo insisted was an argument for the continued need of British colonization, especially in the face of mounting Indian nationalist mobilization. Both Mrinalini

Sinha and, more recently, Asha Nadkarni help us to analyze the tricontinental controversy engendered by Mayo's sensationalist tract as evidence for the continued role that representations of "the" Indian woman had to shifts within Anglo-American capitalist imperialism.[18] Both authors also mention the longstanding and often back-door connections that Mayo had to the Rockefeller Foundation (RF), evidenced by the imprint of the foundation's priorities on her work. In particular, they help me to link her rehearsal of the "woman question" to the prominent place that public health had in Rockefeller's philanthropic works during the decades between World Wars I and II (the interwar years). This is the aspect that I take up in more detail, analyzing the shadiness of Mayo's unofficial connection to the RF as symptomatic of "open door imperialism."

In his classic *Tragedy of American Diplomacy*, historian William Appleman Williams outlines Open Door policy as promulgated by the U.S. power elite at the turn of the twentieth century in relation to China. The strategy represented a shift in the mechanisms of U.S. imperial expansion in that, ideally, it should proceed without war and without the administrative burdens of direct governance.[19] This was imperialism without colonization, and its aim was to proceed through the creation of new markets for capitalization and the inclusion of indigenous actors through imperial networks. The practices of corporate philanthropy pioneered by the RF closely mirrored open-door methods, even as they built upon the institutional and ideological groundwork developed by U.S.-based Protestant medical missionaries. Highlighting their work is a contribution to the analytic work begun by historians of Filipino nurse im/migration.[20] In *Empire of Care*, Catherine Ceniza Choy argues for the role that U.S. colonization had in creating the links utilized by the Philippine and U.S. governments, recruitment agencies, professional nursing organizations, and individual migrants to position Filipinos as the largest pool of foreign nursing labor in the United States. Her work opens an important chapter in the consideration of imperialism, immigration, and the racialization of FNGs in the United States. And yet, the historical ties between the United States and the Philippines add an intuitive strength to Choy's argument that clearly does not transfer to a case such as that of India, which was never a direct colony of the United States. Instead, recognizing the "hidden hand" of open door imperialism helps me to reframe the critical, cumulative role played by private U.S.-based interests in British-dominated India into the American Century.

In the case of India, both missions and the RF existed in a complicated mix of cooperation and competition with the project of British Empire.

The place of missionaries began with what I identify as a process of sub-contracting, in this case of the Christian civilizing mission and the spread of colonial medicine among Indians. As Protestant medical missions became the primary institutions to undertake the latter, which was never a priority for the British colonial government, they developed an infrastructure that was available for the RF to capitalize on during the interwar years, decades when the permanence of Britain's global dominion came more sharply into question. The RF used public health and scientific medicine to insinuate themselves alongside the Indian nationalist elite as the latter found a modicum of space within changes to the structures of colonial rule during the interwar years. This was one critical way in which the version of scientific medicine backed by the RF became part of the package of modernity implemented by the postcolonial Indian state. It thus helps to explain how, in the emerging postindependence landscape, capitalist imperialism did not disappear so much as reconfigure. In *Nursing and Empire*, I trace this reconfiguration as a means to understanding the emergence of a Cold War global market in nursing labor, a market that included Indian nurses.

If the development of an international division of medical and nursing labor began with metropolitan workers traveling to colonized locations, the RF's International Health Division (IHD) reversed these routes by promoting an emerging Third World elite through access to professionalization via metropolitan institutions. In turn, their migration in search of higher education helped to resolidify the links between postcolonial knowledge and metropolitan power through the replenishment of a network that shifted the balance away from Great Britain and toward the United States. It is important to recognize that this process was not inevitable. Professional standards, developed through the structures of a global medical system that was itself a product of capitalist colonization, were not outside the domain of struggles for decolonization. The fact that they were not—by and large—overturned speaks to the hegemony of the RF model of biomedicine and its success in cultivating an international cadre of biomedical professionals. This was not a disinterested operation. The RF and its inheritors were no less interested in questions of conversion than their Protestant predecessors. Their achievement was to shed Christian conversion as the goal and replace it with the uptake of their version of public health and scientific medicine. The result was the establishment of a global biomedical system that set the standard for health care and medical professionalization the world over in such a way that its authority persisted through independence movements.

In the case of Indian nursing, what this meant was that professionalization remained key to authority and upward mobility, and that what it meant to professionalize depended on standards increasingly set by U.S. interests. This ongoing relationship between Indian nursing leadership and a U.S.-centered global medical market prompts questions about the position(s) of Third World women workers and woman's work in processes of recolonization as these affected the formation of what I will call India's "diaspora of decolonization."[21] With this phrase, I reference a most specific lineage for diaspora, one that began with the most brutal forms of forced displacement as these have accompanied and indeed enabled the spread of capitalist imperialism. The signal moments and movements here were conquest of the Americas through indigenous genocide, the enslavement of Africans, and the indenture of Chinese and Indians. In comparison, migration in the pursuit of professionalization appears rendered through reward and based on a most capitalist version of "choice." And certainly, the bodies of its beneficiaries do not bear the brunt of the violence endured by their predecessors. By invoking "diaspora" here, I do not mean to diminish the deep imbrication between capitalist imperialism and violence. Indeed, this is why I want to be careful not to naturalize or neutralize the coming together of modern medicine (biomedicine) and national liberation. Instead, "diaspora of decolonization" references the ways in which open-door imperialism—or what would become known more commonly as neocolonialism—produced a forced exile from the full promise of a definition of decolonization (understood as an end to the inequities of colonial extraction and expropriation). Recognizing this as an as of yet unfinished task destabilizes the "post" in postcolonial and recasts the commencement of immigration to the United States as part of the (at least) century-long relationship between Indian nurses, the international division of nursing labor, U.S.-based medical interests, and the domestic space of the imperial nation.

Clarity around the United States as an imperial nation allows me to contextualize the immigration of Indian nurses as coinciding not only with struggles for decolonization across Asia and Africa but also with struggles for desegregation in the United States. In the mid-twentieth century, U.S. racial formation was, in the formulation of Michael Omi and Howard Winant, entering into a new period of "unstable equilibrium," when the racial state reshaped its legal apparatus as a result of pressure from movements for racial justice.[22] In the case of nursing, the fight against racialized apartheid met head on with the ways in which the legacies of chattel slavery included the ways in which white nurses worked to distinguish themselves from the forms of domestic labor associated with black women. This had taken place around the time of the Civil War, after which the rapid rise of industrial capitalism met head on with the project of reconstructing the southeastern states (the U.S. South), viewed as a kind of "colony within." I investigate the latter as more than a metaphor, as the U.S. South became the crucial testing ground for the public health work that Rockefeller wealth utilized to spread its philanthropic wings across the stretch of Anglo-American empire. In this way, Rockefeller wealth had "opened the door" at home before using its public health work as an "entering wedge" into the shifting contours of British governance on the Indian subcontinent.

In *Nursing and Empire*, I detail the ways in which this transfer was explicit, strategic, and grounded in the imperial objectives of U.S. capital during the interwar years. It was also enormously consequential as Rockefeller wealth became the single largest force behind two deeply interrelated projects: the promotion of Jim and Jane Crow segregation within U.S. health care and the reconstruction of colonial medicine around the world through the promotion of what we now know as biomedicine. Exploring the interconnection between these two operations allows for a consideration of the ways in which racialized segregation was itself a form of "integration,"[23] a form that was to shift shape but not lose function as the British Empire crumbled, India and Pakistan became independent nation-states, and the United States reached new heights of imperial dominance.

African American women and Third World nationals began entering formerly all-white hospitals and nursing organizations in the United States during the 1960s, just when middle-class white women were abandoning the field to move into professions that had previously been the preserve of white men. This did not result in integration, inasmuch as that could signal an end to the inequities of racialized apartheid and colonization. Instead, as they became a permanent feature of the U.S. nursing workforce, FNGs faced stigmatization as a "cheap(er)" solution to recurrent crises in what was cast as a chronic nursing shortage. Their stigmatization as such led to increased testing and regulation, causing some to experience forms of downward mobility, including employment in nursing's nonprofessional ranks where Third World and especially African American labor was disproportionately concentrated. Most also found their labor relegated to the shifts, units, and hospitals least able to retain their white colleagues—such as Thankam Vellaringattu's night shift in the CCU. Thus, while im/migration offered the possibility of professionalization for Indian nurses, it did so while instituting FNGs as a permanent, if inherently unstable (due to immigration/citizenship status), part of the workforce. This was but one piece of a puzzle where the boundaries around race, class, and nation within U.S. nursing were rearranging in ways that were more stratifying than equalizing, raising the specter of resegregation alongside that of recolonization. The same can be said of Indian nurses' relationship to resettlement in the imperial nation—where we move from the "problem" of cheap(er) labor to the "solution" of the model minority.

## Model Minority Exceptionalism

Model minority discourse as it concerns me here has its roots in the story of immigration and assimilation drawn from the (selected) experiences of turn-of-the-twentieth-century southern and eastern European immigrants. These were the "poor, tired and huddled masses" who were not quite white Anglo-Saxon Protestant (WASP) enough upon arrival but who, after a generation or two bred in the shadow of restrictive immigration legislation, had become the bedrock of the normative U.S. middle classes.[24] The consolidation of this unmarked white center coincided with the liberalization of U.S. immigration law, legalizing what became large-scale professional-managerial immigration from the former "Asiatic Barred Zone." The rapid rise of these "new immigrants" into the ranks of the middle classes became evidence that the American Dream was now an equal opportunity employer, regardless of race. It also provided a critical foundation for the stereotype of the Asian American model minority, a figure that helped to put the "post" in post–civil rights U.S. racial formation.

Professional-managerial immigrants from India were a particularly potent example of what was a broader Asian American model minority. For a variety of reasons, unlike other members of this pan-ethnic identity, Indians had had a relatively smaller, geographically isolated, and/or largely invisible presence in the United States prior to the Cold War. It was thus easier to disconnect them from histories of Asian exclusion in the United States (even as these were a critical factor in limiting the nature and scope of their settlement) and from other locations in the Indian diaspora as it had formed under the system of indentured labor across British and (to some extent) French empire. These disconnections served to reinforce some cold hard facts. As a generalized group, the Indians who immigrated via Hart-Celler's occupational preference quotas were among the most highly educated and economically successful in the United States.[25] The relative speed and apparent ease with which they entered the ranks of the U.S. middle classes positioned them as exemplars of a re-racialized model minority.[26]

This image rests on a largely unacknowledged but critical separation between professional-managerial Indian emigration and the forces of U.S.-dominated capitalist imperialism. Thus, the explanation for the arrival of Indians (specifically, as it would vary from nation-state to nation-state) remains that India overproduced skilled labor that it could not retain when U.S. immigration laws changed and potential migrants could make the "rational choice" to migrate where the money was. Absent a sense of how the long history of U.S.-based institutions and ideologies worked to structure and channel the choices of the migrants who would immigrate through Hart-Celler, the United States all too easily figures as an "exceptional" (i.e., nonimperial) immigrant destination in a diasporic circuit that was still otherwise largely centered on the then crumbling British Empire. The distinction of the United States as separate from the circuits of imperial Britain was also an image quite in line with the Cold War aspirations of the U.S. power elite, an establishment that was, at precisely this moment, working to fashion itself as the bearer of freedom and democracy for the decolonizing world. The ideological disconnect between India and the United States vis-à-vis histories of territorial colonization made Indian immigrants a prime location for what I will call "model minority exceptionalism." This was where American exceptionalism met the American Dream to pose as the ultimate horizon for decolonization *and* desegregation.

*Nursing and Empire* disrupts the reign of model minority exceptionalism by analyzing the seminal role U.S. medical interests played in establishing colonial medicine's global infrastructure and constituting its racialized inequalities—in India and the United States. Connecting open door imperialism to the emergence of an Indian American model minority opens an "unexceptional" version of Cold War labor im/migration and one that has clear implications beyond a study of nurses alone. Indeed, during the Cold War, Indian physicians were perhaps the consummate representatives of both brain drain and model minority discourse. Indian doctors were seemingly everywhere. As medical professionals, they were also necessarily products of global shifts within colonial medicine. In this sense it is not enough to stop at biomedicine's colonial career when we turn to the work of the RF. The foundation's work was also about professionalization and institutions, as well as ideologies, of higher education. Biomedicine was but one area of its work globally, and it was not alone but one of the primary U.S.-based corporate philanthropists as work in India and around the world. For instance, its work around the world was certainly rivaled by that of the Ford Foundation and a counterpart to entities such as the United States Agency for International Development (USAID). Recognition of this landscape raises critical questions about the connections between Indian scientists and engineers to an imperial and specifically U.S.-centered market.

It is insufficient, however, to merely add another name to the list— doctors, engineers, scientists, *and nurses*. Nor is it sufficient to (implicitly/ explicitly) fill in the gap solely by launching separate studies, particularly if these continue to employ the framework of a heteropatriarchal model minority exceptionalism. This is not, in other words, a matter akin to multiculturalism where we must fill in all the slots of difference as if we are counting heads. Instead, in different ways, all of these "solutions" end up shortchanging the disruptive potential that a focus on nurses has to the making of the Indian and Indian American middle classes.

In India, a certain configuration of gender and sexuality worked along- side the normalization of region (North India) and religion (Hindu) to produce "the" Indian middle class. During the Cold War, these features were largely, if implicitly, reproduced in the re-formation of an Indian American middle class. Nurses troubled these parameters on multiple lev- els. Their im/migration pattern was not simply female led, but it was also primarily associated with Indian Christian women from South India in general and from Kerala, India's southernmost state, in particular. Dur- ing the 1970s, Kerala nurses emerged as "the" Indian nurse migrant in a way that continues to dominate Indian diasporic imaginaries. I explore this regional specificity further in the chapters that follow. For now, what I can say is that when I first began discussing the current project with friends and colleagues within South Asian diaspora circles, virtually every- one told me that an investigation into Indian nurse migration to the United States was, de facto, an investigation into the movement of Kerala Christian nurses. This was repeated with such authority by such a range of individuals that it appeared to function as a kind of "common sense" within the diaspora circles to which I am privy. As I wound my way through the research, I found this characterization fortified by represen- tations in the ethnic press, mainstream media (in both India and the United States), and the emergent academic literature on Indian nurses in the United States. As this material accumulated, I was certainly left with the overwhelming impression that Kerala Christian nurses probably com- pose the single largest regional/religious group among my potential subject pool. I say "probably" because I have not yet been able to find statistical evidence to verify the regional/religious makeup of Indian nurse migration to the United States.[27]

Rather than take Kerala Christian nurses for granted as the center, this book historicizes the emergence of Kerala as a primary center for Indian nurse emigration. This involves accounting for the specificities of Christianity in Kerala, the differences and relationships between princely states and British presidencies, and the rise of anticaste and communist politics in what would become the state of Kerala after Indian independence/partition. By the time that Indian nurses began to access colonial nursing's international circuits, Kerala was becoming an internationally renowned conundrum. Its combination of high social indicators (in health and literacy) and low economic indicators gave birth to "the Kerala model" of development. It also gave rise to mass out-migration, including nurses. These women workers, in particular, bore the stamp of a society that valued women in particular (and thus its high social indicators), even as their departure signaled its inability to retain key sectors of its workforce. Thus, we can begin to question how the Kerala model encapsulated contradictory and overlapping processes of decolonization and recolonization, and "the" Kerala nurse became an embodiment of these contradictions. This is also how we can begin to understand the regional and religious branding of "women in the lead" in relation to global shifts within women's workforce participation and the re-racialization of the nuclear family ideal.

The model minority was but one pillar of the inferential racism that came to dominate discussions of post–civil rights U.S. racial formation. At the same time, and in the face of ongoing uprisings for justice within communities of color, academics and the media collaborated to popularize the image of Puerto Rican and African American women (women from the so-called domestic minorities) as "bad mothers" and/or "welfare queens." The hypervisibility of these images was part of dominant efforts to explain away the continuity of racialized poverty through recourse to a discourse of bad family values and overbearing women.[28] It also served as rationale for the post–civil rights criminalization of poor communities of color. The result was a "culture of poverty" discourse that relied, critically, on constructions of gender, class, race, and sexuality and stood in direct contrast to the Asian/American "model minority."

The pattern of Indian nurse im/migration straddled the divide between "good" and "bad" families. The fact that it was female-dominated meant that it could find full fit with the family form necessary for inclusion within the model minority. The compulsion to conform to the norm of a heteropatriarchal nuclear family in order to receive the benefits of this status was also certainly a factor in the stigmatization of Indian nurses and nurse families within the immigrant bourgeoisie. This is not the same thing as saying that the stigmatization of nursing in India does not also reproduce through immigration and transnational circuits, despite processes of professionalization and upward mobility. Instead, we must also understand the ways in which this rearticulation was not immune from the pressures of U.S. racial formation. It was in critical ways compounded by them so that the families, communities, and social networks engendered through nurse immigration, through their very composition, could come to defy the Indian immigrant bourgeoisie's complicity with the antiblack, anti-Latino/Latina, antipoor, antiwomen, and adamantly heteropatriarchal forces within post–civil rights U.S. social formation.

At the same time, as I explore in the book's final chapter, the reracialization of immigration to the United States away from Europe and toward the Third World was recast as an attack on the institution of the American family and, consequently, the nation. Rather than announcing a moment beyond racialized oppression, for Asian immigrant women, these arguments recalled those made during the era of Asian exclusion, when anti-Asian movements and legislation cast their sexuality as an explicit threat to the body politic. The anti-immigrant fervor of the 1980s reincarnated the specter of the "bad families" that "women in the lead" bear, casting the threat in terms that targeted the family reunification preferences that are actually at the heart of Hart-Celler. This backlash occurred at a time when the United States was undergoing deindustrialization and the shift toward a service sector economy where female-led migration was increasingly the norm, not the exception, particularly in the low-wage sector. In this way, my analysis of Indian nurse immigration opens a critical window onto the ways in which race, class, sexuality, and nation reconfigured during a period where the increasing feminization of wage labor and labor migration became tantamount to the degradation of labor standards for all workers, male and female, "skilled" and "unskilled."

## Beyond Stigma: A Note on Source Material

This book draws on material gathered from interviews, archival materials, and secondary sources. I don't privilege any one source over the other and, on the whole, rely on them in approximately equal measure in what has become *Nursing and Empire*. This synthesis, however, belies a process where, in many ways, the nurses I interviewed were the ones who led me to the archives and to particular secondary sources/literatures. I want to conclude by dwelling for a moment on the details of my interviews and what my interviewees have meant to this work.

In 2003, I conducted a series of life history interviews with sixteen Indian nurse immigrants in the United States. I recruited them through individual references as well as through contacts I made with hospitals, churches, and community organizations, primarily in the New York metropolitan area. I used the snowball technique to increase my sample by asking every nurse I interviewed for references to other potential participants. I interviewed every nurse at least once and several multiple times. Most of the time, we met in individuals' homes, although at times I also met nurses at their places of work. Our interviews focused on their experiences of work and immigration, although they easily slipped into conversations that encompassed their lives at home, with family and community. The format was conversational, and nurses did not hesitate to ask me questions about my work, family, and life as well. This added dimension to our dialogue and signaled the multiple kinds of relationships at work in these interviews. I was not only an academic researcher but also a member of a general Indian immigrant community and, in many cases, the same generation as their own children. All to say that in many (although not all) of the cases, the ice broke relatively quickly, and we relied on multiple scripts and roles throughout the interviews.

Vasantha Daniel was the first nurse who agreed to participate in the project. Through informal conversations and interviews with her, I learned how she first migrated to the United States on a fellowship from the Rockefeller Foundation that she received through her alma mater, the College of Nursing at the Christian Medical College, Vellore. Daniel remains connected to Vellore through her role as a member of its USA Board. I accompanied her to two of the annual board meetings in New York City, where I made contacts with more nurses to interview and also spoke with the director of the USA Board, the Reverend Lou Knowles. It was thus Daniels's own story, as well as those of other Vellore graduates, that led me to investigate further the link between Rockefeller and Vellore, a link that proved seminal to detailing the "hidden hand" structuring Indian nurse immigration to the United States.

I also made contact with Coney Island Hospital in Brooklyn early on in my recruitment process. There I was introduced to Aleyamma James, an Indian nurse immigrant who I interviewed for the present project and who introduced me to several other nurses who also participated. One of these was Aleyamma Eapen, who led me to the Reverend Sunder Devap-rasad. The reverend is a longtime leader in the Indian Christian community of New York City and proved a valuable resource for more nurses and for community history. Aleyamma James was also the source for contacts I made in India with nurse recruiters and nursing leaders. In addition, Dr. Suwersh Khanna (RN, EdD) linked me to the current leadership of the Trained Nurses Association of India, who I also had the opportunity to visit over the course of my time in India.

Throughout my recruitment process, I was careful to diversify my interview sample as much as possible in terms of gender, region, and religion—in other words, the variables that are often taken for granted in the little literature that exists on Indian nurse migration. As I detail and analyze further in the chapters to follow, I did not end up interviewing a male nurse, but I was able to cut across the other variables to include Hindu nurses and nurses from across India. My sample also includes nurses who were not married, had never been married, and/or were divorced. This was critical, for it complicates questions of upward mobility and settlement as they have been framed thus far.

As alluded to above, one of the key stigmas surrounding "women on the loose" is that they are unmarriageable or, at the very least, that they are less desirable on the marriage market. This did not mean that nurses in India did not marry; in fact, most of them did. However, when nurses gained preferential access to the international market in general and immigration to the United States in particular, they became much more desirable matches, especially for those who could not so easily gain legal entry. Marriage thus accompanied professionalization to position nurse immigrants and their families as part of a model minority composed largely of those who would have excluded them from their ranks on the subcontinent. If their subsequent stigmatization as "women in the lead" marked the limits of their acceptability even after immigration, it also, simultaneously (and implicitly), maintains marriage as the ultimate unit of social reproduction.

And yet, the nurses I interviewed revealed to me other vistas. I gathered from them the ways in which being single was a source of isolation from immigrant communities where marriage to a man is the point of entry. I also learned that certain nurses remained single in order to support their natal families and how immigration allowed them to do so through the maintenance of extended and often transnational kinship networks. Nurses revealed to me the space that immigrations created for alliance, intimacy, and support outside of blood relations. These were often female centered and enabled by the access that women had to adequate wages. I explore these in further detail in the epilogue of this book—a piece that moves beyond nurses' potential stigmatization as "women in the lead" and into the ways in which they understand and enact social reproduction most broadly construed. For now, I want to stress that my ability to hear even portions of these stories and gain some access to the horizon that they draw was a product not only of the nurses who remained single and/or divorced through immigration. Many of these interviewees were in fact referred to me through others who occupy more socially sanctioned situations. In other words, the recruitment process itself was a form of female-centered networking and solidarity that collectively gestured toward possibilities other than those proscribed by dominant institutions and discourse.

## Structure of the Book

The first two chapters of *Nursing and Empire* focus on Protestant medical missionaries in general and the establishment of the Vellore Christian Medical College (Vellore) by Dr. Ida Sophia Scudder in particular. Chapter 1 details the work of U.S.-based Protestant medical missions on the Indian subcontinent and looks at the intersection of "woman's work for woman" and "the woman question" as it affected social reform among missionaries, middle-class Indians, and the colonial government. Chapter 2 excavates India's first pool of Indian nursing labor, reading archives against their grain and positioning these workers within an international division of nursing labor. The next three chapters examine the rise of Rockefeller wealth at the forefront of corporate philanthropy, public health, and colonial medicine. Chapter 3 begins in the post–Civil War United States and examines how the U.S. South was a crucial testing ground for the "open door" philanthropy that the foundation exported to India during the interwar years. Chapter 4 returns to India through the public health work of the RF and the promotion of the first generation of Indian nursing leaders through international migration during the transition to Indian independence/partition. Chapter 5 continues to analyze the opening of international nurse migration to Indians, the particular place of Kerala nurses within that process, and the particular place of the United States on that map. The next two chapters analyze the workforce participation and settlement patterns of Indian nurse im/migrants in the United States during the Cold War. Chapter 6 looks at the establishment of "foreign nurse migrant" as a category within a restratified "post–civil rights" nursing workforce. Chapter 7 focuses on how Indian nurses narrated their navigation of black, white, and foreign as racial categories at work. Chapter 8 examines the formation of Indian nurse im/migrant families and communities, the particular place of Kerala nurses and the Kerala model within this settlement pattern, and the relationship of these to renewed negotiations over the intersections of race, family, and nation within U.S. imperial formation. And last, in the epilogue, I take pause to reflect on the spaces that nursing and nurse im/migration have provided for nonnormative forms of community and family building and how these connect to the history of nursing's gendered "out-casting" on the subcontinent.

CHAPTER ONE

# Feminizing the Christian Medical Mission

In 1900, at the Ecumenical Conference of Missions in New York City, U.S. President William McKinley addressed the crowd: "I am glad of the opportunity to offer without stint my tribute of praise and respect to the missionary effort which has wrought such wonderful triumphs for civilization."[1] McKinley spoke to an audience in their prime. The late nineteenth century had been an unparalleled period of activity for Protestant missions around the world. Much of the scope and momentum of missionary activity during this period owed itself to the consolidation of Anglo-American capitalist imperialism through processes of territorial colonization. Twelve years after the end of the Spanish-American War, and in the midst of the bloody Philippine-American War, President McKinley's invocation of "civilization" had a decidedly acquisitive tone, one connected to the imperatives of a Christian "civilizing"[2] mission that served to justify conquest and colonization. Within this global framework, U.S. missionaries played a role not only in the growing number of U.S. colonies but also across the British Empire, including the "jewel in the crown," India.

Protestant missions from the United States remained second only to their British brethren throughout the reign of the British on the subcontinent.[3] The American Board of Commissioners for Foreign Missions (ABCFM) formed in 1810, a scant three years before the British East India Company began the limited granting of licenses for missions to operate in its territories. U.S. missionaries were in India and Burma as soon as the doors opened.[4] Their presence escalated in the 1830s, following the Charter of 1833, which lifted remaining restrictions on the entry of missionaries. In general, U.S. missions tended to concentrate in the *mofussil* (district level, rather than urban) regions, areas where British missionaries were less likely to already be established. In this way, they established a significant presence in both the Bombay and Madras Presidencies as well as in Punjab, the North-Western Provinces, and Assam. By 1910, what had begun with six U.S.-based missionaries in 1813 expanded into nearly 1,800.[5]

In its 1913 annual report, the ABCFM estimated that by 1910, half of all Indian Protestants had converted through American missionary efforts.[6] By 1925, three-quarters of all Protestant missionary work in India was undertaken and financed by churches in the United States and Canada.[7] One early twentieth-century missionary source also estimated that three out of four Americans in India before 1930 were missionaries.[8] Coming as they do from missionary sources, these numbers are, of course, motivated. This is not to say that they are entirely disreputable so much as to put them in perspective and to underline what they point to most clearly, which is a global network that Protestant missions expanded and operated through in the colonial period, a network that created a space for the substantial presence of U.S.-based individuals and institutions in the operational fabric of British territorial empire. Indeed, in addition to the deputation of U.S. missionaries, church members in the United States also provided funds for British missionary efforts throughout this period.

How are we to understand the role played by U.S. missions in the colonization of the subcontinent? Certainly, we cannot rely on the straightforward equation suggested by President McKinley's salutation, cited above. This was not only because, in the case of India, U.S.-based institutions and individuals were most decidedly "junior partners." It was also because the aims and objectives of missionaries and the British colonial government[9] did not necessarily align in a straightforward manner. This was the case regardless of where missionaries hailed from, and it manifested at several critical junctures when the colonial government explicitly sought to distance itself from their proselytizing activities. Most significant among these was the Indian Rebellion of 1857 and the subsequent shift from rule by the British East India Company to rule by the British Crown. Historians have complicated the prominent narrative that characterizes 1857 as, primarily, a mutiny of Indian sepoys (soldiers) within the British army in response to an insult to their caste and religious practices.[10] The rebellion was neither limited to sepoys nor sparked by caste and/or religion alone. Recognizing this is not the same as dismissing the importance of explanations rooted in religion, custom, and caste. At the time, their circulation served to justify a governmental policy of religious tolerance/noninterference and an official end to the goal of civilizing Indians by Christianizing them.

The British Crown's revised stance toward Christian evangelism did not translate into the end of missionary activity. Both before and after the rebellion, the colonial government enabled missionary activity by the granting of licenses, land, and financial support. Protestant missions gained their basic foothold from British administrative power, a power that grew rather than diminished under the consolidation of colonial power that characterized Crown rule. Thus, while not entirely reducible to governmental imperatives, Christian missions (including those from the United States) were a consistent, if at times contentious, facet of the colonial power structure. In a relationship that amounted to the subcontracting of the civilizing mission, Christian institutions took up a good deal of the work (including evangelism) that the government could not or did not do itself. In turn, there were also instances when the effectiveness of mission work prompted government action in certain areas, particularly the "secondary services" that grew over the turn of the century.

Unlike the colonial government, missions could not abandon their goal of converting India. It was their raison d'être. And yet, years of not living up to their own goals for conversion, coupled with instances of open hostility to their presence, prompted several shifts in mission strategy. One of these was the greater acceptance of more indirect approaches, primarily through the provision of social services that could act as "entering wedges" into communities that had proven hard to convert. In the early nineteenth century, the dominant missionary mode in India was one of "muscular Christianity," or direct evangelism. Service activities such as medical care were viewed as secondary, if not suspect, methods for recruitment. Medical practitioners were generally deputed not as evangelists but to attend to the health needs of missionaries in the field. This reflected the role of colonial medicine as a historically and culturally specific practice meant to protect European health in tropical climes. The racialized dimensions of this focus were made explicit as British colonial medical policy did not concern itself even with the Indian troops in British employ until it began to take questions of public health and contagious disease seriously. Thus, even as colonial medical practitioners turned their attention first to Indian troops and then to Indians living near British quarters, it was only to the degree to which either group posed a potential threat to British health.[11]

Within this context, Protestant missionaries became the first to seriously take up spreading colonial medical care to Indians. This was a development of the second half of the nineteenth century, but one where U.S. missionaries led the way. In 1819, the Reverend Dr. John Scudder Sr. simultaneously became the first medical missionary ever deputed by the ABCFM and the first U.S. medical missionary to work in India. A member of the Reformed Protestant Dutch church, Scudder began work in Ceylon (present-day Sri Lanka) before moving in 1836 to British colonial India. There he and his two sons (also medical doctors) founded a mission at Vellore in the Arcot district of the Madras Presidency. By 1900, twenty-seven Scudders had been stationed in India, and one, L. R. Scudder, addressed the crowd at the Ecumenical Conference: "We believe that the first aim of medical missions should be the relief of suffering from motives of brotherhood. Medical missions are the natural and inevitable expression of Christianity, that is, of the Golden Rule. They are the pioneers of evangelism. They can be planted where no other branch of evangelical work is possible. They are founded on a need which is universal and felt by all. Every human being is sometimes ill, and when not ill himself, is usually anxious on account of the illness of some relative or friend. The doctor therefore has immediate and welcome access to vast numbers who neither wish nor will have any intercourse with other missionaries."[12]

Scudder was at the time on furlough from his position at head of the Ranipet Hospital at the Arcot Mission in the Madras Presidency. The Ranipet Hospital had opened in 1866, under the direction of Dr. Silas Scudder, who wanted to push the medical work of his family further onto center stage. Even in a family full of physicians, this was something of a battle, for at the time the missionaries of Arcot still saw evangelism of the word—not medicine or institution building—as their primary purpose. In his history of the Arcot mission, Eugene P. Heideman describes how, within a few years of the hospital's opening, and while it was still very much struggling, some Christian medical personnel working within the colonial government petitioned the Inspector General of Hospitals to close the government dispensary in Ranipet. They wanted the whole Arcot district delivered over to the mission hospital. The Inspector General not only acceded but also allocated half of the funds previously set aside for the dispensary to the mission hospital and allowed the missionaries to use a government building for the hospital rent-free. This arrangement lasted until 1928, and in the intervening years, the government of the Madras Presidency regularly stepped in with money and grants-in-aid when the hospital hit precarious points.[13]

The Ranipet Hospital was in many ways at the vanguard of the shift toward working to heal Indians in both body and soul. Its evolution was also exemplary of how mission institutions worked through government aid. And by the time the Reverend Dr. L. R. Scudder took the stage in New York, he was speaking to a crowd of the converted. Medical work had become common mission strategy in India (as well as across the colonized world), and U.S.-based missions and missionaries had been in the lead of this development on the subcontinent. Their early embrace was not only evidenced by Scudder, but also by the residing "patriarch" of the gathering, the Reverend Dr. Jacob Chamberlain, who had himself spent the past forty years working as a missionary in the Madras Presidency. Also in attendance were members of the American Medical Missionary Society, formed in 1885 in Chicago, and made up of members who worked primarily in India and China.

It is no accident that all of the figures mentioned thus far were men. To begin with, only men could be ordained and thereby gain the official title of missionary, and in the early to mid-nineteenth century, only men were admitted to medical schools in the United States (as well as in Europe and England). However, increased missionary acceptance of social service work not only opened the field further to medical doctors but also allowed women to take up more prominent, and paid, positions. In addition, as women gained entrance to medical schools in the United States, medical missionary work became a preferred vocation, giving birth to the figure of the single female medical missionary. And again, in this incarnation, U.S. missionaries were at the forefront of a movement that reached new heights at the turn of the century.

### "Woman's Work for Woman"[14] Meets the "Woman Question"

In 1868–69, the Woman's Union Missionary Society of New York received an appeal from a Methodist Episcopal missionary wife stationed in Bareilly, North India. Mrs. D. W. Thomas wrote to request a woman doctor to provide medical training for the girls in her orphanage.[15] Her letter made its way to the Woman's Foreign Missionary Society of the Methodist Episcopal Church, who then contacted Dr. Clara Swain, a recent graduate of the Women's Medical College, Philadelphia (WMC), and an active church member. Prompted by this request, Dr. Swain set sail for India alongside her missionary colleague, Isabella Thoburn.[16] Swain arrived a full ten years before Dr. Fanny Butler, the first fully qualified (by colonial standards) British female physician on record in India.[17] Swain's deputation thus marked the continued centrality of India to the U.S. missionary landscape and of U.S. physicians to the evolution of colonial medicine on the subcontinent. It also augured changes to the prominence and place of women and "woman's work" in the Protestant church and its global mission.

By the late nineteenth century, women constituted the majority of the rank and file within U.S. Protestant churches.[18] Their numerical dominance has prompted historians to describe the Protestant church at this time as an essentially "women's domain," despite continued control at the top by men.[19] In response to the limits on their ascension, women created their own church networks. Mission work played a particularly prominent role within these women-only societies. Early efforts in this regard consolidated in 1861, with the founding of the Woman's Union Foreign Missionary Society in New York. In the decades that followed, the clout of women's foreign missionary societies expanded as separate mission boards sprung up in different denominations across the United States. Women's contributions to the late nineteenth-century mission revival in the United States were substantial. By 1910, the financial support coming from Methodist women alone neared one million dollars.[20] By 1915, women's societies counted more than three million members on their rolls.[21]

The phenomenal growth of this women's movement depended, critically, upon longstanding images of the "other" woman within U.S. missionary circles. Well before the meteoric rise of the global Protestant mission, women church members had used descriptions of their "heathen sisters" to mobilize sympathy and financial support. India and Indian women figured prominently in these accounts, most of which were from British and U.S. missionaries working on the subcontinent. In the early nineteenth century, the selected brahmanical practice of *sati*, or widow immolation, was the most common image used to describe "heathen" women's degradation. Books on sati appeared in circulation and were even taught in Sunday school. In 1859, when the Reverend Dr. John Scudder Sr. published *A Voice from the East to the Young*, he devoted three whole chapters to the subject.[22] By the late nineteenth century, a panoply of Indian images, including the *zenana* (a generalized term used to indicate Indian women's seclusion/the woman's quarters), child marriage, and the deprivations of brahmanical widowhood, had become staples for describing the horrors of the "heathen other." And in 1910, when Helen Barrett Montgomery published her wildly successful *Western Women in Eastern Lands*, she reserved her harshest criticism for the state of Hindu women in particular.[23]

Images of heathen women pervaded U.S. print and church culture over the fin-de-siècle, their reach extending well beyond the churchwomen who made up the membership of women's foreign mission societies.[24] The prominence of India and Indian women within Protestant missionary literature spoke to the global, and specifically Anglo-American, imperial dimensions of U.S. public culture. This is important to underscore because of the motivated domestication of this public culture in ongoing attempts to render invisible the deep, constitutive relationship between capitalist imperialism and the formation of the United States, as well as that nation's imperial role in the world. Undoing the naturalization of this domestication is one of the central tasks of this book. It is also necessary for grasping the mind-set among the Protestant churchgoers and missionaries who made up one of the largest and most powerful social movements during the turn-of-the-century United States. The deputations of the Reverend Dr. John Scudder Sr., Dr. Clara Swain, and Isabella Thoburn have already drawn our attention to the centrality of India to U.S. missionary ambition. Missionaries' longstanding attention to the status and state of Indian women is also evidence of how colonial contests over the "woman question" in India had a global, Anglo-American framework for their articulation.

Numerous postcolonial historians and critics have documented how the debates over the position of Indian women were central to processes of colonization on the subcontinent. As mirrored in the themes circulated through missionary literature, these debates focused most prominently on the selected brahmanical practices of sati, the age of consent (child marriage), and enforced widowhood, as well as sex work inasmuch as it affected the health of British troops. In all cases, the degraded and potentially degrading status of Indian women served as an allegory for Indian society at large, where "woman" stands in for "civilization" (or the lack thereof, as the case may be). For colonists, the low state and status of Indian women indexed India's social backwardness and justified colonial rule by casting it in a beneficent light. Anglo-American colonization would, in effect, save Indians from themselves and prepare them for a far more civilized (if perpetually distant) future.

The women's missionary movement clearly aligned itself with the civilizing mission embedded in the "woman question," while arguing for the particular place of metropolitan women in that project. This was not, however, a place marked by equality of the sexes. Women church members rejected egalitarianism and set themselves up in opposition to movements for women's rights and suffrage. Instead of demands for equal rights, the women's foreign mission movement framed itself around Victorian ideologies of womanhood and gendered "separate spheres." Members emphasized the "special" public role that emanated from woman's essential(ized) nature, a role that men could not replicate. This was the argument memorialized in the story of how Ida Sophia Scudder, granddaughter of the Reverend Dr. John Scudder Sr., came to embrace her family's medical mission on the subcontinent. Her revelation has become the stuff of legend, its details recorded in endless tracts and biographies and enshrined at the heart of the institution she founded, the Christian Medical College, Vellore (hereafter, simply, Vellore).[25] My interest here is to recapitulate the tale as it has been most prominently told in order to highlight the ways in which it exemplifies key facets fueling the feminization of medical missionary work over the turn of the twentieth century.

## *"The Night of the Three Knocks"*

The story begins in the United States, where the young Ida had been sent to complete her elementary and secondary education. By then, Ida had already decided that neither India nor the missionary life were for her. Bucking two generations of Scudder family tradition, she refused to return to the land of her birth, determined instead to live out her days in the United States. Just then, as fate would have it, her mother fell ill. The only female child among her five siblings, Ida had to return to India to attend to their mother. Her trip was meant to be a short visit, and the story picks up with Ida sitting alone in her family's mission home, penning promises to her friends in the United States of her imminent return. Just then, there came a knock on the door, followed, in succession, by two more. Three Indian men—first a Brahman, then a Muslim, and finally another privileged caste Hindu—arrived in succession, each seeking help for his wife. Each woman was in the throes of childbirth, and all three were in perilous positions. Each husbanded pleaded with Ida to accompany them to his wife's bedside, but Ida was at a loss. Having no medical training herself, she insisted that she could be of little service on her own but told them that her father was a doctor and she would gladly accompany him to their wives' bed. One by one, each husband refused to break with custom and allow a foreign man to attend upon his wife, no matter how dire the circumstances. There could be no compromise solution. In Ida's memorialized words,

> I could not sleep that night—it was too terrible. Within the very touch of my hand were three young girls dying because there was no woman to help them. I spent much of the night in anguish and prayer. I did not want to spend my life in India. My friends were begging me to return to the joyous opportunities of a young girl in America, and I somehow felt that I could not give that up. I went to bed in the early morning after praying much for guidance. I think that was the first time I ever met God face to face, and all that time it seemed that He was calling me into his work.

Early in the morning I heard the "tom-tom" beating in the village and it struck terror in my heart, for it was a death message. I sent our servant, who had come up early, to the village to find out the fate of the three women, and he came back saying that all of them had died during the night. As a funeral passed our house during the morning, it made me very unhappy. I could not bear to think of these young girls as dead. Again I shut myself in my room and thought very seriously about the condition of the Indian women and after much thought and prayer, I went to my father and mother and told them that I must go home and study medicine, and come back to India to help such women.[26]

"The Night of the Three Knocks," as it has come to be known, is classic women's missionary fare, capturing many of the central themes that animated mission rhetoric throughout the height of the movement: the dire need of Indian women, the deathly stranglehold of ossified Indian custom (both Hindu and Muslim), and the duty that fell upon Western women as a result. Encapsulating the global call of "woman's work for woman," it speaks in tones that would have been legible to the women's missionary movement. The tale relies heavily on colonial constructions of the zenana, where Indian women, Muslim and Hindu, were presumed locked away and left to languish. This invocation of female seclusion was a tried-and-true tactic of zenana evangelism, revealing what had long been a bias toward the privileged castes and classes within the Protestant civilizing mission.[27]

What dismayed missionaries was not only their lack of a substantial quantitative impact in India but also the fact that the majority of Indians who did convert came from the oppressed castes and classes. Even though missionaries at times actually prioritized these populations for conversion, they were also wont to reject them and/or remain suspicious of how pure their motivations were. This contrasted sharply with the publicity and pride displayed in the instances when a member of the privileged castes and classes converted.[28] Every single version of the "Night of the Three Knocks" that I found (and there are numerous versions given its wide circulation in multiple forums) explicitly mentions the background of the three Indian men who approach the mission door. Each of the three husbands is always characterized as privileged caste and/or class (and significantly, this cuts across both Hindu and Muslim Indians). His status serves as the explanation for the inaccessibility of his wife, and his strict adherence to "custom" justifies the stance that he would rather see her die than allow a foreign man to attend upon her. The ensuing tragedies underscore the zenana as the height of heathendom while also linking the penetration of this inner sanctum to the gendered order of Victorian separate spheres.

Most accounts of Scudder's story emphasize how her determination not to become a missionary and not to return to India were borne out of a strong will and rebellious nature. The realities of mission life for women, however, offer an additional layer of interpretation. When her mother's illness called Ida back to India, it called her back to act, in part, as an unpaid nursemaid within the privatized sphere of a mission family home full of men who were paid medical professionals. This arrangement of paid and unpaid, productive and reproductive labor was essential to the Christian civilizing mission. Indeed, the mission family was meant to be a form for Indian converts to emulate. The ABCFM had even made it an early policy that most male missionaries had to be married, thereby linking evangelism and family form.[29] Adherence to the gendered divisions of a heteropatriarchal conjugal family also served many missionaries, who, in the early to mid-nineteenth century, often hailed from working-class/lower middle-class metropolitan backgrounds. Their ability to fit a middle-class family form thus helped to mark migration as a moment in their own upward mobility. For those missionaries who hailed from more solidly middle- to upper middle-class backgrounds, it helped to buffer the relatively low position that all missionaries occupied within the colonial social hierarchy.[30]

When Ida returned to heed her domestic duties, however, she also did so as a short-term missionary, an option that spoke to the professionalization of mission work for both men and women. By the late nineteenth century, missions in the United States and Great Britain increasingly required specific training and/or preparation before deputation. Women's training stressed social background and the inculcation of "ladylike" qualities, and the specific work that women were trained to do continued to be cast as a "natural" extension of their feminine qualities and family duties. The key distinction between their work and that previously undertaken by missionary wives and daughters was that it was waged. Missionaries found a way to sidestep the potential challenge posed by women's paid work to the authority of the male breadwinner by demanding that women who received wages for their work had to remain single. If they married, they could continue to work in ways that extended the field for their domestic labor, but they would not be paid.[31] These conditions produced the "Miss Sahib," a figure whose work built upon the foundations already laid by mission women working as wives and daughters.

Mission women had long used aspects of their homework as a channel to reach out to Indian women and children. They combined Bible study and literacy with skills such as needlework and basic hygiene/medical and some, like Mrs. D. W. Thomas, also opened orphanages and provided education for girls. Such forms of domestic evangelism were convenient in that they could be cast as an extension of "naturally" feminine roles, reinforcing existing gendered notions of work and separate spheres while simultaneously expanding the scope and purpose of "women's work." In 1855, at the Arcot mission, Sarah (Mrs. Ezekiel) Scudder took three orphaned girls into her home for schooling. By 1860, her efforts had grown into a Female Boarding School, later renamed the Female Seminary. Mary Anna (Mrs. Silas) Scudder had also begun a Bible study for women in her home. It was into this field that the first single female missionaries deputed to the Arcot mission, Martha Mandeville and Josephine Chapin, arrived in 1869, the same year that brought Dr. Clara Swain and Isabella Thoburn to India.

Mandeville and Chapin were zenana evangelists, although shortly after their arrival they made the bold move of opening a Hindu girls' school on the wealthiest and most elite street in Vellore. The school observed caste practices with the idea that former students would continue taking classes after puberty/marriage, when they would no longer attend school outside the home. This would give missionaries access to Hindu homes. The school became part of a controversial network of sixteen caste girls' schools across Arcot. The mission board and missionary societies in the United States soon grew skeptical of pouring energy and resources into a project that was not for Christian converts and that did not seem to produce many either. Doubt escalated to near defeat as mission finances experienced a sharp downturn in 1896, and the decision was made to close the schools. Just then, the Woman's Board of Foreign Missions stepped in with the necessary financial resources and with vigorous arguments against a decision that was taken by male missionaries. The women won the day in what amounted to a testament to the strength of their movement and its importance to the vitality of missions generally.

Local opposition to the school, however, continued to grow. In 1887, a group of Hindu men started their own school for girls across the street, one that would provide a Hindu education for Hindu girls.[32] The controversy over the evangelical intent of mission education climaxed when, in 1890, a zenana pupil from the city of Bangalore arrived at the mission after having converted to Christianity. Julia (Mrs. Jared) Scudder, then head of the Female Seminary, reported that when news of the woman's conversion and desertion from her own home reached the townspeople of Vellore, the vast majority of zenana pupils in town closed their doors to the missionaries.[33] The effect was quite the opposite of the general argument put forward for zenana evangelism and the caste girls' schools, which was that they would *open, not close*, doors.

The elite Hindu boycott of the missionaries in Vellore took place in 1890, the same year that Ida Sophia Scudder returned to India to attend upon her ailing mother. This evangelical crisis was the unacknowledged context for the "The Night of the Three Knocks," a story that flipped the script on closed doors. A central part of the potency of Dr. Ida's revelation lay in the fact that she was actually not trying to enter that inner sanctum of the elite Indian household. She was trying to get back home—to the United States. It was in spite of her adamant looking away that women from the zenana called out to her through their tragedy and awakened her from her reverie. The centrality of the perils of childbirth was also significant to that fateful night, for the tools of domestic evangelism were clearly inadequate to the task confronting Ida Sophia. This was not about needlework; it was a matter of life and death. And the primacy of *this* need was what distinguished medical missionaries in general and single female medical missionaries in particular within the field.

The "Night of the Three Knocks" sent Ida Sophia Scudder back to the United States to attend medical school. Her ability to do so was also a product of the second half of the nineteenth century. In 1850, the WMC became the first school to train women as medical doctors in the Euro-American system.[34] It was an all-female institution, and its opening inaugurated an era when women's medical colleges flourished. It was only toward the end of the century that traditionally male medical institutions began to accept female candidates. Thus, while Ida Scudder started at the WMC, she transferred to Cornell University's Medical School when that institution first opened its doors to female candidates. Most of the women who graduated from medical school in this period found work in feminized specialties such as obstetrics, gynecology, and preventive medicine. Yet even here, opportunities for upward mobility and/or professional autonomy were limited by a profession that remained overwhelmingly male dominated. It was, in part, in light of these limitations that mission work appeared as an attractive alternative. Throughout the first half century of its existence, the WMC maintained strong links with missionary societies, gaining an international reputation for sending hundreds of its graduates to work abroad, primarily in India and China.[35] Colonial migration offered these newly minted physicians a degree of professional authority and autonomy that was as of yet unavailable at home. In the words of Dr. Ida (as she affectionately came to be known) herself,

> One of the compensations and opportunities of medical work in the East is that one has her own hospital where there is the chance to develop work along the lines she wishes. Complete control of all the work, and being chief in the hospital puts the western doctor on her metal. Having to do the most difficult operations and maternity cases, and being up against something one never dreamed of having to attempt, having to do the work alone and without consultation soon develops whatever gifts one may have. All the responsibility falls on her shoulders. Operations are often undertaken which at Home would be sent to a Specialist. In the East the doctor has to be a Specialist in all things, and it is often gratifying to see the results that are obtained. There is never any lack of stimulants to the medical interest.[36]

Dr. Ida returned to Arcot in 1900, when the link between medical women and zenana evangelism had also already been made there before her. Since its founding, the hospital at Ranipet had had the goal of accessing privileged caste and class Indians as patients. Accommodations were made for caste practices, including separate wards.[37] The advantage of having female physicians to work at the hospital had been part of this strategy. In 1894, the hospital employed its first female licensed medical practitioner (a lower grade doctor), Mary Rajanayagam Gnanamoni. Gnanamoni had graduated from the Madras Medical College that same year, and her job was to be a bridge between mission medicine and the Tamil- and Telugu-speaking population of the Arcot district. One year later, the hospital welcomed its first single female medical missionary, Dr. Louisa Hart. Dr. Hart was a fully qualified (according to colonial standards) physician of Canadian origin. She was the one left in charge of the hospital in 1899 when the then director, Reverend Dr. L. R. Scudder, went on furlough.

During her year at the helm, Dr. Hart began to argue for the need for a separate hospital for women, owing to the difficulty of securing women patients (particularly privileged caste and class women) at a hospital that also served men. She approached the Woman's Board of Foreign Missions for funds. Her request reached Ida Scudder, who was just then completing her final year of medical school. This is usually where the legend picks up, with Ida securing ten thousand dollars from a Mr. Schell, who made the donation in memory of his wife. This became the seed money for the Mary Taber Schell Memorial Centre for Women and Children, which opened in 1902. The establishment of a female medical mission at Vellore under the direction of Dr. Ida Sophia Scudder was thus the product of a network of female missionaries, medical and otherwise, who had been at work at the Arcot mission for almost half a century but who have been rendered invisible by the "Night of the Three Knocks." Instead, what emerges is a picture that could compete with Indian patriarchal practices while negotiating with the civilizing mission of the heteropatriarchal conjugal family.

## Birthing a "New Patriarchy"

The medicalization of "woman's work for woman" refined the delicate balance that the female mission movement sought to strike between its promotion of women working for wages and its insistence on the gendered separate spheres that placed women within the realm of reproductive labor. The focus on the importance of maternal health became the source for the ultimate argument women missionaries could make regarding the critical nature of reproductive labor—or the hand that rocks the cradle—to the Christianization of Indian society. At the same time, for single female medical missionaries, it raised a "woman question" of their own. For if female medical missionaries could not marry or raise their own biological children while remaining paid professionals, how were they to retain and express the "essential" femininity rooted in reproductive labor that was so central to the "separate spheres" that structured the heteropatriarchal conjugal family and that fueled the women's foreign missionary movement itself? In "Picture the Home Life in India," Dr. Ida Sophia Scudder offers her answer: their task was to get rid of the grandmothers.

In this piece, Scudder stereotyped India's grandmothers as bigoted, uneducated, indomitable, caste bound, and steeped in superstition—but far from inconsequential. When she declared that "theoretically women hold a low position. Practically they have a tremendous position,"[38] it was to the grandmothers that she referred. This was because, according to Scudder, grandmothers were the ones who carried the torch of zenana tradition. Their authority to do so stemmed from a communal, as opposed to conjugal, family form. To the missionary mind, the former degraded Indian wives and children while at the same time undercutting the authority of Indian husbands. It emasculated Indian men who then became a sign of heathendom's reproduction. When Scudder declared that "what India needs is a new grandmother,"[39] she implicitly offered herself and her cohort of single female medical missionaries as the resolution. This worked through a kind of racialized matriarchy, where Indian wives themselves became the child-like recipients of missionaries' own femininity as it sought to convert the extended family forms associated with the zenana into the gendered "separate sphere" of the heteropatriarchal conjugal family. As part of this process, single female medical missionaries also converted their own exclusion from the heteropatriarchal conjugal mission family form of Christian "civilization" into a means for becoming its privileged purveyors. In this task, their designs entered into a complicated conversation with those of privileged caste and class Indian men.[40]

If the status and state of Indian women were the ultimate justification for female medical missions, it was also absolutely critical to what Sanjay Joshi has analyzed as the making of a self-conscious Indian middle class within the crucible of colonization.[41] In this context, "middle" is a potentially misleading label, for this was the same segment of Indian society that I have been referring to as "privileged caste and class."[42] The degree of "privilege" was of course relative to a context where all Indians were subjected to the racialized hierarchies and violence that constituted British-led capitalist imperialism on the subcontinent. This should not, however, blind us to the hierarchies that did exist among the colonized, or render us unable to account for how these distinctions mattered. Colonization functioned in large part through the elaboration of difference, and this was not limited to race but also and at the same time cut across by caste, class, religion, region, gender, and sexuality in complicated ways that need to be untangled rather than assumed. As a step in the process of clarifying the complexity, it is important to stress that references to the Indian "middle class" in colonial India are references to those who occupied a position in between colonizers and the vast majority of Indians. When it came to differences among Indians, said middle class was not middling in terms of income, access, or status. Instead, "most of them were male, upper caste Hindus, *ashraf* (high-born) Muslims, or other such high-status groups, and many came from so-called 'service communities,' that is, from families and social groups that had traditionally served in the courts of indigenous rulers and large landlords. Not only did this mean that they had sufficient economic resources, but they also possessed sufficient educational training to shape and participate in public debates during the colonial era."[43]

Middle-class Indians, so defined, were a tiny portion of a population whose impoverishment and lack of access to formal education were key to the perpetuation of capitalist colonization on the subcontinent. In this sense, they were, numerically at least, the "microscopic minority" slighted in 1888 by the then departing viceroy to India, the Marquis of Dufferin and Ava, in his farewell speech. But numbers were not entirely the point. The marquis's need to publicly diminish these men was central to his justification of British rule, as well as a sign of the growing strength of their public presence.[44] My reference to "men" in particular is also purposeful. Beginning in the early nineteenth century, the public presence of the Indian middle class was overwhelmingly male. This was but one piece of what became a central tenet in the making of the middle class: its insistence on gendered divisions between public and private, even as these transformed through a multilayered interaction between Indian middle-class men, British colonial authorities, and Protestant missionaries.

The "woman question" laid important, although not exclusive, terrain for middle-class men to enact these divisions. It is indeed important not to assume that shifts in gender and sexual relations among Indians of any class, caste, religion, or community occurred solely due to an encounter with colonizers. To do so is to also assume that the forces of/accompanying capitalist colonization were the forces of change in all its incarnations. It is to assume that the colonizers were the motor of history rather than to see them as one piece of a larger process that had roots also in the decline of Mughal rule and the continuity of other forces that preexisted British imperial ascendancy and continued to exert influence during the period of British domination. In what follows, I want to keep this complexity in mind, even as I turn to the points of most obvious contact with the colonial civilizing mission.

One of the first and most prominent mobilizations of middle-class Indian men around "woman" was a response to the early nineteenth-century colonial fixation with sati. For colonizers, images of hapless Indian women flinging themselves onto the funeral pyres of their tyrannical husbands provided moral justification for colonization. Such images were also a direct attack on the authority of privileged caste and class Hindus, as widow immolation was associated with them, in particular. In the face of their own condemnation, some Hindu men responded by defending a practice that was actually neither common nor prevalent when the controversies first began.[45] Despite its relative disuse, they argued that sati's ancient religious roots made it a tradition that colonizers had no right to interfere in. Others, most prominently the Bengali social reformer Rammohan Roy, lobbied for and supported its legal abolition by the British East India Company. These differences in relation to the role of colonial regulation should not blind us to an underlying commonality. While Roy pushed for reform, he too invoked a vision of an ancient India where women had enjoyed a powerful, high status. Their fall from grace was not due to anything fundamental to brahmanical Hindu scripture but was the product of invasion and conquest. As this interpretation strengthened and spread, India continued to be understood as essentially Hindu, and the corrupting invasion in question became not British but Islamic. The Hinduization of "India" and "the" Indian woman subsequently became a critical component of "the woman question."

The mix of reform and reverence for reconstructed versions of "Indian tradition" elevated the husband-wife relationship within middle-class households.[46] It entailed a shift away from joint family models and from the authority that older women might retain within those structures. In a way, middle-class male reformers shared Dr. Ida Sophia Scudder's disdain for Indian grandmothers who were, in their case, also their mothers-in-law. Indian women from the previous generation were in some sense too recent to have had access to India's ancient unsullied glory and too old to serve as that past's redemption in the present. What was needed was a "new Indian woman," one who could fulfill the role of wife in an idealized companionate marriage and thus return Indian (especially Hindu) womanhood to its state of glory. Unsurprisingly, education, so central to the mobility of middle-class men themselves, became a key tool in their efforts to produce this "new woman."

As we have seen in the case of the Arcot mission, zenana evangelism spurred the growth of Indian efforts toward educating privileged caste and class women, albeit in ways that were meant to supplant rather than supplement what was increasingly viewed by middle-class men as missionary encroachment into their households. Competition between the two groups persisted as they both moved out of Indian homes and built schools and colleges for women. Christian institutions thus grew up alongside (and in critical ways prompted the production of) schools founded by middle-class Indian social reformers as they battled over the education of the "new Indian woman." Privileged caste and class Indians were critical of missionaries first for their evangelical intent and then, when mission colleges increasingly opened to non-Christian Indians, for the fact that they were foreign. Yet in the main, middle-class male social reformers also operated through a vision of women's education that emphasized notions of femininity and domesticity and did not prepare women for wage work or address the needs of women workers. The critical difference between their vision and that of the missionaries was that the role of the woman at home was not to be the bearer of Christian civilization. Instead, the preparation of a companionate wife as part of privileging the conjugal couple over and above the joint family was, for these men, a chance to model a gendered authority that would develop into the hegemonic blueprint for middle-class Indian nationalism.

In his by now ubiquitous formulation, Partha Chatterjee outlines how, by the end of the nineteenth century, middle-class male nationalist leaders resolved the "woman question" by conceptualizing their India in two parts: an outer, material realm dominated by colonists and an inner, spiritual realm where Indians reigned supreme.[47] Such separated spheres afforded middle-class men a space to call their own, one where they could exercise an authority that capitalist colonization otherwise precluded them from assuming. The spiritual sphere was also cast as the proper domain for the "woman question," marking this as an Indian affair, under the control of Indian men, and one that should remain properly off limits to a colonial state that had declared a noninterventionist stance when it came to community/communal concerns.

For Chatterjee, this second space of community/tradition/woman was a space of resistance. However, as several subsequent critics have pointed out, Chatterjee's separation of spheres needs to be complicated rather than assumed, particularly (although not only) because he leaves unexamined the ways in which the colonial state had itself formally ceded the domain of family, religion, and tradition to Indians. Colonial power structures did in some general sense support the sense of autonomy claimed by middle-class Indian men in this sphere even as they retained ultimate authority to administer law and intercede as necessary.[48] Others have also pointed to the way in which Chatterjee uncritically assumes the position of his subjects: the Hindu (and even more specifically in this case, Bengali) men who dominated middle-class Indian nationalism.[49] This limitation, in particular, is actually helpful for my present purposes inasmuch as it allows me to read his claims as a reflection of the middle-class Bengali male worldview (albeit somewhat anachronistically) and, accordingly, use his argument to plot how the middle-class men who led dominant versions of Indian nationalism understood, and exercised, their own sense of authority.

Within this schema, then, the sphere of religion/community/tradition became a space for nurturing a nation that was birthed out of India's ancient roots as represented and reproduced by an essentialized, Hinduized Indian woman. By the turn of the century, the idealized Indian woman was no longer primarily cast as a companionate wife. She was now, for many nationalists and religious revivalists, a mother goddess. Recourse to goddess imagery amplified the articulation of an India that was, at its core, rooted in brahmanical Hinduism. The mother goddess allowed Hindu men to valorize and conflate "woman" and "tradition" while containing women within the realm of unpaid reproductive labor, even as this labor expanded from the heteropatriarchal family to the nascent nation. The figure of "woman" thus enabled an expanded private sphere, one that became the means for middle-class Indian men to develop a gendered sense of authority within the context of capitalist colonization. In this, their project bore a family resemblance to that of the single female medical missionaries.

As we have seen, the question confronting the Miss Sahibs was how to operate within a feminized private sphere while at the same time professionalizing and earning wages for their work. Their resolution came in two parts. The first was to expand the extent to which a feminized private sphere operated so that it could include "woman's work for woman," an endeavor that troubled the lines between public and private even as it relied upon them. The second was to use the figure of the heathen woman to convert this expanded private sphere into a space for missionaries' own upward mobility and increased authority. Because they focused on women from the privileged castes and classes, single female medical missionaries actually sought to enter and transform the same space that middle-class Indian men claimed as theirs. In this sense, the mother goddess was, in part, an antidote to the memsahib, or colonial woman, of whom single female medical missionaries were but one variety. Here was where Indian tradition was a counter to Christian civilization and where the projects of these two groups found their most obvious antagonism. And if we take the contest on these terms, it must be said that missionaries were the clear losers.

The historical record reveals that the primary effect of the Miss Sahibs was not, in the end, converting their privileged caste and class Indian "sisters" to Christianity and thereby spreading the seeds of Christian civilization to all of India (or all of India that mattered). Zenana evangelism was not a marked improvement over previous missionary methods. And yet, this conclusion is only valid inasmuch as we take the biases of both groups that I have been focusing on as the limits of our own vision. For if middle-class Indians did not rush en masse to the nearest church, they did, as I have been detailing, adapt and reformulate elements of the colonial civilizing mission, including the heteropatriarchal conjugal family, as part of their own becoming. Again, this is not the same as saying that this was a one-way, unilateral, or wholly subservient process. It was instead a complicated, overlapping, and contradictory terrain, as scholarship on the complexities of colonization has made us well aware of by now. Indeed, sole attention to the confrontation, competition, and/or antagonism between these two groups masks the way in which a reformulated, gendered private sphere that adapted versions of the heteropatriarchal conjugal family enabled both middle-class Indian men and white women the ability to expand the spaces allotted them by white men and, in the process, to build an authority that challenged their own subordination. In order to achieve this, both of them used the figure of privileged caste and class Indian "woman" as cover for the creation of a space where they could incubate their own power.

In her seminal analysis of the early nineteenth-century debates surrounding sati, Lata Mani astutely argues that Indian women were actually neither the subjects nor the objects. Rather, "woman" provided the ground for a discourse on sati (specifically) or tradition (more generally). In turn, the discursive ground they provided became "the occasion for struggle over the divergent priorities of officials and the indigenous male elite."[50] I am, in a sense, making a similar argument in my comparison between the discourse of middle-class Indian men and single female medical missionaries. To this we must also add that for both groups, constructing "the" Indian woman was not only a means for articulating themselves but also a way to devalue a series of "other" Indian women.

There was one type of woman who threatened the sanctity of the conjugal couple meant to reproduce the newly emergent Indian middle-class family even more than the grandmothers, and that was the "common" woman. "Common" is code word for those who did not fit the small and selected categories of educated elites, as explicated above. It was a category cut across by caste, class, region, and religion. And it was especially aimed at women workers, those who could not afford to function solely as the unpaid reproducers of either a biological family or a nascent nation. Thus, it was that the vast majority of Indian women—and their labor— were effectively excluded from the purview of the nationalist resolution to the "woman question." Missionaries marginalized them also, but in a slightly different way.

Inasmuch as the practice of gendered separate spheres was an ideal that they maintained, the Miss Sahibs also challenged it—not because of their religion, but because of their profession. If recourse to a racialized matriarchy cast their labor within the realm of reproduction, it did not do away with the fact that these were, after all, women working for wages. In the latter role, it was not the grandmother who they sought to replace but, more specifically, the *dai* (like the zenana, a generalized colonial description, this time for Indian birth attendants). And if the grandmother was the bastion of backward tradition, it was the dai, most castigated of all, who purportedly perpetuated dangerous medical practices and was characterized by an ignorance only enhanced by her oppressed caste and class background.[51] Her outcasting by missionaries echoed the exclusion of oppressed caste and class women from constructions of the middle class—with a crucial difference. Colonial medicine sought to retrain and/or replace the dai with women workers who practiced colonial midwifery and colonial nursing. The majority of these were not, for logistical reasons, metropolitan women. They were Indian women who were overwhelmingly from the oppressed castes and classes, most of whom were also Indian Christian converts. They thus fell outside of the class, caste, and religious parameters of the women who constituted the objects of zenana evangelism and the middle-class resolution to the "woman question." They have also, and not for unrelated reasons, fallen outside of the historical archive and, therefore, outside of most historical accounts. And yet, for my present purposes, Protestant female medical missionaries were important for the way in which they point us toward a recovery of this group of Indian women workers, and so it is to their historical presence that I will now turn.

CHAPTER TWO

# Searching for Salome

On August 12, 1960, a group of nursing faculty and students at Vellore performed *"A Pageant Depicting the History of the Christian Medical College Hospital and The School of Nursing" for the Golden Jubilee of Vellore's School of Nursing (1909–1959) and the Diamond Jubilee of Its Mission Hospital (1900–1960).*[1] The *Pageant*'s storyline drew from the many biographical and autobiographical writings, stories, and anecdotes that had become central to the institution's own sense of itself.[2] Its performance was part of a gala celebration that included speeches by the then president of India, Dr. Rajendra Prasad, and the governor of Madras, H. E. Bishnuran Mehdi. All were there to celebrate the phenomenal growth of Dr. Ida Sophia Scudder's medical practice—from a single-bed dispensary to one of the premier biomedical institutions in all of independent India.

I open this chapter with a scene from the *Pageant* because it offers us the most vivid description I have found of Salome, a woman who is repeatedly named as Dr. Ida's first-ever assistant. Salome (or Salomi; there is variation in the spelling of her name) appears in accounts of Dr. Ida setting up her first dispensary. She also sometimes makes mention when the Mary Taber Schell Memorial Center for Women and Children opened two years later. Shortly thereafter, her name drops out. Her appearance in the historical record is thus brief and, ultimately, passing.[3] My intent here is to introduce the entry of Indians into colonial nursing by offering a preliminary excavation of this specific Salome. This will require reading in between the lines of available English-language source material.[4] The scanty and scattered nature of this material (with regard to Salome) is what prompts me to turn to the *Pageant* as a source that, while clearly a product of motivated remembering, also offers a base from which to embark upon an educated exploration of otherwise scattered, if surviving, sources. So let us begin, then, with the *Pageant*'s reenactment of Dr. Ida's first day on the job in India.

Salome Saves the Day(?)

SCENE III

*A downstairs room in the Mission Bungalow, Vellore. One table is prepared for writing, with a big register and files of papers and pads. Another holds basins, pus basins, a tray of instruments. In the rear is a table holding bottles, scales, etc. for compounding of drugs, also a microscope with slides ready. A taped cot is also in the rear.*

*Mrs. John comes in holding a tray of sterilized dressings, puts them down and arranges things on the tables.*

ENTER DR. IDA BY DOOR FROM VERANDA, WEARING TOPI:

DR. IDA: Good morning, Ma-mee! What are you doing in my dispensary?

MRS. JOHN: Your dispensary, is it? Don't be worried, I have been well trained, I won't bring in any germs, I brought the dressings from the sterilizer. Your father let me attend to the sterilizer when he was busy.

DR. IDA: (Hugging) Bless you! You miss him even more than I do! Oh, Ma-mee—now the day has come. I looked forward to the day all through my years at medical school—the day when father and I would work together here. No. I am here and he is gone. . . . It was a beautiful drive down to the town, Ma-mee! The sky was all pink and gold behind the palm trees. I needed that beauty in my soul before I went into those dark, dark houses to see my patients. How I longed to carry them all out into the fresh air and sunshine. The poor woman with a big abscess between her shoulders. If only father were here to tell me if it is a spinal TB as I suspect and whether I should operate or not—Oh dear how can I make such decisions alone?

MRS. JOHN: You will be guided by God and your own good sense. Now I'll leave you unless I can be of some help.

DR. IDA: No.—You have your own work to do and I must not keep you here. But I do need some help.

(ENTER WITH A KETTLE OF HOT WATER)

Thank you, Salome!

MRS. JOHN: Would you like Salome to help you? I am sure the cook can get another helper for himself. I think Salome could at least hand you things. . . .

SALOME: (Nods agreement gladly)—

DR. IDA: (Taking up another apron & trying it on Salome) My first Assistant! Eh?

MRS. JOHN: Try to finish by lunch time, Ida! Make a habit of it from the first day. It is so hard on the servants to have irregular meal times. And harder on you.

DR. IDA: (Shrugging, Smiling) I'll do my best!

(EXIT MRS. JOHN)[5]

There we have it, a depiction of the moment when Salome stepped in to help inaugurate the dawn of a new day at the dispensary. What can we know of her? Her name alone offers us a rich starting place. "Salome" clearly signals to us that its bearer was an Indian Christian.[6] As the cook's assistant, she also occupied a decidedly humble position within both mission and Indian social-economic hierarchies. These orienting details also mark her as a real representative of the Indian workers who served as the first assistants at medical missions during their rise on the subcontinent: they were largely Indian Christian women who were, or were the descendants of, converts from the oppressed castes and classes.[7] Their proximity to mission institutions—as believers, students, and workers—afforded them access to the expanding employment opportunities that accompanied mission growth. These were the women most directly affected by mission presence on the subcontinent, and their numbers spoke to a different genealogy than that of the privileged class and caste Indian women who were the objects of zenana evangelism.

Turning to Salome is turning, also, to the much longer history of Christian education aimed at the Indian women who did convert. For Protestants, records date at least as far back as 1712, with the founding of the German mission in Tranquebar.[8] There the earliest students were the daughters of enslaved Indians and Dalits. Mission education for converts was meant to socialize students into the Christian fold, as well as provide them with some basic skills for employment and, in the case of girls, the "domestic arts." While the latter was the focus of what became zenana evangelism, the former was critical among a student body who had to work outside their homes. In addition to already existing poverty, conversion often meant the loss of whatever small property or inheritance rights individuals may have held within the dominant Indian social order.[9] As mission educational institutions grew in size and scope, there was heated debate over the purpose and place of Christian education. Many missionaries voiced repeated concern over the danger of educating Indians beyond their required station in life, proscribed in caste and class terms.[10] The *Pageant* dramatizes the details of what it might mean to retrain a worker who also needed to "stay in her place."

In the play, Salome's first day is a bit of a disaster. She begins by sticking her finger into the water that's being heated for sterilization. Dr. Ida immediately scolds her. Salome replies by wiping said finger on her skirt and states that it is now "clean," to which Dr. Ida responds by snapping, "Not clean enough for this work."[11] As if that wasn't enough, Salome proceeds to throw a used cotton swab (full of pus from a patient's eye) onto the floor. When Dr. Ida reprimands her, she says she'll sweep the floor later. Her seemingly casual response prompts a lesson in how to use a garbage can for the disposal of waste *now*, not later. Salome's ignorance of basic sanitation contrasts directly with Mrs. John's assured competence. It also opens a portal onto a potentially larger problem that she posed to Dr. Ida's budding practice.

One of the first patients to enter the dispensary is an "Old Lady" who is so weak that she can barely walk. After evaluating her ailments, Dr. Ida goes over to the pharmacy table to mix up a prescription. While they are waiting, the "Patient's friend" turns to Salome and asks her about Dr. Ida: "She very young. Knowing anything? Not feel pulse at all?" We don't get Salome's reply, but what follows are a few lines in Tamil and hesitant English between the Old Lady and her friend about how foreign doctors work differently and that while Dr. Ida is a "young girl," she is also "clever," and her father was a famous doctor, but now he's dead. Meanwhile, Dr. Ida returns to the scene, prescribes the medication, and attempts to give the Old Lady her first dose. The sick woman refuses it, turning her head away. Salome then tries to administer it, at which point the Patient's friend grabs the medicine from Salome and snaps, "Give it to me, You Low caste!" She proceeds to pour the medication into the Old Lady's now open mouth.[12]

The details of this episode highlight a clear sense of trepidation combined with hopeful anticipation on the part of the Old Lady and her friend as they attempt to assess Dr. Ida and the practice of colonial medicine. She is young—but she is clever. There may be something to this—but we don't actually know. This is different. Can we trust her? It is significant that, as they wonder, they turn first to Salome for a bit of guidance. While we never get Salome's answer, and the two continue on their own, this gesture toward her is a window onto the role that Indian Christians played as cultural brokers within the multiple modalities of female missionary work, medical and otherwise. Female missionaries needed Indian women workers for their language skills, for their knowledge of cultural mores, and to help soften the distance between them and their patients, students, and potential converts.[13] In the *Pageant*, Salome serves as this kind of a bridge—up to a point.

The script flips when it comes time to take the medicine mixed by Dr. Ida. It is at this point that the potential for Salome to act as a bridge abruptly ends, and her hand becomes more potentially poisonous than the foreign medication itself. The Patient's friend's refusal to let a "low caste" administer medicine to the Old Lady becomes the first in a chain of events that emphasize the unclean nature of Salome's hands. A few moments later, Dr. Ida asks Salome to hand her a sterilized dressing. When Salome goes to grab it with her fingers, Dr. Ida exclaims, "Oh, no, no! Look!! Those dressings have been boiled. . . . They are clean. Your hands are not clean." Salome then "indignantly wipes her hands on her skirt," demonstrating their cleanliness, to which Dr. Ida replies, once again, that they are still "Not clean enough for this work." To reinforce the point, Dr. Ida begins scrubbing her own hands with soap. After the demonstration, she turns to Salome and issues the order: "Clean your hands."[14]

Will soap be enough to clean Salome's hands? Not if we read this series of events for their full implications. Salome's hands are not unclean simply because she has not washed them. They are also unclean because she is a "low caste." Her subordinated position in relation to caste and class hierarchies is already implicit in her position as a servant. Her insistence that she will, eventually, sweep the swab soaked in pus off the floor also invokes the work of sweepers, among the most ritually impure according to the dictates of brahmanical patriarchy. This association is critical as Salome transforms from the cook's assistant into Dr. Ida's aide, a job that entails doing the "dirty work" of health care. In the gendered division between doctors and nurses constitutive of colonial medicine, this work had been subordinated through its feminization. In India, colonization compounded this subordination through its intersection with caste oppression. Workers and work became mutually constitutive here—with polluting work and polluted workers reinforcing each other in a way that persisted at the moment when colonial medicine introduced primarily oppressed caste and class Indian women workers into its proto-nursing labor force. As the twentieth-century Dalit leader, intellectual and freedom fighter B. R. Ambedkar famously explained it, "The caste system is not merely a division of labour. *It is also a division of labourers.*"[15] In the case of nursing, both laborers and specific forms of labor—sweeping, the removal of polluting materials (especially human waste), and so on—got absorbed into this "new" workforce at the moment of its historical origins on the subcontinent.

The most prevalent explanations for the stigmatization of Indian nurses reduce it to the caste practices of brahmanical patriarchy. The reason most commonly offered for why Indian Christian women did take up nursing within the system of colonial medicine is that they were less bound to caste prohibitions around pollution and gendered seclusion. What the incorrigibility of Salome's unclean hands emphasizes for the *Pageant*'s viewers and readers is that conversion to Christianity alone was not enough to wash away the "stain" of this form of social sanction—a stigma that was not reducible to matters of ritual purity or pollution. It was also a matter of workers and work. Salome's hands were hands that worked, and attention to them reminds us of the manual labor they performed—the dirty work. This is what they shared with the hands of most other Indian Christian women of their time. The majority of Indians who were employed as nursing assistants were women who already had to work outside of their homes. Many (although not all) of them also would have already been involved in potentially "polluting" labor. Recognizing this makes explicit another dimension of the explanation that Indian Christian women were more "willing" to do the work. They were often the ones already doing it (in one way or another). The implicit comparison is with a middle-class Indian subject, for it is only she who would have lost the "privileges" of ritual purity, gendered seclusion, and an exclusive relegation to the realm of unpaid reproductive labor (where she too would most likely have had servants to do the dirty work). Explanations that start and stop here run the risk of assuming that what this means is that caste, understood in some essentialized and transhistorical way, persisted through colonization unchanged. We must be careful to differentiate between (the absolutely) necessary attention to the inequities inherent to brahmanical patriarchy and the potential trap laid for us by colonial epistemology, a trap that renders caste the intractable marker of Indian difference, shame, and inferiority without analyzing the ways in which colonization itself also became a factor in the making and remaking of caste hierarchies.

The nineteenth-century Indian anticaste social reformer Jotirao Phule saw the complicity between caste and colonialism clearly. While he never converted, Phule had completed his secondary education in English at a mission school run by the Free Church of Scotland in Pune, then part of the Bombay Presidency.[16] In 1848, he visited the girls' boarding school in Ahmadnagar begun by Cynthia Farrar, a single female missionary deputed by the ABCFM to work at the American Marathi Mission. That same year, Phule and his wife, Savithribai, founded a girls' school on that model in Pune. They would later also begin a home for single mothers and child widows as part of the series of educational institutions that they founded and taught in for the purpose of wielding education as a weapon in the struggle against caste and for the liberation of the majority of Indians.

Phule saw colonial education as an opportunity for Shudras (those who would today be known as the "other backwards castes") and Dalits to break through the barriers to schooling and textual knowledge that were so central to the stranglehold of brahmanical power. He also testified that this potential was undercut by the government's deference to, and active recruitment of, Brahmins. His argument was that because of this, the civil service (and, we can add, the colonial professions) did not do away with caste privilege so much as remake it in ways that strengthened the stranglehold of brahmanical patriarchy.[17] In what ways might we read nursing as a site for the remaking of caste oppression? And how does the crucible of colonization connect the position of colonial nursing's earliest Indian recruits to a global workforce constituted through conquest and colonization and reconstituted through the elaboration of hierarchies based on gender, class, race, and caste?

## Colonization, Racialization, and the Rise of the Trained Nurse

In the early decades of the nineteenth century, hospital nursing was in its infancy in Europe, the United Kingdom, and North America. It consisted of menial and servile tasks that none but the most marginalized—or religious—women would perform. Nurses came in two prototypes. The first was famously captured by Charles Dickens's Sarah (Sairey) Gamp, the elderly, impoverished, drunk character working with little regard for the actual care of her poor patients, from whom she was barely distinguishable.[18] The other descended from the work of the Sisters of Charity, founded in France in the seventeenth century. The Sisters of Charity undertook care of the sick as central to its mission, beginning with home visits but eventually also becoming hospital staff. In 1840, the Protestant Sisters of Charity (later known as the Nursing Sisters) also organized across the Channel. Both Catholic and Protestant sisterhoods spread their wings alongside European colonizers. The global reach of their work laid an institutional and ideological foundation for the development of nurse training, begun under their auspices before it became associated with the figure of Florence Nightingale.

Nightingale's nursing résumé began in 1850 with the Sisters of Charity in Alexandria, Egypt. From there she went to Europe to complete her training in Kaiserworth, Germany, and then to work with the Sisters of Charity in Paris before becoming the superintendent of English General

Hospitals in Turkey. From Turkey, Nightingale went to serve the British troops fighting in the Crimean War. It was her service there, in the midst of a war that marked the shifting sources of global imperial power,[19] that the "lady with the lamp" gained the fame that launched her career as the most prominent leader of the push to promote trained nursing. Returning to England, she founded the Nightingale Training School for nurses at St. Thomas's Hospital in London. Shortly thereafter, she published her wildly influential *Notes on Nursing*, which spread her ideas about sanitation, military health, hospital planning, and the necessity for nurse *training*.[20]

Nightingale's insistence on training was firmly linked to her belief in sanitation as a separate sphere of medical work, one that could and should be the preserve of nurses. Nursing's "sanitary mission" was a means to literally clean up the stigmatization of nurses as "loose and lowly" women à la old Sairey Gamp. For Nightingale, the cure to this "disease" was a kind of class reformation that was enacted through the framing of nurses as the handmaidens of doctors in a gendered, sexualized division of labor where men cure and women care.[21] She rejected neither this sexual division of labor nor its purportedly biological roots. Instead, she famously insisted that a "good nurse" was, first and foremost, a "good woman." Her emphasis on the "good" and the "virtuous" secularized the Christian mission of the nursing sisterhoods while framing nursing as a way for women to actually *enact and embody* the ideals of Victorian femininity. A nurse's duty became the "natural" extension of a Victorian lady's role within the private sphere of the patriarchal family: to the doctor, she was absolutely obedient; to the patient, she was selflessly devoted; and to the lower level hospital employees, she exercised the harsh discipline of a household manager. Thus, even as sanitation was marked as the especial preserve of nurses within the hospital, it was not figured as a separate and equal sphere so much as a subordinate and obedient one. Nurses did not threaten the work of doctors so much as enable it. It was in this way that Nightingale figured trained nursing as appropriate for middle-class women, especially those who had not, for whatever reason, married. In the words of the grand dame herself: "How many good women every one has known, who have married, without caring particularly for their husbands, in order to find—a natural object—a sphere for their activity. . . . The want of *necessary* occupation among English girls must have struck every one. . . . In the middle classes, how many there are who feel themselves burdensome to their fathers, or brothers, but who, not finding husbands, and not having the education to be governesses, do not know what to do with themselves."[22]

Nightingale insisted that training made nursing acceptable to a "better sort" precisely by seeking legitimacy through rather than against the heteropatriarchal norms of the bourgeoisie. Thus, the earliest nursing leaders distinguished themselves as "good nurses" not only by their training but also by remaining unmarried. Their status as single certainly drew from the legacy of the sisterhoods, but it was also the final way in which they entered the world of wage work through a compact with the norms of the bourgeois heteropatriarchal conjugal family. It allowed their wages to remain a separate affair, one that did not threaten the privileged ideal of the male breadwinner as head of household. At this point, we are standing but one step away from the call for "woman's work for woman" that animated Ida Scudder's return to India as a fully qualified medical physician. The step is imperial in its dimension, positioning white women's work in relation to the "backwardness" of the women whom Anglo-American capitalist imperialism set out to colonize.

Even a cursory glance at the map of "the lady with the lamp's" own evolution—from Egypt to Turkey to Crimea—makes clear the constitutive relationship between her promotion of trained nursing and empire. Her abiding concern with the health of Britain's own troops extended to India, itself a major outpost of the British army. In the late nineteenth century, Nightingale issued recommendations regarding nursing and sanitation in India, corresponded with Indian social reformers, and made sure she was consulted in major public health debates.[23] Despite this deep imbrication, or perhaps because of it, most accounts naturalize empire as the grounds upon which Nightingale nursing took shape, thus obscuring its imperial origins and ambitions.

Highlighting the imperial scope of Nightingale nursing reveals a critical foreclosure. In what has been handed down to us as a classic case of the race-sex stereotyping of jobs, trained nursing in the post-Nightingale period became the preserve of "white women in white."[24] It was an image that willfully erased the Afro-diasporic women who worked as nurses in the very same fields, at the very same time. When the Crimean War broke out, the Afro-Jamaican nurse Mary Seacole applied to serve but was refused. Undeterred, she gathered up her own means and traveled to the warfront independently, setting up a nursing station for soldiers just behind the battle lines. Eliminating Seacole from this moment disables an analysis of the systematic ways that post-Nightingale trained nursing produced itself through the racialized exclusions and hierarchies of capitalist imperialism. This becomes clear as we return to India and contextualize the employment of Salome.

It was not until post-Nightingale models of nurse training emerged that colonial nursing became an occupation that could be compatible with the colonial "civilizing mission." Over the course of the nineteenth century, the denigration (both materially and ideologically) of nursing labor that held sway in Europe, the United Kingdom, and North America also marked the tenuous and marginal status of the white women who took up colonial nursing in India. The investigative research of Rosemary Fitzgerald is invaluable for helping to give us a sense of these women workers. She describes their numbers as small and asserts that while this may account for the lack of information we have about them, it is not a sufficient explanation. From what we know, this was a "highly variegated assortment" of "socially inferior" white women.[25] They were the deserted wives and widows of British/European soldiers and low-level colonial officials. They were Anglo-Indians and East Indians (those descended from British/European and Indian parents).[26] They were, as the century wore on, also single women working within mission structures. They were all women who had, in one way or another, fallen or opted out of the structures of the heteropatriarchal family and into the world of waged work. They were the subcontinental counterparts of Sairey Gamp, "women on the loose," performing a historically stigmatized and stigmatizing form of feminized "dirty work."

Neither the already outcasted and impoverished white women who worked as nurses in nineteenth-century India, nor the nursing sisterhoods who had become a cheap source of labor for government hospitals, could serve the reproductive, regenerative role assigned to whiteness as it came to be its own justification for the right, indeed the duty, to rule over "others." The *Pageant* makes this manifest when it erases the "lesser" white women who worked as nurses in nineteenth-century India and presents us instead with the image of Mrs. John Scudder, whose training in sanitation had to have taken place in the context of a patriarchal husband-wife relationship. There were no nursing schools in India during her day, as there were not in most of the rest of the world. Her elite background[27] and the representation of her as a model of middle-class respectability allow her to maintain the status of white women as the bearers of a heteropatriarchal Christian colonial civilizing mission in a way that these "other" white women could not. As Fitzgerald points out, this was another reason why the presence of these earlier nurses may not have been deemed fit for preservation.[28] They threatened to undo the imperial function of bourgeois white femininity.

The erasure of these "other" white women did not mean that the stigmatization of nursing labor ceased. Instead, it was transferred—to Indians. This becomes manifestly clear when Mrs. John suggests Salome for the job, and Salome becomes the one who bears the burden of representing the unfit, unready, unclean—and low caste. Contextualized in this way, we can move caste away from its status as an absolute marker of "Indian difference" and raise, instead, the question of how caste hierarchies informed the particular way in which the stigmatization of nursing labor took shape in India. How did this vary according to caste's regionally specific manifestations? What difference did conversion to Christianity make? How did Salome's position relate to the divisions within metropolitan nursing between Old Sairey Gamp and the sisterhoods? In what way was Salome an inheritor of Sairey's position as stigmatized servant? In what way was her outcasting related to Seacole's? What role did easy recourse to caste as the explanation of Indian inferiority play in the erasure of lesser whites and the privileging of middle-class white femininity? What was the relationship between caste and race in the context of colonization? And how were both related to the position of missionaries within the colonial social order? To the dismal wages and meager working conditions characterizing most mission institutions and government hospitals in India?[29]

Instead of a field opened by this type of questioning, what has prevailed is an essentialized rendering of caste as the ultimate marker of "Indian difference" in a way that actually upholds brahmanical patriarchy as the ultimate source of "Indian tradition." It was now no longer the gendered division of labor inherent in the development of colonial medicine that was the source for stigmatizing this form of "dirty work." The stigmatization of Indian nurses became an Indian problem, one rooted in an a historical rendering of caste, gender, and religious hierarchies in India and one that opened a space for the upward mobility of a new category of white women: the trained colonial nurse.

## Hospital Nursing and the Rise of India's Colonial Nursing Leadership

In 1902, Miss Lillian Hart, sister of Dr. Louisa Hart of the Ranipet Hospital, became the first nursing superintendent of the newly minted Mary Taber Schell Memorial Center for Women and Children. The hiring of a trained nursing supervisor reflected emergent trends in the evolution of metropolitan hospitals. There, post-Nightingale nursing was ushering in a new division of nursing labor. Instead of simply leaving hospitals for private duty nursing upon graduation, nursing graduates were filling the ranks of nursing superintendents. This was a role that emphasized the importance of nurses to hospitals, positioned trained nurses at the helm of the nursing workforce, and distinguished them from the majority of nurses vis-à-vis their access to a certain level of education.

Miss Hart's migration to work at the Schell Hospital indicated that Dr. Ida's institution was in conversation with developments within metropolitan hospitals and supported trained nursing in a way that was very much still in the trenches there. This latter point is not to be taken for granted. First, the necessity for nurse training (and with it, nursing superintendents) was not yet fully accepted or established—anywhere in the world. It was very much still in development. In 1893, Isabel Hampton of the Johns Hopkins Hospital spearheaded a meeting of nursing superintendents at the World's Fair in Chicago. The resulting organization included both Canadian and U.S. nurses and went through several permutations before giving birth, in 1911, to the U.S.-only American Nurses Association (ANA).[30] Let us be clear that this was not unionization. These were not attempts to organize the overwhelming majority of the nursing workforce. All of this organizing was for nursing superintendents and alumnae of nurse training programs, and it was a push toward professional recognition over and against complaints about the exploitation of student nurses by hospitals. This was the context that brought Miss Lillian Hart to the Schell Hospital, to replace Mrs. John Scudder.

Hart was the superintendent of nursing at the hospital for its first five years, during the decade that ushered in the peak period for the migration of metropolitan trained nurses to India. Most were from Britain, the United States, and Canada, and they brought with them their drive to elevate trained nursing and, alongside it, themselves. Events in India were thus roughly contemporaneous with those in metropolitan locations. The main difference in India was that female medical missions became the primary institutions to house trained nurses, particularly as they grew from dispensaries into hospitals during the first decades of the twentieth century. Single female medical missionaries, themselves at the forefront of struggles for female access to education and professionalization, were predisposed to be the allies of nurses pushing for status and authority based on their training. The promotion of nursing also helped to bolster their own status. As women working in a system of medicine that had subordinated women as nurses, promoting and employing trained nurses ensured that female physicians would not be mistaken for nurses themselves.

In 1905, in a move that resonated with contemporaneous developments in the United States, nine nursing superintendents who were working across India met to discuss the difficulties of their own isolated work situations as well as the future of colonial nursing on the subcontinent. Out of this meeting, they formed the Association of Nursing Superintendents of India (ANSI) and began to hold annual meetings. In 1908, ANSI spawned the Trained Nurses Association of India (TNAI), comprising nurses who were trained but not necessarily working at the supervisory level. The two organizations met and worked in tandem, jointly publishing the *Nursing Journal of India* and eventually amalgamating while retaining the name TNAI.[31]

In both North America and India, the organization of trained nurses was a process marked deeply by racialized exclusion and/or segregation. White hospital nurses in the United States had from the beginning worked to distinguish themselves from African American women and the latter's association with enslaved forms of domestic labor. Mainstream nursing accounts position women such as Dorothea Dix, white hospital reformer and superintendent of Army Nurses for the Union during the Civil War (1861–65), as Nightingale's U.S. counterpart. They fail to mention that Seacole too had her counterparts during this war. Two of the fiercest Afro-American freedom fighters of the era, Harriet Tubman and Sojourner Truth, also worked as nurses on the frontlines. After the war was over, Truth continued to work as a nurse for the Freedman's Relief Association in Washington, D.C.[32] And in 1879, African American nurse Mary Eliza Mahoney graduated from the New England Hospital for Women and Children's Training School for nurses, just six years after the first white woman, Linda Richards, did.[33] Mahoney was also in attendance at that first meeting at the World's Fair in Chicago. However, as the brief period opened by postwar Reconstruction came to a close, hospitals and trained nursing in the United States quickly fell in line with Jim and Jane Crow segregation. Since that time, U.S. nursing history has, by and large, followed suit in a way that naturalizes segregation by either erasing Afro-American nurses or segmenting them off into a separate book or chapter. This is clearly insufficient for my present purposes.

I have found no archival evidence of African American nurses (formally trained or not) migrating to work in India at this time. This does not mean that there could not have been a few who did. Afro-American women had long been involved in Protestant evangelism. In 1823, Miss Betsey Stockton went to Maui as an evangelist and a teacher. She was the first single female missionary that we have a record of in U.S. history.[34] As the century wore on, missionary work offered many Afro-Americans an opportunity for mobility that few other venues did at the time. For a variety of reasons, most went to either the Caribbean or Africa, but at least one did make it to India.[35] Mrs. Amanda Smith was a member of the Methodist Episcopal Church and an ardent evangelist. Once she became a widower, her passion led her deep into the missionary circuits of the United States and then on to the United Kingdom, India, and eventually Liberia. She visited India in 1879, where her travels intersected with Dr. Clara Swain. Both Smith's autobiography and Swain's collected letters contain descriptions of a mudslide that occurred while the two of them were staying together as part of a missionary group vacationing in the hill station of Nainital. Dr. Swain went on to pen no end of praise for Smith.[36] And James Mills Thoburn (the aforementioned Isabella Thoburn's brother and a missionary based in India) wrote in his preface to Smith's autobiography, *"During the seventeen years that I have lived in Calcutta, I have known many famous strangers to visit the city, some of whom attracted large audiences, but I have never known anyone who could draw and hold so large an audience as Mrs. Smith."*[37]

These historical flashes are exciting for the possibilities they raise about expanding our sense of subaltern histories as well as overlapping and intersecting worlds. And yet, the presence of Afro-American missionaries had to be the exception, not the rule, on the Indian subcontinent, where colonization was constituted through racialized hierarchies. This was especially so when it came to the single female medical missionaries and missionary nurses who are my focus here. As we have seen in the case of the former, the opportunity for upward mobility and professional authority offered them by migration to India depended, critically, on their position over and above Indians as racialized "others." And while Protestant evangelism did offer African Americans some space in certain instances to partake in a "civilizing" mission, they could not have established a concerted presence in India without at the same time unduly complicating if not calling into question the racialized foundations of colonial rule in India. With this in mind, we can then return to understanding the distance that white nurses took from black nurses in the United States as both a symptom of the racialized apartheid that has been constitutive of settler colonialism *and* a preparatory step for the Anglo-American imperial turn that trained nurses self-consciously took at the turn of the century.

In 1899, the International Council of Nurses (ICN) formed, with Ethel Fenwick of England as the first president, Mary Agnes Snively of Canada as treasurer, and Lavinia Dock of the United States as secretary. The ICN had been preceded by the Colonial Nursing Association, founded in London in 1894,[38] and was followed in 1903 by the Nurses Missionary League. These organizations found their counterparts in the literature authored by these same nursing leaders where they cast their work within a self-consciously global, imperial framework.[39] India figured prominently in their imagination, due in no small part to the focus built up around it through "woman's work for woman."[40] Rosemary Fitzgerald analyzes this moment as a sign that trained nurses had arrived at a point where they could be seen as bearers of a colonial "civilizing mission."[41]

In the United States, the first decade of the twentieth century saw the successful passage of nursing registration acts based on educational attainment and testing, producing the earliest batches of registered nurses (RNs).[42] Dr. Ida was on top of these developments. While on a fundraising furlough to the United States in 1907, she met and recruited Delia Houghton, RN, to come and work at Schell (where Houghton remained for thirty-two years). Her deputation was part of the successful effort to upgrade nursing education at the hospital. In 1909, the hospital inaugurated a diploma nursing school of its own, with Houghton as its head instructor. This put Vellore at the vanguard of nursing education in India.

The opening of the nursing diploma school at the Arcot mission took place just one year after ANSI had brought a resolution to upgrade nurse training in India via standardization to the South Indian Missionary Medical Conference (SIMMA). Members of SIMMA then conducted a survey of mission medical institutions and, in 1911, met to start planning standards based on these. The resulting recommendations included proscribed textbooks, a minimum age for probationers (nursing students), and a set course for a three-year training program.[43] The decision by ANSI (which was not, by definition, a missionary organization) to go to SIMMA is significant for understanding the primary place that missions—not the colonial government—had in the development of training Indians in nursing.

The government hospitals that did have nurses (many did not) employed women who were mostly white or Anglo-Indian. Missions were where Indians working in colonial nursing found employment but not authority. In 1912, the TNAI became the first non-Western member of the ICN. It was also, technically, the organization that broke the ICN's race barrier. Two years earlier, the TNAI had opened to Indian nurses who met its requirements for training, which meant that this milestone was mostly on paper. When it joined the ICN, only one Indian, Rosie Singh of Ludhiana, was a TNAI member. Her membership was exceptional at a time when India's colonial nursing leadership was primarily missionary and resolutely not Indian. The question that Rosie Singh's presence in the historical records helps to raise is the following: how did the move toward more standards, enacted as it was by white nursing leaders, affect the status of Indian workers? The *Pageant* dramatizes the possibilities.

### But My Daughter Is a "Good Girl"

By the time the Schell Hospital opened its first nursing diploma school, the Arcot mission already featured a web of day and boarding schools providing elementary, secondary, and vocational education as well as junior colleges, a seminary, and a normal (teacher training) school. The hospital had also begun a course for compounders (pharmacists) in 1903. In the midst of all this, the nursing school had to compete for students. That this was something of an uphill battle is made manifest in a scene from the *Pageant* depicting a day in Miss Houghton's classroom.

Class is about to begin when the father of a new student, Jaya, comes barging in. He demands that his daughter come home with him at once. Miss Houghton intervenes, trying to convince him to let Jaya stay, adding that nursing school was tuition free *and* came with a stipend to cover all related expenses. Jaya's father replies, "My daughter is educated up to the 8th class! You ask her to do sweeper's work! . . . Let others do it if they wish, but not my daughter! I want her to make a good marriage. No good family would ask for a girl who earned her living by this menial work."[44] Miss Houghton counters with the conviction that nursing is Christian work, and his daughter's desire to engage in it is a mark of her desire to provide Christian service. Jaya's father remains unconvinced, saying that he would prefer her to become a teacher in order to fulfill her duty to Christ. The rest of the scene is worth quoting in full:

> MISS HOUGHTON: Teaching does not appeal to her. It is not the talent God has given her.
>
> FATHER: She must obey her parents. You are a foreigner, Madam, and you are ignorant of Indian customs. In India it is only women of loose morals who are midwives and nurses. I cannot let my daughter get a bad name. We are a respectable family.

MISS HOUGHTON: (Trying to be patient) In England it was the same until Florence Nightingale, daughter of a high family, defied her father and took up the work. She made Nursing an honourable profession in every land.

FATHER: Not in India.

MISS HOUGHTON: Salome,—you talk to him. We must overcome this bad idea of nursing!

SALOME: Sir, do not be afraid to follow this new path! Our ancestors walked on foot paths and dirty roads or rode in bullock carts. In this generation we go by train or in horse carriages. Our doctor has even a new and faster bandy, a horseless carriage, called a motor. Do we continue in the old ways and refuse the new?[45]

FATHER: You were very good to my wife when she was Dr. Scudder's patient.

SALOME: Of course, I was! I consider it a privilege to make my patients happy and comfortable. I am not an 8th Standard girl. A girl with that much education can understand all of these Science lessons and become almost a doctor! Is that dishonourable? I am happy to follow in the footsteps of our Master, JESUS who gave HIS LIFE to serve and heal others. If HE could wash their feet, why can't I bathe those who are too weak to stand up?[46]

Given the scarcity of actual details about Salome as a historical person at the Arcot mission, it is indeed a powerful moment when Miss Houghton hands the fictional conversation off to her in this scene. The drama of the gesture—"Salome,—you talk to him"—and the following speech that emphasizes the movement from a relentlessly retrograde Indian custom to Christian progress refer me back to the significance of her name. In Christian literature, "Salome" (or "Salomi") is a liminal figure associated with both devotion and transgression. Salome is the name of the sister of Jesus, one of his three female followers who witnessed his crucifixion and the second midwife at his birth. The last of these three is the most relevant for furthering our understanding of the significance of "Salome" in this scene. The first midwife, Zelomi (a variant of Salome), was the one who declared that a virgin has just given birth to a child. Zelomi tested this truth with her finger, upon which her hand burned. An angel then came to tell her to touch the child so that she would be healed. When her hand healed in this way, she became a believer (and thus blurred into the figure of Salome, the follower of Jesus).[47]

These biblical references offer a guide to analyzing the evolution (so to speak) of Salome over the course of the *Pageant*. Salome's unclean hands are marked by the detritus not only of caste or even devalued forms of labor but also of disbelief. In this particular case, it is not a disbelief in Christ, as Salome, Jaya, and her father are all Indian Christians. However, it was, if we recall the opening scenes, a disbelief in the importance of hygiene and sanitation, thus breaking the link between nursing and Christian service that Miss Houghton here insists on and that Jaya's father disputes. In this later scene, when Salome speaks, we find her utterly transformed into a model nurse. Her invocation of new modes of transportation associates colonial nursing with technological progress. Further implicit in her speech and her person is the admonition that Indians must give up their reluctance to nursing on the basis of "custom." She is thus a midwife to the birth of a new Indian nurse, one who can represent medical progress in a colonial context where Christianity still held sway over the field. Salome is not advocating for a return to the sisterhoods, however. Her admiration for Jaya's level of education emphasizes the impact of trained nursing at Vellore. It is also, at the same time, a stepping aside, for with the introduction of a diploma program, Salome could no longer herself make the grade.

In the Indian context, the invocation (however indirectly) of a midwife also returns us to the "problem" of the "demon dai." The "Grand Finale: Part I" of the *Pageant* makes this connection vividly clear. The Commentator takes the audience back to the "old days" when "the devils of Ignorance, Fear, Superstition and Disease ruled the land."[48] The consummate scene that captures all of these evils is the moment of the birth of an Indian child, when the only ones to watch over him are "2 old crones in dirty clothes and disheveled hair and dirty hands. One is the midwife who holds a newborn infant. The other is the grandmother of the baby."[49] Both characters believe the child may be possessed by evil spirits and almost throw him away in an ash heap. The midwife goes on to smear the infant in cow dung and then stuffs mother and child in a dark and airless corner while she wipes her rusty sickle on her skirt (a gesture that resonates with Salome's actions earlier). Before leaving for her next hob, she instructs the grandmother to brand the baby sixteen times if he shows more signs of being possessed.

The scene represents a fantastical reenactment of what missionaries imagined happening behind those three doors that had been locked to the young Ida Scudder on that fateful "Night of the Three Knocks," now many moons ago. This scene reminds viewers and readers of the central place that childbirth, and hence processes of biological as well as social reproduction, had to the establishment and growth of female medical missions. It also reminds us of the two figures that Dr. Ida had to clear from her path: the Indian grandmother and the dai. In the first chapter, we saw how figuring a racialized matriarchy allowed single female medical missionaries to rechannel their reproductive labor into patient care, thereby retaining the sanctity of the white heteropatriarchal family and replacing the Indian grandmother at the same time. Replacing the dai took a slightly different path—one that left a definitive mark on the way in which trained nursing came to be established on the subcontinent.

If rescue and conversion of the new mother by single female medical missionaries was the cure to the Indian grandmother as bastion of backwards tradition, the dais presented a different sort of problem. For as polluted and polluting as "the demon dai" purportedly was, she was also a figure with a certain kind of authority within the Indian social structure, an authority that had to be broken in order for colonial medicine to assert itself as "progress."[50] Thus, in addition to demonizing the dai, from the mid-nineteenth century onward, colonial governmental officials and missionaries also launched different kinds of dai retraining schemes. Historian Geraldine Forbes describes how poor planning and implementation limited the impact of most of these programs. She also cites four reasons why, from the perspective of the Indian workers who were meant to participate in one such scheme, the training was of little use: "First, they regarded their time as money and wanted to be paid to attend. Second, they found the training schemes interfered with their ability to practice their craft. Third, they did not recognize the superiority of the Western way of childbirth. And finally, clients were satisfied with their services."[51]

The Madras Presidency took the lead in creating a corps of midwives when, in 1854, it implemented a training program in its government-run Lying-In Hospital. The application form asked candidates for their name, age, whether they were European or East Indian, whether they were married women or widows, their husbands' corps or departments, and a copy of a certificate of character.[52] The third question revealed an expectation that candidates would be the wives or widows of British soldiers. In addition, "East Indian" referenced those of mixed European and Indian ancestry. The lack of emphasis on Indians is borne out by the record of the actual candidates who applied. By 1871, the school had graduated 122 Europeans or East Indians and five "natives."[53] This was still the same population who made up the earliest recruits to sick nursing on the subcontinent.

In the mid-nineteenth century, training in midwifery was actually prioritized over and above sick nursing. This emphasis followed from the focus on maternal and infant health that fed into the "woman question" and gave rise to the space opened by "woman's work for woman." It was not until the 1870s that sick nursing began to be prioritized, as part of the global influence of Nightingale-style hospital nursing. Rather than doing away with the prior emphasis on midwifery, trained nursing in India absorbed it.[54] Nursing courses retained special sections on midwifery. In this way, Indian nurses came to be cast as the antidote to traditional Indian birth attendants and as the particular contribution of female medical missions to the Christian colonial civilizing mission. This history of midwifery as it relates to "woman's work for woman" adds weight to a woman named "Salome" preaching the path of Christian progress.

Jaya's father's resistance to his own daughter following in these footsteps also brings us to another "Salome," one who is rooted in the erotics of female temptation and transgression. The origins of this figure are multiple, and within Christian literature, there are two primary references. In *The New Testament*, the daughter of Herodias, who is here unnamed, dances before King Herod and pleases him so much that he grants her any wish she wants. She asks (on behalf of her mother) for John the Baptist's head on a platter. King Herod, husband of Herodias and stepfather of the dancer, must abide by his word and thus behead John. Herodias' motivations are supposedly to revenge John the Baptist for stating that her marriage to Herod was unlawful (because she was a divorcé). The other, contemporaneous occurrence of this character is in Flavius Josephus' *Jewish Antiquities*, where she is explicitly named Salome. Since that time, Salome the seductress has come to be associated with, specifically, the dance of the seven veils. The seven veils is possibly also a reference to the pre-Christian Assyrian/Babylonian fertility goddess Ishtar, who, when she went to visit her sister in the underworld, had to pass seven gates by shedding an item of clothing in front of each. By the time she passes the seventh door, she is naked and imprisoned. Salome thus came to represent a kind of compendium of female sexuality as inherently dangerous, deceitful, and pagan.

There is, in the scene with Jaya's father, a translation of the dangers of female sexuality "on the loose" in relation to the emergent pool of Indian nursing labor when he flatly states, "In India it is only women of loose morals who are midwives and nurses. I cannot let my daughter get a bad name. We are a respectable family." His statement is a twist on the insistent, consistent refusal of each of the three fathers in the "Night of the Three Knocks." There, it is absolutely inadmissible for a "foreign man" to attend upon a privileged caste and class Indian woman. Here, it is the inadmissibility of a "good girl" to perform the "dirty work" associated with nursing. Sex work was part of the insinuation here, as some (although not all) nurses worked with male patients.[55] For Jaya to enter this work would thus render her unmarriageable: "No good family would ask for a girl who earned her living by this menial work. . . . We are a respectable family."

The imperative to reproduce respectability allows me to differentiate even further the characteristics of the first Indians to work as nurses within colonial medicine and to see how this moment of the introduction of trained nursing was poised to be an "upgrade." It was not just that the earliest Indian nurses were primarily Indian Christian converts and, therefore, likely to come from the oppressed castes and classes. They were also often widows, orphans, survivors of famines, and other individuals who had been economically and socially dispossessed. The prevalence of widows, in particular, raises the distinct possibility that Salome was one herself. This status would have doubly outcast her—first by the structures of brahmanical patriarchy—and then from the support systems offered by family and community (regardless of position within dominant social orders). Their status as abandoned by social structures was what they had in common with their white predecessors/counterparts who also did not, by and large, make it into the archives of the civilizing mission.

We do, however, have mediated glimpses. In *Meet the Indian Nurse*, Ethel Bleakley, single female medical missionary in Bengal, introduces readers to her first three assistants—Hemila, Shoila, and Shorojini (all widows)—and describes how they built up their own dispensaries and became semi-independent practitioners. Their work was especially important in providing a bridge between her work and the work of conversion among local Indians.[56] Bleakley's testimony adds nurses to the suggestion made by historian Geraldine Forbes that Indian "lady doctors" (a lower grade of doctor than the Miss Sahibs) performed a form of hybrid medicine, one that we need to look more closely at in order to understand how Indians practiced and responded to colonial medicine in complicated ways.[57] In addition, in her aptly titled work, *Outside the Fold*, Gauri Viswanathan elucidates Christian conversion as a conversation rather than a total erasure. It is an invitation to dialogue between existing social structures as converts attempt to make meaning and space for themselves.[58] We can add nursing to this list, and also recognize that Indian uptake of colonial nursing was not always borne out of being abandoned. Some of the Indian women who became nurses actively chose to leave social structures they found abusive or unsatisfactory. The story of one of these, Vidyalakshmi (known more commonly as Vidyaben), comes to us through that of a most (in)famous Indian woman, Dr. Rakhmabai.

A nineteenth-century child bride, Rakhmabai had refused to consummate her marriage after she reached physical maturity. In response, her much older husband, Dadaji Bhikaji, filed a case with the Bombay High Court for restitution of conjugal rights in 1884. The trial and ensuing verdicts became a flashpoint for debates around child marriage and the age of consent. It was also embroiled in controversies over the effects of women's education on their ability to fulfill their role as wives. Rakhmabai had had access to schooling at her parents' home, and when she stressed the she and her husband were incompatible, it was partly in reference to the difference that this education had made for her. Despite adverse rulings, the threat of imprisonment, fines, and her eventual excommunication, Rakhmabai persisted in her refusal. Instead of consummating her marriage, she went to England, studied medicine, and returned to set up a medical practice in the city of Rajkot (part of present-day Gujarat).[59] While working there, she encouraged Indian women to take up nursing, going so far as to fundraise for that purpose. One of the women she convinced was Vidyaben, a mother of two who was estranged from her husband. Vidyaben began by assisting Dr. Rakhmabai but eventually took up employment with the local chapter of the Red Cross and became an advocate of birth control. She also eventually returned to her husband but refused to have more children.[60]

The fictionalized Jaya presents us with a different picture. Here is a young Indian Christian woman who comes from a family and a community that wants to keep her in their fold. The question is not one of abandonment but respectability—and upward mobility. Jaya's family is also clearly not of the sort of Indian introduced to us through the "Night of the Three Knocks." They are of the working classes. The question is not whether Jaya is allowed to leave her home but what kind of a home hospital work would allow her to make. Her father insists that as a teacher, she could fulfill her duty as a Christian *and* make a good marriage. This is apparently not something that a foreigner like Miss Houghton would understand. It is, he asserts, an Indian thing. His stubbornness in this regard can be read as a reiteration of the stubbornness of "Indian tradition" as analyzed above in regard to Salome's caste status. And indeed, caste is not far away from the picture here even as it remains unnamed. As historian and feminist theorist Uma Chakravarti emphasizes, endogamy, and proscriptions over female sexuality as a means of ensuring it, have historically been absolutely central to the reproduction of caste. Caste groups only maintain themselves through marriage within the group, thereby making female sexuality a key to the maintenance of caste purity. This is what makes caste a system organized by productive *and* reproductive labor.[61]

This double duty frames Jaya's father's insistence that his daughter make a "good marriage." For members of the oppressed castes and classes, education offered a means for upward mobility in economic terms. It did not necessarily confer the dignity that had heretofore been denied them on the social, cultural, and spiritual plane. While conversion to Christianity could take care of the last of these, it did not necessarily provide for social and cultural dignity within Indian social structures as dominated by brahmanical patriarchy, particularly as it continued to be associated with members of the oppressed castes and classes. Nursing complicated this even more, as the labor itself had associations with menial work and exposure to men outside of one's kinship structures. In light of this, the desire for a form of productive labor that could ensure a "good marriage" within the "respectable" community was also an insistence on the ability to reproduce the kind of dignity that Christian education could offer converts of the "right sort"—those already within the fold of family and community.

There is a danger here, once again, of assuming that the association between nursing and "women on the loose" was a particularly Indian thing. That is, after all, what Jaya's father says—indeed insists on. The intractability of "Indian tradition" is underscored when, in rebuttal to Miss Houghton's invocation of the global impact of Florence Nightingale, he flatly states, "Not in India." And yet, the critical link between women's productive and reproductive work is not limited to India or Indians. It has been, as I have repeatedly pointed out, central to the kind of upward mobility offered single female medical missionaries and colonial nurses in India. Neither Dr. Ida nor Miss Houghton could marry at all. They had to remain single if they wanted to retain the privileges of their profession and uphold the heteropatriarchal conjugal family that was part of their Christian civilizing mission. They were not alone. In the United States, during the early decades of the twentieth century, the majority of women entering the occupations that were opening up to women—teaching, clerical work, and nursing—were single. The expectation was that they would work for wages until they married, at which point they would have the protection of a male breadwinner and thus leave the workforce.

What we have here in the case of Jaya is a movement from *unmarried* to *unmarriageable* and thus somehow still outside the fold of feminine respectability in a manner that recalls the stigmatization of Salome despite access to a nursing diploma. The association between nursing and "women on the loose" was thus once again the specific—not exceptional—way in which colonial nursing manifested in India, among Indians. Recognizing this also leads me back to the United States, for an undoing of its exceptionality within colonial nursing's global map.

# CHAPTER THREE

# Reconstructing the Imperial Nation

In 1881, two white women, Sophia Packard and Harriet Giles, moved from Worcester, Massachusetts, to Atlanta, Georgia, where they founded the Atlanta Baptist Female Seminary. The seminary was a school for freedwomen, and its founders were among the many white northerners who made their way south following the U.S. Civil War. The Friendship Baptist Church had agreed to house the fledgling school, offering its basement for the first classes. The American Baptist Home Missionary Society promised the funds. This was "woman's work for woman" at home, in a nation constituted by conquest, the machinations of settler colonization, and the legacies of chattel slavery. By the late nineteenth century, the imperial nation was both newly conquered and reunited. The Treaty of Guadalupe-Hidalgo in 1848 completed conquest of the contiguous forty-eight states by usurpation of a large chunk of Mexico, and the Civil War that ended in 1865 prevented the secession of the Southeastern states (or "the U.S. South" as it is referred to generally). The South was thus in a period of heightened transformation—from an economy based on chattel slavery and the production of raw materials to one that was being integrated into an economic system dominated by northern industrialists. Missionaries were thus but one part—the "soft side"—of a larger movement of northern industrial capitalists and carpetbaggers into the region during its reconstruction.

A year after the establishment of their seminary, Packard and Giles met John D. Rockefeller Sr. at a church conference in Ohio. Rockefeller was moved enough by their work that in 1884, he paid them a visit in Atlanta. By that time, the seminary had grown in size and had also gained the support of many local African American individuals, churches, and organizations. Rockefeller was so impressed that he decided to single-handedly settle the seminary's debt, with the intention of putting it on a firm footing for future growth. In homage to his patronage, the Atlanta Baptist Female Seminary was renamed after his wife, Laura Spelman Rockefeller. The name Spelman Seminary was also meant to invoke her Ohio-based family's history as abolitionists active on the Underground Railroad.

In 1886, Spelman Seminary opened a two-year nursing diploma school, the first nursing school in the United States to be housed primarily within an academic institution rather than a hospital. The distinction, while important, was not absolute. Soon Spelman nursing students had to take a four-year course, with three of the years devoted, essentially, to staffing the seminary's hospital infirmary and providing private care for local, mainly white, families. Most of the graduates would continue in this second line of work. The nursing school continued to receive periodic support from Rockefeller, but despite this, it struggled. In 1927, when Spelman Seminary became Spelman College, the newly minted board of trustees voted to close the nursing school.

I open this chapter with a thumbnail sketch of the founding of Spelman College and its (relatively) brief-lived nursing school because it allows me to begin to enumerate two different, and deeply interrelated, processes of reconstruction. The first was the transformation of emancipation from chattel slavery into the institutionalization of a new system of racialized apartheid, which in the United States went under the name of Jim Crow segregation. The second was the reconstruction of colonial medicine's global infrastructure in a way that promoted nursing's professionalization and repositioned North America as the center of colonial nursing's global map. Rockefeller wealth was the single largest source of capital behind the interconnection between these developments. Rockefeller, his advisors, and his emissaries achieved this not by simply elaborating upon the structures of Protestant medical missions or British Empire. They wielded Rockefeller wealth to work within the interstices of already existing imperial structures through idioms that drew upon, translated, and exported structures of U.S. racial formation as these themselves were shifting following the end of the Civil War. The story of how they achieved this began not with their public works but with the accumulation of Rockefeller's own fortune.

### The Seeds of Secularization

During the U.S. Civil War, John D. Rockefeller Sr. moved from New York to Ohio, a state that the railroad had connected to the oil boom and that the Mason-Dixon line had made a borderlands between a plantation economy fueled by chattel slavery and one where corporate industrialization was forging ahead with abandon. In 1865, the same year that the war ended, Rockefeller bought out his business partner to become the sole owner of one of Cleveland's most successful oil refining enterprises. The buyout set the stage for a rapid and ruthless growth spurt, with Rockefeller continuing to buy and/or drive competitors out of the market by any means necessary. In 1870, Rockefeller combined his holdings to form the Standard Oil Company, and by 1879, Standard controlled 90 percent of oil refining in the United States, as well as having a lock on the major pipelines and dominating transportation.[1] Standard Oil's increasingly successful monopolization of the industry did not go uncontested. Opposition ran the gamut from exploited workers to irate (and often dispossessed) competitors and came to include muckraking journalists and eventually the courts. The company came under attack for a combination of exploitative work conditions, underground railroad rebates, and drawbacks to, ultimately, the impeding of free and fair trade. The fine point on arguments regarding this last charge was that Standard owned most of the industry at a time when, technically speaking, corporations could not legally own stock in other corporations. Rather than quitting what was an illegal practice, Rockefeller and his associates created the Standard Oil Trust Agreement of 1882. The agreement created a structure in which stockholders—not the corporation—held shares in other firms. These collected shares were then held in trust—not for Standard Oil—but on behalf of said stockholders. This structured evasion allowed Rockefeller to sidestep the law as he monopolized the industry, inaugurating a new phase (what many would deem a "craze") of monopoly capitalism in the United States.

Rockefeller, who was in many ways the face of monopoly capitalism, remained a devout Baptist his whole life. His participation in the same circles as Packard and Giles and his beneficence toward the ladies' project were components of his belief that his wealth was God's gift and that it was God's will that he distribute it according to his own conscience.[2] Rockefeller thus combined, in his own person and practice, two dominant strands of late nineteenth-century U.S. imperial culture: Protestant evangelism and monopoly capitalism. He was both the iron fist and the velvet glove. As a calculation made out of this double-sided punch, in 1891 he hired the Reverend Frederick T. Gates as his chief advisor in matters of both business and charity. And it was Gates who, taking note of the success of medical missions, convinced Rockefeller that human health should be at the center of his giving: "If science and education are the brain and nervous system of civilization, [said Mr. Gates] health is its heart. It is the organ that pushes the vital fluid into every part of the social organism, enabling each organ to function, and measuring and limiting its effective life. . . . *Disease is the supreme ill of human life, and it is the main source of almost all other human ills—poverty, crime, ignorance, vice, inefficiency, hereditary taint, and many other evils.*"[3]

The emphasis is mine. It is illustrative to lay out the generative connection made here between health and wealth. The identification of health as the supreme source of all human ills relied on a definition that severed it from its social context, posing it as solely biological. Naturalized thus, it became the a priori cause of social conditions. Namely, it was ill health that caused poverty, not impoverishment that created the conditions for sickness (through a deadly combination of dangerous working conditions, low wages, and inadequate access to social resources). Wealth created through capitalist exploitation was more than merely erased from this formulation. It was actually transformed into the cure, as it stepped in to ameliorate conditions that, more often than not, it had had a strong role in creating. Truly though, even if it did not create the particular conditions at stake in a direct or discernable way, its position as the curing and caring hand served to draw scrutiny away from the ways in which capitalist wealth accumulation affected the shape of social reality and indeed the conditions for life itself.

Gates's logic was different from that of the Christian medical missions from which it clearly took its cue. Protestant missionaries justified their use of medicine as a means to Christian conversion. Rockefeller and Gates, while remaining religious men, represented a pivotal force pushing forward the seeds of secularization already inherent in Protestant medical missions. They were not alone in pursuing this path but were part of a trend that had sponsors in India as well, proponents who, like the missionaries they took their lead from, were very much a product of the circuits of Anglo-American capitalist imperialism. Most well known among these seedlings on the subcontinent was the National Association for Supplying Female Medical Aid to the Women of India, more commonly known as the Countess of Dufferin's Fund.

Launched in 1885, the fund's aim was to provide medical care for Indian women and children, to offer medical training to women, and to supply trained nurses and midwives for both hospitals and private homes. One of its primary effects was the establishment of Dufferin hospitals as well as female-only wards in already existing hospitals. These were staffed by women, many of them trained through Dufferin funds. Throughout its existence, the overwhelming majority of women trained and employed at Dufferin institutions were of European descent.[4] Even so, missionaries were prohibited from receiving either training or employment through the fund. Dufferin set itself up as *the* secular alternative to medical missionary work. This was despite the fact that it took many of its cues and contours from the Protestant medical missionaries who were the progenitors of the field.

Missionary influence was nevertheless reflected in the rhetoric surrounding the fund. Maneesha Lal describes how it was from British female medical missionaries that Queen Victoria first heard of the "plight" of her "Indian daughters." She subsequently mandated the fund and, in the process, took the "women of India" into her heart and under her care. The imagery of this legend clearly drew from "woman's work for woman." Indeed, in this scene, Queen Victoria figures as the ultimate matriarch in what I have already described as the racialized matriarchy undergirding the feminization of colonial medicine in India.[5]

Given its royal and official pedigree, which included the likes of then-Vicerine Lady Curzon, the Countess of Dufferin, and of course Queen Victoria herself, one might assume that the fund was a project of the colonial state. From the outset, however, it was made explicit that funding this initiative was not necessarily a government function. Thus, while the countess's efforts received some degree of financial support from the colonial state, it could not rely on this. This close relationship underscored the critical way in which colonial domination was the condition that enabled other elements in colonial civil society to take on these tasks. Thus, rather than totally abandoning the Christian civilizing mission, the colonial government had in effect subcontracted these duties to missionaries. This was also the case with the Countess of Dufferin's Fund. In addition, many of the fund's primary benefactors were members of the Indian aristocracy. This was a strategic alliance that fit in with a post-1857 strategy of colonial power: courting India's princely powers as "partners" in Crown rule. The hope was that this would give the appearance of sharing power with Indians while actually trying to enlist Indian aristocrats as bulwarks of empire in the face of the first inklings of middle-class nationalism and the constant battle against subaltern protest. Instead of alienation, the Dufferin Fund would allow the wealthier of these men to become the active sponsors of such work and thereby retain their patriarchal patina. It was through this version of subcontracting that the colonial state could claim Dufferin's victories while retaining the ability to shift the blame in the face of any potential fallout.[6]

In the Bombay Presidency, the Dufferin Fund was not the only secular force at play. There, Parsi businessmen played a seminal role in promoting colonial medicine through their sponsorship of hospitals.[7] One, Mr. Pestonjee Hormusjee Cama, specifically sought to build a women's hospital. Cama was willing to put up the funds if the colonial government would provide the site and agree to an all-female staff. This last stipulation proved potentially prohibitive, as government officials preferred to have male supervisors, at the very least. In the end, the ability for the Cama Hospital for Women and Children to meet its founder's vision was through an alliance not with the colonial government but with Mr. George T. Kittredge, a U.S. businessman resident in Bombay.[8]

In 1882, Mr. Kittredge read an article about the lack of medical women in the Bombay Presidency that moved him to establish the Medical Women for India Fund, Bombay. Through the fund, Kittredge gathered contributions from wealthy Indian men in Bombay and set off to recruit medical women for Cama's hospital. In 1883, he met with Dr. Edith Pechey (later Pechey-Phipson) in Paris. Dr. Pechey was one of five women who had fought to end the gendered barriers to medical education in the United Kingdom by demanding admittance to the University of Edinburgh Medical School. She eventually completed her degree in Berne and was also certified by the Royal College of Physicians of Ireland. Kittredge was able to convince her to come to India and become the first senior medical officer at Cama Hospital, in charge of an all-female staff.[9] From there, she was the one who spearheaded efforts to raise money so that the (in)famous child bride Rakhmabai could cover her legal fees and study to become a doctor in England. Dr. Pechey-Phipson also worked with Kittredge to persuade the University of Bombay and Grant Medical College to admit Indian women candidates. By 1889, the fund itself had ceased its operations, having played a critical intermediary role between government and private openings for women in medicine in the Bombay Presidency.

Kittredge recognized the lack of medical women in Bombay the very same year that Rockefeller met Packard and Giles in Ohio. They were men of the same moment, moved to similar ends. And while Kittredge fell on the side of secular giving, and Rockefeller was moving through church circuits, it was ultimately Rockefeller's wealth that was to do the most toward secularizing colonial medicine. Here I want to return to a key detail in the story of Spelman's nursing school, that it was not only the first school for African American nursing students in the United States but also the first to be housed within an academic institution, not a hospital. This was a time when nurse training was still nascent, and when and where it did exist—it was hospital based. The decision to launch a nursing school at an academic institution was ahead of its time, but it was to be the model favored by Rockefeller wealth as it became the single largest force behind the remaking of medical education in the United States over the turn of the twentieth century.

*Scientific Medicine and Rockefeller's Medicine Men*[10]

In the late nineteenth century, scientific medicine as we now know it—by the term "biomedicine"—had achieved neither clear dominance nor full coherence in the United States. Instead, it was in competition with multiple medical systems, and there existed no clear standard for medical education or for what constituted a medical doctor. It was within this confused context that Rockefeller wealth funded the Johns Hopkins University (JHU) to become the first medical school to employ full-time scientific researchers on its faculty. This was a major move toward exalting the researcher over the practitioner in medical education, a hierarchy that found its fullest early expression in the Rockefeller Institute for Medical Research (RIMR, later Rockefeller University), founded in 1901 as a pure research facility. The emphasis on research was controversial, even for some who supported scientific medicine among the competing systems contemporaneously in use. There were those who believed that the focus of medical education should remain, as it had been, on the clinical side. Alongside this was the argument that medical research should be application oriented rather than produced primarily for the accumulation of knowledge.

The first few decades of the twentieth century saw the JHU model of medical education prevail in the United States. The coup de grâce for this development was publication of the Flexner Report, commissioned in 1910 by the Carnegie Foundation and authored by Dr. Abraham Flexner. After surveying medical schools across the United States, Flexner made a series of recommendations that emphasized higher admission and graduation standards as well as strict adherence to the protocols of science in teaching and research. In his view, the university-based medical school with hospital attached (the JHU model) was the ideal institution. Historian Paul Starr concludes, "Whatever its influence on public opinion, the Flexner Report crystallized a view that proved immensely important in directing the major foundations' investments in medical care over the next two crucial decades. In a sense, the report was the manifesto of a program that by 1936 guided $91 million from Rockefeller's General Education Board (plus millions more from other foundations) to a select group of medical schools."[11]

It is not incidental that Starr foregrounds the contributions of Rocke-feller's General Education Board (GEB). In addition to the large sums of cash that the GEB invested, it also created a network of what historian E. Richard Brown has dubbed "Rockefeller medicine men": men who graduated from the JHU model of medical education and continued to promote its expansion through their network. Most remained employees in one of Rockefeller's medical initiatives. Key members were also selected for the board of the Rockefeller Foundation (RF) when it began opera-tions, including Dr. William Welch, dean of JHU and later president of the RIMR; Dr. Abraham Flexner himself, who after his report went on to work for the GEB from 1912 to 1925 (after 1917, he was its secretary); and Dr. Simon Flexner, brother of Abraham, RF trustee, and the first director of the RIMR. The model of medical education promoted by Rockefeller medicine men was explicitly elitist in intent, positioning a class of profes-sionalized white male medical doctors over and above other health care workers and patients.

The recommendations of the Flexner Report rang the death knell for most of the already existing commercial, women's, and black medical schools. The decades following its release saw a drastic decline in the peak of women's medical colleges that had occurred at the turn of the century[12] and the closing of all but the two black medical schools recommended for survival by the report (Howard University and Meharry Medical College). The shuttering of these options was largely due to the fact that they could not compete with the institutions that, in the wake of the report, became the prime recipients of corporate philanthropy. The racialized, gendered, and classed dimensions of medical education were another crucial di-mension of the program spearheaded by Rockefeller medicine men in the United States.

The fallout from the Flexner Report took place over the very same time period that Rockefeller's wealth hit a potential stumbling block. In 1911, the Supreme Court of the United States invoked the Sherman Antitrust Act, ruled that Standard Oil was an illegal monopoly, and ordered the cor-poration to split. The thirty-four resulting companies included many of those that continue to dominate the industry into the twenty-first century: Exxon-Mobil (initially two separate companies), Chevron, the U.S. arm of British Petroleum, Amoco, and Conoco. At the time of their creation, these corporations remained basically friendly to each other, undermining the idea that Standard's dissolution would necessarily increase competition in the field. And while Rockefeller Sr. had already retired as Standard Oil's manager before the ruling, he retained major holdings in the resulting companies and emerged from the breakup richer than ever, having increased his wealth to 900 million dollars (a large sum in the twenty-first century—an astronomical one in the early twentieth century).[13] Two years later, in the face of his public notoriety as a "robber baron," Rockefeller received an official charter from the state of New York, and his foundation was born.[14]

The creation of the RF was, in a very real and legal sense, a consummation of the form of the corporate trust, which was itself an adaptation of a structure that was originally intended to protect white widows and children in matters of inheritance. When transported into the corporate setting, the trust structure did not lose but rather expanded its ability to enable the intergenerational transfer of wealth. From their inception, critics have consistently pointed out how corporate foundations provide a tax shelter for wealth that has been accumulated through the labor of workers who are also tax payers. Money set aside in the form of a foundation was not and is not subject to estate taxes or any governmental regulation. Foundations did not and do not spend the majority of their holdings but only a small percentage annually. The amount they spend was (and remains) largely tax exempt. In the same year as the birth of Rockefeller's foundation, the Revenue Act of 1913 created 501(c)(3) tax-exempt status for nonprofit organizations. This dual birth created a symbiotic structure where the limited spending of largely tax-exempt corporate foundations is also tax exempt as long as they focus their giving on 501(c)(3)s.[15]

The RF was among the first and, due to the extensive scope of Rockefeller wealth, largest of the many corporate foundations that would become a mainstay of capitalist expansion over the course of the twentieth century.[16] Its inaugural president was John D. Rockefeller Jr., who was his father's sole son and the heir who decided to devote his life's work to the humanitarian arm of his family's wealth accumulation. On the surface, his leadership would seem to confirm the argument that this corporate foundation was indeed a matter of the retention and intergenerational transfer of wealth, but that is actually too narrow of a reading. Corporate foundations were a critical development in the consolidation of a capitalist class that would soon come to manage not only their own industrial empires but also many aspects of the same state that had, in the not too distant past, ordered some of them to dissolve. Foundations were key to this development for the ways in which they countered the brutal excesses of capitalist exploitation with their articulation of a corporate humanitarianism. The birth of the RF makes this point crystal clear.

In 1913, the same year that the RF received its official charter, thousands of miners working for the Colorado Fuel and Iron Corporation went on strike in response to the assassination of one of their organizers and as a sign that they would not relent in their battle against low wages and poor working and living conditions (they were housed in a company town). Rockefeller owned 40 percent interest in the company and was instrumental in breaking the strike. First, he hired gunmen to raid, threaten, and kill strikers. When that didn't work, the governor of Colorado called in the National Guard while Rockefeller supplied their wages. The National Guard brought in strike breakers, killed organizers, and eventually burned down strikers' tents, resulting in the death of men, women, and children. Their actions created a national uproar, with sympathy strikes and actions spreading across the country. Eventually, President Wilson sent troops to Colorado in order to break the strike a year after it had begun. In the aftermath, Rockefeller tried to block publication of reports and sponsored speakers to deny the massacre. *At the very same time*, representatives of the newly minted RF were setting about their first major organizational task: prioritizing and globalizing their work in public health by setting up the International Health Commission (IHC).[17]

The IHC divided the world into four target areas: the U.S. South, Latin America, and British colonies in the West Indies, and the Far East. The conformity to a map drawn by the contours of Anglo-American Empire was not coincidental but deeply considered. Rockefeller was at the forefront of U.S. industrial capital as it sought to consolidate its hold on the entirety of the United States and the dominion claimed by the Monroe Doctrine, while at the same time setting itself up as a concerted presence within the fabric of the British Empire.[18] The emphasis on the latter served a dual purpose. On the one hand, foundation officers publicly admired and approved of the global reach of Britain's rule and desired to work with and through its offices in London and the colonies. On the other hand, especially in the years following World War I, their aims were not entirely collaborative but also increasingly competitive. This tension was indicative of a moment signaled by what Mrinalini Sinha describes as "a shift from the 'illusion of permanence' that characterized the high imperialism of the late nineteenth century to the recognition of the conspicuously altered state of metropolitan-colonial ties at the advent of the 'American Century.'"[19] Within this context, U.S. corporate interests worked to defend the general premise of the British Empire while simultaneously promoting the expansion of U.S.-based capital through "open door imperialism."

Open door imperialism derives from U.S. foreign policy in relation to China at the turn of the twentieth century. It was most famously articulated in the "Open Door Notes" penned by U.S. Secretary of State John Hay in 1899 and 1900. Historian William Appleman Williams describes Open Door policy as the solidification of a strategy whereby U.S. business interests firmly linked the well-being of the U.S. domestic economy to the continual expansion of U.S.-based capitalist markets externally. Williams's work ties this doctrine to Frederick Jackson Turner's "frontier thesis," wherein the closing of the continental frontier served as the stimulus for extension beyond the borders of the settler colonial nation-state. The modification in the modus operandi of U.S. imperialism made by the Open Door policy was that it would proceed without war and without the administrative burdens of "traditional" territorial colonization. Thus, "the Open Door Notes" advocated a "classic strategy of non-colonial imperial expansion" in China, one that desired a China strong enough to resist outright colonization, yet weak enough to allow for economic penetration. While this was the ideal situation, proponents of open door imperialism also understood that it would be "necessary to open the door into existing colonial empires as well as unclaimed territories."[20] The latter was the way in which British-controlled India became a target of U.S. capitalists, especially during the decades between World Wars I and II (the interwar years).

U.S.-based corporate foundations were key institutions in the practice of open door imperialism, accompanying and often paving the path for their business benefactors. They did so through a secularized humanitarian rhetoric that was, in many ways, directly indebted to the colonial civilizing mission of Protestant missionaries. However, by the turn of the twentieth century, the men at the helm of the RF were key to the development of the form of corporate philanthropy that superseded Christian charity in the civilizing mission of capitalist imperial expansion. They promoted philanthropy as an investment, not a form of relief. Its goal was not ameliorative so much as preventive. Philanthropic grants were meant to be of limited duration, and their primary purpose was to stimulate "self-help," not continuing dependence. Philanthropists saw their contributions as seed money that would then continue to grow after the initial investment. The ideal outcome was the creation of institutions and initiatives that would have a life beyond foundation monies. This would occur through the ability to attract further/matching funds from other sources and by maintaining a set of appropriately trained personnel who could contribute to the initiative's continuity and replication. The practice of corporate philanthropy thus premised itself on a type of disappearing act that was in fact a mirror of the tried-and-true tactics of evasion pioneered by monopoly capitalists. It also proved to be an effective "hidden hand" that could arrive first and stabilize social situations in target locations in a way that "opened the door" to U.S.-dominated capitalist imperialism. Naming this function is crucial for understanding the role played by the RF in restructuring the map of colonial medicine through the promotion of its version of scientific medicine and its relationship to public health.

## Public Health and the Corporate Civilizing Mission

In 1902, the *New York Sun* ran a headline that began by screaming, "GERM OF LAZINESS FOUND? DISEASE OF THE 'CRACKER' AND SOME NATIONS IDENTIFIED."[21] The "crackers" in question were poor Southern whites, and the "germ of laziness" limiting their productivity was hookworm. The Rockefeller Sanitary Commission for the Eradication of Hookworm Disease (RSC) formed in 1909 to combat this threat. The RSC estimated that hookworm infected almost half of the white people in the South and that it was concentrated especially among impoverished whites in whom it caused an unmistakable demeanor and an unshakeable lethargy that rendered them unfit for productive labor and left them with a propensity to eat dirt.[22] Researchers, however, located the source of hookworm not among whites but among blacks. Their theory was that Africans had carried the disease with them during their enslavement. This, apparently, accounted for their far lower rates of infection. It also accounted for the infection of whites who had not built up the same level of immunity. Black proximity to poor whites in the South was what made this latter group particularly susceptible to the "germ of laziness" and what set the South aside as a "country within a country" even after the end of the Civil War. The justification for the work of the RSC was thus the rescue and redemption of poor Southern whites, so that their healthy bodies could be folded into a robust image of white America.

Hookworm was the perfect disease to set out to eradicate in that it was actually relatively easily cured. All it required was a basic medication and, in order to prevent reinfection, education regarding sanitation and hygiene—hence, the Rockefeller *Sanitary* Commission. The RSC's emphasis on building public health demonstration units to model sanitation and hygiene was in fact the legacy that it most effectively left behind, and in this sense, its work harkened back rather directly to that of Florence Nightingale. The RSC had two main institutional inspirations: the British Sanitary Commission that Nightingale worked for during the Crimean War and the United States Sanitary Commission that incubated many of the earliest white nursing leaders during the U.S. Civil War. Nightingale's mission to promote colonial nursing took its cue from the germ theory of disease in a way that prefigured the uptake of that theory by the RSC. In turn, Rockefeller wealth proved critical to the establishment of professional nursing within scientific medicine and its attendant hospital system, an outcome that took the trained nursing led by Nightingale nurses one step further up the ladder of respectability.

Public health and professionalization went hand in hand throughout the work of Rockefeller philanthropies. Thus, JHU was not only home to model medical education but also became *the* model public health program in the United States. The JHU model thus included public health nursing as a crucial component of its model of university-based nursing education. The RSC drew public health officials from the ranks of professionalizing medical and nursing programs, reinforcing the link between the two and posing the one as subjects over a field where distinctly non-professionalized and often racially subordinated groups of people were the objects. The essential dirtiness of these "objects" was the source of a scourge that threatened white health while enabling white wealth and professional mobility.

The RSC was meant to have a limited life span of five years, during which it set out to entirely cure the U.S. South of hookworm. As John Ettling describes in his analysis of its work, what the RSC did more than anything was model a practice of professionalized public health that the IHC then globalized. This was the reason for the inclusion of the U.S. South in the agency's division of the world. It was both a hangover and a homage, one that connected the way in which Rockefeller wealth—both the iron fist and the velvet glove—had already "opened the door" to the U.S. South before it set out to conquer the world.

It was the Reverend Frederick T. Gates's explicit vision that hookworm be the "entering wedge" for the IHC outside of the United States. As he eyed the British Empire in particular, the ultimate source of the disease shifted from Africans to Indians, particularly to Tamil indentured laborers (or "coolies"[23]). The word at preliminary IHC meetings was that "every Indian coolie already in California was a center from which the infection continued to spread throughout the state."[24] In 1915, Victor Heiser, the IHC's inaugural Director of the East, commissioned a study revealing that

63 to 90 percent of Indian immigrants to the United States carried the disease.[25] The cry of "coolies as cause" participated in the anti-Asian movements that were spreading from the Pacific Coast to the halls of Congress, where in 1917, legislators passed the Asiatic Barred Zone excluding Indian labor from legal immigration. It also helped to justify the globalization of public health on the RSC model and allowed the IHC to launch its first international hookworm campaign in British Guiana, a colony where Indian indentured labor had arrived in large numbers after the abolition of the trade in enslaved Africans. Meanwhile Madras, birthplace of the "Tamil coolie," became the first place that the IHC took its hookworm campaign in the Far East.

Arriving in Madras via the Rockefeller Foundation's IHC allows me to approach, anew, a few of the central points that I addressed in the last chapter when I was searching for Salome. As an oppressed caste and class female Tamil laborer, Salome bears more than a mere family resemblance to the group of workers who became indentured laborers on the plantations of the British and French Empires during the nineteenth century.[26] Even while still in India, Salome's impoverishment and her caste background contributed to her association with seemingly incorrigible dirt, an incorrigibility whose only cure was the repeated, insistent lectures on sanitation and hygiene provided by Dr. Ida Sophia Scudder, exemplar of professionalizing white womanhood in "heathen" India. The RSC/IHC also fixated on dirt and pollution from explicitly enslaved and indentured black and brown laborers as the condition that propagated hookworm disease and exemplified its effects (one of which was, as noted above, actually eating dirt). If we take the logic of the RSC's reports and research at face value, black and brown workers *were* the disease. The question remained whether the same "cure" would work in India as it purportedly had in the United States. Here was where the earlier example of George Kittredge, and his navigation of the cracks in the infrastructure of colonial India, could serve as a kind of premonition for the politics of the possible.

## Public Health and Shifting Imperial Formations

Between 1879 and 1915, the Indian Medical Service (IMS), part of the British colonial apparatus, had already conducted surveys of hookworm incidence in India, with particular attention to plantation areas such as Assam. They reported high rates, but efforts at eradication would have to wait until the Rockefeller Foundation stepped in. Between 1916 and 1919,

International Health Board (IHB, as the IHC had been renamed in 1916) officers surveyed plantations, jails, hospitals, and asylums in the Bengal and Madras Presidencies for the disease. They continuously reported high rates of infection and, unlike the IMS, they had what they considered a "tried-and-true" plan for action. It was a plan that the foundation had incubated within the context of post–Civil War reconstruction in the U.S. South, and that they now attempted to inject into the particular situation confronting India at the end of World War I.

The war had altered the political economy of the British Empire and India along with it. Indians had played a critical role in maintaining Britain's war efforts. A million and a half had served in British-led combat. Those who remained behind bore the burdens of increased taxes and a sharp spike in the overall price index for essential goods. This came at the same time that there was a decrease in the prices paid for the raw materials produced by Indian labor. Those Indian soldiers who were not killed off in the war returned to face unemployment, food riots, a failed monsoon in 1918–19, the global influenza epidemic of 1918, and imperialist fears over the effects of the Bolshevik Revolution on politicized Indian mobilizations. Indeed, the exacerbation of endemic impoverishment created the conditions for widespread protests that cut across class, caste, region, and religion, often exceeding the confines of elite-led Indian nationalism.

British fear over their hold on India manifested in two ultimately interrelated ways. In early March 1919, the Imperial Legislative Council in London pushed through the Rowlatt Act, which extended the wartime measures of warrantless arrests, indefinite detention without trial, juryless trials for proscribed political acts, and secret evidence (including the identity of accusers). Rowlatt focused specifically on the imperial dictum to suppress revolutionary activity, yet its passage met with protests across India, culminating on April 13, 1919, with the Jallianwala Bagh massacre, where British troops fired mercilessly on unarmed Indians who had gathered in Amritsar to protest the arrest of two leaders through the act. The rampage showcased the brutality of the British and enflamed Indian resistance.

At the end of that very same year, the Parliament of the United Kingdom passed the Government of India Act of 1919. Under the act, British authorities were to retain absolute power in London and in Delhi (the central government of India), while British Indian provinces were now to be ruled through a system of dyarchy. What this meant was that provincial government split into two levels, one that remained within the full control of British authorities and the other where administrative control devolved to Indians who were appointed from the ranks of elected Indian Legislative Assemblies. British provincial governors retained items on the "reserved list," which included the police, courts, land revenue, communication, defense, and foreign affairs. Administration of the "transferred list," including public health and education, fell to Indians. As Sumit Sarkar describes, dyarchy was a limited and limiting structure that "transferred only departments of less political weight and little funds to ministers responsible to provincial legislatures, skillfully drawing Indian politicians into a patronage rat-race which would probably also discredit them, as real improvements in education, health, agriculture and local bodies required far more money that the British would be willing to assign to these branches."[27]

The question of money was indeed paramount. The colonial government devolved areas linked to human development at a time when its own economic presence on the subcontinent was in a process of postwar reconstruction. Wartime conditions had strengthened Indian industry such that Indian textile mill production now surpassed that of Lancashire. It was the beginning of an irrevocable shift. Thus, by 1919, space had opened up within British colonization of the subcontinent for limited collaboration by selected Indian politicians and businessmen, even as the vast majority of the population suffered increasing impoverishment and the whip of colonial brutality. While most histories of colonial and postcolonial India emphasize these shifts in relation to Indian freedom struggles and British colonization, a few also emphasize the ways in which the postwar restructuring of empire also opened up more space for U.S.-based capital on the subcontinent. What this meant, concretely, was that increased U.S. economic presence occurred alongside limited power sharing with Indians. This was to prove particularly important in the face of constrained finances, and it was in this way that the IHB maneuvered its first hookworm campaign in the Madras Presidency in 1920.

As it had in the U.S. South, the campaign linked eradication to the inculcation of hygienic and sanitary practices among infected populations. This entailed preventive education through demonstration units, which the IHB established in seven locations across India: four in the provinces, one in Delhi, and two in the princely states of Mysore and Travancore. Hitting the heartland of hookworm, however, proved less immediately rewarding than anticipated.[28] While some plantation owners in Darjeeling did report a healthier workforce, IHB officials cited the intractable dirtiness of targeted Indian populations as all but insurmountable outside of the most tightly controlled conditions.[29] In addition, the foundation had difficulty finding adequately trained staff. While it initially invested in educating startup staff for the work by sending them abroad to its own model institutions and programs in the United States and the United Kingdom, there was difficulty with retention upon return.[30]

The shutdown of the IHB's initial public health campaigns in India did not mean that the foundation abandoned its ambitions there. Instead, this first phase of work gave way to a second phase that concentrated on institutionalizing the connection between public health and professionalized medical education on the subcontinent. These efforts officially began in 1926, when William S. Carter, associate director of the Division of Medical Education at the RF, conducted a yearlong tour of India. At the end of his subcontinental survey, Carter recommended the establishment of the All India Institute of Hygiene and Public Health (AIIHPH), to work in conjunction with the already existing Calcutta School of Tropical Medicine (CSTM). The AIIHPH was meant to be an academic institution on the model of those that the RF had supported in the United States and exported to China with its promotion, in 1906, of the Peking Union Medical College.[31]

Carter's tour and recommendation had been set up in a manner that highlighted the kind of backdoor negotiations that had become RF protocol as the foundation navigated the spaces opened up by the Government of India Act of 1919. In 1922, Lt. Col. J. W. D. Megaw, director of the CSTM, had proposed to the Surgeon General of the Bengal Presidency that they approach the RF for funds. His request had been prompted by a prior, informal meeting that he had had with Victor Heiser of the RF. At that meeting, Heiser had apparently suggested that if the government were to make a request to the foundation, it would likely meet with approval. My use of the conditional tense is pointed, for none of this was, strictly speaking, official. Our knowledge of this chain of command comes from a sifting through of the RF's own archives, not pronouncements at the time or the foundation's official history.[32] Thus, it would seem that when the All India Conference of Medical Research Workers passed a resolution urging the government of India (GOI) to invite the RF to do a survey of medical education in India, it came wholly from the volition of British colonial medical practitioners. The result of this elision was (and is) a naturalization of the power of the RF model of medical education as inherently progressive, rather than politically constructed through the shifting circuits of Anglo-American capitalist imperialism on the Indian subcontinent.

William Carter returned to India again in 1928, at which time he entered into talks with various government officials over the nature and constitution of a public health institute and the role of the RF in its establishment. Because of the logistics of dyarchy, the RF and British colonial authorities had to at least formally negotiate with Indian members of the Legislative Assembly in Bengal in order to establish the institution. They did so within a context of growing Indian mobilization against British colonization. In fact, Carter's second trip might appear as a mere blip in a year overshadowed by the arrival of the infamous Simon Commission. Their subcontinental tour was the product of a provision in the 1919 act stipulating that a commission be set up to study constitutional reform in India. It was composed of seven members of the parliament of the United Kingdom, and no Indians. Their absence from representation outraged Indians across the political spectrum, with all major Indian political parties vowing to boycott the commission upon its arrival. Their boycott had the force of mass public protest behind it. Everywhere the commission went, it faced seas of Indians chanting "Go Back Simon" and waving black flags of protest. Anti-Simon agitation also led to an India-wide *hartal* (strike), and British repression of Indian protestors led, most famously, to the death of well-known Congress leader Lala Lajpat Rai after he sustained beatings at an anti-Simon protest in Lahore.[33]

Meanwhile, throughout the negotiations, Carter insisted that the proposed institute be in Calcutta, be situated across from the CTSM, *and* be "all India." This last point was a complicating factor within a landscape where both public health and medical education had devolved to provincial control, making Carter's "all India" proposal one that posed a constitutional challenge according to the provisions of dyarchy. What were Carter's justifications for this demand? On the surface, his rationale rested on his assessment of the massive public health needs of the general population across British-dominated India. According to RF assessment, these were such that they demanded an all-India scope. However, if Indian health was the object of RF investment, the foundation was adamant that this was not an endeavor that could be entrusted to Indian leadership or control. In the negotiations over the constitution of the AIIHPH, "all India" appeared as a thinly veiled marker for "not Indian," inasmuch as it placed the proposed institute under the purview of the central government of India, which remained autocratic and entirely British. For the RF, this would ensure that their investments remained safe from becoming "political" playthings, "political" being another codeword for "Indian."

The crux of the RF's argument against Indians, however, was not actually its insistence on an "all India" institute. It was its infamous insistence on "standards." The RF argued that the closer its investments got to provincial politics, the greater the risk of an inability to maintain that the standards were linked to the foundation's definition of scientific medicine as the product of research-oriented institutions. The emphasis on research actually positioned the proposed institute in between the reserved and transferred lists of the 1919 GOI Act. While public health and medical education were on the transferred list, and thus subject to the involvement of Indian politicians, medical research remained on the reserved list and was thus limited to the control of British colonial authorities. The foundation's equation between "standards" and medical education that prioritized scientific research over clinical applications proved crucial to ensuring that the AIIHPH evaded Indian control. The RF insisted that management reside with the governing body of the Indian Research Fund Association (IRFA), which remained the stronghold of colonial medical men who would have been the only ones in India to have had access to the requisite training. This was what the Indian call for more Indians and more medical men contested, with "medical men" representing medical practitioners as opposed to researchers in their case.

Once it became clear that the RF would not broker its "standards" and that these standards included both postgraduate training and research, Indian legislators agreed to overriding constitutional objections and establishing a public health institute under the jurisdiction of the central government. Accompanying this acquiescence was also the issue of money, for provincial governments utterly lacked the resources for such an undertaking, and the central government was notoriously stingy in this regard. The RF walked the line between these two realities, insisting that its funding come attached to acceptance of its medical model and, consequently, to the continuity of colonial control.[34]

The needs of the AIIHPH provided the framework within which the RF began to pay attention to the state of nursing on the subcontinent. One year before its opening, the Indian Red Cross Society held a meeting with Victor Heiser of the RF on the subject of nursing. As follow-up to the meeting, the Red Cross convinced the GOI to formally extend an invitation to the RF, asking that it conduct an informal survey of nursing on the subcontinent. In 1935, the foundation complied by deputing Miss Mary Beard. Beard noted that India lacked all of the requirements of "modern nursing education." Her reference was to the tenets of professionalized nursing education as it had come to be practiced in the United States, a standard that in her estimation even India's trained colonial nursing leadership largely failed to live up to.

Beard's criticism of India's colonial nursing leadership must be understood as a product of the shift from trained to professional nursing, a shift that was part of the larger restructuring of medical education in the United States. This takes us back to the tendencies condensed within the Flexner Report and the ways in which it repositioned the relationships between women, men, whites, and blacks within U.S. health care. The drastic curtailing of women and African Americans from medicine during a period of the reconsolidation of white, male elite leadership did not mean that the newly emergent medical model entirely abandoned either group. Instead, it positioned them in specific ways that were also, actually, underwritten by the same sponsors. So, for instance, in 1920, the RF funded research into the conditions of nursing education in the United States, which resulted in the 1923 publication of the Goldmark Report. The report's recommendations proved provident for the aspirations of white U.S. nursing leaders, in that it promoted the establishment and expansion of university-based degree programs over and above hospital-based diploma programs at a time when the latter were at their peak in the United States. Diploma nursing, captured as it was by hospital administrators, left graduate nurses with minimal authority. For U.S. nursing leaders, university-based education was a culmination of their decades-long quest for a higher standard of nurse training and, thereby, a clearer stratification within an evolving workforce. It would, they hoped, pave a path to the acceptance of nursing as a specialized field of knowledge, one where nursing leaders could claim a larger degree of autonomy from hospital administrators and control over nursing students and subsidiary categories of nursing labor. The development of baccalaureate nursing thus found fit with the desires of a national nursing leadership that sought to separate itself from the bulk of hospital-based, working nurses (and indeed the category of "worker" itself). This was also in line with thinking at the RF, where, in a 1925 meeting regarding nursing, officers insisted that the foundation did not exist to supply the rank and file of any occupation. Its programs were meant to train leaders, as leadership was what the RF saw as its mandate across all its investments.[35]

Even as Rockefeller support proved critical to the aspirations of U.S. nursing leadership, it did so in a way that continued to reinforce the gendered division of labor between doctors and nurses. Throughout its work in scientific medicine, medical education, and public health, the RF continued to place nursing within a feminized realm of service, as opposed to the masculinized realm of knowledge. While the differential allocation of attention and resources can certainly be read as discriminatory, it was actually compatible with the gendered division of labor that had been a key part of nursing leaders' push for recognition of their work as its own area of feminine expertise. This was thus one instance of the contradictions within the Victorian ideology of gendered separate spheres that created space for a kind of autonomy within "woman's work" while at the same time subordinating that work within a male-dominated public sphere. The rise of corporate-backed scientific medicine did not undo this gendered division of labor so much as reaffirm it within its preferred health care system. What this translated into was a subordinated concern for professionalized nursing alongside the final strokes that decimated women's medical colleges. If nursing leaders both wittingly and unwittingly accepted the terms of this bargain, they did so in a way that allowed them to exercise the privileges that professionalization afforded them within the nursing market. In the United States, a nation whose social formation has deep roots in the racialized imperatives of settler colonialism, this translated into the privileges of not only class (inherent in professionalization) but also race. Here, too, the invocation of "standards" was key.

### Jane Crow Nursing

One year before the closing of Spelman's nursing school, the RF had altered its mandate from "the well-being of mankind" to "the advancement of knowledge." In order to survive this shift, the foundation's health divisions reoriented themselves even more firmly under an academic research rubric. From the perspective of the RF, this was not a radical move as the foundation had already been promoting this shift within medical and nursing education for at least a decade and a half prior. What the reorganization did signal was the final removal of any vestiges of "charity" within the RF's rhetoric. The "well-being of mankind" was not that far removed from the missionary impulse that animated much of late nineteenth-century and early twentieth-century U.S. imperial culture at home and abroad. "The advancement of knowledge," on the other hand, completely secularized corporate philanthropy and tied it more closely to science for the sake of science. This was not the same thing as saying that the impulse to evangelize disappeared. Instead, science and especially scientific medicine functioned as its own kind of secular theology within the foundation and a civilizing tool when promoted across the shifting contours of Anglo-American Empire.

The "advancement of knowledge" certified the demise of Spelman's nursing school. The school's promise, according to Rockefeller priorities, was its situation in an educational institution rather than a hospital at a time when hospital-based nursing schools dominated the market. A key problem with the school at Spelman Seminary was that it was never able to fully achieve the academic standards that its later white counterparts did at institutions such as Yale, Columbia, and the University of Toronto. It remained beholden to a beleaguered infirmary cum hospital with its students receiving minimal theoretical instruction and serving primarily as a source of cheap labor both inside and outside of the school. By the 1920s, the RF had made clear that its goal was to fund university-based nursing programs. In this sense, the location of a nursing *diploma* program (as opposed to a degree program) within an academic institution (albeit not a university) could be cast off as an early experiment that ended as something of an anomaly.

The shutdown of Spelman's nursing diploma program was also part of a larger shutdown around African American nurses and nursing within the RF. This was signaled by the repression of a devastating report, "A Study of the Present Status of the Negro Woman in Nursing, 1925," produced by the British-born nurse Ethel Johns and recovered in the 1980s by historian Darlene Clark Hine. In this report, Johns found that "the average [African American] nursing student was ill-housed, overworked, under-or-unpaid, and badly exploited."[36] The hospitals where they studied admitted African American nursing students oftentimes against their own stated standards, thereby cultivating a pool of nursing students who had not had access to adequate prior schooling. In the South, they worked in segregated hospitals. In the North, they also worked in some hospitals that were only for African Americans, or in segregated units, or under racialized quotas. Regardless of their location or particular situation, nursing students—both black and white—provided the bulk of the labor that kept hospitals running, and they did so virtually for free as they were technically students, not wage laborers. Another key feature of African American nursing schools and hospitals was white, not black, nursing superintendent/supervisors. The latter also led a movement to create a lower grade of certification for a nursing attendant and to channel African American students into this category and away from the possibility of upward mobility.

Johns's report was clear and concise, and it painted a picture that was actually inseparable from the general state of black hospitals under Jim and Jane Crow segregation in the South and, more or less, also in the North. And yet, if it were not for Hine's investigative work within the RF archives, the report may still be lost to our collective knowledge. The foundation actively suppressed it and never followed up on its conclusions or suggestions.[37] The result was a de facto decision *not* to pour money into the often desperate situation that African American nurses found themselves in—with one exception.

In the North, selected African American nurses had access to postdiploma education through the allotment of quotas. These graduates formed the nucleus of a black nursing leadership, women who were not a focus within the Johns report but who had been making moves of their own toward greater access and recognition since the beginning of the century. What began with a letter writing campaign spearheaded by Martha Minerva Franklin in 1906 coalesced into the first meeting of the National Association of Colored Graduate Nurses (NACGN) in New York City in 1908. By 1920, the NACGN had gathered 500 members but remained run on an all-volunteer basis.[38] African American nurses' struggle for professional recognition gained momentum in the 1930s, aided by an infusion of support from white philanthropists. The opening gesture came from the Rosenwald Fund, which of all the foundations had made African American issues one of its primary foci. At the end of the 1920s, black nursing leader Carrie E. Bullock met with representatives from the fund who subsequently set up a fellowship to offer the opportunity of advanced training for one black nurse a year. By the middle of the next decade, the Rosenwald Fund, Frances Payne Bolton, and the GEB agreed to collectively underwrite the NACGN's organizing efforts.[39] In the end, however, it was the GEB that "saved the day." In 1934, the GEB stepped in to provide the money for the NACGN to hire its first salaried executive director. It also offered the NACGN office space at Rockefeller Center in midtown Manhattan, the same building that hosted the headquarters of the American Nurses Association (ANA), the premier professional nursing organization in the United States and a group that was effectively barred to African Americans.[40]

What was it about the NACGN that was of interest to the same philanthropists who had all but abandoned addressing the systematic impoverishment of the bulk of African American health care workers, let alone African American health? The conscious and willful neglect of the latter clarified the limits of the humanitarian rhetoric surrounding white corporate philanthropy. Meanwhile the support of the NACGN took shape out of the same logic that, while promoting two black medical colleges, basically doomed the rest to dissolution for lack of funds. White corporate philanthropists insisted on an elite strategy that emphasized the creation of a small group of hierarchical, professionalized, foundation-supported

leaders. In the United States, their promotion of processes of professionalization was simultaneous to the institutionalization of Jim and Jane
Crow segregation in education and health care. Foundations were key
to both. They invested in separate institutions to accommodate white
racism (their own, as well as that of the general population) and to disregard the needs of the majority of formerly enslaved Africans and their
descendants.

Racialized segregation was the norm in both the South and the North,
even though it took a different form in the latter. So, for instance, while
according the NACGN status in the South was still out of the question, in
New York City, it was only thinkable within limits that clearly acquiesced
to white exclusion and (often) outright hostility. Recognizing this requires
us to shift our thinking about segregation as solely a form of separation
and understand it, instead, as a form of integration predicated on the continuity of racialized oppression and structural inequality. Herein lies the
symbolic power, and structural limits, of housing both the NACGN and
the ANA at Rockefeller Center. This arrangement allowed the RF and its
associated philanthropies to support the NACGN *and* respect the racialized exclusions in operation at the ANA.

I want, at this point, to take a cue from the longstanding debates about
the benefits and disadvantages of white corporate philanthropy among African Americans.[41] It was not as if Rockefeller had invented health care or
education for African Americans. Enslaved Africans and their descendants
had practiced self-education and community health care since their arrival
in the Americas, in the face of prohibition and violence. What corporate
philanthropists did do was provide much-needed funds to communities
that were otherwise systematically denied avenues for wealth accumulation
themselves. We should be clear here, though, that these funds were not intended to aid in a process of emancipation following the legal end of chattel
slavery. Quite to the contrary, they were meant to institutionalize a system
that catered to the continuity of the possessive investment in whiteness.[42]
For Rockefeller, this was money for "education not agitation," a point that
many African Americans made as they took a stance against what they
saw as the pernicious effects of white philanthropy in keeping African
Americans "in their place."[43]

With regards to nursing, let us remember that distinguishing between
the forms of domestic labor and care work associated with black women
was one of the first moves that white nurses in the United States had made
toward the elevation of their own status. In the 1920s, white nursing
leadership was still struggling to establish itself above the mass of diploma

nurses who provided the cheap labor that white hospitals ran on. Johns herself reported that, "if the influence of race conflict could be eliminated from the situation the problem of the negro [*sic*] nurse would not differ greatly from that of the relatively inferior type of white nurse, and a common solution might possibly be found for both."[44] Here Johns stated an "if" that has shadowed the course of U.S. history, from its origins as a British settler colony through to our "postracial" present. When addressed to officers of the RF at a time when they were literally investing in Jim and Jane Crow segregation, such a statement fell on purposely deafened ears.

Johns concluded her report by stating, "The present study has convinced the writer that the things which need doing more are, first, to induce a superior type of negro [*sic*] woman to enter nursing, and secondly to provide sound training for them."[45] It was a curious conclusion given the damning evidence throughout her report of the miserable conditions under which African American nurses—both students and graduates—labored under. Here at the end, however, there was not a word about wages or working conditions. Instead, the representation of African American nurses implicit in her *first* proposition frames African American women themselves as the problem. The African American women who worked as nurses were inferior; until and unless they improved, nothing else would. African American women thus came to bear the burden of representation of their degraded working conditions, a fact that they themselves were well aware of and that Johns's report also made clear. One African American graduate nurse interviewed explained that "nurses are looked down upon in the South . . . the social position of a teacher is much higher."[46] Johns went on to explain that those who did work as nurses had a reputation for being of a "low moral character," a reputation evidenced by entrance requirements that many black hospital diploma programs had for applicants to test for syphilis and tuberculosis, as well as produce a "certificate of moral character."

The requirement for a certification of moral character raised the question of who or what entity could provide such a thing. The answer was not predetermined and far from readily forthcoming. Black applicants had no clear way of producing such certification, and the (most often) white nursing and hospital supervisors were all too often willing to overlook it. The laxity in this instance was but one part of the categorical failure of almost every hospital surveyed to meet its own stated requirements. This is not to say that the requirement did not serve a real purpose. Rather than proving a bar to entrance, what the "moral character" requirement (evidenced in terms of physical as well as character-based certification) achieved was a clear and continuous suspicion of African American women and, consequently, a justification for their strict supervision. In this sense, it further justified and empowered the role of the mostly white supervisors of black nursing labor. Hine describes how Johns's interviews with white nursing supervisors revealed their deep disregard for black nursing students and their depictions of them as lacking in the intelligence and moral character required for "proper" nursing. In the Southern states, this disdain sat right next to the preference that many white patients, both inside and outside of hospitals, had for African American nurses. Theirs was a preference born out of racism, the same racism that categorically associated black women with domestic labor and with systematically degraded if not anymore technically enslaved and unfree working conditions. It was, in other words, a preference born out of the same images that white nursing leaders had set themselves up against. In the case of white nurses supervising African American nursing students, the cost-benefit ratio of this distancing was vividly clear. By continuing to insist on degrading black women, black womanhood, and the "dirty work" of the sick nursing that was relegated to them, white supervisors justified the need for their own supervisory role over and above the purported mess. White nurses thus became the entity who could provide moral certification, both by the example of their own womanhood and by the authority that this purified womanhood wielded in the Jane Crow South. This was a critical component of the "sound training" that Johns also recommended as a surveyor of the situation.

The resemblance between the stigmatization of African American nursing labor in the Jane Crow United States and that of Indian nursing labor in colonized India presents me—at this point—with an almost rote exercise in repetition. Here again was the trope of dirt and an explanation that rendered it an attribute of colonized peoples rather than a product of the systemic impoverishment and dehumanization produced by colonization. Here also was a reincarnation of the imminent threat posed by "women on the loose," as African American women's sexuality was a sign of the need for white control over their labor. In fact, when the black graduate nurse quoted above referred to teaching as a preferable career to nursing, we are brought right back to the scene where Jaya's father insisted that his daughter was a "good girl" and that she should become a teacher, not a nurse, in order to preserve her moral character. And if we'll remember, the argument was between Jaya's father and Miss Houghton, a colonial nurse who had migrated from the United States to India in order to supervise Indian students. All of this is not to say that the situations of Af-

rican American and Indian nurses in the early twentieth century were reducible to each other. Differences existed, and they do matter. However,
in the face of the force of American exceptionalism, difference also has a
tendency to take on a hue of distinction that I want to avoid inasmuch as
they force us to separate analyses of situations that the global, colonial
span of the imperial nation and its agents such as the RF connected.

# CHAPTER FOUR

# Remaking Mother India

In 1928, Sarojini Naidu, the poet and freedom fighter who Mohandas Karamchand Gandhi had affectionately dubbed the "Nightingale of India," wrote a lyrical letter to the Mahatma from the hills of Chittoor (in the Telugu-speaking portion of the Madras Presidency). The tone was intimate as she described the lush setting surrounding the tuberculosis sanatorium where she was attending upon her eldest daughter. Naidu's focus then shifted to the state of the Indian nationalist struggle and her particular commitment to the cause of Hindu-Muslim unity. And then, with what reads like a rhetorical sigh, she wrote, "Now about America: it seems to be written in the book of fate that I must go. You and everyone else in India think that I should go. The calls from America are incessant and insistent. I am not very happy at the thought of leaving India at such a critical point: but I have given my word and I mean to keep it. Maybe I shall be a good ambassador. I go not to refute the falsehoods of an ignorant and insolent woman but to interpret the Soul of India to a young nation striving to create its own traditions in a new world."[1]

The "ignorant and insolent woman" that Naidu referenced is U.S. journalist Katherine Mayo, author of the incendiary *Mother India*. Published in 1927, Mayo's book sent shockwaves across three continents (North America, Europe, and India) as it revitalized, spectacularly, the "woman question" that had served as a justification for British colonization. *Mother India* focused on brahmanical practices such as child marriage, reporting on the degrading and degraded status of Hindu women, which, subsequently, emasculated Hindu men and degenerated biological and social reproduction. Hinduism's defilement of women's sexuality was thus rendered the root cause of India's social, political, and economic problems. Mayo's focus on Hindus, while actually explicit and specific, quickly expanded to encompass all Indians who, under the presumed dominance of brahmanical Hinduism, were in no shape for independence. At its heart of hearts, as Mayo would freely confess, *Mother India* was an argument about Indian unfitness for self-rule and a clarion call for the continuity of British colonization.

*Mother India* created an immediate uproar among the Indians that it attacked, spawning a veritable subindustry of books, tracts, and speaking tours in its wake, across both the United States and the Indian subcontinent.[2] Naidu's U.S. tour was one of the most famous of these. Few prominent Indians could have figured so well as a living incarnation of the *other* "Mother India," not she of Mayo's vitriolic prose but the mother-as-goddess who had become central to the imagery of Indian nationalism. In the above letter, Naidu continued, "India has an imperishable gift to make to the new world as it has made to the old worlds age after age."[3] Here the glory of Indian womanhood was both a matter of ancient pride and a future promise being forged within the struggle for independence.

Katherine Mayo, herself a U.S.-based single, white woman traversing the terrain of colonized India in order to critique the natives in the name of capitalist colonization, bore more than a mere family resemblance to the likes of Dr. Ida Sophia Scudder and the many missionary women—medical and otherwise—who had launched themselves through the "woman question" during the high noon of British colonization. And indeed, Mayo's work found such favor with British colonial officials that they successfully pushed publication forward so that each member of the Simon Commission held a copy of *Mother India* in his hand before leaving for India. Connections such as these brought frequent charges that Mayo was in cahoots with the colonial government and that her book had even been commissioned by them. Such accusations added fuel to the fiery international scandal caused by the publication of *Mother India*. They also ended up largely shielding Mayo's connections to the Rockefeller Foundation (RF) and the specific logics of U.S. imperialism.[4]

*Mother India* began as a journalist's self-professed inquiry into the state of public health in India. Evidence of this remains laced throughout Mayo's analysis, as she reports on malaria, cholera, and hookworm among Indians. Degenerate sexuality became another disease in this order and one that added to the list of what made Indians a "world menace."[5] The latter characterization drew less from "woman's work for woman," which ultimately urged white women to travel the world in order to save their "sisters," than it did from the public health work of the RF. In the former, the opportunity was *for* circulation—the circulation of white women who could save their heathen sisters. In the latter, circulation, this time of infectious brown bodies, became a threat to white health. Diseased brown bodies had been central to the justification for the launching of the International Health Commission (IHC), when RF officials specifically cited indentured Indian labor as a primary hazard to global health. In 1920 they began broadcasting this threat through the educational film *Unhooking the Hookworm*, which was translated into Spanish, French, and Portuguese and distributed to locations across the world. The film began by displaying specimens of male and female hookworms, and then these words appear on the screen: "Their victims are counted by the millions, from India——" It then cuts first to a screen crowded with Indians and then moves directly to a shot of a poor white southern family in the United States, whose members all bear the mark of the disease in their lethargic pallor.[6]

In her analysis of *Mother India*, Asha Nadkarni reminds us that Mayo's concern was not simply with upholding British colonization of the subcontinent. It was also, explicitly, a strategy of containment. Indians were not only unfit for self-rule, but their circulation also posed a danger around the world. Mayo's own ideas about Indians came from her childhood years spent in Surinam (Dutch Guiana), where her father had worked as a mining engineer in the late nineteenth century. It was there that she first began to characterize indentured Indians and their descendants as "sly and mysterious," in contrast to the "docile" descendants of formerly enslaved Africans and the "upstanding" white bearers of "civilization." For Mayo, Indians were the threat to adjacent white and black populations. This was especially the case in an "immigration nation" such as the United States.[7] Accordingly, when she returned to the United States, Mayo would go on to establish her journalistic credentials by writing for the expansion of policing and against the presence of Catholics, African Americans, and Asians. She was a nativist through and through, defining that term through a naturalization of White Anglo-Saxon Protestant (WASP) settler colonialism as the central motor for the imperial nation. This was, ultimately, the public whose health she was concerned with. Her emphases clearly found fit with the arguments of the RF as both sought to elaborate the particular convergence between the concerns of an imperial nation "at home" and abroad. Indeed, the film by the International Health Board (IHB, as the IHC had been renamed in 1916) came out just after anti-Hindu mobilization had helped to secure Indian exclusion and just before the Supreme Court of the United States also definitively ruled Indians ineligible to naturalization (in the United States at this time, the word "Hindu" referred to all Indians).

From the available evidence, it seems that Mayo's working collaboration with the RF began after she was an already established journalist, when foundation officers suggested that she write a book on public health in the Philippines.[8] The context was one where the Jones Act of 1916 had set up conditions for the election of a Philippine legislature, one step toward a still vague commitment to the goal of "autonomous government." The act granted limited room for Filipinos while retaining all the essential safeguards for U.S. imperial interests. Mayo's 1925 book, *The Isles of Fear: The Truth about the Philippines*, would add its argument to the weight of empire. It was in this work, actually, that Mayo first submitted diseased, colonized bodies as evidence against self-rule and as objects for the "benevolence" of colonization.[9] Her argument gained strength from the special place that public health work had within the U.S. Empire. In the Philippines, it was a place embodied by Dr. Victor Heiser himself. Before being named Director of the East for the IHC, Heiser worked for seventeen years with the U.S. Public Health Services. For ten of those years, he served as chief quarantine officer in the Philippines. Mayo dedicates a whole chapter of *Isles of Fear* to Heiser, who, as historian John Farley observes, was both a purveyor of public health and "a passionate advocate of the white man's burden."[10] In the Philippines, according to U.S. colonial logic, the two converged through public health's emphasis on sanitizing diseased bodies so that they could function as productive, and docile, labor. It was a task that required U.S. colonial control before the prospect of self-rule could be considered. This was a particularly U.S. spin on the civilizing mission.

Mayo's intention to pronounce a similar thesis on public health in India may also have been at the suggestion of RF officers. The connection was not formal. *Mother India* was not an officially funded foundation project. However, Mayo's previous work with the foundation and other extenuating details, such as the fact that RF president George E. Vincent was apparently the only one to have read the full manuscript before its publication, are, at the very least, revealing.[11] Indeed, the murkiness of the details serves as its own kind of metaphor for the linkages between public health, corporate philanthropy, and open door imperialism. Mayo's change of focus—from cholera to an oversexed India—did not ultimately change the argument of her book, an argument that linked colonial control to the spread of sanitation, hygiene, and public health as methods for containing the threat of Indian contagion. The real trouble was that this particular colonial logic didn't work in India as it had in the Philippines. The link between imperial benevolence and public health was difficult to maintain in the face of the sustained, systemic neglect of Indian health under British rule. Indians had already branded the British as an obstacle to public health. As Mrinalini Sinha repeatedly points out, Indian critics did not argue against Mayo's facts but with her explanatory framework. They did not dispute that the conditions for Indian women needed improvement, yet improvement, they argued, would only come through the promise of self-rule.

The failure of public health to provide adequate grounds for the justification of colonization in India revealed a critical difference in its place within the colonial civilizing mission of U.S. imperialism. In India, this difference allowed the RF to have its cake and eat it too. The flak resulting from *Mother India* was Mayo's to bear, as she and her alleged connections to British officials became focal points for middle-class Indian mobilization. In the process, Mayo's connections with the RF fell to the wayside within a construction of colonizer-colonized that did not, in the main, account for the Anglo-American contours of capitalist imperialism. Rockefeller officials were quite conscious of the way in which this could position their work within what RF medical man Dr. John Black Grant identified as a political situation that was "probably more labile socially than anywhere in the world, with the possible exception of Russia."[12] Grant toured the subcontinent to assess the possibilities for public health work in 1935 and already by then indicated that some form of independence was imminent. This was the same year that Miss Mary Beard did the first full survey of nursing in India, and her comments even more explicitly outlined the relationship between the foundation, Indian anticolonial mobilization, and shifting imperial formations: "In spite of American unpopularity following Katherine Mayo's book (and I noticed a lessening of the antagonism to MOTHER INDIA, so apparent when I visited India three years ago), Indians are frequently sympathetic with what comes to them from America. Whenever Indian people entertained us and there were no English present, we were sure to hear very different and much more confidential talk. Congress has been suppressed but it is not dead. Indians say to an American, "Congress is our only hope.""[13]

The Indian National Congress Party was a manifestation of the same Indian middle class that I have traced since its origins as a "miniscule minority" within processes of colonial social formation. Its leadership included, at one point or another, many of the "great men" of Indian and Pakistani nationalist history: Jawaharlal Nehru, Sardar Vallabhai Patel, Bal Gangadhar Tilak, Gopal Krishna Gokhale, Muhammad Ali Jinnah, Maulana Abdul Kalam Azad, C. Rajagopalachari, Subhash Chandra Bose, and Mohandas Karamchand (Mahatma) Gandhi. It was the shrewd politics of the Mahatma that led the transformation of the Congress from a party of the Indian elite (albeit under colonization) to an organization that could mobilize the masses of Indian people. As many scholars have pointed out, the people's participation enabled Congress' (and the Mahatma's) ascendancy, while at the same time constantly threatening to exceed the limits placed upon it by Congress' (and the Mahatma's) control. Nevertheless, it was the power of mass mobilization that signaled the political instability of the decades between World Wars I and II (interwar years) in India and set the stage for a series of negotiations that would lead to passage of the Government of India Act of 1935.

The 1935 act was a follow-up to the Simon Commission's survey and a series of hotly disputed Round Table conferences. It replaced provincial dyarchy with a principle of "responsible government," theoretically in all departments. It extended the franchise to include approximately thirty million Indians (from six and a half million) and allowed Indians to form majorities and be appointed to forms of government. British provincial governors, however, retained unchecked power to suspend "responsible government." And at the center, in Delhi, while the act instituted dyarchy in some departments, the British retained full control over key areas such as finances,[14] foreign affairs, the military, and the railways. These safeguards, as well as the lack of a mention of even Dominion Status, left Indians from across the political spectrum unsatisfied and unenthusiastic. However, when elections were held in 1937, the Indian National Congress Party won nearly half of the overall available seats and held absolute majorities in Madras, Bihar, Orissa, the Central Provinces, and the United Provinces, with a near majority in Bombay. This assumption of power within the structures of British colonial rule was a major step in what Sumit Sarkar characterizes as the process whereby "the Congress . . . while fighting the Raj was also becoming the Raj, foreshadowing the great but incomplete transformation of 1947."[15]

Sarkar's formulation benefits from the hindsight of a historian's ability to analyze years marked by uncertainty over the fate of India's future. Certainly, the safeguards that bulwarked the limited power sharing in the 1935 act spoke to the insistence of British colonial control. And yet, the winds of change were also in the air, and it was to these that RF officers in India attended. Beard's assessment highlighted how, once again, the crack in the colonial infrastructure, opened by pressure from Indians, also appeared as an avenue to the RF. If Congress was the hope of the Indians she interviewed, public health was the tool of the imperial interests that Beard herself represented. Indeed, public health become a critical way in which the RF successfully courted middle-class Indian nationalists. This was a critical convergence, and one that had constitutive implications for the shifts in the status and position of Indian nurses and nursing.

*Nursing the Nascent Nation*

In many ways, the crux of *Mother India* was the eponymously entitled chapter nested toward the beginning of the book. In it, Mayo resuscitated the tried-and-true scene that was at the heart of "woman's work for woman": the moment of the birth of a (male) Indian child. The moment was one that for Mayo, as for the missionaries who preceded her, encapsulated the utter savagery at the core of Hindu heathenism. It was also a scene that allowed her to differentiate between the Indian woman giving birth and the Indian woman attending upon her. The first was "the" Indian woman who represented "Mother India," and the other was the dai, "the half-blind, the aged, the crippled, the palsied and the diseased, drawn from the dirtiest poor, as sole ministrants to the women of India in the most delicate, the most dangerous and the most important hour of her existence."[16] The dai was, here again, the ultimate source of contamination.

In her analysis, Asha Nadkarni points out how this splitting of "Indian woman" into Indian women positioned "Mother India" as simultaneously a threat and a victim.[17] There was in this picture one woman worth rescuing from the contamination of "the other." This partitioning of pollution from the perspective of a self-styled purveyor/protector of public health compounded the caste- and gender-based oppression constitutive of brahmanical patriarchy. In this, it echoed the broad outlines of the movement of middle-class Indian women that took shape during the interwar years. As evidenced by Naidu's North American tour, Katherine Mayo's *Mother India* proved a critical catalyst for the mobilization of middle-class Indian, and mostly Hindu, women as political subjects in their own right. And yet, in the arguments that ensued, the specificity of the practices of brahmanical patriarchy threatened to masquerade as universal under the "all India" umbrella in a way that specifically marginalized the positions of religious minorities as well as oppressed caste and class women. Dalit and Shudra activists were the first to point this out.

In the controversies over *Mother India*, the pages of *Kudi Arasu* stand out for their multifaceted challenge to structures of oppression on the subcontinent. This challenge made sense given that *Kudi Arasu* was the journal of the Self-Respect movement founded in Madras by E. V. Ramaswami Naicker (more popularly known as, simply, Periyar). Self-Respecters challenged Brahmins to prove Katherine Mayo wrong.[18] In doing so, they joined fellow anticaste activists in differentiating between an attack on all of India or Indians and one that focused specifically on practices propagated by brahmanical patriarchy. What this clarification achieved was that it posed the overthrow of not only British rule but also brahmanical patriarchy as the condition for liberation. It also pointed to the way in which the two could collaborate to continue, anew, the subjugation of oppressed caste and class Indians.

The tension between the representational politics of "all India" and the lived reality of all Indians came to the fore during the debates that led up to passage of the Government of India Act of 1935. At stake during the series of Round Table conferences held was a revision of colonial rule, and up for debate was the creation of an Indian electorate. During the discussions, Dalit intellectual and political leader Dr. B. R. Ambedkar demanded a separate electorate for Dalits so that they could represent themselves and work to undo the oppression of their material, spiritual, and social out-casting by Hindus. The initial acceptance of Ambedkar's demand by British authorities led to the declaration of a fast-unto-death by Gandhi. Gandhi opposed separate electorates for Harijans (Dalits), claiming that it would fracture "Hindu unity." The Dalit counterargument was, of course, that Hindus had never considered Dalits part of their fold. However, faced with the prospect of the Mahatma's death laid at his doorstep, which would almost certainly result in an unprecedented increase of attacks on Dalits across the subcontinent, Ambedkar eventually relented. When he signed the Poona Pact in 1932, Dalits became part of the general Hindu electorate, with special representatives elected out of a constituency within which they remained minoritized. This was a crucial step in the creation of a Hindu majority to stand over and above the separate electorates allotted to India's other major religious groups (including Christian).

Indian middle-class attention to the state of Indian nurses took place within a post–Poona Pact Indian political context. It also took place during a period when the influence of the International Health Division (IHD, the final and best known name of the IHC) and imperial discourses of "public health" offered an avenue for the secularization of colonial medicine in general and colonial nursing in particular. Globally, Florence Nightingale's insistence on the links between sanitation, hygiene, public health, and "woman's work" had sown the seeds of secularization in the field, seeds that benefited from the later work of the RF. In India, since medical missionaries were the primary purveyors of Nightingale nursing, there developed nevertheless a deep and lasting association between it and the Christian civilizing mission, a mission that was cast as antithetical to an Indian nationalism dominated by privileged caste and class Hindus. In contrast, the secularization of these self-same concerns through the idiom and practice of public health was part of what rendered them palatable to a Congress-led middle-class nationalism and allowed them to be packaged as part of the subcontinent's modern Indian future. This convergence of factors is important to note because the majority of women (and men) working in colonial nursing were members of India's Christian minority and/or the oppressed castes and classes. The general mandate given to their minoritization in the face of a privileged caste and class Hindu-dominated "all India" struggle compounded the hierarchies already institutionalized within colonial medical practice. It created a context for privileged caste and class Hindu women to rescue themselves at the expense of their subaltern "sisters."

In 1934, the All India Women's Conference (AIWC) passed a resolution calling for legislation that would mandate the compulsory registration of all dais and midwives. The AIWC was at the time the premier organization representing middle-class women within the Indian nationalist movement. Historian Geraldine Forbes argues that the AIWC's resolution regarding dai registration was a clear indication of how the "new woman," embodied by the middle-class Indian women now fighting for the nascent nation, had come to accept colonial medicine in general and colonial birthing practices in particular as part of the package of progress. They thus aligned themselves with the medicalization of the colonial civilizing mission over and against certain "disposable" versions of Indian custom, superstition, and tainted tradition. Disposability was most clearly embodied by the figure of the dai, who they too cast as the "evil witch of progressive India."[19]

In keeping with the dictates of colonial medicine, dai registration was an intermediary step on the way to their replacement by doctors and nurses trained within the system of colonial medicine. Accordingly, in 1941, the AIWC conducted a survey of nursing in India. The results prompted the organization to pass a resolution supporting better salaries and housing as well as more extensive training facilities for India's overworked, underpaid, and undervalued nurses. Rather than reading this as a sign of solidarity across class (and caste) among Indian women, it is actually most useful to understand this as an act of social sanitation. The AIWC turned its attention to nursing under the leadership of Rani Laxmibai Rajwade,[20] an Indian medical woman with a commitment to social and personal hygiene, as well as the promotion of birth control. In her work, Sanjam Ahluwalia makes clear that as it emanated from middle-class women, birth control in India was "rhetorically more a critique of less-privileged sections of Indian society rather than the glorious march towards' women's emancipation."[21] As part of this larger project, the call for better nursing conditions and upgraded education echoed what, around the world, had since the late nineteenth century been the call for a "better sort of woman" to enter nursing and thereby remove it from its association with variously outcasted women.

It's useful at this point to remember that Indian medical women had themselves once been the source of scandal. I have already introduced the historical figure of Dr. Rakhmabai, the child bride who refused to consummate her marriage in an earlier moment in the making of the Indian middle class. When she went on to reverse the routes of colonial medicine to become a medical doctor, she did so at a time when her degree and the independent practice it enabled upon her return would brand her, to many, as a consummate "woman on the loose."[22] Dr. Rajwade's leadership of an organization such as the AIWC was proof of how, by the 1940s, the status of Indian medical women had consolidated into one where they had now become standard bearers for respectability.

And what of Vidyaben? In what ways does her story, submerged as it is in the historical archives, offer up a set of possibilities for transformation? What can we say about a woman who left her abusive husband, found shelter in the practice of nursing, and eventually returned to conjugality but with a degree of independence, autonomy, and authority that fortified her refusal to bear any more children? Certainly, there were shades of "woman on the loose" *and* "woman in the lead" here. And like Rajwade after her, she found her place in the world of waged work through a commitment to public health and birth control. Her access occurred through the Red Cross, an agency that came of age alongside Nightingale nursing, even as trained nurses came to see its work as something of a menace to their mission. This was not because of the Red Cross' association with the exigencies of war (this it shared with Nightingale, after all), but with the way in which those exigencies came to associate Red Cross nursing with hastily prepared care workers, workers whose proliferation threatened the standards that bodies such as the International Council of Nurses struggled to promote.[23] Would the "better standards" called for by organizations like the AIWC transform the nurses who followed Vidyaben into public health and birth control from an association with the ill prepared? Where were the borders between agency, conformity, and/or cooptation by colonizing projects? These are important questions to bring forward into an examination of the 1940s, which proved to be a critical decade for the promotion of India's first generation of Indian nursing leaders through the institutionalization of professional nursing in India—for Indians.

In 1941, the same year that Rajwade led the AIWC's survey of nursing (the survey itself being a form central to the public health work of the RF, dating back at least to the Rockefeller Sanitary Commission), the IHD deputed one of its senior nursing advisors, Miss Mary Elizabeth Tennant, to do the same.[24] Tennant's tour was related to the overhaul of the All India Institute of Hygiene and Public Health (AIIHPH) under the leadership of the aforementioned Dr. John Black Grant. Prior to Grant's arrival, the institute had been in a protracted leadership crisis, beginning in 1935, when its initial director, Lt. Col. Dr. Stewart, rather abruptly resigned. After Stewart's departure, the institute ran under Dr. Lal, a professor of vital statistics and epidemiology who had received his training in part through a fellowship from the RF. Despite his colonial accreditation, Dr. Lal was never seen as more than a temporary replacement. The RF even went so far as to break with its official protocol and hire Dr. John Black Grant in a move that would "rescue" the AIIHPH from the threat of Indian control that Lal embodied.[25]

Turning to John Black Grant was, in many ways, like turning to the sum total of the routes that had led to the establishment of colonial medicine on the subcontinent and that marked the particular place of North Americans in that process. Grant had been born and raised in neighboring China, the son of Canadian Baptist missionaries. He eventually attended medical school in the United States and then worked for the RF in its campaigns against hookworm, first in China and then in Puerto Rico and North Carolina. After his work across a swathe of U.S. Empire, Grant earned a master's in public health from Johns Hopkins University's (JHU's) newly opened School of Hygiene and Public Health. The RF then hired him as a professor at the Peking University Medical Center, as part of their move to promote that institution as "the Johns Hopkins of China."

Political instability in China due to the second Sino-Japanese War cut Grant's ambitions short in the land of his birth. In 1939, the RF transferred him to India, where he became the head of the AIIHPH. As a Canadian, he was the perfect "compromise candidate." The logic was that since he was neither British nor Indian he would not necessarily inspire Indian ire—or fan the flames of Indian independence. As a Canadian, he was also a British subject and so could retain a permanent position under institutional regulations. At the same time, his birth in China and his prior absorption into U.S.-led medical circuits positioned him as an envoy of the U.S. RF in a way that made his status as Canadian ultimately a useful technical detail.

Grant was a complicated figure within the foundation. Known as the "Rockefeller Bolshevik" by some, during his time in North America he had become an adherent of Fabian socialism, a commitment that brought him into repeated conflict with his employer.[26] However, his formative association with the RF meant that he would maintain what was an implicitly imperialist vision even as he was not directly tied to British rule—a vision coded through RF "standards." His education and fieldwork had made of Grant a firm believer in the foundation's standardization of medical and nursing education—he was, in effect, a preacher of professionalization. Immediately after his arrival in India, Grant assessed the education on offer at the AIIHPH as insufficiently superior to that offered elsewhere even on the subcontinent and its research activities as insignificant. If conditions were not able to improve, he recommended that the institute be closed. Improvement for Grant meant making the institution into the "JHU of India." Such a task included a command to bring public health nursing up to the standards of professionalization promoted in the United States. Tennant's tour took place as part of this project.

The opening of Tennant's "Summary of Impressions of Nursing in India" placed the prospects for professionalized nursing firmly within the particular permutations of the "woman question" in India. She opened by stating, somewhat flatly, that "nursing in India is backward because of the inferior status of women." Her explanation then quickly linked this classic racist colonial generalization to its corollary understanding of caste: "The caste system in India is such that nursing is looked down upon. Low caste women have been the nurses and midwives."[27] Caste again appeared as the ultimate marker of Indian difference and the means to distinguish between the generalized Indian woman of the "woman question" and the oppressed caste women who made up the ranks of India's nursing workforce. The rest of the report further specified this distinction, as Tennant described how middle-class Indian women refused to become nurses because performing the tasks associated with the occupation would make them "untouchable." She noted their particular fear of the association between the removal of bedpans and the removal of night soil, tasks associated with those most marginalized by caste oppression. The preponderance of Indian Christian women within nursing also had a caste-based explanation, as Tennant summarily categorized all Indian Christians as converts coming from the most oppressed "sweeper class" because of the Christian interest in uplift. This "uplift" had its clear limits, as Indian nurses were virtually absent in leadership roles at any of the civil hospitals that she visited. The only exception Tennant made note of was not at a mission or government hospital but at the J. J. Hospital in Bombay, where T. K. Adranvala, a Parsi nurse, was superintendent.

Tennant contrasted the lack of professional status and social position of Indian nurses with the momentum among middle-class Indian women within medicine. She reported that in India, young middle-class women who were motivated toward medicine went to school to become subassistant surgeons. This was an intermediary degree, which was, by 1941, in the process of being discontinued and replaced by the MBBS (the British equivalent of an MD in the U.S. system). In her report, Tennant framed this switch as a moment of opportunity for professional nursing. If upgraded according to RF standards, nursing could serve as an alternative for the middle-class women who would have otherwise gone for the subassistant surgeon training.

It is only later that one reads, briefly, that this analysis of the situation came to Tennant through a Mrs. Mitra, the only Indian who Tennant noted as participating in the Trained Nurses Association of India (TNAI) conference that she attended in Delhi. Mitra was at that time the principal of the Lahore Health School.[28] She was also, it was noted, an Indian Christian from a family of Brahmin converts. Her caste background made her fit the definition that both the TNAI and Tennant had of an Indian woman of "good family and education," and her presence and voice at the TNAI conference was notable in a field that otherwise remained overwhelmingly dominated by India's old-guard colonial nursing leadership. Nevertheless, Tennant's mention of her was brief and passing, and the limitations to the scope of Mitra's voice become evident for us as Tennant basically usurped it without reference when she made her own recommendations.

If Mrs. Mitra's voice, however submerged, allows us to begin to recognize the role that Indian nurses themselves had during the denouement of British rule on the subcontinent, Miss Mary Elizabeth Tennant also serves as a reminder of the reincarnation of the colonial nursing leader in the form of the international nursing advisor. Unlike their predecessors who populated the TNAI, Tennant and Beard came to India to survey, not to stay. Their job was to assess, but theirs was not an assessment of what kind of programs would work given local conditions. It was a determination of what kind of opportunity a particular location offered for developing a university-based nursing program along the lines modeled by the same institutions that had conferred upon them their own authority and expertise.

Tennant echoed Beard's prior observations when she noted that all of the nursing schools in India were hospital based, working on the "earning while learning" model and thereby positioning nursing students as a cheap source of hospital labor. India's colonial nursing leadership was also in an unremarkable state, as Tennant drew a clear distinction between the kind of diploma-based trained nursing that prevailed among them and the kind of university-based professional nursing that had developed among nursing leaders in the United States. Unsurprisingly, she recommended that what India needed was a nursing college attached to a university. Such a college should be under the control of professionalized nursing leaders and become a model program that would address "the great need for young Indian women of good family and education to enter nursing."[29] While the concern to draw in better "quality" nursing students had been a constant refrain, and one that allowed for the establishment of India's colonial nursing leadership, the difference here was that Tennant and her employer were actually actively advocating for allowing Indians access to professional mobility. Her recommendations thus resonated with the tenor of the times as advocated by the leadership of an organization such as the AIWC but with the addition of the monetary means to actually make it happen.

The central government of India was also, by the 1940s, at long last showing signs of having nursing on its agenda, paving the path for the establishment of a professional program. A year after Tennant's tour, it appointed its own nursing advisor, Miss E. A. Hutchings, and opened a school of nursing administration in Delhi to train sister-tutors and hospital administrators for civil and military hospitals. And in 1943, it formed the Health Survey and Development Committee, headed by Sir Joseph Bhore (whose name the committee and its ensuing report are most commonly known by).[30] The committee's task was already in line with the model set forth by the RF and its IHD, where a survey and recommendations by experts preceded any concrete investments and actions. Here too the subject was primarily public health, and it was on this committee that Dr. John Black Grant, who was by this time fed up with the AIIHPH and aiming to leave India, found an outlet for his vision of public health programming that emphasized both professionalization and centralized national planning. Grant was also crucial to setting up the Bhore Nursing Subcommittee, which met in a conference in New Delhi in 1944. The subcommittee reflected India's colonial nursing leadership in its composition. It included U.S. nurses, but only two Indians were on its roster, one a doctor serving on the Bhore Committee and the other a nurse, the same Miss T. K. Adranvala noted in Tennant's report.[31]

The conference proceedings registered deep dismay at a nursing short-age of such grave proportions that committee members were compelled, against all of their apparently better instincts, to suggest that India may have to *temporarily* emphasize quantity over quality. To do so, it could implement a lower grade nursing certificate along the lines of the subass-istant surgeon phase that Indian medicine had had to go through, but hopefully closing it down within a shorter time span. Nursing would of necessity emphasize public health and also have a top tier separate from this lower grade. This tier would be spearheaded by the inducement of "educated Indian ladies" into the field via access to professional nursing programs in North America. The subcommittee's recommendations thus invited Indian nurses into colonial nursing's global circuits as these had been reconstructed through the system of scientific medicine funded largely by U.S.-based corporate philanthropists.

As we have seen, the establishment of university-based nursing pro-grams in the United States was critical to the consolidation of an elite nursing leadership composed of the "white women in white" who stood over and above the majority of working nurses. Rockefeller investments helped to professionalize colonial nursing via new standards of accredi-tation, while at the same time placing North America at the center of nursing's renewed global, imperial network. As with their public health work, this involved an early association with the British Empire, specifi-cally. Rockefeller wealth initially focused on developing two model nursing programs, one at the London School of Hygiene and Tropical Medicine and the other at the University of Toronto. The idea was that these could serve as beacons for large swathes of the globe, Toronto for North America and the Caribbean, London for the British Empire. Eventually, however, Rockefeller's medical investments in North America made that continent the home of professionalized nursing. In this, no institution loomed as large as the one at the University of Toronto, although programs in the United States, such as the ones at Yale University and Teachers College at Colum-bia University, also became key centers in an international nursing circuit fueled, in large part, through RF fellowships.

The interwar years saw the solidification of the use of foundation fel-lowships for the training of a network of teachers and leaders around the world in many fields, including professional nursing.[32] Just as the RF had made international health work its particular focus throughout the first four decades of its operations, medical practitioners made up the major-ity of its fellowship recipients up until 1950.[33] Fellows were key to spread-ing the version of scientific medicine promoted by the RF. The idea was that as they spread across the world, fellows would do so as emissaries of the education they had received in RF modeled programs. This was philanthropy at its best, with the fellowship recipients functioning as the seeds of corporate-sponsored public health and scientific medicine.

Scholars and analysts continue to debate the impact of the fellowship program. Generally speaking, supporters praise the opportunities it provided and the achievements it enabled. Critics focus instead on its essentially undemocratic and elitist function. In this view, fellows served to maintain the dominance of imperial centers along lines conducive to the spread of the priorities of corporate capital.[34] All sides agree on one thing, though, and that was how critical the fellowships were to the foundation's work around the world. The fellowship program was a central tool in establishing the knowledge networks that Inderjeet Parmar has argued were "*both* the ends and the means of hegemonic social and political forces."[35] He continues, "For American foundations, the construction of global knowledge networks is almost an end in itself; indeed, *the network appears to be their principal long-term achievement.*"[36]

The construction of network through the circulation of fellows was key to the transformation of colonial nursing into what I will call open door nursing. It began with nursing advisors such as Beard and Tennant and continued as they selected Indian nurses for promotion through access to the same metropolitan institutions that were the source of their own authority. The latter began in 1941, when Tennant recommended that Miss Uma Chatterjee receive a fellowship to study at the University of Toronto.[37] Chatterjee was the daughter of Col. A. C. Chatterjee, the Indian medical service director of public health in Bengal. She thus fit the criteria of a "good girl" coming from a "good family," making her an idealized candidate for promotion into a model professionalized nurse. In 1945, in preparation for the inauguration of a BSc course affiliated with the University of Delhi, the RF selected several more nurses for fellowships that would enable them to complete their undergraduate degrees abroad. Indians, however, given their general "backwardness" according to RF standards, would not yet be in the lead of the emergent program. Instead, in 1945, the foundation also deputed one of its nursing advisors, Janet Corwin, to oversee affairs during the remainder of the development phase. The College of Nursing at New Delhi (CON-D), affiliated with the University of Delhi, opened in 1946, offering a four-year degree course leading to a Bachelor's of Science (honors) in nursing. Its inaugural principal was Miss Margaretta Craig, a U.S. nurse, and it had on its startup staff fully one Indian nurse in a leadership role, and that was Miss Uma Chatterjee. The core staff also had on board six Indian nurses who had been RF fellows, two who had received RF travel grants, and two who were still studying at the University of Toronto.[38]

At this point, it's worth pausing and asking what had changed since 1935 when, less than a decade earlier, the threat of Indian control (and that too of a medical doctor, not even a nurse) had created the conditions for the deputation of Dr. John Black Grant. Part of the answer lies in the fact that the RF's heavy investment in the CON-D was, in a sense, a key outcome of the foundation's public health presence on the subcontinent since the lead-up to the founding of the AIIHPH. And like that older institution, the RF was clearly committed to starting up the CON-D, but unlike the decade following World War I, by the 1940s, the foundation was at the end of the beginning of what I will call a "philanthropic transition" of its public health work.

During the interwar years, the RF's IHD emerged as *the* major force promoting public health and biomedical education on a global scale. No other institution could match its range or the wealth it wielded. In 1951, the IHD merged with the RF's medical sciences program and ceased its existence as an independent entity. Success was a major reason for its dissolution. By this time, much of the work it had pioneered had been taken over by a new set of agencies, including, in the United States, the National Science Foundation and the National Institute of Health; on the global stage, the World Health Organization (WHO) and the U.S. Technical Cooperation Administration (later, USAID); and regionally, the Colombo Plan. Many of these organizations were not only modeled after the IHD but were also staffed by former IHD administrators.[39] Thus, by the end of World War II, the RF's versions of scientific medicine and professionalized public health were "going global" such that they no longer needed to go in its name.

Critically, the IHD's philanthropic transition coincided with Indian independence from direct British rule. But in this case, it was not former IHD administrators who were to remain at the helm of the new nation-state; instead, they were to have a critical role as open door advisors. This is the best appellation for the work done by the likes of Mary Elizabeth Tennant and the advisors who followed her into India during the decade after Indian independence/partition. Their work was in keeping with the ideology of philanthropy pioneered by Rockefeller and his advisors and the kind of state-corporate nexus that foundations had already established in the United States. Key to this was the training of leadership in a foundation-approved mold. As a central government project, the CON-D was an ideal regional center for the establishment of foundation-based networks in the new nation and for the inclusion of that nation within a map of Anglo-American capitalism that was, with the end of World War II, undergoing its own period of significant reconstruction.

Nursing scholars describe the end of World War II and the establishment of a Cold War global order as a key moment for renewing international nursing's sense of purpose. That nursing was on the agenda of the new proliferation of international organizations accompanying and enabling this shift was meaningful to the ongoing struggle that professional nurses had to wage for status and recognition. Despite the overall and implicit boost that corporate-backed scientific medicine had given to professional nursing, nurses had long held a secondary, subordinate position within the elite, knowledge-based networks that were, ultimately, the RF's raison-d'être.[40] Their subordination was a clear reflection of professional nursing's class-based struggle to attain status in the face of the gendered hierarchies of scientific medicine. And yet white nursing leaders retained an upper hand when it came to sowing the seeds of their professional network—both in the United States and across the global map of capitalist imperialism.

One year after her visit to India, the General Education Board (GEB) enlisted Tennant to assess the possibilities for developing a baccalaureate nursing program at Dillard University, a historically black institution in New Orleans, Louisiana. At the time, Rita Miller, an African American nurse with a degree from Teachers College, headed the nursing program at Dillard and brought her program to the foundation's notice. Her request initiated the deputation of Tennant, and Tennant's stamp of approval, in turn, helped to ensure the GEB and the Rosenwald Fund that Dillard was a promising investment. Foundation backing then allowed Miller's staff to train through fellowships from the GEB so that eventually all of them had degrees from Toronto or one of the other premier programs developed through foundation imperatives. As Dillard conformed to the patterns of professionalization and education at a place like Toronto, it too became a model institution for the GEB's increasing investment in the development of baccalaureate nursing programs at other historically black institutions.

Dillard's startup staff trained at the same institutions that Indian nursing fellows were sent to for the CON-D. As these newly professionalized workers graduated together, the Indians returned home with a mission that seemed to run straight up against state-sponsored plans that emphasized precisely the parts of the Bhore Report that foundation officials objected to most strenuously. The report noted an absolutely critical shortage of nursing personnel.[41] For the years 1941–71, it recommended increasing the number of medical doctors by four times, but for nurses and health visitors (public health nurses), one hundred times.[42] After independence, the government of India insisted, in its first two five-year plans, on the rapid training of more nurses to meet the massive demand. This training was linked to the rural and public health emphases of the plans and would introduce a lower grade nurse as indicated above.[43] Rockefeller Foundation officers at work in India after independence objected to virtually all of this. In his 1952 "Report on Medical Education in India," Richmond K. Anderson, RF Medicine and Public Health staff member in Bangalore, began by warning of the possibility that in India and Pakistan, medical education threatened to develop with a priority on producing quantity, not quality. He described the hurried expansion of medical schools and colleges and (to his mind) the overproduction of poorly trained personnel.[44] In his view, such a policy would not serve India's urgent health needs. What was more, he wrote, "I believe the RF could exert an influence toward combating this tendency."[45]

As the RF folded its International Health Division, and other agencies, both international and national, took on this work, the foundation found its particular niche in its insistence on the maintenance of professional standards and the cultivation of global networks of professionalized practitioners. The split that occurred in India was figured, and indeed enacted, by the work of Dr. John Black Grant. While the Indian state took on the portions of the Bhore Report that reflected his "Bolshevik" side, his employer maintained his legacy as a preacher of professionalization. Characteristically, rather than focusing on the conditions of work, RF officials fixated instead on the inadequacy of the nurses themselves. With regard to the students, a 1946 report noted their promise but at the same time stressed their poor study habits and inability to obtain adequate exam results. Among the baccalaureate group, several dropped out before completing the first year. In addition, RF returned fellows were not getting properly placed.[46] One year later, in 1947, another report recorded continued problems with staff recruitment and retention.[47] However, as one continues to read the reports of RF officers, for them the primary problem was not retention, but recruitment, and specifically the continued inability to attract enough Indians who they deemed suitable candidates for their fellowships.

One of the problems that foundation officers identified while seeking out "suitable" nurses for their network in the new nation was the persistence of missionary influence on the field. RF representatives set themselves up as beacons for nursing's secularization, a secularization that was tantamount to modernization as they cast mission nursing as antiquated, at best. Their disdain was not reserved, simply, for India's foreign missionary leaders. It extended to their employees, as there was also an equation of Indian Christians with mission nursing and, thereby, poor quality. In 1949, nurse advisor Anna Mary Noll assessed the CON-D: "The College has been able to demonstrate during its short life that Indian girls of good social and educational background can be recruited for nursing. Four Indian communities are represented in the student body; Christians are very much in the minority."[48]

The Christian minority among BSc students at the freshly minted CON-D was meant to reflect their minority status within the general population and thereby position the central government program as genuinely "all India" and "modern." This calculation ran into the problem that at independence/partition, missions employed 80 percent of the Indians working in the field.[49] In the decades that followed, many mission institutions continued to operate because of the Indian government's policy of protecting the rights and institutions of minoritized religious groups.[50] In the face of this, the CON-D, a secular, central government institution, was meant to represent the new norm. And while RF officers attributed the difficulty with staff and students there to the generalized inadequacy of Indian nurses themselves, an inadequacy born out of both Indian (read: dominant Hindu) social norms and mission mismanagement, there was another alternative—and it too was American.

As early as 1927, George E. Vincent, then president of the RF, wrote in his diary that foundation aid to the Protestant medical mission at Vellore would help it develop into a "genuinely Anglo-Indian" institution, as opposed to a British one.[51] Of course, given its origins as a U.S. mission, Vellore was never exactly a British affair but one with definitive U.S. roots that would potentially make it more appealing to the RF at a period when the foundation was just coming off of its work on the backs of missions worldwide. Two decades later, however, the RF had not only shed its association with foreign missions, but in the case of Indian nursing, it specifically shunned their influence. Yet the nursing program at Vellore was one of the primary ones to receive foundation support in India, and it actually opened the first BSc nursing program in India, one month before Delhi.

As a medical mission, Vellore had always relied heavily on overseas funding for its sustenance. During the late nineteenth and early twentieth centuries, when the Protestant medical missionary movement was at its global height, Christian funding circuits were a primary source. During this period, the Vellore boards in both the United States and the United Kingdom first formed for this purpose.[52] Vellore was also chosen as one of the seven women's colleges in the Orient (defined as India, China, and Japan) for the 1911 jubilee celebration of "woman's work for woman" in the United States. From 1913 to 1914, two Baptist women from the United States, Mrs. Lucy Peabody and Helen Barrett Montgomery, went on a tour of these institutions as representatives of the newly created Federation of Women's Boards of Foreign Missions. When World War I was over and their efforts resumed, they turned to the newly created Laura Spelman Rockefeller Memorial Fund (LSRM). In its early stages, the fund's representatives continued to support "woman's work for woman" out of deference to Mrs. Rockefeller's lifelong interest in that cause (she had passed away in 1915). As Mrs. Peabody presented her case to the LSRM, she mentioned that Vellore, in particular, had more applicants than available spots. She also characterized it as both worthy and in need.[53] It thus became one of the earliest recipients of Rockefeller monies in India via the Jubilee Fund, and it remained a regular recipient over the decades when there was an "overall movement from religious to secular missions by Americans in South Asia . . . [and] within the compass of the Rockefeller Foundation's programs."[54]

As foundation documents repeatedly remark, this stream of support had much to do with the ways in which Vellore, unlike other medical missions in India, conformed more closely to the standards of scientific medicine dominant in the United States than any other institution in India. According to historian Meera Abraham, "The winds of change which swept the Vellore School of Nursing in the early 1930's did not appear of necessity to have affected other mission nurse training centres in the same way. From the 1930's very clearly there is a distinction between the way in which the Vellore School of Nursing functioned and other mission schools with a regional outlook and no links with a teaching hospital and a college of medicine functioned."[55] Abraham connects these "winds of change" with the arrival of a new set of nursing faculty at Vellore. In the decade preceding independence/partition, Vellore's nursing program was under the leadership of Vera K. Pitman and Florence Taylor. Pitman was from the United Kingdom and trained at Guy's hospital, generally regarded as the top nurse training program in England at the time. She worked under Florence Taylor, who was the director of nursing education and head of Vellore's Nursing School during the decades surrounding independence/partition. Taylor was a Canadian who had graduated from the University of Chicago and then the University of Toronto and who had served as a nurse in Korea and Manchuria as well as India.[56] At Vellore, such a pedigree would not have been unusual, and it was precisely this level of "quality" that distinguished Vellore for foundation officers.

The changes that Taylor and Pitman helped to usher in at Vellore were critical to the attractiveness of the institution to the RF. Despite the fact that both remained committed to the Christian mission that lay at the heart of the institution, they were also firm believers in the need to upgrade the nursing education offered at Vellore through standardization and models of professionalization that would register with Taylor's own training at Toronto. Vellore's nursing school had long been associated with the hospital and medical school run out of the same mission. However, by the time Vellore introduced the Bachelor of Science (honors) course in nursing, the medical school had been upgraded to a medical college and was affiliated with the University of Madras. As the nursing school itself became a nursing college, it also began to develop more of a program in public health. Much of the credit for this goes to Kathleen Norris, who Vellore recruited as an assistant professor in public health nursing just before it began to offer the BSc in 1946. And finally, in 1947, Vellore's medical college began to admit male as well as female medical candidates. The shift to a coeducational institution signaled the swan song of the phase of Vellore history dominated by the call for "woman's work for woman." It was such a constitutional shock that many of the Vellore U.S. board members resigned in protest. However, coeducation also marked the culmination of Vellore's reincarnation as a university-based medical college, with an attached hospital. Vellore was now institutionally in line with what the RF had helped to prop up as the dominant model of medical education in the United States and Canada. In addition, the institution's constitution and reconstitution through colonial medical networks that centered on North America meant that it was networked. Network allowed it to remain at the vanguard in India, and standards ultimately trumped the religious background of the majority of Vellore's students. In this regard, the student body at Vellore proved the most promising field in all of India.

In the face of their disdain for missions, RF officers stressed that at the very least, the Indianization of Vellore's staff must also be accompanied by a reduction in the preference for Indian Christian students.[57] Publicly, the RF rationale in this regard was that Vellore's reservations for Christian students prevented it from serving as an "all-India" institution and thereby a model for the rest of the nation. RF insistence on this at an institution where Indian Christians formed a majority had an interesting relationship to India's official policy regarding reservations and minority rights. In general, it was precisely to religious minorities, scheduled castes (Dalits in governmental parlance), and women that the government allotted reservations. Vellore authorities used the fact that reservations were official governmental policy to argue for their own policies.[58] And in fact, privately officers seemed to indicate that their emphasis on the problem of Christian reservations was perhaps exaggerated, yet it nevertheless helped them leverage the type of change they wished to further at Vellore.[59]

In the 1952 diary of her Indian trip, Medicine and Public Health Assistant Director Elizabeth W. Brackett comments that there were still no Indians in the top positions at Vellore.[60] This was despite the fact that by then, the College of Nursing had already graduated its first group of BSc nurses. At the time, such a level of nurse training was limited to Vellore and the CON-D, making these graduates among the most elite in the nation. They were thus prime candidates for ascension to these posts. Indeed, it would seem that beyond leadership and teaching, there was not actually much scope for their service within the field. With regard to this, Brackett noted that one of the Indian doctors she spoke to in Madras told her that there was really no need for producing more BSc nurses at the time, for India did not have the capacity to absorb them.[61] Such a line of reasoning was not ultimately of concern to the RF. Instead, Vellore graduates, and most especially its BSc graduates, became the primary source for RF nursing fellowships in India.

Of the twenty-five RF Indian nursing fellows listed in *The Rockefeller Foundation Directory of Fellowships and Scholarships 1917–1970*, over half were from Vellore.[62] RF fellowships enabled this selected group of Vellore graduates to pursue further education in North America (all of them studied in either the United States or Canada or in some instances in both places) and to attain degrees not yet available in India. This training served as an initiation into the network that conferred authority upon the institution's missionary leadership. In many cases, this meant moving beyond the level of a BSc to earn a master's degree. Upon their return, the fellows took up teaching and eventually leadership posts at Vellore. In this way, Aleyamma Kuruvilla, a Rockefeller fellow who earned her master's degree at Columbia University in 1953, was appointed the first Indian dean of the College of Nursing, Vellore. It was under her leadership that nursing education and nursing service were integrated at the institution and that Vellore introduced an MSc program in 1967. She was also the first Indian to be president of the Board of Nursing Education, South India, a position she held from 1972–74 and again from 1978–94. And finally, during her career, she also served as president of the Christian Medical Association of India and the TNAI for four years each.

Clearly, if the RF were to judge its success in fostering Indian nursing leadership on the case of Aleyamma Kuruvilla alone, it would have to conclude that its investment had been a smashing success. However, hers was not the only example of a Vellore grad turned Rockefeller fellow turned nursing leader. Violet Jayachandran, Kasturi Sunder Rao, Ann Rajan Sukumar, and Rachel Chacko were all RF fellows who went on to become professors and department deans at Vellore. And beyond the presence of these specific fellows were the Indian nurses who received international scholarships/fellowships from other agencies and who also went abroad to study and assumed leadership positions upon their return. The ascension of these international fellows was not limited to the changing of the guard at Vellore. The institution was a wellspring for the emergence of India's first generation of Indian nursing leaders. The influence of its graduates spread across the country and lasted throughout the century. In one count from as late as 1994, out of forty nursing colleges operative in India, fully half were headed by Vellore grads.[63]

### Of Course I Must Go

At the beginning of this chapter, Sarojini Naidu stressed how fate seemed to have led her to a tour of the United States. Naidu went to the United States to counter the calumnies of Katherine Mayo through her own embodiment of glorious, articulate, active, and eternal Indian womanhood. Her ardor was unequivocally born out of her commitment to the nationalist struggle in India, just as it was undoubtedly buoyed by her access to language, references, and worldviews accessed through her education at King's College, London and Girton College, Cambridge. Elite education in the United Kingdom was something that Naidu shared with many an Indian nationalist leader, including India's first prime minister, Jawaharlal Nehru. Set next to this, the relationship between the Christian Medical College, Vellore and the RF highlights the critical, cumulative role that U.S.-based institutions, individuals, and ideologies had in shaping the hierarchies of Indian nursing during decades marked by struggles over the content and form of decolonization. It warns us that the changing of the guard at mid-twentieth century was not solely from the British Raj to the Indian nationalist elite. It was also from a capitalist world order dominated by Great Britain to a Cold War that marked a heyday for American ascendancy. These shifts worked through and amplified the significance of the long history of U.S. medical interests on the subcontinent, revamping them through the ideology accompanying U.S.-based corporate philanthropy and persisting through the crumbling of Great Britain's Empire.

Rather than undoing the link between colonial migration and upward mobility, the shifts in colonial medicine during the interwar years eventually allowed selected Indian nurses to reverse the routes. The provision of international fellowships was particularly crucial to the reconstitution of nursing education at Vellore such that the institution could become the Indian hub for including India's first generation of nursing leaders in professional nursing's U.S.-centered global, imperial network and for spreading the seeds of their training in India. I heard about this early period in many ways during the course of my interviews with Indian nurses in the United States. One such story came to me from Rajan (not her real name), a Vellore graduate from the South Indian state of Tamil Nadu (where Vellore is now located). Rajan, like so many other of my interviewees, told me almost immediately that she had not wanted to be a nurse. While growing up, her original ambition was to be a medical doctor. It was a goal that her family could not support, as medical school cost money that they did not have. In contrast, nursing schools offered room, board, and a small stipend, and so it was that upon graduation from secondary school Rajan tested into Vellore's BSc nursing program. For a young girl whose modest means required her to prepare for work that was considered, at best, a low-status occupation, this was as good as it got. The youngest member of her entering class, Rajan excelled among her peers. After graduation, she was hired into Vellore's teaching staff. Soon thereafter, she began contemplating scholarships to further her education in the United States. Rajan stressed, in what will serve as a kind of working-class coda to Naidu's opening quote, "Getting an education abroad is more prestigious, you know, and most of our professors who had a master's degree got their degree in the United States. They were teaching you. They were role models for you. So you wanted to become like one of them by going abroad and getting your education. . . . *It was so patterned at Vellore.* At a certain level, after a certain year, they usually sent staff abroad to get educated and come back. . . . That's how they maintained their *standards.*"[64]

# CHAPTER FIVE

# From Kerala to America

If over half of the Indian nursing fellows listed in the Rockefeller Foundation's (RF's) 1917–79 fellowship directory had Vellore training, half of these went almost immediately to work in Trivandrum, capital of the princely state of Travancore. During British domination of the subcontinent, Travancore was one of three political units that had majority Malayalam-speaking populations: the princely states of Travancore and Cochin and the Malabar region of the Madras Presidency. While administratively separate, these areas remained connected by language, culture, and history. In 1956, almost a decade after Indian independence/partition, they came together to form the present-day state of Kerala.[1] As noted in the Introduction, Kerala nurses have come to represent both "the" Indian nurse and "the" Indian nurse im/migrant in the Indian national and diasporic popular imaginaries. Their predominance has been largely naturalized and/or confined to cultural explanations. Beginning instead with the regional exchange between Vellore and Trivandrum, as mediated by the RF, this chapter begins to reconstruct the historical roots and routes for the establishment of colonial nursing and capitalist colonization in what would become the capital of Kerala.

## Kerala and India's Colonial Nursing Network

Kerala was a crossroads for world trade long before the rise of Europe, let alone the arrival of the British on the Indian subcontinent. It is also home to Christian communities that date back to the landing of the Apostle St. Thomas in the year 52. Legend has it that Thomas converted several local Brahmin families and that these converts were the beginning of Kerala's Syrian Christian communities. This conversion story differs substantially from that associated with most Indian Christians, and it served as a foundation for supporting Syrian Christians' privileged status. They function much as the merchant classes (Vaisyas within the brahmanical varna system) do in other regions and attained a high economic status through their involvement in trade and later in the development of plantation economies. And while technically not a caste, they have had a status akin to privileged castes and also practice some of the restrictions around dining, marriage, and social intercourse that distinguish brahmanical caste groups. They do so in a society that was notorious for having one of the most rigid caste hierarchies on the subcontinent. In Kerala, there were not only those deemed "untouchable" but also those who enslavement marked as "unapproachable" or "unseeable," rendering proximity or the very sight of them from a distance polluting to privileged castes.[2]

The early establishment of Christian communities in Kerala meant that the region has been a beacon for Christianity in a way that distinguishes it from most of the Indian subcontinent. Following Vasco de Gama's arrival in Calicut in 1498, Kerala became a destination for Roman Catholic missionaries throughout the sixteenth and seventeenth centuries. Their presence created fissures and splits among Syrian Christians, and also added large communities of converted fisher-folk along the coast. This last group became known as Latin Rite Roman Catholics, who also have a long historical presence in Kerala, although not one marked by the same degree of caste or class privilege. The conversion of oppressed caste groups in Kerala really began, however, during the nineteenth century when Protestant missionaries flooded the region. These conversions created tensions with the older, more established, and more privileged Christian communities who for the most part maintained a keen sense of their status within the fold. Divisions between churches, within congregations and parishes, and even within graveyards persisted as Protestant missionaries provided new opportunities for education that *all* Christians (and sometimes even non-Christians) accessed. Increasing investments in the spread of Malayalam education by the local rulers of Travancore and Cochin also grew alongside mission education. By the early twentieth century, both states had also formally abolished caste restrictions in schools and allotted some forms of scholarships, although privileged caste Hindus and Syrian Christians remained the overwhelming majority in government schools into the twentieth century.

The spread of Protestant missionaries and mass conversions from the oppressed castes occurred during the same century when Malabar fell to direct British rule, and Travancore and Cochin remained princely states under British suzerainty but with a modicum of autonomy over internal affairs. This was to have an effect on the establishment of colonial medicine particularly in Travancore, where the maharaja, Ayilyam Thirunal Rama Varma, himself became a major proponent. In 1865, the same year he published *An Essay on Health* (in Malayalam) for use in the school system, the maharaja famously had his whole family vaccinated against smallpox. He later mandated that all public servants, students, lawyers, and hospital patients in the state get vaccinated, marking public health as a priority. Rama Varma also oversaw the expansion of hospitals in the state. Coming as it did from royalty, this stamp of approval positioned colonial medicine among Travancore's elite first and foremost. It thus decidedly did not have the same set of caste and class associations that it did in much of British-dominated India. Hospitals here were frequented by privileged castes and classes as early as the nineteenth century. It was what the Protestant missionaries in the neighboring Madras Presidency dreamt about.

One way to understand the elite uptake of colonial medicine in Travancore is through the difference of a princely state. Not to deny any real concern that the maharaja may have had for the health and well-being of his family and subjects, but his embrace of colonial medicine also positioned him as "civilized" and ingratiated him to British officials under whose relative mercy his rule continued. "Mercy" is the appropriate word here, for when Rama Varma took office in 1860, Travancore was in such a state of debt that India's newly empowered British rulers threatened annexation via their "doctrine of lapse." The maharaja staved off this threat by appointing Sir Tanjore Madhava Rao as his Dewan. Rao had studied in British-dominated Madras, and he set in place reforms that allowed him, by 1863, to declare Travancore debt free. In an about-face, British colonial administrators now dubbed Travancore a "model" princely state.

If longstanding Christian communities and royal uptake of certain elements of a colonial civilizing mission might position Travancore as a particular field of opportunity in the eyes of India's British overseers, Kerala also presented a particular challenge to generalized characterizations of the "woman question." It is home to the Nairs, perhaps the most well-known matrilineal caste grouping on the subcontinent. Their system, *marumakkattayam*, was not matriarchal, but it combined matrilineal descent with communal property and polyandrous relationships. Because Nairs are a privileged caste, situated just below Nambudiri Brahmins in Kerala's Hindu hierarchy, marumakkattayam also became a crucial component of how other adjacent castes "purified" their own practices in bids for increased status. Thus, many of the Malayalees across all of what is now Kerala presented a picture that was in many ways the opposite of colonial characterizations of purdah and the zenana, in that for many women, public circulation was not necessarily taboo. Instead, colonial characterizations of "degenerate matriliny" posed many Malayalee women as the consummate "women on the loose," women whose status as such was actually protected by their joint family system.

Digging through the archives, historian Robin Jeffrey mentions that as early as 1871, four women from the Nair caste trained as obstetric nurses under a Scottish doctor working for Travancore state. Jeffrey also notes that later, in 1894, while European medical women were arriving in Kerala, six teenaged Nair women requested training to administer smallpox vaccinations.[3] Jeffrey doesn't make too much of these details or tell us more about who else was drawn into nursing in the late nineteenth century, noting instead that real movement in the field did not occur until decades later. Yet the mention of caste is critical, for it presents a different picture than that offered by Salome and the earliest recruits into nursing on other parts of the subcontinent. There, the association was with the op-pressed castes and classes and privileged caste widows, women whose gen-dered subordination rendered them economic and social outcastes after the death of their husbands. Could it be that in Kerala, matriliny opened up a different kind of space for entry into the field, one not characterized by subordination but instead a product of a greater acceptance of female mobility within public space? Could this have combined with larger num-bers of Christian candidates who would have potentially been less re-stricted by caste taboos to create a larger and more "ready-made" pool of nursing recruits?

It's difficult to say an outright "no" to such an interpretation, particu-larly without access to any sense of why, for instance, these particular Nair women chose nursing. The absence of their subjectivity is perhaps due to the nature of the source material itself. But we nevertheless do have ac-cess to other information that complicates explanations that rest solely on culture and custom alone—and this lies in the realm of economics. First, there were gradations among Nairs such that there was no necessary relationship between caste and what we could call class privilege. In ad-dition, the danger posed by marumakkattayam to the social order sought by Christian, capitalist colonization created a context for its slow but steady abolition, which began in the late nineteenth century and pro-ceeded piecemeal into the postcolonial period when all vestiges of the joint Hindu family system were fully illegalized. Throughout this process, the relationships between caste, gender, and economics were under in-tense contestation and transformation. Along the way, the economic security of women within matriliny was disrupted, creating situations that could lead women out into the world of waged work where they would not have had to venture before. These economic motivations have to be considered alongside cultures of public circulation.

Jumping to the 1930s, economic dislocations on the level of joint family structures were compounded by the impact of the worldwide economic depression on Travancore's economy. By that time, much of the agriculture in the area had shifted to plantation monocultures, and all residents tied to the production of plantation crops were hit particularly hard when prices plummeted. Loss of income meant loss of ability to import food, a necessity in an economy that was dominated by items for export, not for local sustenance. During this period, records indicate a notable increase of Malayalee nursing students at Vellore. Vellore's nursing school, under the leadership of Vera K. Pitman, also appears to have specifically recruited Syrian Christian students. That this particular group of Indian Christians would appeal to Vellore's sense of itself made sense given missionaries' longstanding bias toward privileged groups. The economic tumult of the times meant that for many, status would have to suffice in the face of heavy losses in areas of the economy where Syrian Christians were concentrated. Syrian Christians were thus among the Malayalee nursing students that RF nursing advisor Mary Elizabeth Tennant noted as filling the ranks at Vellore by the time of her 1941 tour.[4]

The movement to the Madras Presidency for training had roots, also, in Maharaja Rama Varma's early commitment to colonial medicine. From the beginning, this involved Malayalees in regional and global circuits of medical migration. In 1872, Travancore state sponsored its first students to attend Madras Medical College, fostering a relationship with the Madras medical establishment that would extend to nursing. Indeed, it was not until 1943 that Travancore, which led the way for what would become Kerala in this regard, opened its own school of nursing in Trivandrum. Even then it was a meager beginning, as noted by Janet Corwin, RF nursing consultant in residence at the College of Nursing, Delhi (CON-D). Corwin visited Trivandrum as part of her 1945 itinerary. She noted that the nurses' quarters lacked beds, linens, and furniture and that the school had insufficient equipment and curricular materials. In short, she said it needed to upgrade everything. Corwin recorded Mrs. Rugmaniamma Iyengar as the only nurse on staff and recommended her for an International Health Division (IHD) fellowship to Toronto. Iyengar was a twenty-eight-year-old Nair nurse, a Vellore graduate, and the wife of a Congress party official. Despite the supposed stature implied by her caste background, she was far from well-to-do. In a letter from her to the secretary general of Travancore state, Iyengar stressed how honored she was by her recommendation for a fellowship and how she absolutely could not meet any related expenses on her own: "My financial circumstances are not at all affluent and in addition to that I have to support my children whom I have to leave with my parents at home."[5]

If Mrs. Iyengar's financial situation was not well-to-do before her IHD fellowship, it threatened to be worse afterward. The RF's philanthropic practices meant that it expected other agencies to put up part of the funding for its ventures. So while the foundation provided much of the means, Travancore state had to come up with the rest. In this case, state support had serious strings attached. It came with a service bond of fifteen years, which, if Iyengar broke, would require her to repay all expenses put forth by the state for her stay in Toronto. This was the flip side of the legacy of affirmation given by the rulers of Travancore to colonial medicine: in the case of nursing at least, it did not come along with adequate pay or reasonable working conditions.

Documentation from the Kerala State Archive reveals the decided consternation of Travancore officials during Corwin's visit. The Dewan at the time, C. P. Iyengar, was horrified that public health officials had "paraded" the nurses' quarters to Corwin. His tone was one of utter obsequiousness as he simultaneously lamented and lambasted them: "Is it not realized that we stand condemned in the eyes of the great Rockefeller organisation which would normally be of the greatest help to us? . . . I own so a feeling of humiliation."[6] The surgeon general admitted in later correspondence that

It is true that there is not as much convenience as there ought to be in this building; but when it is remembered that this class was started for the training of few girls for employment on the termination of their training in the State Hospitals; and on previous occasions there was not even the semblance of a well constituted class, and the girls themselves after training have to accept remuneration and live a simple life and could ill-afford to continue on semi-Anglo-Indian costume and food and above all the conveniences now provided for them is [sic] far better than what most of them are accustomed to in their own homes. I consider that the suggestions of Miss Corwin while welcome, are not to be taken seriously.[7]

Here it was again, the same refrain heard in Delhi and Madras in relation to RF initiatives in the field of Indian nursing: that they were not relevant to the state of the field. The deeply impoverished conditions of nurses across India spoke to neglect by the government and mission institutions. Even in a princely state such as Travancore, the fact of the matter was that the government lacked resources if not willpower (the latter is not to be taken for granted, either) to follow through on its lip service to the field. There was indeed a degree of truth in the denigrating remarks of the secretary general that few nursing students in Travancore could find work that reflected RF standards. In fact, this was a frequent and repeated complaint from RF nursing fellows across India during the pivotal decade of the 1950s, when they had begun to earnestly replace India's colonial nursing leadership. This helped to mark their ascension as troubled, as many of them quit and/or refused to take up the posts offered them upon their return.[8] There was the case of Atula Shroff, who was an RF fellow at the University of Washington in 1951.[9] Shroff refused her government position at the CON-D upon return, saying that she saw "no future prospects" in it. A foundation official, in appraising her refusal, concluded that, "Apart from having an exaggerated idea of her own importance, my feeling is that Miss Shroff never had much intention of joining the College of Nursing, unless she could do so at her own convenience and terms, on her return to India . . . I think we may write Miss Shroff off as a bad fellowship investment."[10]

As Travancore joined with Cochin to form a state in the Indian union, its health officials had something similar to say about Mrs. Iyengar. It was not that Iyengar could be counted as a "bad investment" in quite the same sense as Shroff. She didn't refuse her position. She took up the post as head of the nursing school at Trivandrum upon her return and worked through her bond. What she shared with Shroff, at least according to the assessment of government officials, was a "bad attitude." Their correspondence characterized her as making "exorbitant demands regarding her pay," even though it was better than any other nurse on staff. Her "exorbitance" came across as self-respect when, in 1955, she wrote a letter demanding redress for her exclusion from the list of Non-Gazetted Officers of the Medical Department. As superintendent of the School of Nursing at Trivandrum, she goes on to list her educational credentials and demand a reply to this, her second attempt at formalized respect and recognition. She eventually received a positive response, but this sat next to the fact that this acknowledgment did not address a thing about conditions for nurses in the state.[11] What it did do was perform a strategic move as Travancore-Cochin continued to court the RF for funds.

In 1951, RF officers noted that not only were all of the teachers at Trivandrum from Vellore but that the school actually had more applicants than available slots.[12] In addition, it was government supported, relatively new, in need of funds, and ripe for intervention in RF-preferred areas of development such as public health nursing. All of these reasons fed into the decision to commit RF funds/support to Trivandrum.[13] This began in the 1940s, with the provision of textbooks and educational materials as well as the aforementioned training of its first superintendent. Over the years, the foundation also supplied the school with new buildings, new curriculum, model wards for clinical training and practice, and RF-appointed nursing advisors.

The first RF advisor, Lillian A. Johnson, arrived in 1952. She was a prototype of the colonial nurse turned open door nursing advisor: a white woman from the United States who had been educated at Bellevue hospital in New York and who, by the time she arrived in India, had worked with American company hospitals in Panama, Columbia, and Peru; served in the army in New Zealand, the Philippines, and New Guinea (earning the rank of captain); and worked with the Community Service Society in Puerto Rico. The foundation appointed Johnson for a two-year residency in Trivandrum to work as a consultant alongside, but not in place of, Iyengar. The horizontal arrangement was insisted upon by Iyengar and met with the RF's open door nursing policy.

Apparently, Johnson's global/colonial credentials did not prepare her for the nursing situation in Travancore-Cochin, which she found particularly tough going. In her detailed correspondence with RF officers in New York, she remarked how, "Each day I absorb a bit of the depressed conditions of the nurses."[14] The reference was again to the low pay as well as the long bonds that were attached to foreign training *and* training in other parts of India. In 1950, three of the staff at the School of Nursing in Trivandrum copied the same letter to the government complaining of their pay. All three had been sent by the government to study nursing in Tamil Nadu, two at the Government General Hospital in Madras and one at Vellore. None of them had received a revised pay scale, despite their promotions upon return.[15] The archives leave us no record of a resolution. Instead, two years later, there is record of a group of European matrons and nursing sisters with decades of working experience behind them who appealed to the newly formed state of Travancore-Cochin for the ability to retain their positions and for enhanced pay. Their request was granted. The list attached to this correspondence offered a revealing snapshot of nursing hierarchies in the state, with nurses from non-Anglo countries also prominent. German and Swiss nurses on the list spoke to the longstanding work of the Basel mission and its counterparts in Kerala, while the presence of Italians reflected the work of Catholic nursing sisterhoods.

Indians appeared on the list as well, although it appears that they were paid less.[16] Indian sisters were later also recorded as complaining that their pay had not been enhanced since promotion even though they were qualified, committed, and willing to go without dearness allowance, scale of pay, or pension.[17]

The record of European missionary nurses in Travancore-Cochin was a reminder of the role that missions played in developing nursing there, as well as in British-dominated India. It was also an influence that the RF sought to overturn, at least in terms of position even if that did not translate into pay. In 1952, Miss Johnson recommended one of the 1950 complainants, Miss G. Chandramathy (the Vellore graduate), for a fellowship. In negotiating with the government over the terms, the RF demanded to have her bond waived. After some consternation, the government agreed. The lessening of state bonds for its most professionalized nurses, coupled with the continuing low pay, created a potentially unstable situation. This was the warning issued by the directorate general of health services in Delhi to the secretary general in Travancore-Cochin after he concurred about lowering the bonds: "You are probably aware that the pay scale for nurses in Travancore-Cochin is lower than that in any other state. If the low salaries are coupled with very stringent conditions the result will be that only those nurses who cannot get work elsewhere will work in Travancore."[18]

Despite such warnings, throughout the 1950s, the governments of Travancore-Cochin and then Kerala advertised for BSc nurses to help in the push to further establish professional nursing education in the state.[19] Vellore, being the only institution in South India to offer the BSc in nursing at that time, was the primary source for the resulting recruits.[20] Many of these Vellore graduates were also international fellows, Rockefeller and otherwise. Eventually, one Vellore graduate and RF fellow, Miss Lucy Peters, took over from Mrs. Iyengar at the helm of the School of Nursing in Trivandrum. Under Peters's direction, the school began a two-year postbasic BSc in nursing. The degree was meant to be an intermediary one, above a diploma and in preparation for the full BSc. During its implementation, Miss Peters had the help of another RF-appointed nursing advisor, Jane R. Stewart, who was in Trivandrum from 1963–65. By this time, the development of nursing education at Trivandrum was no longer the task of two women, one an RF nursing advisor and the other a former RF fellow, as in the days of Mrs. Iyengar and Miss Johnson. Instead, by 1963, Trivandrum's entire nursing faculty had been RF fellows.[21] Many other former fellows had also spread across the state alongside the establishment of nursing education. Notably, when Peters took over, Iyengar was transferred to head the nursing program in Alleppy, Kerala. The move marked the end of an era, as Peters had credentials that trumped Iyengar's, and foundation officers felt it was time to move on from the woman who represented an earlier moment in the spread of open door nursing in the state.

### Producing India's "Diaspora of Decolonization"

RF investments in Kerala were not enough on their own to raise nursing education there to the level found at Vellore or the CON-D. Their primary impact was to update the regional connections that had constituted colonial nursing in Travancore and expand those to include Kerala in the open door network instituted by the foundation's philanthropic work across the shifting map of Anglo-American capitalist imperialism. This was the same network Susan George Arakal entered when, in 1955, she began nursing school in Kottayam, Kerala.

During our interview in 2003, Arakal described to me how she did not come to the decision to pursue nursing on her own but was following the strong recommendation of her cousin-sister who was a nurse, a graduate from the prestigious Christian Medical College, Vellore, and recent returnee from the United States where she had earned an advanced degree. Arakal explained how the influence and example of her "very educated," "very modern," and "very strict" cousin-sister was seminal: "I didn't know abcd of anything, what nursing meant you know? I was a young girl, eighty pounds with a skirt and blouse, a small girl. So I said okay, nice to get out of the home . . . I didn't choose. She [my cousin-sister] said it is better for you, you know, to have a good future. That's what she said."[22]

Susan George Arakal studied to become a nurse in the same "Americanized hospital" that her cousin-sister taught in after her return from the United States. Following her graduation, Arakal received a number of grants and scholarships from the World Health Organization (WHO), United States Agency for International Development (USAID), and the United Nations Children's Fund (UNICEF). Through these, she trained to become a public health nurse and lecturer. She was one of the nurses who worked at the WHO-sponsored Public Health Nursing Orientation Center in Gwalior, part of the present-day state of Madhya Pradesh. Both Susan George Arakal's own belief in education and her "kilos of certificates" were largely a product of her association with the government of

India as it worked through the agencies of an always already internation-
alized field. The organizations she worked for picked up where the RF's
IHD had left off, emphasizing public health as a public good and thereby
disseminating practices of biomedicine among Indians. In postindependence India, the public health nurse had come to embody the vision encapsulated by Moti Balsara, writing in 1960 about "The Role of Today's Nurse
in Society": "The modern concept of nursing is the multi-purpose nurse
or the public health nurse, and public health nursing is socialized nursing
and medicine."[23] In this definition, nurses were no longer stigmatized
women who did "dirty work" that cast them beyond the pale of privilege.
They were instead the privileged purveyors of a public good, a public
necessity. They were nurses for the new nation.

The fact that this new nation remained networked to the circuits of
open door nursing, however, meant that many of the nurses trained into
leadership would leave in what I have dubbed a "diaspora of decolonization." Apparently, neither the existence of a small cadre of Indian nursing
leaders trained to meet international standards nor their newfound role
as purveyors of the public good were enough to overcome the difficult
conditions on the ground. As nursing scholar Madeleine Healey argues,
nurses received increased status from a postcolonial state that did not
allocate the resources necessary to make that status more than symbolic.
This created an often contradictory context where the ill pay, poor working conditions, and lack of resources that had characterized colonization
continued.[24] And if this was the case across India, it was especially the
case in Kerala. One result, as predicted, was migration out of Kerala and
out of India. Here is what *Physician and Nurse Migration: Analysis and
Policy Implications: Report of a WHO Study*, published in 1979, had to
say with regard to the field in India: "Nursing, as a profession, is grossly
underrated in India, as it often is in other poor countries. At present the
Indian nurse is faced with difficult conditions: absence of any professional
status, underpaid senior positions, extremely understaffed hospitals which
overwork the existing staff, and poor living conditions in rural areas."[25]

The WHO report was a response to the "brain drain" scare that hit India
(along with much of the Third World) during the Cold War. According to
the brain drain theory prominent at the time, highly trained workers were
investments (vis-à-vis education and social costs) that a particular nation
had made in its future development. Their emigration figured as a net loss
for the sending country and a net gain for the receiving country. The latter received the cream of another country's educational crop without

having borne the costs of producing their worth. This uneven exchange was further characterized by the fact that the movement of skilled laborers was primarily from the decolonizing world to metropolitan centers.

Indian doctors were, in many ways, the consummate representatives of brain drain theory. Indeed, in its section on India, the same WHO report began by stating that "India is, in terms of absolute numbers, the world's largest donor of medical manpower. There is scarcely a recipient country in the world where there are no Indian physicians."[26] The authors estimated that, in 1971, there were 15,000 Indian doctors working outside of India. Such a large number, however, potentially belied the fact that this only constituted an estimated 13 percent of the pool of medical labor in India at the time.[27] As an explanation for the combined magnitude of the pool of Indian medical labor, the report's authors argued that India overproduced physicians. They did not mean that India had too many doctors per se. Instead, they pointed to two complicating factors. The first was that the domestic market could not afford to employ all of the doctors available: "India's problem is that it cannot afford the physicians it needs. By producing more physicians than it can hope to employ, it is inevitable that India should suffer from 'overspill' emigration."[28] This "overspill" was not, however, necessarily constituted by the kinds of medical labor that India actually needed. It stemmed from the fact that the Indian system of medical education remained based on a colonial model and tended to produce a large number of doctors whose skills, specialties, and aspirations were often out of step with the government's health care goals and plans. The report thus implied that it was not simply that India had too many physicians; it was, more precisely, that it had too many of the wrong kind.

Indian nurses differed from Indian doctors in terms of both quality *and* quantity: "As a result of its over-supply of physicians and the poor image that nursing has, there are more physicians than nurses in India."[29] The discrepancy was severe. India suffered an absolute nursing shortage. This fact throws into proper relief the statistics surrounding nurse emigration that do exist, however partial.[30] The WHO study ranked India tenth in terms of international nurse emigration, compared to first for physicians. Emigrant nurses were estimated at less than 5 percent of its domestic stock. However, this amount was not noted as superfluous in the same way that doctors potentially were, according to WHO logic. The nurses who left were absolutely vital. In 1976, Trained Nurses Association of India (TNAI) President A. Cherian reminded her colleagues that thirty years after the Bhore Committee published its recommendation of one nurse to

5,000 patients, India had still not come close to that goal. Nor had it achieved the recommendations of the Central Council of Health for one nurse to three patients in teaching hospitals and one nurse to five beds in nonteaching hospitals.[31] A piece published that same year notes that if India was to fully implement the health schemes contained in its Fifth Plan period, ending in 1979, it would "require more than twice as many effective stock of nurses as exist at present, not to mention additional Public Health Nurses or Health Visitors and Auxiliary Nurse-Midwives who would be utilized as multipurpose workers and Health Supervisors in rural areas. Even if the educational facilities are continued at present rate and not cut back, the shortfall in requirements for nursing personnel would be 53,000 nurses, 27,000 Public Health Nurses, and 84,000 ANMs."[32]

A little over a decade after this estimate, *Nursing Journal of India* editor Narender Nagpal noted the discrepancy in India's stock of physicians and nurses. She estimated a nursing pool of approximately one lakh (100,000), compared to an estimated seven lakh physicians.[33] The vast majority of these nurses would not have been candidates for the international labor market. However, what such scattered data suggest is that the loss of top-tier trained nursing personnel was a matter of national concern, despite the relative lack of official notice let alone outcry over it. In fact, the WHO report reflected the relative neglect of nurse emigration when it stated, simply, "Hardly anything is known about the Indian nurses who have emigrated."[34]

We do know what happened to Susan George Arakal. She eventually received a Rajkumari Amrit Kaur scholarship, which was administered by the central government of India and funded by the WHO and the International Red Cross. The scholarship offered her the choice to study in England, the United States, or Canada. She chose England and departed in 1966. While studying there, she met and married a man from Kerala who was there working as an engineer. When the couple returned together to India, Susan was immediately promoted to what she described as a "premier government post" in public health nursing. Her husband had more difficulty achieving that kind of upward mobility, so he eventually left India for Kuwait, where members of his family had already migrated. After a year or so of a long-distance marriage with child, Susan leveraged her skills as a nurse and found a job so that she could join him there.

Susan George Arakal left her official position in India without a word. She never handed in a formal resignation, a fact that hovered over our conversation with the aura of an incomplete gesture. This was clearly something that continued to haunt her nearly half a century later. Its presence came across first through the silence and strain that pervaded the room when she first told me of her departure. It is not an easy emotion to convey within the confines of this page. Later on in our interview, she admitted that, "Actually, from the heart of heart, I wanted to be in India. . . . You could help a lot of people [doing public health work]. They needed you. So that feeling created so much tension in my heart, saying I must go back."[35] The feeling, apparently, was mutual. Arakal described to me how the government of India eventually tracked her down in Kuwait. According to her, rather than reprimand her for leaving, government officials implored her to return. They even offered her promotions for ever-more prestigious positions as enticement. They would, she insisted, not leave her alone. But her family was in Kuwait, and life there was good. In her description, public health work in India, while necessary, was also incredibly difficult. Working in a Kuwaiti hospital was, by comparison, "Very easy. Very easy and very nice. There was nothing to do but get the money and go. You had a lot of staff, and your functions were very much different [than in India]. I had a seven to one job; by one o'clock I was home!"[36]

Government of India officials were not the only ones courting Arakal while she was in Kuwait. She also eventually received a notice through the U.S. embassy that her visa was about to expire. Somewhere along the way—between all of her scholarships, certificates, and travels—Arakal had applied to work as a nurse in the United States. She had even already received a job offer from a hospital in New York City but had temporarily turned it down due to other considerations. It was this same offer that hunted her down in Kuwait, replete with its expiration date. This time around, she decided to take the job. In an idiom that ran across my interviews with Indian nurses, she spoke of the move as something that happened to her: "They really forced me."[37]

Susan George Arakal's narration of the tug-of-war between Indian government officials, U.S. hospital recruiters, and her employment in Kuwait figured her as a member of the brain drain set. It also introduced a third party to the debate. This was not a contest between only India and the United States. In the same study that I have been citing from, the WHO acknowledged the emergence of oil-producing countries in the Persian Gulf as a destination for nurses from developing countries. Following the oil crisis of 1973, the Gulf became the major exception to the rule that otherwise saw nurses from both developed and developing countries migrating to or in between the United States, the United Kingdom, and Europe. "Gulf fever" hit Kerala particularly hard, and in the case of nurses, it would become an especially important destination.[38] They joined the mass movement of labor from Kerala to the region, a movement that proved to be a critical safety valve for Kerala's underemployed population and quickly became a key engine for the growth of Kerala's struggling economy vis-à-vis Gulf remittances. By the mid-1980s, when Indian migration to the Gulf was at a peak, nurses made up the majority of skilled Indian labor in the region.[39] There they joined colleagues from around the world. Nurses I interviewed who had worked in the Gulf spoke to me of their Filipino, Bangladeshi, Egyptian, Iranian, and South African (among others) colleagues in Saudi Arabia and Kuwait. Also, like Arakal, the Gulf was often only one of several stops where nurses had spent time living and working. One interviewee had worked in Iran as well, and many had also spent time in England, Europe, or Canada before immigrating to the United States. This was the new global map of nurse immigration, one where Indians had a mobility that had, prior to World War II, been denied them.

What distinguished destinations on this map was not solely economics. In its simplest version, "brain drain" theory posits more money as the main motor behind people's decisions to uproot their lives and move across the world. Certainly, any Indian nurse who had access to international migration during the early decades of the Cold War would have had to have economic considerations as part of their calculation. This had its roots in a hard reality. In 1974, when Indian nurse emigration to the United States was at a peak, the average staff nurse in India made $432 per year, according to one estimate. In the United States, the same worker would make $5,472 per year as a nurse's aide and $9,639 per year as a staff nurse.[40] Annie Samuels, a Vellore graduate who immigrated to the United States via the Persian Gulf, put it bluntly: "In India nurses are not paid well. So you knew if you went abroad, you will be better paid. And you have to make some money."[41] But this was not how Susan George Arakal described her decision to move to either Kuwait or the United States. In both cases, she highlighted family first. She left a grand position in India so that she could raise her son with her husband in the same place. And their decision to move from Kuwait to the United States was certainly not about money. Her job in Kuwait was, in her own accounting, as good as it got. Instead, she described to me how, "When I was in Kuwait my husband started thinking of my son's education. We started thinking of the child. In Kuwait, when he passed high school he would have to go to another country for college. He would no longer be with us. If we came to the U.S., he would still be with us. That was the main thing, thinking about the baby. And then, a better education is a better life, you know."[42]

The ability to prioritize social and biological reproduction was at the heart of what set the United States apart from Kuwait. In the case of Persian Gulf countries, nurse *migration* was, by definition, temporary and without access to the full rights of citizenship. This was the reason that the Arakals could not plan on educating their son in Kuwait. The possibility to do so in the United States marked a critical shift in a nation that had excluded Indian labor from legal immigration since 1917. By the 1970s, when Susan George Arakal and her husband decided to move to the United States, Hart-Celler had ended race-based exclusion in the law and included nurses within its occupational preference quotas. The latter meant that Indian nurses could enter the United States as permanent legal residents (green card holders), without being beholden to a particular employer (even the ones who had hunted them down), and with the right to sponsor their family members.

Open door nursing had premised itself on migration, not immigration. The point had been to train individuals from around the world in the United States but to send them back to their countries of origin. If they did not return, the theory went, they would not have been able to spread the seeds of their training. The interdiction against the possibility of immigration was actually written into the law that permitted exchange visitors into the United States, as analyzed in detail in the following chapter. The point worth following up here is the way in which the opening of nurse immigration actually played upon the association between the United States, higher education, and upward mobility that had been fortified through the network of professionalized nurses created by open door nursing. This comes through in the quote above, where Susan George Arakal framed her decision in relation to her son's ability to access education and a "better life." These were all components of "the American Dream," particularly as it was professionalized during the Cold War.

For Indians, open door imperialism distinguished the ideological promise of U.S. imperialism from the death throes of the British Empire that they had helped to unravel. After independence/partition, Indians and Pakistanis joined migrants from the Caribbean and Africa in making the United Kingdom a primary destination in their postwar migrations. In doing so, they turned the tables on a society that was used to expanding its assets by remote, territorial colonization or settler colonialism abroad. That decolonization could involve the Third World coming "home to roost" was not part of that program. Colonial racism plus postcolonial migration thus created a context for the growth of anti-immigrant movements, and these fueled the passage of immigration restriction at approximately the same time that U.S. policies liberalized. Certainly, this made the United Kingdom less attractive. But it was also less appealing even to the degree to which it was still possible. Satwant Malhotra, a Punjabi nurse who migrated to England before settling in the United States, had this to say about her family's decision to move to North America: "We never liked living in England. . . . There, you know, all [of the Indians] were working class. There were very few professionals. In America, in those days, professional people came. There was no [Indian] working class there . . . so we had a very different image of America in that sense."[43]

With this statement, Malhotra joined George in helping to contextualize the liberalization of U.S. immigration law as part of a postcolonial promise that began with the establishment of U.S.-based professional nursing networks in India. The opening of immigration made professionalization through international migration available to a much wider segment of the Indian nursing workforce than ever before and would appeal to nurses from Kerala who were among the worst paid and most mobile in India already. In opening themselves to the opportunities thus presented, Indian nurses created a female-dominated immigration pattern, one where women such as Susan George Arakal and Satwant Malhotra became the ones whose occupational skill set enabled their families to settle in the United States. Their settlement in the United States raises a question that will serve as a turning point for *Nursing and Empire*: In what way would an immigration pattern led by Third World women workers challenge the divisions between open door imperialism and the politics of settler colonialism as the latter played out in the imperial nation?

## Coming to America

Aleyamma Eapen, a Christian from Kerala, was the first nurse in her family. In her own telling, her entry into the field was an act of divine intervention. When she reached college age, she overheard a conversation between her parents that revealed a difficult truth: they no longer had enough money to allow her to continue her studies. The news was devastating. Before confronting her parents, she sought refuge in the pantry. There, instead of plenty, she found the empty teak box where her family usually kept its store of rice. She crawled inside it and prayed, asking God what to do in the face of her newfound difficulties. His voice came to her loud and clear. It said, "Don't confront your father; offer instead to enroll in secretarial school." She took the advice, preempting her parents' disappointing news. Time passed. She was still in secretarial school, and yet her path had not necessarily become clearer. She sought the Lord's advice again. This time he told her to visit her cousin in Madras. Dutifully, she went. While there, she saw an ad in the local paper recruiting nursing students to study/work at the Tata Main Hospital in the North Indian state of Bihar. She applied, and she got in.

The Tata Group has its origins in the same community of business interests that helped bolster George Kittredge's efforts toward the training of medical women in India in the late nineteenth century. Jamshedji Tata was the first businessman in a family of Parsee Zoroastrian priests from what is present-day Gujarat. He began by founding a trading company and then quickly turned to the textile industry. While not all of the projects that followed in his name occurred during his lifetime, Tata had the goal of founding a business empire that would include steel, hydroelectric, and oil manufacturing—all of which was accomplished in his name. In 1903, he built the Taj Mahal Hotel in Bombay, the first in what became a prominent chain of luxury hotels. His industrial empire would come to include Tata Steel in 1907, Tata Hydro-Electric Power in 1910, Tata Oil Mill in 1917, Tata Airlines (now Air India) in 1932, Tata Chemicals in 1939, and TELCO (Tata Motors) in 1945. Postindependence/partition and into the twenty-first century, the Tata Group added industries and has remained India's largest multinational business conglomerate.

From what Eapen indicated to me, the Tata hospital in Bihar was linked to the industrial development in that state. Several of the Kerala nurses that I interviewed had a similar story of their first migration, from a state that lacked an industrial base to hospitals in the industrializing North.[44] Their movement was aided by the fact that these hospitals, often run by or linked to large business interests such as the Tata Group, offered free travel to and from the admission interview as well as free tuition, lodging, and a small stipend while in school. In return, students provided the bulk of nursing labor at the institution, and that too at a relatively low cost.[45] This was precisely the model of "learning while earning" that professional nurses had set themselves up against because it attracted the "wrong" kind of student. And yet, from the experiences of many of the South Indian nurses I interviewed, their northern migration ended up serving as the first stop in their access to professional nursing's global routes.

Tata Main Hospital was Eapen's introduction to the United States. She described to me how all of her teachers there were actually from the United States, as were many of the materials and methods that they used for instruction. It was at the school's library, while she was browsing through nursing journals from the United States, that she spotted an advertisement recruiting students to a hospital in Brooklyn, New York. Again, she applied. This time, she was competing against other nurses and graduates from her hospital in India. When she was chosen over them, it was something of a coup, for Eapen had not yet graduated. She was only a second-year nursing student in a four-year program. Beyond that, she owed four years of service to Tata after graduation. That was her bond. Despite all of these extenuating circumstances, Eapen discontinued her Indian education and left for Brooklyn, where she completed her degree. Four decades later, when I met her for this project, that borough of New York had remained her home base.

The cumulative impact of U.S. nursing standards in postindependence India is clear in Eapen's story. And yet, in her telling, access to the institutional routes of international nurse migration alone was not the only or even primary force that motivated her im/migration. She was driven by divinity, and then a dream. It was a dream that she had declared to Dr. Barucha, the administrator who first interviewed her for Tata Main's nursing program. For its application process, the hospital initially accepted thirty-six students. After three months of training, it cut that original number down to thirteen, who would enter the full four-year program. Eapen made the second cut. However, even after this, Dr. Barucha wanted to interview each remaining candidate one more time. It was then that he asked Eapen, "What is your dream?" She replied, "To get as much education as I can. I want higher education, and I want to do that in America."[46] To which Dr. Barucha scoffed (in an echo of his male medical colleagues in Delhi and Trivandrum), "You just came here; you don't have any money; we have to give you a stipend to study. How can you dream this big?" Ripe with determination, the young Aleyamma replied, "Why can't I dream? It is my right to dream, whether it comes true or not. You asked me what my dream was, and now I told you."[47] And with that she immediately earned the doctor's respect, shook his hand, and walked out the door.

As she described it to me decades later, this dream remained her motivation when, two years later, Eapen boarded the plane for New York City. I asked her how, at the time and under the circumstances, she developed this particular ambition to go to America. She began by explaining to me the impact that John F. Kennedy's assassination had had on her. Eapen remembered hearing all the stories of how he fulfilled his own dream to become president of the United States, a dream that seemed impossible because of his religion and Irish American background. U.S. history had been an inspiration to her even before she entered nursing school. During primary school, she had chosen to recite the "Gettysburg Address" for a school competition. She won the first prize. "So that's why I wanted to come to America; because I loved Kennedy's history and Abraham Lincoln's. I loved Kennedy's idea that immigrants can come to America. So I would like to go and study there, to see it."[48]

Part pilgrim, part pioneer. . . . Called to nursing by divinity, and to the United States by the legacies of Lincoln and Kennedy, Aleyamma Eapen's story positions her in line with the long history of the "American Dream." Indeed, she reminds us that this dream had decidedly Christian incarnations before it encompassed emancipation or Ellis Island, including those tied to the Puritans' "city on a hill" and the divine drive of Manifest Destiny. It is only after introducing us to her own divine destiny that her conversation with Dr. Barucha invokes the turn-of-the-twentieth-century Horatio Alger–style saga of American immigrant success. Here, the world's weary and downtrodden arrive in the United States with nothing more than their determination and aspiration. And while these were not enough to see them through in their home countries, they were all that is necessary to take advantage of the opportunity that is America. At mid-twentieth century, there was perhaps no greater example of the historical culmination of this ideologically driven narrative than the election of John F. Kennedy to the presidency of the United States.

A question that Aleyamma Eapen's story raises for us is, what happens when an Indian woman and an Indian nurse take up the main subject position in this story? On the surface, it might seem that her ability to do so reinforces the myth of the post–civil rights model minority even more clearly than it would if told by other members of India's third preference cohort—most of whom were not, it should be emphasized, drawn from India's downtrodden. Urmil Minocha characterizes the South Asians who were able to take advantage of the third preference in the following manner: "Recent immigrants from South Asia are predominantly young, highly educated, and professionally well-trained male urban elites who have come to the United States not to escape poverty or political turmoil in their homelands but mainly to seek educational and economic opportunity for themselves and their families."[49]

Here, Minocha essentially references the Indian physicians described above with reference to the WHO report on international medical migration. His description *does not* include nurses. Indian sociologist T. K. Oomen spells out the different social origins of the pool of physician and nurse labor in postindependence India.[50] His observations are based on his study of ten public hospitals in New Delhi, where he and his students collected data between 1966 and 1970. His distinction begins with the definition of nursing as a "semi-profession" and medicine as a "full-fledged profession." Further, he finds that the majority of nurses came from lower middle-class backgrounds, with Christians still forming the majority, followed by Hindus.[51] In terms of the latter group, most nurses were from the "clean castes."[52] And finally, the overwhelming majority of nurses in India were women.[53] This contrasted with the doctors in Oomen's study who were (again) predominantly male, middle class, Hindu, and from the privileged castes. These distinctions created what Oomen terms two distinct "*social islands* of privilege: One inhabited by urban middle class, upper caste Hindus born of fathers who pursued professional and higher administrative occupations from which doctors are recruited and another inhabited by urban and rural, lower-middle class, upper castes and Christians born of fathers in semi-professional and lower administrative occupations from which nurses are recruited."[54]

The privileges that Oomen associated with both physicians and nurses included, seminally, the possibility for emigration during the period of his investigation. For nurses in particular, Oomen underscores how the opening of the international field enabled the "transformation of nursing from a *socially stigmatized occupation* to that of an instrument of social mobility . . . [where] high instrumental valuation and *low social prestige* co-exist."[55] That this combination had the makings of a primetime postcolonial *and* post–civil rights uplift story came to me clearly during an interview with Aleyamma James. When I first met James, she was a nurse educator and a colleague of Eapan's at Coney Island Hospital in Brooklyn, New York. She too originally hails from Kerala but shifted to North India to pursue nursing education, in her case at the prestigious CON-D. After graduating, James remained at the college as a teacher before moving to Iran, the Persian Gulf, and finally the United States. The following is a description of a recent (in relation to our 2003 interview) reunion James had had with one of her former students at the CON-D:

> She was from one of the villages near Delhi, and she was the first one who graduated from high school in her community. She was nominated [to the College of Nursing] as a scheduled caste/scheduled tribe. When she came into the College she could not speak a word of English; she was a "typical village girl." And the transition! I watched for three years and then I left. I saw how she transformed. . . . And then I didn't know anything about her. We have an alumnae association based here in the

United States. Unfortunately I have been to only one meeting, and that was in '94 maybe. . . . The meeting was in Long Island so I went with my family. As I'm walking into this place where the meeting is being held I hear someone calling me by my maiden name, "Ms. John!" I said no, no, that's only my imagination. And then someone turned around and called me "Johnnie!" I said okay this is happening. So I turned around and looked at this young—beautiful looking young woman— very sophisticated. She was holding the hand of a five or six year old girl. I asked her, "Did you call me?" She said "Yes, you didn't recognize me?" I said "No I don't." She gave me a hint. I couldn't believe it was the same girl! Who was from the village who was nominated . . . I bring her as an example even to my children. She made such progress in her life! She finished nursing college; she met a Malayalee doctor; got married; moved to the United States. She went to Yale and got her master's in public health. Now she is a consultant in the Department of Health in Maryland. So with determination she made such progress![56]

"A typical village girl." As a rural, marginally educated ("she could not speak a word of English") Dalit girl, James's former student was truly among the most multiply oppressed Indian subjects. What was more, her caste, class, and gender positions combined to embody the historical stigmatization of nurses and nursing in India. And yet, in the United States, she appeared so utterly altered as to be unrecognizable. The stain of her stigmatization no longer read as a catalog of her condemnation so much as a mark for the extent of her transformation. She now served as a lesson in what hard work, individual determination, and attention to opportunity could achieve—for anyone. The fact that in this case, the "anyone" was a rural Dalit woman summarizes the historic opportunity that immigration to the United States presented for Indian nurses, in particular. No longer were these workers left to toil under the leadership of colonial nursing leaders who had themselves migrated to the subcontinent in order to circumvent their own share of stigmatization. No longer was international migration an option open to a mere handful of selected Indian nurses who were meant to inherit leadership of the field from their colonial predecessors. After 1965, international migration, upward mobility, and the "good life," American style, were available even to one who could have otherwise been deemed a successor of Salome.

And yet, it would be untrue to the meaning of the message that I received from James, Eapen, or many other of my interviewees if we left it at that. They offer us a critical edge—both implicitly and explicitly. This story is not a simple or straightforward affirmation of the "American Dream" at precisely a moment when that dream was taking on renewed global dimensions under the aegis of American ascendancy. James's student's story of transformation began not in the United States but in India and, more specifically, at the CON-D. While the CON-D was, on one hand, an open door outpost for professional nursing connecting the Indian workforce to the global market, the political terrain in postcolonial India was not as simple as that. As a central government institution, the CON-D was required to admit students from every state in India, as well as to allot reservations for students from the Scheduled Castes (SC) and Scheduled Tribes (ST). (SC/ST is government of India parlance for Dalits [ex-untouchables] and Adivasis [indigenous] peoples.) These reservations are one legacy of Dr. Bhimrao Ramji Ambedkar's historic fight for justice as it linked up with his study of U.S. constitutional law at Columbia University and his role as the primary architect of the Indian constitution.[57] In many ways, they parallel the post–civil rights affirmative action programs in the United States and make a double claim—on India and the United States—to follow through on the promises of decolonization and desegregation.

There are several dimensions to this convergence. One is the overlap between model minority discourse and the discourse of Dalit advancement voiced so often by India's postcolonial elite and middle classes. The latter's arguments turn the banning of caste-based discrimination and the institution of reservations as positive discrimination—against them. In this view, Dalits and "other backward castes" (OBCs) are favored to the degree to which it has become much easier for them to succeed than for others—with middle-class and elite Indians falling under the category of "other" in this instance. Clear material evidence of privileged caste and class reaction of this sort could be seen in the riots that ensued after the implementation of the Mandal Commission recommendations by Prime Minister V. P. Singh in 1989. The commission's reservations for OBCs sparked massive protests by privileged caste students who argued that these spelled an end to their own life chances. Their reaction culminated in a series of self-immolations on college campuses across the country. The fury over the Mandal Commission was widely cited as a primary reason for the eventual resignation of Prime Minister Singh.

In my inquiries into caste, particularly the position of Dalit nurses, I heard many rehearsals of this line of reasoning by my interviewees. Its resonance with the post–civil rights rhetoric against race-based affirmative action in the United States most certainly formed part of the narrative context of my conversations with nurses and our discussions of caste. And yet, the invocation of Ambedkar is important also for the way in which it serves as a reminder of another genealogy. Aleyamma Eapen was not alone in invoking Abraham Lincoln from a school setting in India. Here I want to return to the life work of Jotirao Phule and the inscription opening his seminal work *Gulamgiri* (*Slavery*). It reads, "Dedicated to the good people of the United States as a token of admiration for their sublime disinterested and self-sacrificing devotion in the cause of Negro Slavery; and with an earnest desire, that my countrymen may take their noble example as their guide in the emancipation of their Sudra Brethren from the trammels of Brahmin thraldam."[58]

How can we read such an appeal? Is it simply a glorification of white abolitionists—"the good people of the United States"—over and above the agency of the formerly enslaved? One would be hard-pressed to push that interpretation given Phule's limited and partial exposure to U.S. history through missionary education. Indeed, the top-down view of emancipation clearly reflected the kind of view that white Christian abolitionists held, and that missionaries would impart in a colonial context. Coming from the pen of an Indian anticaste activist who was himself from a humble caste and class background, however, these same sentiments are not reducible to their source material. Instead, they reveal another dimension to Phule's politics, a politics of subaltern solidarity that understood and articulated the struggle against caste in India alongside the struggle against racism in the United States. This was the strand picked up by Ambedkar in his constitutional politics, and it is the lineage through which I read Eapen's retelling of her own American Dream. Her story thus helps me to raise a question about what kind of critical, subaltern edge Indian nurse immigration opens into Cold War Indian immigration to the United States.

# CHAPTER SIX

# Putting the "Foreign" in Nurse Im/migration

At the end of my last formal interview with Vasantha Daniel, I asked her if there was anything about her immigration history that she felt we had not adequately addressed. After a thoughtful pause, she replied,

> My big thing is that when I came [to the United States] as a student my experience was totally different. Again, we are talking way back in the sixties . . . I came in '62/'63. And now we are here forty years later. At that time I was a novelty and so I felt that there was this whole group of people taking care of us and making sure that we got involved in the American way of life. They had a family taking care of us and we got invited to a lot of events. I felt then that I was intermingling a lot more with the American population. And truly they were treating me as a novelty. You got included in things and then you went back. Okay, you did what you did, you shared your culture, and you were gone. When I came back here as an immigrant to work I felt that the attitude was completely different. It was more like "now you're trying to compete with us." I didn't expect it at first, so it came as a little bit of a surprise to me. But then again, it was '67 when I came back. And as time is moving on I find that that kind of a feeling, "well here are these foreigners here," is increasing. I don't think it is diminishing.[1]

These reflections chart Daniel's own transition from a foreign student to an immigrant in the United States. She first arrived in 1962, under the auspices of the Rockefeller Foundation (RF). After earning her master's degree in nursing, she returned to India, to fulfill her bond at the Christian Medical College, Vellore. This form of "institutional insurance" did not ultimately work to retain Daniel's expertise.[2] Instead, the connections that she had made while at the University of Washington in Seattle drew her back to the United States. She returned in order to study for her PhD, an option not yet available for nurses India. Because she pursued this degree without financial sponsorship, she had to teach in order to support herself. In her experience, it was this switch—from visitor to employee—that moved her from "foreign novelty" to "foreign competition" in relation to the very same colleagues at the very same institution. Vasantha Daniel's history thus opens a critical window onto the ways in which immigration solidified the status of primarily Third World immigrant nurses as "foreign" in the post–civil rights United States. An inquiry into how this happened begins not with the opening of immigration post-1965, but with the Exchange Visitor Program (EVP) that was the U.S. side of the international fellowship programs that had helped to cultivate India's first generation of Indian nursing leaders.

*The Exchange Visitor Period: Neither Immigrants nor Employees*

The EVP developed through the colonial medical map drawn by the RF and its priorities, as these shaped professional nursing's international circuits during the onset of decolonization across much of Asia and Africa. Thus, in 1947, at their annual meeting, member organizations of the International Council of Nurses (ICN) agreed to act as official sponsors of exchange nurses in their respective home countries. In the United States, this meant that the American Nurses Association (ANA) was the program's first official sponsor. Its participation was made possible by passage of the EVP (which was not limited to nurses but included them) as part of the Information and Education Act in 1948. The act was modeled on the fellowships pioneered by the RF, and represented something of a coup-de-grâce during the foundation's philanthropic transition, as detailed in chapter 5. In the wake of the new legislation and throughout the program's peak, the ANA remained the EVP's most prominent promoter. However, once it was incorporated under U.S. federal law, the ANA was one among a multitude of organizations involved. Universities, hospitals, and foundations could and did also apply to become sponsors of exchange nurses, and different sponsors offered different experiences. These ranged from the opportunity to earn advanced degrees to gain additional clinical experience (sometimes leading to a certificate) and to engage in short periods of observation. It would also not be uncommon, especially under ANA auspices, for a particular exchange nurse to divide her stay between several sponsoring hospitals in order to gain a wider variety of experience and exposure.[3]

Like the corporate foundation-sponsored fellowships that preceded it, both the law and its language emphasized that exchange nurses were temporary migrants, *not* immigrants. Immigration was explicitly made a violation of exchange visitor status. Nurses were issued visitor visas for a maximum of two years. These were tied to a specific sponsoring institution and were categorically ineligible for adjustment to immigrant status. Anyone who overstayed her visa or engaged in what was deemed political activity while in the United States was subject to immediate deportation.[4] Furthermore, in 1961, the U.S. Mutual Educational and Cultural Exchange Act stipulated that exchange visitors could not reenter the United States as immigrants for two years after their initial departure. This order remained in effect until the passage of Public Law 91-225 in 1970.[5] These prohibitions regarding foreign nurse immigration were buttressed by the EVP's own justifications, which centered on educational exchange, leadership training, and the creation of goodwill between the United States and the world. In order for this last piece to manifest, migrants had to return to their countries of origin to distribute the professional network that they had been inducted into.

If exchange nurses were meant to be temporary migrants, their limited time in the United States was further restricted by their definition as visitors and not employees.[6] Regardless of the sponsoring institution, nurses on exchange visitor visas were considered students or, at most, trainees. They did not receive a salary but a stipend.[7] This was despite the fact that their experiences within U.S. institutions often amounted to taking on the same tasks and hours required of other nurses formally considered and compensated as workers. This was especially the case with those nurses who were sponsored by hospitals. Nurse historian Barbara Brush outlines the contradictions that emerged from such a situation: "Although foreign nurses visiting the United States on a two-year exchange visa were treated and expected to act as workers, hospitals behaved as though their visitor status justified lower wages. Further, despite the EVP's de-emphasis of nursing capabilities and skills, nurse's stipends and status were often contingent upon them. For example, a foreign nurse deemed poor in language skills or clinically inept was paid a reduced stipend or relegated to a lower paid nurse's aid position until she was 'brought up to the standards required of the nursing profession for the safety and welfare of patients.'"[8]

The quote at the end of Brush's statement is taken from Jeanne Broadhurst's 1962 study of the EVP, *Nurses from Abroad: Values in International Exchange of Persons*. The study was singular for the period and was funded jointly by the RF and American nurses' foundations. The latter represented U.S. nursing leadership, led by the ANA. Given this, the emphasis on *standards* was no accident. It was a clear signal that the EVP and foreign nurses along with it were being brought under the language and imperatives of U.S. nursing leaders' historical drive to professionalize as this intersected with the imperatives of corporate philanthropy. Increasingly strictly defined "standards," as institutionalized through licensing, credentialing, and the division of labor that these engendered, had long been key to this convergence. The inclusion of exchange nurses within this language was a clear signal of the controversy that was brewing over the use and potential abuse of these temporary "visitors."

Two years prior to Broadhurst's study, the ANA published a statement in its official organ, the *American Journal of Nursing*, clarifying its position on the EVP. As its title implied, *"Protecting* Our Exchange Visitors and Nursing Practice" (emphasis in the original) began by underscoring the ANA's support of the EVP as part of its broader commitment to the profession. It continued by listing a series of by-then common complaints regarding the program's implementation (as opposed to its stated intention) by hospitals in particular: the use of misleading advertisements that promise educational experiences but do not fulfill them, programs that were inadequately supervised, the use of foreign nurses to meet the needs of sponsoring institutions, and the low stipends received by exchange visitors. From the perspective of the ANA, "Such practices, representing deviation from the original intent of the Exchange-Visitor Program, lead to serious consequences. *This is especially true when the program is used as an employment instrument rather than an educational program.* It can lead to disappointment and frustration for nurses who come to this country to improve their knowledge and skills. It can impair our country's international relationships. *It endangers the safe care of patients. It unfairly affects the professional and economic status of nurses in the United States"*[9] (emphasis added).

The controversy surrounding the slippage between education, employment, and the EVP took place within the context of what hospital administrators deemed the first-ever crisis in the supply of U.S. nursing personnel. This shortage had actually begun during World War II and was widely heralded by its conclusion. Historian Susan Reverby identifies several overlapping factors for the seeming exodus of white nurses from hospitals at the time: the war effort drew many into its service, others left due to the availability of better paying war-related jobs at home, and the postwar marriage boom engendered "the forced exodus of white women to hearth and home."[10] At the same time, the postwar years saw passage of the 1946 Hospital Survey and Construction Act (Hill-Burton). Hill-Burton was a state-based program that provided federal grants and guaranteed loans to expand the nation's hospital system. It did so along lines that prioritized the foundation-supported, research-oriented, university-based hospital as the pinnacle of the expanding health care system. Its implementation, alongside the expansion and reformation of the Veterans Administration (the VA, which was also modeled on Hill-Burton), prompted a massive boom in hospital construction.[11] This simultaneous contraction and expansion created an increased need for nursing labor, and it was in light of this that hospital administrators were accused of using exchange visitors as an easy solution to their growing labor needs. Positioned in this way, exchange nurses took their place in the long history of the division and redivision of U.S. nursing labor as this intersected with the politics of im/migrant labor.

## Nursing Education, Student Nurses, and the Division of Nursing Labor

As examined from various angles in previous chapters, it was not until the eve of World War I that a need for nurse training had begun to gain general acceptance in the United States. The result was a massive proliferation of hospital-based diploma programs, which reached their peak in the 1920s. In this model of education, hospitals offered students room, board, and a small stipend (not a salary). In return, students received training while also constituting the bulk of the hospital workforce: "Nursing education was called training; in reality it was work."[12] It was such hard work that, outside of a few who stayed to serve as nursing superintendents, graduates did not continue to work in hospitals. Most did their best to find work as private-duty nurses. Such an outcome suited hospital administrators and graduate nurses alike. The former preferred the cheaper labor of student nurses, and the latter preferred not to have to continue working under such exploitative conditions.[13]

The working conditions facing the vast majority of student nurses were not what moved U.S. nursing leaders to action. For these leaders (understood as separate from the majority of working nurses), unionization and worker demands were out of the question.[14] Instead, their first tactic was actually to argue against giving nursing students stipends at all during their training. Their belief was that the offer of room, board, and a stipend attracted too many of the "wrong" kind of nursing student. In other words, they attracted working-class women—precisely the sort of women who nursing leaders saw as the stumbling block in their drive to professionalize and, thereby, transcend the stigma of the working girl. And yet, as diploma schools proliferated, these were the students who provided a veritable surplus of labor for hospitals. Such an expanding workforce ran directly counter to the goal of professionalization, which is based in large part on the ability to control entry into a field. Nurse training, captured as it was by hospital administrators, had in this instance proved an inadequate path to professionalization. In addition, leaders' efforts to gain state recognition through the passage of licensure and registration laws were still only partially successful. While many states had laws on the books, few if any actually enforced them.[15]

The 1920s were not only the highpoint for hospital diploma schools and student nursing labor, but it was also during this period that hospitals were rationalizing health care through their uptake of the production models set forth by industrial capitalism. This clearly affected the use-value and working conditions for student nurses. It also offered nurse leaders another means through which they could stake their argument for nursing as a profession: efficiency. It was through a call to more efficient nursing practice that leaders attempted to link their fates to those of rationalization and thereby hospital administrators, physicians, and the corporate foundations that funded them. Efficiency became a new way for nursing leaders to enumerate, categorize, and elaborate on what constituted nursing practice and to assert their own place within it.[16]

With efficiency as their catchword, nursing leaders sought to attract graduate nurses back into hospitals in order to replace diploma students at the center of hospital care. This strategy prevailed, but not by their efforts alone. Instead, the exigencies of the national economy following the stock market crash of 1929 created the incentive for graduate nurses to seek employment in hospitals rather than on private duty. Their reentry was rapid, and by the eve of World War II, they were the decisive majority. Licensed and credentialed graduate nurses (more commonly known as registered nurses, or RNs) professionalized into the role of hospital supervisors vis-à-vis their access to university-based graduate programs. This was the core recommendation contained in *Nursing for the Future* (the Brown Report), commissioned in 1948 by the National Nursing Council and authored by Esther Lucile Brown of the Russell Sage Foundation. The report recapitulated and updated the original agenda of U.S. nursing leaders. Its final recommendations upheld the baccalaureate degree and projected an ultimate end to all diploma programs. Recognizing this as an immediate impossibility, Brown went on to assert that so long as diploma graduates remained an "interim solution" to staffing problems, they should be considered second-class citizens. Baccalaureate nurses should be at the top of the hospital nursing division of labor.[17]

The rise of the RN entailed the promotion of two new categories of nursing personnel: nurses' aides and licensed practical nurses (LPNs). These employees performed much of the "dirty work" historically associated with the occupation. Their work was deemed unskilled, and they were paid less for it than the RNs they worked alongside. In this way, auxiliary nursing personnel served as another partial "solution" to the crisis in nursing labor that followed World War II and the passage of Hill-Burton.[18] However, even as these workers took up some of the tasks shunned by professional nursing, RNs felt threatened by their presence within the hospital. Battles over jurisdiction, professional authority, and the distinction between "skilled" and "unskilled" labor ensued. Finally, in a compromise with hospital administrators, nursing leaders (all RNs) agreed to a division of labor where RNs would serve as the managers of auxiliary nursing personnel. The work of the former required education and skill and could thereby be deemed professional. The work of the latter did not. This division of hospital nursing labor came to serve U.S. nursing leaders precisely because "their strategy and their tactics were built upon limiting the opportunities and devaluing the labor of other women workers."[19]

This was the situation, broadly speaking, when foreign nurses began arriving in U.S. hospitals and universities through the EVP. Despite appellations to the contrary (visitor, guest, etc.), the position of exchange visitors closely resembled that of the aforementioned student nurses: apprenticed to the institution for educational purposes and provided with a small stipend as well as, at times, room and board. And it is out of this resemblance that we can now reread the ANA's response to the charge that the EVP was being used for employment rather than education. The allegations about cheap labor and unfair competition drew upon idioms crafted in response to the "problem" that the abundance of student nursing labor had posed to the professional aspirations of U.S. nursing leaders in the earlier part of the century, as well as the perceived threat that subsidiary nursing personnel continued to represent by mid-century. Thus, through its arguments against reported abuses of the EVP, the ANA aligned foreign nurses with the working-class women who continued to constitute both the majority of U.S. nursing personnel and the perceived limit to the professional agenda of nursing leaders.

There were, however, important differences between exchange nurses and U.S. nursing's rank and file. The first had to do with exchange nurses' arrival during a nursing shortage. This was in stark contrast to the historical association of diploma nurses and a labor surplus. In addition, while foreign nurses entered the U.S. market as, ostensibly, apprentices, they did so at the upper echelons of the occupation. Most exchange nurses were already beyond the level of diploma nursing or were well on their way along a U.S.-centered path to professionalization. In this sense, they were the peers of U.S. nursing leaders, with the exception of their visa status. The fact that exchange nurses could not become citizens leads us to, rather than encompasses, another difference that I wish to highlight: the re-racialization of the foreign nurse population during the height of the exchange visitor period and just before the introduction of foreign nurse *immigration*. In the decades leading up to 1965, this occurred primarily through the intersection of racialized restrictions on immigration and naturalization law and the racialization constitutive of the nursing profession itself.

## The EVP and Racializing Foreign Nurses in the United States

The racialized segregation that characterized both U.S. hospitals and the nursing profession persisted beyond passage of Hill-Burton, despite the fact that the act specifically prohibited the allocation of funds to institutions that discriminated on the basis of race, color, national origin, or creed. This was because it also contained a "separate but equal" clause that remained in operation until the U.S. Supreme Court ruled it unconstitutional in 1963.[20] This was buttressed by segregation at the top, as the ANA did not allow African American members until it finally merged with the National Association of Colored Nursing Graduates (NACGN) in 1950. In 1956, when the U.S. Supreme Court declared racialized segregation in public schools illegal, only 721 of 1,141 non–African American nursing schools accepted African American students, and the Florida state association retained its ban on African American membership. Even after passage of the Civil Rights Act of 1964 and Voting Rights Act of 1965, diversification remained "sluggish."[21]

The formal integration of the NACGN and ANA occurred roughly at the same time as the inception of the EVP. However, during its initial years, the EVP did not pose a racialized challenge to the profession. Women from northern Europe dominated the earliest pool of foreign nurses in the United States. The national origins of exchange nurses from 1948–51 have been reported as follows: 54 percent from Denmark, 11 percent from Sweden, 9 percent from Great Britain, and 6 percent from Norway.[22] While these nurses certainly differed from their U.S. counterparts in terms of culture and language, their presence did not challenge the historically entrenched image of U.S. nursing as the domain of "white women in white." Their difference lay instead within the realm of U.S. immigration law and the prohibition it placed upon their immigration vis-à-vis the exchange visitor visa. Yet this too had its distinctly racialized dimension, one that did not affect all exchange visitors equally.

Within the context of early to mid-twentieth century U.S. immigration law, the restrictions of the EVP were not exceptional so much as indicative. The Immigration Act of 1924 had instituted a national origins quota system that restricted the southern and eastern European im/migrants who had dominated immigration from that continent since the turn of the century. It also capped off an era of exclusion that had already deemed all migrants from a legislatively defined "Asiatic Barred Zone" ineligible for both immigration and naturalization. With regard to this history, northern and western Europeans were clearly the favored lot. Their immigration was explicitly sought as a way to stem the tide of "undesirables" and settle the nation in a way that would reproduce a white majority. Cast in this light, the immigration restrictions surrounding the EVP were less notable than the fact that the majority of early exchange nurses had origins that allowed them to legally migrate at all and that they retained the possibility, albeit through other means, of eventually immigrating to the United States. That hospitals and/or foreign nurses utilized these "other means" was written into the ANA's 1960 response to reported abuses of the EVP. Their position statement extended its concern over the use of foreign nurses for labor needs to those recruited under immigration visas, stating that "the ANA recognizes as acceptable practice the employment of graduate nurses who wish voluntarily to immigrate to the United States, provided they have adequate educational preparation for the functions they are expected to discharge, are able to meet the licensing requirements for registration in a state, and possess a sufficient command of English to permit them to practice safely."[23]

By 1960, however, this wary recognition of foreign nurse immigration spoke to an increasingly non-European pool of exchange visitors. By this time, the tide of the EVP was already turning from Europe to Asia and specifically to the Philippines. The EVP was the primary instrument that enabled this transformation. Indeed, the 1960s proved seminal as "Filipino nurses, along with Filipino recruiters and U.S. hospital administrators, transformed the EVP into an avenue for the first wave of Filipino nurse mass migration into the United States."[24] At the decade's end, Filipinos formed 80 percent of the exchange nurses entering the United States.[25] Examining this switch is especially critical given the fact that

Filipino nurses came to dominate the foreign nurse population of the United States in the twentieth century. With regard to this, Paul Ong and Tania Azores assert, "It could be argued that a discussion of immigrant Asian nurses, indeed of foreign-trained nurses in general, is predominantly about Filipino nurses."[26]

Indian nurses never approximated the numbers of their Filipino colleagues during the exchange visitor period (or afterward).[27] For example, in 1958, ANA statistics list six Indian exchange visitors, compared to twenty-six for the Philippines.[28] Neither number is overwhelming. Even twenty-six nurses is hardly cause to take especial note, especially when Australia sent nearly three times as many that same year.[29] But an emphasis on numbers alone does not offer an adequate explanation for the fact that India emerged as one of the top sending countries in the immediate aftermath of the 1965 Immigration and Nationality Act Amendments.[30] As I have argued across these pages, this was not because the United States was an "exceptional" destination that "naturally" attracted immigrants when its doors opened (wider). Instead, Indian im/migration was a product of a critical, cumulative history that had connected U.S.-based institutions and individuals to Indian nursing labor through the circuits of Anglo-American capitalist imperialism. While these ties were less readily apparent in India than for other nations topping the list, such as the Philippines and South Korea, they are nevertheless crucial for understanding how the workings of capitalist imperialism abroad affected the reracialization of foreign nurse immigration to the United States during the Cold War. The domestication of this into the contours of a shifting U.S. racial formation occurred at the overlap between the categories of "Asian" and "foreign" nurses.

"Asia" was in many ways the creation of U.S. immigration law as it worked to exclude groups we would now consider "Asian" from immigration and naturalization prior to World War II. The 1917 Immigration Act constituted an "Asiatic Barred Zone" by drawing a line from the Ural Mountains to the Red Sea, encompassing the Indian subcontinent, Afghanistan, the Middle East (including the Arabian Peninsula), and most of the Pacific Islands.[31] By this time, Chinese and Japanese migrants had already been subjected to exclusion and/or restriction, with Koreans subsumed under Japan vis-à-vis their colonized status, and Filipinos left to enter as colonial subjects of the United States. This left Indians and migrants from what to Europeans had become the "Middle East" as the major groups affected, until the Tydings-McDuffie Act of 1934 instituted a ten-year timetable for self-rule in the Philippines. In this case, independence meant that Filipino migrants would also fall into the category of those ex-cluded by the Asiatic Barred Zone, and be limited to a quota of fifty legal entries per year.

The minimal quotas allotted by the Asiatic Barred Zone ran into the related problem of the racialization of naturalization. Since 1790 this had been restricted to "free white persons," and later, after the Civil War, ex-tended to the descendants of formerly enslaved Africans. In the postwar period, during the mass migrations that accompanied industrialization in the United States, the question of who could lay claim to the category "white" came up for serious debate. Asian Indians, in fact, became one of the most successful groups in suing for citizenship primarily on the basis of claims to Caucasian and/or Aryan ancestry. The Supreme Court ren-dered this rationale impermissible in 1923 when it declared Bhagat Singh Thind ineligible to naturalize. Thind sued for citizenship based on his Aryan ancestry, which made him Caucasian according to contemporary scientific classifications of race. The Supreme Court ruled that he could not naturalize because while he may have been Caucasian, he was not white in the understanding of the common American. Critically, the Thind decision came on the heels of the same court's ruling against the natural-ization claims of Takao Ozawa on the basis of the fact that his skin color was white and that he had all the trappings of American civilization. In Ozawa's case, the decision declared that while he was white, he was not Caucasian and therefore remained ineligible. Cumulatively, both cases barred all legislatively defined Asians from naturalization whether they claimed status as white or Caucasian. The decisions were compounded by the categorical exclusion of "aliens ineligible to naturalize" contained in the 1924 Immigration Act. Thus, while the 1924 act ushered in a period of immigration *restriction* for southern and eastern Europeans, it finalized race-based *exclusion* for Asians.[32] And indeed, Asian/Pacific/American studies scholars have long argued that it was this combination of immi-gration exclusion and denial of the right to naturalize that effectively lumped all "Asians" together, racializing them as perpetually and indeli-bly "foreign" within the processes of U.S. racial formation.

During World War II, the United States Congress began to slowly and partially lift the ban on Asian naturalization, beginning with the 1943 Magnuson Act, which repealed Chinese exclusion and allowed for a quota of 105 immigrants per year as a goodwill gesture to a wartime ally. This was followed by the 1946 Luce-Cellar Bill, which lifted the ban on natu-ralization for Filipinos and Indians. In addition, the legislation allowed for a quota of one hundred immigrants per year from each country. Its passage was again seen as prudent postwar foreign policy, occurring as it did just days before Filipino independence from U.S. colonial rule and one year before Indian independence/partition.[33] This was the situation when the EVP began in 1948, and it did not change until the liberalization of immigration law in 1965.

Given this history, the increasing number of Filipino exchange visitors meant that more and more foreign nurses were de facto excluded from immigration and the full rights of U.S. citizenship. This all but ensured the temporary, if elite, emphasis of the EVP itself. At the same time, it tied the status of temporary migrants to a history of the racially inassimilable, marking a turning point in the racialization of foreign nurses within the U.S. workforce. We can now read the ANA's 1960 statement regarding the EVP in two interrelated contexts. The first drew on the long history of racialized hierarchies within the field of nursing itself. Within this racially segregated field, charges of "cheap labor" had historically been leveled at hospitals with regard to their use of student nursing labor. However, as these same criticisms were brought to bear on an increasingly Asian exchange visitor pool, they also resonated with the long history of nativist, anti-Asian, and anti-immigrant sentiment that had cast Asians not only as perpetually foreign but also, and thereby, as a perennially cheap(er) source of labor. It was in this way that the exchange visitor period set the stage for the creation of a new category of distinction within U.S. nursing, one tied to the exigencies of U.S. immigration law. "Foreign" was thus a racially loaded category that would mark Indian nurses in a way that did not apply to their white American or European immigrant counterparts. It also took its place alongside the racialized segregation that had characterized the U.S. division of nursing labor since its inception, and that continued to characterize its reformulation during the period when foreign nurse migrants became a permanent presence in the workforce.

### Post-1965: Foreign Nurse Graduates, Nursing Shortages, and the Racialized Division of U.S. Nursing Labor

Nursing was not originally named in the third preference's list of professional occupations. Its inclusion was settled through case law, in "Matter of Gutierrez," decided on July 5, 1967. At issue was a Filipino nurse who petitioned for a third preference visa on the basis that nursing was a recognized *profession*. Her argument began with the distinction between an RN and an LPN, and it continued with the observation that, despite the fact that professional status is usually equated with higher education (in this case, a baccalaureate degree), "registered nurses have traditionally been regarded as professional persons. Authoritative sources such as various state licensing authorities and the American Nurses' Association, which are interested in maintaining high standards for practicing this profession, require a specified amount of education and training, not necessarily including a baccalaureate degree, for recognition as a professional nurse."[34]

The petition was approved, thereby recognizing RNs as professionals within U.S. immigration law and paving the path for nursing's inclusion in the third preference's Schedule A. For foreign nurse graduates (FNGs), this meant they could immigrate with permission to work but without being bound to the offer of a single employer. From the perspective of U.S. hospital administrators, this certification enabled them to employ FNGs at a time when they were once again lamenting a critical shortage in the domestic supply of nurses. Their calls took their cue from the massive growth within the U.S. health care sector, fueled most ostensibly by the 1965 passage of two federally funded programs, Medicare and Medicaid, and alongside these the increased access to private health care through employer and individual plans. At the same time, many U.S. nurses and physicians were being sent to serve in the Vietnam War. In the case of white nurses, wartime-induced domestic labor shortages coupled with gains made by feminist struggles expanded work opportunities for women. Nursing thus lost some of its appeal, as it was no longer one of the few options open to the middle-class white women who had constituted the overwhelming majority of RNs. The ensuing nursing shortage was actually specifically in reference to the supply of RNs in particular, not their subordinated auxiliary coworkers. This had racialized implications.

The post–World War II compromise between nursing leaders (RNs) and hospital administrators condoned a job hierarchy that was cut across by race as well as class. Following World War II, there was a gradual lifting of segregation within U.S. nursing. Yet the formal integration of the NACGN and the ANA did not translate into African American RNs sharing management responsibilities with their white colleagues. Instead, African American women were primarily channeled into auxiliary nursing positions, to work under predominantly white, if female, management. The result was the post–World War II model of "Team Nursing," characterized by RNs as the managers of LPNs and nurses' aides. In this model, racialized segregation gave way to "integration" via stratification by race and class, in a hierarchy secured by a system of credentialing and licensing that hospital administrators left in the control of a predominantly white nursing leadership. RNs continued to primarily be white middle- to upper middle-class women who held a baccalaureate degree, LPNs were mostly lower middle-class white women who held diplomas, and aides were mostly women of color. The latter two categories made up for their lack of authority through their numerical dominance. In the heyday of Team Nursing, RNs composed only one-third of hospital nursing labor, while auxiliary workers comprised the majority, with the other two-thirds.[35]

If Team Nursing emerged in the context of the first major crisis in the supply of U.S. nurses, its reign was coming to an end at the onset of the post-1965 nursing shortage. In the late 1960s and early 1970s, hospitals began moving toward Primary Nursing, a switch that RNs themselves initially advocated.[36] Unlike Team Nursing, this model prioritized RNs, aiming to place registered nurses back at the center of nursing care and thereby in the numerical majority. This did not spell the end of aides or LPNs but instead found RNs taking up more and more of the "dirty work" formerly ceded to these subsidiary workers. This emphasis on RNs was bolstered by the 1964 Nurse Training Act, which mandated federal funds for the expansion of resources related to nursing education, recruitment, service, research, and practice. The result was that, between 1972 and 1983, RN production increased by 100 percent.[37] By the end of the 1980s, the Team Nursing ratio had flipped so that RNs constituted two-thirds of hospital nursing labor, while LPNs and aides were increasingly employed in nonhospital health care facilities.[38] This reallocation of nursing labor did not substantially alter the racialized stratification set in place in the era of Team Nursing. As late as 1996, a full 90.3 percent of RNs were white. Of the remaining, less than 10 percent, 4.2 percent were African American, 3.4 percent Asian, 1.6 percent Hispanic, and .5 percent Native American.[39]

The shift to Primary Nursing had mixed results for RNs. On one hand, it resolved many of their jurisdictional disputes with aides and LPNs. The labor of RNs became absolutely central to hospital nursing and provided them with a larger degree of professional autonomy/authority than they had previously been allotted. However, Primary Nursing also dramatically increased their workload as they had to take up many of the tasks formerly allocated to aides and LPNs.[40] These additional responsibilities combined with relatively low salaries to produce disincentives for entering a field increasingly characterized by high rates of burnout and dropout. Thus, the statistics on the higher rate of production of RNs tell a partial story, focusing on recruitment alone rather than recruitment and retention.[41] Beginning in the late 1960s and extending, intermittently, into the 1970s and 1980s, the problem of high exit rates resulted in hospital administrators continuing to sound recurrent alarms of a crisis in their supply of RNs. From the perspective of RNs, these shortages allowed them some leverage to demand better wages and working conditions. Indeed, by the late 1980s, they were the single largest line item in hospital budgets.[42] In the face of this, hospital administrators began once again to look for ways to cut their costs. However, in the era of Primary Nursing, they did not return to the large-scale use of LPNs or aides. Instead, the RN shortage of the mid-twentieth century also allowed hospitals and their recruiters to lobby the U.S. government for the use of FNGs as another possible solution to their staffing needs.

In 1975, nearly a decade after the Gutierrez decision, FNGs still constituted only 3.5 percent of the total number of RNs working in the United States. Moreover, 75 percent of these nurses were concentrated in only five states: New York, New Jersey, Michigan, Illinois, and California.[43] Even here, their work was concentrated in the hospitals that suffered the most from problems with RN recruitment and retention: urban hospitals serving predominantly low-wealth people of color. Within these institutions, FNGs were concentrated on the least desirable units and shifts, such as intensive care and the night shift. Their labor was absolutely essential to the provision of services in these locations and at these times. So, for instance, between 1970 and 1980, New York saw a five-fold increase in the presence of FNGs, and as early as 1974, one out of every three RNs practicing in the state was a foreign nurse graduate.[44] And, as Janet Henning puts it in the opening of her 1975 *Modern Healthcare* article, "In metropolitan Chicago hospitals, getting along without foreign nurses is like trying to get along without bedpans. Nobody would dispute the fact that they are needed, but some people might be more comfortable without so many of them."[45]

Henning's analogy between foreign nurses and bedpans is certainly jarring. It is also, given its referents, racist. As the rest of the article made clear, by this time, the majority of foreign nurses in the United States were Asian, and those who might wish them away were generalized members of the U.S. national body (and, therefore, presumably white). Her language is thus a strong example of the mounting reaction of U.S. nursing leaders to the predominance of foreign nurse graduates within certain sectors of the U.S. hospital system. Their response had two major, and ultimately converging, strands. The first was coded in terms of cultural differences (and deficiencies) between foreign nurses and their U.S. counterparts. In this regard, the most common concerns and complaints found in U.S. nursing journals characterize foreign nurses as unable to communicate effectively due to English-language difficulties, of being cliquish, of having shy and/or unassertive personalities, and of being insensitive to death and disease.[46] By the early 1970s, when these criticisms began to gain momentum, they were often aimed specifically at the increasing numbers of foreign nurse graduates from the Third World. These were the women workers who were regarded as unable to effectively assimilate into mainstream U.S. nursing. One article, quoting a U.S. nursing professor who had worked in several Asian countries and consulted with U.S. hospitals regarding their recruitment of foreign nurses, put it this way: "There's no doubt, she says, that nurses from Great Britain and Ireland—indeed all of Western Europe—find acceptance more readily than those from the Philippines and other third-world countries. An Irish accent is charmingly familiar. A Filipino accent may sound a bit strange."[47]

These concerns over culture, language, and other forms of racialized difference converged with a second strand of criticism that charged U.S. hospital administrators and nursing recruiters with using foreign nurse graduates to fill their labor needs during a self-proclaimed nursing shortage. Here, the criticism was actually quite resonant with that which surfaced in relation to the EVP: that foreign nurses provided a cheaper and more easily exploitable workforce than their U.S. counterparts. As one article put it, "In some states, there is some feeling that foreign nurses are recruited by hospitals and other institutions not because there is a nursing shortage, but because they can be paid less and are not inclined to make demands on the employer."[48] With regard to the latter, the common characterization of foreign trained nurses as docile, timid, and unassertive due to alleged cultural differences ignored the structural conditions of their employment. By 1974, when that statement was first published, FNGs were increasingly put into a position of imposed docility and vulnerability. Again, this has to do with their position vis-à-vis U.S. immigration and naturalization law.

By the mid-1970s, the majority of FNGs entering the U.S. market were doing so through the use of temporary, or H-1, visas.[49] This requires some explanation, as it occurred at roughly the same time that the opening initiated through the 1965 legislation had begun to narrow. The Immigration and Nationality Act Amendments of 1976 required that immigrants have firm job offers upon arrival, and, even more specifically, the Health Professions Educational Assistance Act of 1976 required proof of employment before immigration. In this context of tightening demands, the appeal of the H-1 visa was its expediency. In 1970, the average waiting period for a third preference, or permanent legal resident, visa was thirteen months. This compared to only a thirty- to ninety-day wait for an H-1.[50] By this time, temporary visas had also become the preferred recruiting mechanism for hospitals. Unlike the third preference, where nurses arrived as legal permanent residents with the right to switch employers at will, the H-1 not only was temporary in duration but also restricted FNGs to employment with their initial sponsor. In this sense, it echoed, if not imitated, the conditions of the EVP. Here again, if migrants switched sponsors (without first petitioning to do so) or overstayed their visas, they would be subject to immediate deportation. However, in the case of post-1965 H-1 visa holders, the possibility of adjusting their status to legal permanent resident not only existed, but in 1970, it was facilitated by an amendment that allowed H-1 holders to fill permanent positions. In that same year, the law also changed so that nurses who arrived as exchange visitors could adjust their status without the previously required two-year foreign residency requirement.

From the perspective of U.S. hospitals, H-1 nurses were appealing because they solved, at least for the duration of their visa, the problems of both recruitment and retention. Their retention was made possible not only through the mandates of the H-1 employer restrictions but also because FNGs often came through nursing recruiters. Recruiters charged a set fee that nurses had to repay before they could leave the employment of their sponsoring hospital. It was, in part, in response to these easily exploitable conditions that U.S. nursing leaders raised their cry of "foul play" on the part of recruiters and hospitals. And yet, the concrete form that their response took had mixed results when it came to protecting foreign nurse graduates from further exploitation. The primary tool that nursing leaders fought for and employed with regard to FNGs was an insistence on the same system of licensing and credentialing—standards— that had maintained the hierarchical and racialized division of nursing labor all along. Their increased efforts in this direction coincided with the three overlapping phenomena detailed above: the establishment of FNGs in the U.S. market due to the collusion between immigration reform and hospital recruiters; the predominance of Third World women, especially Asians, among FNGs; and the increasing use of H-1 rather than permanent resident visas for their employment. In the end, it was these developments, combined with targeted licensing and credentialing, that finally carved a permanent place for FNGs in the division of U.S. nursing labor.

*Standardizing "Foreign"*

When nurses first began immigrating to the United States, they were slotted into the nursing hierarchy without, by and large, having to take the exams required of U.S. nurses. In 1968, 90 percent of FNGs were able to practice as RNs through the endorsement of their employers rather than by state examination.[51] However, as the permanence of immigrants within the U.S. market became more apparent, U.S. nursing leaders pushed states to require that FNGs take the State Board Test Pool Examination (SBTPE) in order to practice as an RN. According to their arguments, this would not only ensure FNG competency but also safeguard U.S. nursing practice and, thereby, patient care. The insistence that immigrant nurses pass the SBTPE in order to practice as RNs in the United States marked the switch from the period of exchange visitors to occupational im/migrants. New Jersey required it as early as 1966. New York began in 1971. By 1977, all fifty states required FNGs to pass the exam if they were to work as RNs.

The SBTPE was developed by the National Council of State Boards of Nursing, which was part of the ANA until 1978. Individual states used it by contract in order to credential the registered nurses practicing within their dominion. The test had five subject areas: medical, surgical, psychiatric, obstetric, and pediatric nursing. In order to take the exam, foreign nurses had to have an occupational visa and proof of registration or licensure as professional nurses in their countries of origin. They also had to show evidence that they had already met the prescribed amount of education required in all five areas to qualify as a "first-level nurse" as defined by the International Council of Nurses (ICN). Similar to RN certification in the United States, the ICN standard was meant to differentiate between professional and auxiliary nursing personnel vis-à-vis educational certification.

It became apparent almost immediately that use of the ICN definition did not ensure RN certification in the United States. FNGs failed the SBTPE in notable numbers. From 1970 to 1972, only 22.5 percent passed the first time they took the test, with two-thirds of second-time takers failing again.[52] In New York State, from 1972 to 1974, failure rates for first-time takers ranged from 63.6 to 90.9 percent and from 52.2 to 86.6 percent for repeat takers.[53] This range contrasted sharply with the success rates of U.S.-trained nurses during the same period. From 1969 to 1978, 85 percent of FNGs taking the SBTPE failed on the first try, compared to only 17 percent of U.S. nurses.[54]

For FNGs and U.S. nurses alike, failure meant the inability to practice as RNs. However, among FNGs, there was a marked contrast between the fate of green card holders and the H-1 nurses who increasingly constituted the bulk of the foreign nurse population. If a green card holder failed the SBTPE but still desired employment within the field, she (or he) could work on a permit until that person passed the exam. In real terms, this translated into downward occupational mobility. Nurses who were used to working at the level of RN found themselves demoted into the ranks of nurses' aides. Several green card holders also described to me their employment as licensed practical nurses before, or instead of, becoming an RN. Their ability to do so depended on the licensing rules during the period of their immigration and attempted certification. These would also vary from state to state. For instance, Ms. Dhas, an Indian nurse who immigrated to New York in 1978, received an LPN license after the first time she took the SBTPE and failed. Her score was past 400 and therefore qualified her for the lower certification. She did, however, eventually pass the RN exam two years later: "For twenty-two years, I was an RN. That was nice, otherwise as an LPN you make so much less money for the same work."[55]

The consequences of failure for H-1 nurses were much more severe. Since their H-1 was tied only to their work as RNs, failure to take or pass the SBTPE meant that their temporary visa would be revoked—and that they were subject to immediate deportation. Their situation was complicated by the fact that the recruiters and hospitals who hired H-1 nurses did not always inform migrants of the testing requirements in the United States or the time frame within which these needed to be completed. This compounded migrants' chances of slipping into unauthorized status. However, the hospitals that hired H-1 nurses in significant numbers were often so reliant on their labor that instead of being deported, migrants would often continue working. Because they were no longer in the United States legally, they could neither become LPNs nor take the SBTPE again but became (or remained) nurses' aides who now worked "under the table." As described by Ms. Dhas above, the change in position did not always translate into a change in duties. Workers would often still be responsible for many of the same tasks. The primary difference would be, instead, the increased probability of exploitation due to the looming threat of deportation.

The mounting reaction of U.S. nursing leaders to foreign nurses' high SBTPE failure rates climaxed at the ANA's 1974 biennial.[56] At the convention, a group of nursing leaders pushed a twelve-point platform that would remove FNGs' preferential immigration status and support state nurses associations' efforts to continue to evaluate FNG practice via the SBTPE. Their position stressed that FNGs were insufficiently prepared to practice as RNs. Their test scores were all the proof that was needed. Their position thus relied on nursing leadership's historical use of licensing and credentialing as a path to professionalization and, concomitantly, racialization. The latter was not explicit in the rhetoric opposing the use of FNGs. Instead, complaints were coded in terms that harkened back to the original complaints voiced against the use of exchange visitors as cheap hospital labor and, especially, a threat to patient safety (and, by extension, the U.S. public).

The original anti-FNG platform was defeated. In its stead, another group of ANA members, including one Filipino nurse, floated an alternative resolution that passed. This platform emphasized the role that hospital recruiters and administrators played in FNG recruitment, thereby positioning aspects of U.S. nursing within an international frame. It also proposed the creation of a prescreening exam, to be administered before applicants arrived in the United States.[57] This last item led to the creation of the Commission on Graduates of Foreign Nursing Schools (CGFNS) in 1977.

The CGFNS was a private nonprofit organization, cosponsored by the ANA and the National League for Nursing and underwritten by a one-time federal contract grant of $346,173. In the words of two of its leaders, the organization developed "in response to a direct need: on one hand, to insure safe nursing care for the American public and, on the other hand, to protect foreign nurse graduates from employment exploitation."[58] In October 1978, CGFNS tests were administered for the first time in thirty-two cities around the world. The exam was found to dramatically increase FNG success rates with testing in the United States. In 1983, the CGFNS reported that 70 percent of FNGs who passed the exam went on to pass state licensing exams.[59] By 1980, the Immigration and Naturalization Service (INS) required candidates to pass the CGFNS in order to obtain an occupational visa, either preference or H-1. In addition, in 1977, a CGFNS study determined that 0.7 percent of FNGs entering the United States as dependents were nurses.[60] It followed that they too were required to take the exam, and testing centers were set up in Chicago, Los Angeles, and New York City. And finally, the CGFNS applied retroactively. This meant that nurses already licensed in the United States had to take the

CGFNS in order to retain their status. If they failed, they had to take the SBTPE again and were demoted accordingly until they passed.

By the 1980s, the SBTPE was itself on the way out. This time, questions of racialization and professionalization had a clear voice in the debate. In California, a coalition of groups spearheaded by the Filipino-led National Alliance for Fair Licensure of Foreign Nurse Graduates organized a campaign against discrimination in the SBTPE.[61] In 1980, a study in California had found the test to be both racially and culturally biased. This helped account for the racialized pass rates in the state: with 45 percent Asians, 62 percent African Americans, 55 percent Filipinos, 40 percent Latinos, and 40 percent Native Americans failing compared to 12 percent of whites.[62] In 1981, California broke away from the SBTPE. And in 1982, the test was replaced with the National Council Licensure Exam (NCLEX) across the country. This did not change the rules regarding the CGFNS and, now, the NCLEX, both of which were still required of FNGs in order to practice as RNs in the United States.

The intersecting systems of immigration regulation and labor certification define the position of foreign nurse graduates in both the U.S. labor market and nation-state. Their history is one that all FNGs living and working in the United States share, to some degree. The partiality of this statement was already in evidence during the exchange visitor period, when race- and nation-based exclusion and restriction created a different set of (im)possibilities for Asian nurses. While the post-1965 period substantially altered the legal landscape vis-à-vis immigration, the increasing battery of tests that FNGs had to clear in order to work in the U.S. health care industry created another set of barriers. Again, these were not equally applicable. This was especially the case with regard to the CGFNS, an exam that required the establishment of testing centers around the world. The reintroduction of a global framework returns us also to the specificity of Indian nurse migration. Of the thirty-two cities that first hosted the CGFNS exam in 1978, none were in India. As a measure to prevent the loss of nursing personnel to more lucrative markets, the Indian government refused to allow the test to be administered within its borders. Its refusal persisted through the end of the twentieth century, only reversing in 2001, when it approved the opening of a CGFNS center in the southern city of Bangalore.[63] This ban had its effect on the shape of Indian nurse migration to the United States. In particular, it seems to have affected the routes taken by potential migrants after the wait for a green card became prohibitive. In his review of Indian nurse immigration to the

United States, historian Raymond Brady Williams reports that in the 1970s, U.S. hospital recruiters were active in facilitating Indian nurse immigration, but by the 1980s, fewer Indian nurses immigrated and more relied on family reunification as a means of entry.[64]

The decline in Indian nurses entering the United States as nurses in the 1980s was a result of both the increasingly prohibitive waits for third preference immigrants (reportedly up to a decade) and the inability for potential migrants to take the CGFNS in India. In general, the former was one cause for the increase in H-1 nurses in the U.S. market. The latter, however, accounted for the fact that U.S. hospital recruiters no longer looked to India as a primary source for this category of temporary worker. This did not mean that Indian nurses no longer looked to the United States. First, options other than labor immigration were also available. Many of the nurses who came as third preference immigrants in the 1970s were able to sponsor whole families and communities through the family reunification provisions of the 1965 amendments. Individuals who went to work as nurses were among those sponsored. In addition, the inability for nurse graduates to take the CGFNS in India did not mean that they could not take the exam somewhere else. Examination centers operated in nearby countries such as Sri Lanka, Pakistan, and Thailand. Reports are that Indian nurses took advantage of these.[65] Nurses who had already migrated to countries in the Persian Gulf, Australasia, and Europe could and did take the exam and gain admittance from countries in these regions. The trails that nurses made across continents and countries offer one way to chart the shifting position(s) of Indian nurses within the global division of nursing labor. They also serve as a clear reminder that the racialization of Indian and foreign nurse labor in the United States was part of the changing contours of this global, imperial map.

# CHAPTER SEVEN

# Indian Nurses Navigate the U.S. Division of Nursing Labor

Prior to immigrating to the United States, Subhashini (not her real name) had been the head nurse in the pediatrics unit of Mumbai's prestigious Sir Jamshedjee Jeejeebhoy (J. J.) Hospital for nearly a decade. In a country where nurses still had little if any respect in the public eye, Subhashini stressed to me how her position at one of India's top hospitals conferred authority, and the quality of her work garnered esteem. The income she earned also allowed her to live an independent life as a single woman in a big city, while at the same time supporting her widowed grandmother. She summarized her situation by simply stating that, "There was nothing better than what my life was at that time."[1] In contrast, she described her decision to immigrate to the United States in 1975 as one that was, in a curious way, unintentional if not accidental. There was no agency in her explanation. When pressed, she eventually offered two reasons. The first was the bidding of her sister and brother-in-law, who were both medical doctors already working in New York State. The second was her firm decision to remain single and the difficulty that presented for living long term in India. Her move was aided by the fact that it took place during the height of the first full wave of foreign nurse immigration to the United States. In this context, she was able to arrive having already cleared the hurdle of obtaining a green card and with a permit to work until she passed the State Board Test Pool Examination (SBTPE). In a sense, she had nothing to do upon arrival but stay with her relatives and study for the exam. However, knowing nothing about the U.S. system, she was convinced that she would fail unless she gained some work experience in the United States. Her sister advised her not to take a job: "You were a Saab there; and all of a sudden over here you will be a nurse's aide."[2] "Saab" is an alternative for "sahib," a title that denotes respect, authority, and, indeed, superiority in India. The distance that her sister's warning charted was thus the difference between being at the top of the field in India and starting at the bottom of the hierarchy in the United States. This was not a matter of money per se, but respectability. In India, a head nurse would have been able to pass on the "dirty work," whereas in the United States, joining the lower ranks of the nursing hierarchy meant that one would be performing precisely those tasks.

Subhashini disregarded her sister's advice. She contacted a friend who was working as a medical resident in Kentucky and got a job as a nurse's aide in a pediatrics ward there. She had only just begun this job, however, when she was due to take the SBTPE in New York (where she was still taking it despite her temporary move): "So naturally I failed. I knew I was going to fail. It was so terrible, my God! And I wasn't dumb like this. I was a first-class student in India. So that was another blow to me. How dumb can one be in this country?"[3] At this time, and in her case, failure meant that she had passed only two of the five required subject areas. Subhashini cited several factors for her results: she had studied for her nursing diploma (not a BSc) in India well over a decade earlier, she had to pass certain subject areas such as psychiatry and medical-surgical in which she had not worked since her studies in India, and the multiple-choice format of the test was both unfamiliar and demanding. These issues were not unique to her case. With the addition of language competency, they were the most common factors used to explain low foreign nurse graduate (FNG) success rates with the SBTPE.[4]

Given these combined difficulties, it took Subhashini two years to pass all sections of the exam and get a license. She could afford this time because she already had a green card. In the interim, she continued working as a nurse's aide in the hospital and later in a nursing home in Connecticut. After passing the SBTPE, she found employment as a staff nurse in pediatrics at a public hospital in New York City. During her twenty-five years at that same institution, she earned several promotions as well as a bachelor's degree in community health and health administration. When I spoke with her, she had retired but maintained her apartment across the street from the hospital as her home base.

Subhashini's work history is, in many ways, representative of those related to me by Indian nurses who entered the United States on occupational visas (with their green cards). However, in their retelling, my interviewees also acknowledged the world of those who did not arrive with green cards and/or who were not able to eventually pass the requisite exams and legal hoops. The latter's exclusion from my sample pool was in many ways a product of the snowball technique that I employed and the persistent, consistent struggle that Indian nurses have had to wage against their own stigmatization. This last point made it even more difficult to get recommendations to interview nurses who worked "under the table," never mind the vulnerability that might also prevent unauthorized nurses from themselves feeling able to speak out. Their presence is the shadow to the stories that I have been able to include. It is a reminder of the ways in which the politics of im/migration added another layer to the structural factors shaping the status of Indian nurses.

While all of those I interviewed eventually obtained a license and thereby a means to degrees of upward mobility, the process commonly took several years.[5] In the interim, they found employment at the unlicensed end of the nursing hierarchy, which meant that they worked primarily as nurses' aides. Interviewees described this work as grueling, involving heavy lifting and long hours. For most, this came as something of a shock, especially as it relegated them back to the type of care work that they had not performed since their days as students or entry-level nurses in India. For some, like Susan George Arakal, the difference between "then" and "now"/"here" and "there" was earth-shattering: "It killed me, killed me. When I used to go to work, I used to think, 'Oh my, let the earth go into two pieces so I can go down.'"[6]

Immediate, if temporary, downward mobility was not the only shock that greeted Indian nurses in the U.S. workplace. Those I interviewed started work either in large urban hospitals serving impoverished communities or in nursing homes. Nurses routinely described these facilities as "disgusting," for both workers and patients. Several left their jobs for this reason. One nurse described to me the resignation letter she wrote, where she listed, in horrified and horrifying detail, all of the problems that her employer presented for adequate health care delivery. These were conditions that did not change after nurses received their licenses and moved up in the nursing hierarchy to the ranks of licensed practical nurses (LPNs), registered nurses (RNs), or administrators, often within the same institutions. Instead, they provide the detail necessary for understanding what it meant that most FNGs were employed in underserved urban institutions, in the least desirable units, and on the least desirable shifts. The remarks I heard were indeed the flipside of Janet Henning's comparison of foreign nurses and bedpans, cited in the last chapter. Her description was actually in specific reference to the high rate of FNG employment at Cook County Hospital in Chicago. Separate accounts of this particular urban institution describe how, in the 1960s,

Because of rapid expansion, organizational disarray, and shortages of physicians and nurses in the 1960s, Cook County Hospital earned the reputation of "an unsanitary dumping ground" in which quality patient care was deemed impossible. In the wake of public condemnation, Cook County Hospital could not attract U.S.-trained nurses, who preferred care of the acutely ill in hospitals in which staff morale was higher and professional challenges greater to staff positions. As an urban hospital caring for low-income, chronically ill minority patients, Cook County Hospital was particularly vulnerable to nurse shortages.[7]

This "vulnerability" describes many of the hospitals where my interviewees found employment. The same hospital where the above-mentioned nurse resigned offered her a choice of five positions there if she would return to work and clean up the mess as best she could. Indeed, my interviews made clear the preference that certain hospitals had for the labor of foreign nurse graduates. Nurses did not, however, describe their employability as tantamount to equal access to the upper tiers of the nursing division of labor. Instead, they described their employment as both tenuous and, after a certain point, limited. Their descriptions fortify some of the observations made in the previous chapter, as well as flesh them out from another angle.

Generally, critiques of the exploitability of FNGs rested on the case of those who, arriving unprepared and/or underinformed, failed to pass the requisite licensing exams and faced either deportation or unauthorized employment. This was (and is) the case for H-1 nurses and certainly represents the most tenuous existence of foreign nurse graduates in the U.S. market. However, green card holders revealed to me the way in which their status as legal workers was also limited by hospitals' reliance on nursing employment agencies for the placement of FNGs. These agencies were used in addition to the recruiters who were sent abroad in search of new labor. Even some of the nurses I interviewed who arrived without the aid of international recruiters turned to employment agencies in order to find their first jobs once in the United States. This was the case when Thankam Vellaringattu went out looking for a job after arriving in New York City.

Vellaringattu had come to the United States with a green card and years of work experience as a nurse in India, Saudi Arabia, and England. She approached hospitals armed with all of the above. In addition, and in her view as a kind of proof of her ability to both live and work in the United States, her husband Tom and her baby daughter Tanya accompanied her on the search: "I kept giving applications everywhere. I was going with Tom and Tanya and the stroller. I don't know, seeing us new to the country or whatever, they wouldn't. . . . Maybe they thought I won't be able to function here. They would say okay, we will call you."[8]

Frustrated, Vellaringattu finally followed the advice of an uncle who suggested that she may have more luck finding work if she went through a temporary agency first and then, with that experience, have more leverage for a job. The agency she signed up with sent her to work in one of the very same jobs for which she had just applied and been told there was no vacancy. The message was now clear. Her strategy to show seriousness through her attachment to a husband and child had backfired precisely because it highlighted her claim to stability and permanence. The hospital had vacancies but preferred to fill them with temporary, contract labor regardless of visa status. Vellaringattu thus began her agency-based assignment without any orientation or training. However, much to her amusement and their surprise, she found the system in use quite familiar. The hospital where she worked in Saudi Arabia had been run by a California-based company and followed U.S. standards. She was therefore able to jump into the new job routine quickly and proficiently. With this confidence in her abilities, Vellaringattu mentioned to a coworker that she had already applied for this same job at the hospital and been told that there was no vacancy. Word got back immediately to their supervisor, who asked her if she wanted the full-time regular position. "Now I realized that they were in need of nurses, so I gave a little demand. I told them I also had an offer from another place."[9] They countered, and when Vellaringattu was offered the job, she again met with the same hospital administrator who had initially denied her the opportunity: "She [the administrator] asked me, 'Whom do you know here?' That's what she asked. I think somebody got really annoyed with her for sending me away. . . . So when I went back she was like . . . a little . . . not like a jolly . . . I could see some anger on her face."[10]

Thankam Vellaringattu is an extremely good-humored, animated, and attention-grabbing storyteller. When she recalled this experience to me, we were both laughing at her audacity and the strength of character that worked her potential exploitation to her advantage. Yet, even as she overcame this particular challenge, her story also highlights the way in which hospitals and nursing agencies worked in collaboration to keep foreign nursing labor in precarious positions even after their legal validation. In this case, the distinction between working the same position through the agency or through the hospital itself was the difference between temporary and permanent employment: job security, relative stability, and benefits. However, even after securing full-time, nontemporary positions, nurses repeatedly described to me the limits placed upon their mobility. I heard recurring stories of untenable workloads, the absence of promotions and/or promotions that were essentially undermined, and lack of recognition for the work—above and beyond—that nurses performed. Together, these amounted to a collective description of the "glass ceiling" that limited their job mobility within the U.S. workplace. The specificity of this upper limit constituted the second major way in which nurses narrated their occupational mobility within the United States.

The ability to retain FNGs as employees could also serve as an attractive feature with regard to their employment by hospitals that were otherwise plagued by high rates of staff turnover. Some degree of job loyalty was ensured by the technicalities of their immigration status, as well as by the fees that many had incurred through recruiters. FNG stability was in contrast to the patterns of U.S. citizen nurses, who have displayed historically high rates of institutional mobility and/or attrition—particularly in relation to the jobs where foreign nurses tend to be hired. Certainly, Subhashini's story provides one example of the institutional longevity attributed to foreign nurse graduates. On its own, her example speaks simply and strongly to a kind of dedication and stamina to survive in a job that might otherwise suffer from high rates of burnout. Such an interpretation may also be fortified by the fact that several other nurses I interviewed spent their careers at the first institution in the United States where they were hired and/or began training as students. The work histories of other nurses I interviewed provide, however, a wider window onto this phenomenon.

Many interviewees expressed dissatisfaction with the first fully licensed jobs they found, even as they were able to move up beyond the position of aide. Instead of staying put, they chose to explore their options elsewhere. This translated into a shuttle between a series of jobs that were, ultimately, not in significantly different sectors of the health care industry. This was the case with Satwant Malhotra, who had already worked at two different institutions before getting her RN license. After receiving her certification, personal and professional reasons took her through two more positions until she finally spent eighteen years working at a psychiatric institution in Long Island. She described the workforce there to me in this way: "At that time, American doctors didn't want to work in mental institutions, so there were a lot of Indian doctors there. Ninety percent of the doctors were Indian. . . . It was a stationary kind of job."[11]

Malhotra's description focuses on the physicians at her workplace. However, institutions that hired large numbers of foreign medical graduates (FMGs) were also often the same ones that hired large numbers of FNGs, and these were the same institutions that most of the nurses I interviewed worked in throughout their careers. In this way, what the postlicensing segment of their work histories tracked is a kind of lateral mobility within a certain segment of the U.S. health care sector. For U.S. nurses, leaving institutions with poor working conditions and high attrition rates could mean finding a job in a more desirable location. For Indian nurses, such a possibility was limited by the realities of a market that largely contained FNG labor in particular kinds of institutions and positions therein. This reality shaped, in part, nurses' decisions to eventually settle on a position within this spectrum that suited their needs. For many, this translated into a long-term commitment. In some of these cases, nurses were able to find job (and even career) satisfaction. In others, they did not. The latter was evidenced by the fact that, while interviewees stayed in certain positions longer than their peers with more options may have, many of the near-retirement nurses I interviewed had still switched jobs and institutions at the end of their career. It is thus against this backdrop that we must read hospital and recruiter claims regarding higher rates of retention with regard to FNGs.

It would be inaccurate, however, to claim that Indian nurses experienced no upward mobility within their places of work. Instead, it is to be understood that these lateral limits defined the scope within which their promotions took place. And indeed, several of the nurses I interviewed eventually achieved positions of prominence within the institutions where they worked. They found regular work not only as staff nurses but also as supervisors, administrators, and educators. Given the fact that U.S. nursing's hierarchy was historically structured through licensing and credentialing, it is not surprising that much of this upward mobility was enabled through the acquisition of advanced degrees. Subhashini explained to me that this was the reason she pursued her bachelor's degree while working full-time. The implication was that being an Indian diploma graduate limited her professional mobility. The advanced degree allowed her to be competitive according to U.S. standards and thereby securely hold the position of head nurse within her department.

For the nurses I interviewed, the acquisition of advanced degrees was not always sufficient to ensure promotions commensurate with an individual's qualifications. One nurse, Dr. Suwersh Khanna, took this particular strategy to the highest possible level. Khanna earned her doctorate while working full-time, but this did not translate easily or immediately into the type of mobility and/or authority that such an achievement might otherwise confer. Dr. Khanna summarized her work history to me when she stated, proudly, that "I have done it all at different stages."[12] And indeed her range is vast, covering everything from work as a live-in housekeeper while earning her degree to retiring as a professor emeritus. In between, and after earning her PhD, she had a job teaching at Pace University in New York City. Here she described to me how she was repeatedly passed up for promotions. After filing a grievance and still being denied, she decided to prove her point in another way. She took a leave of absence and went to work in St. Louis as a visiting professor: "I was an associate professor. I wanted status; I got it there. I could not get tenure there because I was visiting but I still wanted to prove that I am as good as anybody else. If they published one article and get such a long mileage out of it, how come I wrote so much—fifteen things—and did my post-doctorate and still not get it? So to prove my worth I lived through hell again with separation from my husband and family . . . but when I returned in December I became an associate professor right then."[13]

If Dr. Khanna's story could be construed as just another tenure battle in an industry constituted by such struggles, Aleyamma Eapen helps us understand the achievement, appreciation, and promotion of immigrant nurses in another light. Like Suwersh Khanna, Eapen pursued a doctorate while working full-time. Illness prevented her from completing the full degree. She stopped her study after earning her master's. When I met her, she was working as the head nurse at Coney Island Hospital's cardiac catheterization lab. Here, she had pioneered the technique of using music rather than sedatives to calm patients during their angiograms. Given the diversity of patients served at Coney Island, she makes sure that she has on hand music from many of their home countries/cultures. This innovation formed the basis of her master's thesis. And it went largely unnoticed and/or undervalued by her colleagues and hospital administrators: "I'm telling you the hospital never recognized it. They knew I was doing this because I had to get permission to do the research. And they knew I was not doing it for academic reasons alone, but for the patients."[14]

Eapen's work finally came to light when hospital inspectors doing a tour of Coney Island took note of both her technique and the fact that she was pursuing it almost entirely on her own. They were so impressed that they asked for her research abstract and brought it to the attention of Coney Island's administration and the New York City press.[15] The ensuing publicity garnered her several awards, and her work transformed into a point of pride at the hospital and part of how it publicizes itself. However, the New York Times piece profiling Aleyamma Eapen quotes her as saying that the cardiac catheterization lab welcomed her when she first started working there, "partly because most hospital staffers do not like to work there."[16] It was not a desirable position, in part because of the risk that regular exposure to radiation might entail. Her story thus reiterated the fact that, of the nurses I interviewed who reached the position of head nurse or administrator, most did so in units and/or on shifts that were not generally desirable.

In our conversation, Eapen took the analysis of this containment a step further by explicitly drawing attention to race. When she described to me the troubled process of recognition for her work, she did so in order to illustrate why she wants to write a book based on her work experiences as a foreign nurse in the United States: "If you come to Coney Island, you will see every department there is owned by Indians. Every department head is an Indian; all the good workers are Indian. These are highly educated workers, not the bottom ones, the top ones. But they will never recognize your knowledge. They will use your knowledge to get things done, but the topmost person will be that white person. And if you blow the whistle, if you don't see things in their way, you will be fired. You understand what I am saying?"[17]

Her compatriot, Mrs. Parmar, did understand. As a BSc nurse from India who went on to earn her master's degree at New York University (again, while working full-time), Mrs. Parmar rose to the rank of nurse educator and supervisor on a night shift at Maimonides Hospital in Brooklyn, New York. As much authority as this position entailed, she described to me how the most difficult work still fell onto her shift. As a teacher, she was in charge of orienting new nurses to the hospital. Part of this involved taking care of some of the hospital's sickest patients, in order to cover as many facets of nursing care as possible: "They'll give me three patients, bad patients, so that my nurses can learn everything about the patients. For three months I'll have all the sickest patients. Then my student becomes an RN and graduates to work in critical care and I have a new nurse to train. So every three months I am the one who is taking care of all of the sick patients, and meanwhile all of these nurses—white nurses— they have the recovering patients. I got tired of doing this."[18]

Mrs. Parmar got so tired that she started having health problems and switched to work as the director of nursing on a day shift in the geriatric unit. Here her authority was again undermined. This time the hospital brought in a white nurse as an assistant director and, eventually, through a series of departmental reorganizations, authority was eventually shifted over to her coworker and away from her. Mrs. Parmar's description of these machinations was thoroughly racialized: "She was white, and I was Indian.

There is always something going on."[19] She defined this "something" to me earlier in our conversation when she told me, "The higher you go in nursing, the more discrimination there is. Lots of discrimination."[20]

In the case of her own history of positions and promotions, Mrs. Parmar articulated the discrimination she experienced mostly through the idiom of jealousy. It was the jealousy of supervisors who resented her presence and thereby attempted to contain it. This was her most specific explanation for the repeated cap that was put on her mobility. And it was the persistence of this glass ceiling that eventually compelled her to step out of the field entirely. When I met Mrs. Parmar, it was for an interview in the offices of the Parmar Financial Group, an insurance firm that she heads and runs out of her own home in Brooklyn. The business allowed her to be both an independent agent and a community resource, two roles that she relished and sustained in full measure. Her decision to opt out of nursing marks the limits of job mobility and confirms a pattern of self-employment often noted in relationship to skilled immigrants who are unable to find and/or sustain employment commensurate with their qualifications.

Jealousy, competition, interpersonal and intergroup rivalry, and resistance were among the most common descriptions of workplace experiences that I heard from nurses. Significantly, this was not only in relation to stories describing limits on upward mobility. Relationships between nurses and their subordinates were also, and even more commonly, described to me in these terms. And these descriptions were also thoroughly racialized, but this time mostly in reference to African Americans.[21] An example from Rajan, who was working as a nurse administrator in Queens, New York, at the time of our interview, illustrated the way in which interviewees experienced "jealousy" from the other side.

Rajan first arrived in New York City on a visitor visa in the late 1960s. At the time, the nursing shortage was acute and she had already graduated from the Vellore College of Nursing's bachelor's and newly minted master's programs. She was thus rather quickly and easily able to convert her visit into an opportunity for employment in a critical care unit in the city. While working there, she received an offer to be an assistant director and nursing educator at Meharry Medical College in Nashville, Tennessee. Rajan described her work at Meharry as difficult: "That place was hard. The thing is, almost all of them, ninety-nine percent of them are black. Their ways are set. . . . They didn't like you because you are from another country and you are trying to disrupt their routine."[22] The problem with "their ways being set" was that many of their "ways" were what Rajan characterized as bad work habits. And these formed one of the many qualities that she found substandard to the quality of care she was used to from working at Vellore.

Meharry is a historically black medical college and one of the few to survive the overhaul in U.S. medical schools that followed publication of the Flexner Report in 1910. It was also, consequently, one of the few historically African American medical and nursing colleges that the Rockefeller Foundation (RF) chose to support and promote during Jim and Jane Crow. This placed it alongside Vellore on the roster of institutions that the RF had decided to invest in. It was RF practice to send administrators from one institution to another in order to provide models and pathways of communication between foundation projects/prospects. While I have no direct evidence of this in the case of Vellore and Meharry, Rajan did explain to me that the director at Meharry knew about Vellore and had actually already met the Vellore graduate who Rajan was living with in New York City. This was how she had been hooked into the job. It is not too much to suppose that the director's knowledge came from historical connections between the two institutions that were in fact first promoted by the foundation and its followers.

At the time when Rajan began working at Meharry, the long struggle for black freedom had recently seen victories in the courts and in federal legislation with regard to desegregation. Despite these achievements, at Meharry, as in much of the rest of the U.S., racialized segregation was still very much a fact of life. This explained, in part, the racialization of the workforce when Rajan started working there. However, as the rest of my interviews made clear, it would be a mistake to characterize the racialization of workplace tensions at Meharry as something specific to the mid-twentieth century U.S. South. Instead, the jealousy, competition, and resentment interviewees felt from African American nurses was a complaint that ran across my interviews with nurses, the majority of whom worked in the northern United States and the New York City metropolitan area specifically. In general, Indian nurses did not feel that they could inhabit positions of power with full authority, and this came out in racialized complaints about the difficulty of managing African American nurses' aides and/or other auxiliary nursing personnel: "They are set in their ways." "They won't listen." "I found it impossible."

These racialized complaints began in descriptions of the period when nurse immigrants worked as aides and auxiliaries themselves and extended into their later role as managers of this same sector of the workforce. While Rajan, with her educational qualifications and institutional

connections, was able to straightaway attain this latter position, her experience of it conformed to that of her fellow interviewees. Resistance to
change, incarnated in her presence as a *foreign* nurse, was the common
theme that Rajan used to characterize her staff at Meharry. This not only
prevented her from instituting the type of change she saw as necessary
but also eventually led her to resignation. Again, she joined other nurses
I interviewed, several of whom also opted out of their role as managers in
situations where they felt unable to bridge, specifically, the racialized divides of the U.S. nursing workforce.

The manner in which interviewees racialized intractability and insubordination is just as troubling as their descriptions of the racialized limits placed upon their own upward mobility. Both are manifestations of
racism in the workplace and between workers. In the context of the long
history of professionalization and racialization that characterizes nursing,
this is sadly not surprising so much as it is predictable. First, as we have
seen, the professionalization of RNs was wrought through the subordination of auxiliary nursing personnel and solidified through reliance on
systems of licensing and credentialing. This division between nursing personnel was manifest on a nationwide scale during the period of Team
Nursing, when RNs were placed in positions of management above LPNs
and nurses' aides. In a manner that mimicked this in the miniature, the
foreign nurse graduates who were able to successfully navigate the tests
that awaited them also moved beyond their initial positions as coworkers
in the position of aide or LPN. They thus reenacted this historical subordination in the miniature in a way that white RNs were less likely to have
to do on the individual level. And yet their experiences also reveal something of the racialized workplace within which all nursing personnel
functioned.

The distinctions between aides, LPNs, and RNs were not, in fact, as
clear in practice as they were on paper. The division between tasks often
entailed a large degree of overlap and created a large degree of distrust
and workplace tension:

Although RNs viewed auxiliaries as members of inferior occupations,
their perceptions of auxiliaries was itself contradictory. On the one
hand, RNs commonly believed that auxiliaries were not responsible or
dedicated. They could not be trusted, did not work conscientiously, and
required close supervision. On the other hand, RNs also complained
that auxiliaries were excessively ambitious, did not stay in their place,
and engaged in tasks they were not supposed to be doing. . . . Auxiliary

nurses also held derogatory views of RNs. LPNs and aides commonly felt that they did all the "real" work. RNs processed doctors' orders, made entries in patient charts, and maintained the nursing care plans while auxiliaries performed the bulk of bedside care: making beds, emptying bedpans, giving baths, passing meal trays, and doing a variety of other tasks essential to patient care.[23]

This description comes from Robert Brannon's ethnographic study of the nursing workforce in "Pacific Hospital"[24] in the 1980s. It makes clear how the comments I heard from Indian nurses were manifestations of the larger tensions prevalent between RNs and auxiliary nursing personnel in U.S. workplaces. Indeed, my interviewees expressed their experiences in the same idiom of intractability and insubordination that Brannon found among the nurses in his project. What Brannon does not fully account for, however, is the way in which these same divisions were historically racialized, so that these complaints were not only about divisions within an occupation but also manifestations of the way in which nursing in the United States has been part of the pattern of U.S. racial formation and, indeed, U.S. racism. In other words, RNs' comments about LPNs and nurses' aides were also, more often than not, white middle-class women's comments about working-class white and African American women. And Indian nurses' first jobs as aides, auxiliaries, and managers were also their initiation into this racialized hierarchy. However, even as their experiences articulated the racialized divisions within U.S. nursing, their presence also signaled a shift in these parameters.

Rajan worked at Meharry in the late 1960s, at a moment when the arrival of foreign nurse *immigrants* in the United States had just begun. By the 1970s, it was clear that FNGs were, in one form or other, becoming a permanent feature in the division of labor. That their position would be distinct from those already in place was signaled by the confluence of licensing, credentialing, and immigration law that solidified around them, as outlined in chapter 6. What my interviews helped to further explain was the way in which the institutionalization of this separate status was also a process of racialization. A snippet of my conversation with Mrs. Parmar captures the complexity of the position that Indian nurses occupied in this regard: "When you work with black nurses, you are not black. You are not one of them because you consider yourself different. When you are with white nurses, they do not think you are black, but you are also not white."[25]

The quote makes clear that Indian nurses are neither African American nor white, while at the same time making evident the power dynamics inherent in U.S. nursing's black-white binary. Indian nurses get to name themselves as not African American and, as part of that process, move further up the occupational ladder than the majority of African American workers. In fact, the relative immobility of African American workers must be understood as part of the conditions of possibility for Indian nurses' advancement. At the same time, white nurses affirm Indian nurses as not African American while denying them full access to the privileges of whiteness. This back and forth renders the "lots of discrimination" that Mrs. Parmar emphasizes above as a multifaceted phenomenon, flowing both up and down the nursing hierarchy and positioning Indian nurses on both the perpetrating and receiving ends of racism. It also raises the following question: if Indian nurses are neither African American nor white, who/what are they within this racialized field? The answer that the nurses I interviewed gave me was: foreign. In fact, their descriptions of their workplace experiences help to flesh out what this status meant on the ground.

The particularities of this status as foreign cut across the specific job positions that they occupied throughout their individual and collective work histories. Indeed, it was the institutional fact of their foreignness that inducted them into work as nurses' aides and rendered some of their compatriots perpetually vulnerable employees. And it was the continued perception of them as foreign that characterized the resentment they received within the U.S. health care system. Again, Vasantha Daniel helps us to make the link. As one of the most credentialed nurses I interviewed, she described to me her postimmigration move away from the University of Washington as resentment about her presence there began to grow: "I think I was the first non-white faculty there. They had one black lady; only one mind you—in 1967. And then I was the other non-white . . . I was considered a very strict instructor but students appreciated the increased learning. These positive comments from students caused resentment in some of the other faculty members and that seemed to increase the resentment against me as a foreign faculty."[26]

Coworkers, subordinates, and supervisors were not the only ones to cast Indian nurses as "foreign" within the workplace. Patients did as well. All of the nurses I interviewed took great pride in patient care, with almost all of them citing it as the heart of their nursing practice. However, many of them also spoke to me of the racialized tension that cut into the care they have been able provide at U.S. hospitals. For instance, Ms. Dhas described how an elderly patient in one of the nursing homes where she worked didn't like her: "Some way she didn't like me, I noticed. So she said to me, 'You're a very good nurse, why don't you stay in your country?' See that means she didn't like me."[27]

Ms. Dhas's recollection is a reflection of the reality that the hospitals and nursing homes where the majority of FNGs find work are also centers where interactions between racialized minorities were the norm, not the exception. This exposed and implicated nurses to the realities of U.S. racism on multiple, interrelated levels. Aleyamma Eapen described to me how at one of the hospitals where she had worked, the emergency room did not operate on a first-come, first-serve basis. Instead, black patients were routinely, and as a matter of course, treated after white patients, regardless of the urgency of their need. It was within this context that she witnessed a young black man, about sixteen years of age, brought into the emergency room (ER), handcuffed, by six police officers. While being held captive thus, he was administered a new drug that the hospital was testing. The drug made him wildly violent, to the point where he was actually frothing at the mouth. Meanwhile, as she bore witness to such scenes (this was not recounted as an exceptional instance), Eapen was under pressure from the hospital's staff to file a report against her boss. The director of the ER, a white doctor, was addicted to prescription drugs. Everyone at the hospital knew. He abused drugs on every shift. Yet everybody was pressuring Eapen alone to report it, so that she would become the one responsible for whistleblowing. Under such pressure, Eapen couldn't take it anymore. She resigned, sold her home, and left Brooklyn: "I made up my mind that day. I will never take any position anywhere to do dirty work for others."[28] With this, the "dirty work" of nursing has shifted from the clearing of bedpans to being complicit in perpetuating racist violence and shielding racist privilege.

It must be said that despite the setup for conflict provided by the division of labor within nursing, explicit and implicit racism were not the only experiences that nurses described. There were also clear instances of appreciation and acknowledgment of the critical labor that Indian nurses provide in what often amount to underserved sectors of the nursing workforce and education sectors. For instance, at the same time that Vasantha Daniel described to me the growing resentment of her work at the University of Washington, she made clear that her strict standards had a very different reception when she shifted to a position at Bellevue Community College. At the time, in 1969, Bellevue's nursing program needed both state and national accreditation. It was her job, along with two other foreign nurses who were hired at the same time (one from Canada and one from Egypt), to bring the program up to speed. To this end, her years of experience and her high degree of education were seen as a boon, and her reception was much warmer and more welcoming. In Daniel's own estimation, "when they need something from you, they will embrace you," and it was this need that gave rise to her very different reception at Bellevue.

Nurses also made clear to me that learning to live with and through difference was part of their daily work. Significantly, this did not begin in the United States. Instead, as several nurses emphasized, it began when they entered nursing school. This was as true of those who went to school in India as those who entered programs in the United States. In both cases, nurses spoke to me of their exposure to difference through the diversity of their fellow students and their teachers. Aleyamma James told me of the culture shock she experienced when she first entered the BSc program at the College of Nursing, Delhi (CON-D): "It was a rude awakening to me because I was in a very close knit society back in Kerala, and I was transferred into this cosmopolitan setting. . . . It helped me grow as a person. I learned a lot of things about India and the world. We had students from all over India. We even had foreign students, mostly from Africa. We also had Indians who were based in South Africa. It was a very shocking idea to us you know. You are Indian but you cannot speak any Indian language. They were fluent in English and they wore Indian dress but they couldn't speak. . . . It was a learning process for me. It was not easy but it really shaped me."[29]

In James's case, it helped prepare her for her eventual emigration, which began with her employment in Iran helping to set up a new nursing school and went through her time in Kuwait, where she met and married her husband. She described their marriage as a do-it-yourself, multicultural affair, with all of their friends and coworkers taking part. "It was a combination of all of the cultures. I had Iranian, Filipino, Bangladeshi, Indian friends attending our marriage. So my Filipino friends and Iranian friends also wore saris. It was just . . . a beautiful thing."[30] It was with all of this experience working and living with people from all over the world that James arrived in New York and found employment in the education department of Coney Island Hospital. There she has developed and piloted cultural diversity training, in conjunction with the City University of New York, for staff and for refugees to the U.S. as prospective employees. When I asked her to explain to me what her training entailed, she replied, "It is based on my own personal perspective. In Kuwait my colleagues were from all over the world. I worked with Americans, Britishers, Filipinos, Nigerians, of course there were Indians, a few Libyans, a few from Arab countries, and other Europeans. So at that time I thought I knew everything about culture. Little did I know that I didn't know so much. After I came to Coney Island [Hospital] there are so many other people . . . Coney Island is like the United Nations. There are people from so many different countries. So I said this is a very good opportunity to share information and learn. The program I wrote up was geared toward employees and toward patients."[31]

As her explanation makes clear, Aleyamma James understands that dealing with difference entails understanding your own perspective and knowledge as always partial and incomplete. Her experiences around the world have helped her not only to admit difference but also to make working with it the center of her career. The map of her own work experience reminds us that nursing is multiracial and international around the world. It also helps us to connect the immigration of FNGs and the increasing diversity of U.S. nursing as part of this global picture. It is not, therefore, difference that is novel, so much as the specific meaning attributed to it. And in the United States, this meaning is not confined to the equation between "foreign" nurses and "cheaper" or "dangerous" labor, as articulated by U.S. nursing leaders and/or hospital administrators. Indian nurses, as immigrants and workers, offer definitions that redefine "foreign" as a contribution, collaboration, and form of belonging. Aleyamma James summarized it to me in this way: "I've always been in the majority. It's the same experience here [in the United States]. Even though I am a foreign nurse, I am in the majority."[32]

Aleyamma Eapen, James's colleague, extended this reframing of the "foreign." She did so through her "coming to America" story as recounted at the end of chapter 5. She also offered another telling incident from the ER room that she eventually quit because of its racist practices. She recalled how the waits in this hospital were long, given the number of patients needing care. A man, an "almost six-foot tall white guy," who had been waiting for longer than he thought was his due, eventually came storming into the ER and demanded to know who was in charge. When Eapen told him that she was, he shouted, "You are in charge? Go back to your own country!" To which she replied, "You first go back to your own country! I belong here. I am the Indian." When she told the story to me, she added, "I didn't say American Indian or the other Indian. I said, 'I am the Indian. You pushed us out first. You go out first. You go back and then I'll tell you when I have to go back.' I said, 'I belong here. You go back.' He just looked at me like. . . ."[33]

The end of the quotation is hard to capture because it was not verbal. The inference was that the man looked at her with fear, and rage, and . . .

like she was crazy. But Aleyamma Eapen's retort was meant to turn "crazy" on its head in order to remember, instead, the contours of this imperial nation. Immediately after telling me this story, she went on to explain the multiple theories that connect Native Americans and subcontinental Indians genetically. Her awareness of these connections extended to an engagement with the indigenous communities who inhabited, and inhabit, the land where she has made a home. When I first visited her home in Canarsie, she asked me if I knew whose land we were on before proceeding to pull out a collection of mementos and tokens she had received for making regular financial contributions to Native American organizations in Brooklyn and New York City. This whole episode of our conversation was imbued with a respect for Native Americans that she wished to pass on to me.

Who was schooling who? Eapen's insistence that "I am the Indian" turned normalized definitions of who is "American" on their head, invoking, instead, the link between genocide and this cradle of capitalism. As long as we stay on the level of founding myths, it's worth remembering that Christopher Columbus and his crew were in search of a trade route to China and India when they sailed the ocean blue. What they found was the Caribbean, and "Indians." Eapen's retort plays on concepts of "the Indian" in order to call out notions of belonging within normalized processes of European settler colonialism, conquest, genocide, and immigrant exclusion/restriction. Her engagement with indigenous communities is more than an act of solidarity. It explicitly crosses the lines that constitute immigrant as settler and indigenous as disappeared. With this conscious practice, she simultaneously claims and critiques the imperial nation.

# CHAPTER EIGHT

# Immigration and the Return of the "Woman Question"

Ani Mathew (not her real name) fell in love with her husband's hand-writing before she had ever met him. She saw it first when she was in her fourth year of nursing school in the North Indian state of Bihar. Like so many of the nurses I interviewed, she described to me how she had not, initially, wanted to go into nursing. Prohibitive fees and the priority of her brother's education had prevented her from becoming a teacher. She initially enrolled in secretarial school in her native Kerala and was busy taking typing courses when her cousin, who was already a nurse, urged her into the field. It took a while for Mathew to warm up to the work. Over the course of the four-year program, she met inspiring teachers and "started to enjoy it more and more. And the more enjoyment you get, the more patients will heal and then they admire you."[1] Mathew's growing appre-ciation of her occupation was soon clouded over by her father's increasing discomfort. His eldest daughter's entry into the field forced him to con-front what the work of nursing entailed: "My father was very upset about it, you know. He didn't want me to . . . he didn't know what I was doing in nursing. When he came to know that I was giving showers to the patients and taking all kinds of work—clinical work—he was so upset. But it didn't bother me. I knew it already, you know. He didn't even imagine what we were doing, so when he came to know a little bit about it he was getting upset. But it didn't bother me."[2]

Her father's discomfort apparently abated when he discovered that the opening of immigration to the United States offered him an opportunity to levy his daughter's occupation into the means for securing a socially sanctioned marriage. He accepted a proposal from a young man who was already in the United States on a soon-to-expire visa. Since there was no way to meet in person before the marriage, Mathew began a cautious cor-respondence with her suitor. It was then, when she saw his handwriting, that she decided that he couldn't be that bad. Her acquiescence was also prompted by the "bad reputation" that nurses had: "Even one of my aunts said that I am going to be a . . . that I am going to end up in a love marriage because I might end up with one of the, you know, like they talk, gossip. . . . So I decided I won't end up with a love marriage because I wanted to prove that nurses are not spoiled women. They can do good things, you know."[3]

On the Indian subcontinent, "love marriages" have a long history of association with "women on the loose." Love and romance do not necessarily conform to the strict endogamy that otherwise regulates the reproduction of caste and caste-like groups. Love marriages thus bear the mark of couples who somehow manage to make a potential break from the strictures of the caste, class, gender, and sexual norms that otherwise might constrain social and biological reproduction. This was the context within which Ani Mathew decided that it was a "good thing" to follow through on the match that her father had arranged. So, in 1974, she boarded a plane for New York City with nothing but a picture and a handwritten name with which to identify her fiancé. It was an arranged marriage in the extreme: "I was very shy and fearful. I had never been out of my house or nursing school and the local environment. I was never exposed to the outside world. But I had promised him, you know, that I will come and marry him. And through me I knew he was going to get a visa, so I didn't want to lose his visa. At the time I had that as a goal. I didn't even think about a job or anything, even though they were hiring nurses at that time."[4]

When Mathew disembarked at John F. Kennedy airport, she walked into a new role, a new life, and a new nation all at once. Unbeknownst to her and her husband, she also walked into a script where the parts had been played by generations of Asian immigrants before her. This had begun with the exception allowed to Chinese merchants within Chinese exclusion, but even more so within the terms of the 1908 Gentleman's Agreement negotiated between the United States and Japan.[5] Rather than outright exclusion, the Gentleman's Agreement terminated all labor immigration from Japan (and, by extension, Korea, as U.S. legislators deferred to Japanese colonization) but allowed for Japanese and Korean men already resident in the United States to send for their wives, children, and parents. Through this provision, many men arranged marriages with women from home and then sent for their wives to join them in the United States. Some of these women entered as "picture brides," women who, like Ani Mathew, had nothing but a photo and perhaps some letters to guide them to their husbands-to-be.

The phenomenon of "picture brides," or "mail-order brides" as they were sometimes also known as, legitimated the entry of otherwise excludable women on the basis of their status as wives, not workers. Their prearranged marriages ensured, or so it was assumed, that conjugal control would prevent them from posing the inherent danger to public health and morality that had cast Chinese women in particular, and Asian women in general, as threats to the sanctity of the white American family (understood as *the* reproductive and representative unit of the imperial nation). The stereotyping of Chinese women as de facto prostitutes had been critical to passage to the Page Law of 1875 and fed into the Chinese Exclusion Act that followed in 1882. It formed a central component of the multiple ways in which Asian exclusion emphasized gendered and sexualized constructions of deviance that then became central to the normalization of the white nuclear family. This occurred at a time when neither whiteness nor nuclear families had consolidated in ways that we would recognize from a post–World War II vantage point.

The ability for some Asian men to use family reunification provisions during the exclusion period highlighted how class status and/or the ability to conform to notions of gendered propriety were also avenues of permissibility.[6] Neither of these would have carried their weight without, first and foremost, the a priori legal power of men over their wives. This was rooted in the legacies of coverture, which positioned wives as subordinate to their husbands and vested all legal power in him, not her. In 1855, the U.S. Congress passed a law allowing for the naturalization of any woman who married a U.S. citizen, and until 1907, this law was used to also conversely deprive any U.S. citizen of her citizenship if she married an alien. That year, the Expatriation Act underscored this by explicitly expatriating a U.S. citizen woman marrying an alien. So strong was the notion that a man had the legal right to a wife who he represented in the full that family reunification for U.S. citizens and racially eligible legal permanent resident men was preserved even in the otherwise largely restricting Immigration Act of 1924. Even though the national origins system of 1924 became the centerpiece of U.S. immigration law two years after the Cable Act had granted citizen women independent legal status, family reunification provisions did not extend to women citizen sponsors until 1928, and women still lost their citizenship status if they married a racially ineligible citizen until 1934.

World War II provided context for the fortification of family reunification through immigration law, beginning with passage of the War Brides Act (WBA) of 1945. The act operated within the boundaries of racialized exclusion, so it denied legal entry to Asian spouses and minor children. This too, however, slowly began to lift alongside the institution of minimal quotas for Asians considered wartime allies. In 1946, Congress passed the

Chinese War Brides Act, which allowed U.S. citizen servicemen to sponsor their Chinese wives as nonquota immigrants. In 1947, the Solider Brides Act modified the WBA to temporarily lift the ban on Asian spouses (but not children), but it wasn't until 1950 that the WBA was officially extended, for two years, to cover all military spouses and minor children. Upon its expiration, Congress passed the 1952 Immigration and Nationality Act (McCarran-Walter), which lifted racialized exclusion and allowed Asian spouses and minor children to enter as nonquota immigrants.

Asian inclusion, piecemeal and partial as it was over these decades, privileged geopolitical considerations (wartime allies) *and* the heteropatriarchal conjugal family form already encoded in U.S. immigration law. It did so in a way that fortified the racialized exclusiveness of such family formation. Lawmakers assumed that the extension of nonquota military marriages to Asian spouses was a benefit for Asian Americans.[7] This assumption was backed by a legal landscape that had outlawed marriages across race since the founding of the imperial nation. Fully forty-one of fifty states had had anti-miscegenation regulations as law at some point during their history. All of these laws were meant to prohibit marriages between whites and a series of racialized "others." Coinciding with the period of Asian exclusion, most western and some plains and southern states explicitly banned marriages between whites and Asians. Significantly, the decade or so after World War II was when these were overturned, beginning with California in 1948. It was not until 1967, however, that the Supreme Court of the United States ruled, in *Loving v. Virginia*, against the fourteen southern states (plus Oklahoma) that continued to have anti-miscegenation laws prohibiting, primarily, marriages between whites and blacks. Their rationale explicitly posed the "right to marry" within a civil rights framework: "Marriage is one of the 'basic civil rights of man,' fundamental to our very existence and survival. . . . To deny this fundamental freedom on so unsupportable a basis as the racial classifications embodied in these statutes, classifications so directly subversive of the principle of equality at the heart of the Fourteenth Amendment, is surely to deprive all the State's citizens of liberty without due process of law. The Fourteenth Amendment requires that the freedom of choice to marry not be restricted by invidious racial discrimination. Under our Constitution, the freedom to marry, or not marry, a person of another race resides with the individual and cannot be infringed by the State."[8]

Ani Mathew's marriage took place after the 1965 Immigration and Nationality Act Amendments (Hart-Celler) replaced race-based exclusion and nation-based restriction with an immigration system centered on family reunification. The legal inclusion of Asians—including Indians— was not just a matter of needing more scientists and engineers for the space race or more physicians and nurses for the Veterans Administration, Medicare, and Medicaid. It was not simply a matter of staffing the capitalization of defense and health care. It was also a pivotal moment for reaffirming a particular family form—the conjugal, nuclear family and its gradated extensions—as the unit of belonging to the imperial nation. This was to prove as important to the form and function of Indian nurse immigration to the United States as nursing's inclusion in Hart-Celler's occupational preference quotas.

The Mathews unwittingly walked into the post–civil rights phase of this history on that day in JFK—with a crucial difference. Mathew's arranged marriage was not solely structured by her fiancé's emigration precedence, her father's matchmaking priorities, or even her own personal preferences. It was also underwritten by the second critical piece of paper that she held in her hand: a visa for her own legal employment and permanent residency. Her green card was what allowed both her husband and herself to stay and build their lives in the United States. Ironically, the degree to which this undercut the position of a "picture bride" was underscored by the way in which the legacy of coverture was retained in immigration law. In 1952, the McCarran-Walter Act formally changed "wife" to "spouse" within U.S. immigration law. However, it preserved the structural advantage of the sponsoring spouse in that it was this individual who retained full control over the legal status of the alien spouse until naturalization. This right remained intact through the 1965 Immigration and Nationality Act Amendments, which left sponsored spouses no avenue for self-petition. This set Hart-Celler apart from many of the other feminist gains that had followed the Cable Act, which by the 1960s had been largely rectified on the books. In this sense, the dominance that sponsoring immigrants retained stood as a distinct instance where coverture's legacy remained encoded in the law to the disadvantage of, primarily, women, and, increasingly, Third World women. Indian nurses and their Third World counterparts turned this supposition on its head, allowing us to read Ani Mathew's arrival as a scene of potential subversion rather than supposed subjection. It opens a window onto the world created by nurses who wielded their immigration preference to form families and build communities.

The role played by nurses in immigrant community formation was made clear to me during my interview with Mrs. Thannickal, a Keralite nurse who lives with her family in Brooklyn, New York. Mrs. Thannick-al's eldest sister was the first in her family to enter nursing and, as in so many of the cases I heard about, her entry into the field was something of a community scandal. However, soon after she earned her credentials, a hospital connection in India enabled Mrs. Thannickal's sister to immigrate to the United States. There she found a job and met a man who was also originally from Kerala. He became her husband, and she became an example that others in her community in India set out to emulate. Mrs. Thannickal's sister then turned to immigration law to bring as many of her brothers and sisters to the United States as possible. For this, the nursing shortage in New York City proved providential.

It was in this way that Mrs. Thannickal and another of her sisters first came to Brooklyn, New York, in order to attend a hospital diploma school. When they completed their course, both sisters immediately took the exam to practice as licensed practical nurse (LPNs) while they prepared for state certification as registered nurses (RNs). They were thus able to work their way up in the system due to the knowledge that their eldest sister had already gained. They also both got married to men from Kerala who were friends of their eldest sister's husband. All of the men were in the United States on student visas, in this case studying to be medical technicians: "They all came to study actually but a lot of them were not able to change their visa status, so a lot of them married nurses. A lot also brought nurses from back home and when they were here they got married."[9] In this way, whole communities of Indian (in this case Keralite, specifically) migrants adjusted their status nearly simultaneously to settle themselves in the United States.

We should be careful not to assume that immigration and labor market preference overturned patriarchal privilege within this immigration pattern. It was most often more complicated than that. One clear example of the potential complexity came across to me when I met with Mrs. Parmar in the Brooklyn home office of her insurance company. I had initially contacted Mrs. Parmar because she was the head of the Gujarati Christian Federation of NYC/USA, and I wanted to know the role that nurses had played in forming that particular regional Indian immigrant community in the United States. As it turned out, Mrs. Parmar was herself a nurse who had since segued into another career. Our conversation took place at a time when her community was under attack in Gujarat, as they too were among the religious minorities targeted in that state when it was under the governorship of Narendra Modi. Modi is a member of the

Bharitya Janata Party (BJP), which is the political branch of the "Sangh Parivar" or blood family of Hindu fundamentalists in India. Mrs. Parmar and her organization had helped raise consciousness around attacks on Gujarati Christians, and we met during the same year that Hindu fundamentalists conducted a pogrom targeting primarily Muslim Indians in that state.[10] This crisis, then, provided the context for her to tell a tale of belonging that began somewhat at the beginning, tracing the origins for me, first, of Christianity in that region of western India.

While her mother's family had been an Indian Christian for four generations (with ancestry that included an Irish great-grandfather), according to Mrs. Parmar the majority of Gujarati Christians can trace themselves back to the aftermath of a massive flood in 1927. By this time, her great-grandfather, a member of a "very Hindu" Patel family that had once been village head, had already been widowed and left with the care of his children. The flood proved to be the tipping point, and he had to drop the baby (Mrs. Parmar's grandfather) off with Methodist missionaries, promising to come back and claim him when things were better. At the mission, her grandfather joined hundreds of others who had been orphaned during the flood to be schooled and raised by the Methodists. Many of these orphans became missionaries themselves, and Mrs. Parmar described them as the "root" of her community.

Through his close association with Methodist missionaries, Mrs. Parmar's father first studied to be a compounder. Soon, a nursing school opened up around the corner, and he switched fields, becoming in Mrs. Parmar's estimation "the first male nurse in Gujarat."[11] His daughters followed in his footsteps, the eldest going to study at Vellore and Mrs. Parmar herself graduating with a BSc in nursing from the University of Bombay.[12] Both sisters initially returned to work in Gujarat, where they were among a mere handful of baccalaureate nurses. Mrs. Parmar soon got a job with the World Health Organization (WHO) and became a self-described modernizer, emphasizing public health and sanitation everywhere she went. She was so ahead of the curve that she updated her uniform to a miniskirt and wore purple lipstick, positioning her as "modern" or a "scandal" depending on who you asked. As she said to me, at the time, "Getting married was the least of my priorities."[13] Her exposure to international nursing through the WHO did, however, eventually implant in her the idea of getting a master's degree in the United States. Conveniently, her parents were able to make her a match with a man whose father was already a nurse in New York City. This was how she came to the United States, on a quest to upgrade her own qualifications but through social networks that were structured by marriage and men who were themselves nurses.

Mrs. Parmar's story is important for the ways in which it highlights how conversion and colonial medicine created spaces for multiple and overlapping renegotiations of gender and occupation. Indeed, it serves as a reminder of the Christian church and the genesis of Indian nurse migration. Raymond Williams's work is exemplary for revealing how a study of Indian Christian communities in the United States is also, largely, a study of Indian nurse im/migration. He outlines some of the ways in which priests, some of whom immigrated on the basis of their own vocation, also became key figures in enabling chain migration and supporting resettlement.[14] In my own research, I met the Reverend Sunder Devaprasad. He was introduced to me by Aleyamma Eapen. She described to me how he had helped her settle in Brooklyn and find a way to reunite, in the United States, with the man who she wanted to marry but who was still back in India. Eapen urged me to meet the reverend because he was a keeper of community history, and indeed he proceeded to introduce me to others of my interviewees.

Sheba Mariam George's ethnographic work in a Kerala Christian immigrant community also reveals the ways in which the husbands of nurses, in particular, have used the church as a location for the restitution of forms of power and authority that might otherwise be denied them within a pattern where many women remain the effective breadwinners.[15] The ramifications of her analysis confronted me when I attended a service at the Church of South India (CSI) in Queens. It was a scouting trip, and I was in search of nurses to interview for my project. This church attracted me because it was made up primarily of im/migrants from Hyderabad, in the southeastern state of Andhra Pradesh (which, as of 2014, has divided into the separate states of Telengana and Andhra Pradesh). It thus offered the possibility for regional variation in a recruiting process that most often led to nurses from Kerala. As the service concluded, I made my way among the crowd looking for an "in." I was immediately met by a man who clearly held some kind of leadership position within the congregation. I explained my purpose to him, and he responded that he himself was a nurse and that he would definitely help me. He gave me his contact information and rushed off to attend to more immediate church business.

This was not what I had expected, yet I was thrilled at the prospect of interviewing a male nurse. His story might provide further insight into the gendering of this immigration pattern. I called him a week or so later to describe my project in a bit more detail, explaining that I was conducting life history interviews, and that these usually began with the question of how a participant first entered nursing and how they then came to migrate. At this, his initial tone of enthusiasm, generosity, and acquiescence shut down, shifting to one of outright refusal: "Oh no, oh no! I won't do that." I explained that of course our interview would be a conversation, that he could refuse to answer any question he didn't like, and that he would have the right to review the transcript and ask that any portion of it not be published. He refused to budge. I then asked if there were other members of the congregation who he thought might be willing and/or able to participate. He hesitated and finally said that while many of the female members had been nurses in the past, most of them had since married and were now full-time housewives. When I insisted that this did not necessarily present a problem for my own research needs, he quipped that he did not think that he could offer me any further help. Our conversation was clearly over.

Freeze frame: domestic harmony reigns through the restoration of a gendered order of things. Women are in the patriarchal home, hidden from our view as anything but the spoken-for housewife. Men are in the lead as patriarchal providers for their resolutely heterosexual families. Men are also in control of community spaces, here the church. Through this, they control access to other members of the congregation and also, even especially, the community's image. In this image, women are not in the lead but in the background, dutifully playing their supporting roles as wives. Such an image recalls the negotiation of gender and class that was so central to the making of the Indian middle class under colonization, and to the professionalization of nursing vis-à-vis Florence Nightingale. In the latter example, women worked, but only inasmuch as it enabled a femininity that met the standards of a patriarchal middle-class morality. Indeed, it was the force of patriarchal authority that was communicated to me most adamantly in this exchange.

My interlocutor's admission that many of the congregation's women had in fact been nurses but no longer functioned as such played upon notions of women's wage work as secondary and/or temporary. It allowed for their labor to enable the movement to middle-class status and disappear in the face of its achievement. The realities of Indian nurse immigration, however, contrast with the implicit assertion of middle-class male authority. Instead, the admission that nurse immigrants and their families make up the CSI congregation leads to several solid assumptions. First, given that nursing remains, to this day, female dominated in the United States and India, it follows that nurse immigration has been as well. What is more, as stories such as that of Thankam Vellaringattu's night shift (recounted in the Introduction) illustrate, women's work does not necessarily diminish in importance over the course of immigrant resettlement. Instead, at best, it just disappears from view. Thus, what was hidden in the picture provided me of the CSI congregation was the centrality of both women workers and women's work to its creation. Such a suppression was not unique to this encounter but instead spoke to a broader anxiety surrounding the configuration of gender, class, and race in the settlement of Indian nurse families and communities in the United States. That this was the case was revealed to me at the beginning of the very first recorded interview I had with a nurse for this project.

The story Vasantha Daniel opened with was not entirely her own; it had been told to her by her friend Joe (not his real name). Joe was a former nurse recruiter and fellow member of the Indian immigrant community in the greater Seattle area. His tale took place in the early 1970s, the "golden years" for nurse immigration from India to the United States. Daniel explained to me that in the midst of the immigration frenzy, many nurses had difficulty navigating the set of professional test and job opportunities that had opened up, and so a business of nurse recruiting sprung up around them. Recruiters promised to take care of all of the paperwork and secure a job and a green card—all for a fee, of course. In many cases, nurses continued to pay off these fees while working in the United States. Joe's story concerned a young Indian nurse who had come to the United States at that time through the help of one such service. And as it turned out, her recruiter not only knew of a job—he also knew of a man in New Delhi who was also trying to come to the United States. So he approached our nameless nurse with a proposal—would she marry this man so that he could gain entry and then legal residency in the United States? The deal was that the marriage would be on paper only and that once her husband had free legal standing, she could divorce him and they could both be on their merry ways—no strings attached. In other words, it would be a typical green card marriage. The nurse agreed.

Things started to go awry after the marriage, when our nameless nurse refused to grant the divorce. As the story goes—the nurse had decided that she couldn't let go of her new husband because he was just too good looking! Unfortunately, her husband was not so smitten. As soon as he got his green card, he left her. But his wife did not let him go without a fight. She tracked him down, repeatedly, only to have him disappear again, repeatedly. Eventually, as Daniel explained, her husband just "didn't know what to do. He got so desperate. So he said, 'How am I going to get rid of this woman?' Then he joined the armed forces and he went away. But you know, she wouldn't keep quiet. She said, 'Well I'm not going to let him get off that easy!' So she somehow tracked him down through the recruiting office somewhere and reported to the armed services that here was her husband who had deserted her, hadn't written or contacted her for so many months or years or whatever . . . I don't know how the story ends. I told Joe to let me know, but I don't know."[16]

That's where Daniel's retelling ended, trailing off inconclusively, concealing as much as it revealed. Filtered through multiple narrators, the story's details are hard to pin down. What sort of obligation was the nurse under to her recruiter? To whom does she really appeal? How might the U.S. armed forces respond to the charge that one of its immigrant members had deserted his immigrant wife? Does the framework of military families carry any weight at this late date? And, ultimately—does our nurse get her man? Or, does he disappear, according to his own plan? We do not know. And in some ways, the facts are not what's at stake here. Instead, Joe's story is best understood as a tall tale, a fabulous fable made for the telling and retelling. And like every good fable, it has its moral. When told to and by nurse recruiters and/or male immigrants, it fairly screams: buyer beware! That nurse with the ticket to ride, she'll have your hide! Visions of the castrating female are front and center here, recalling characterizations of Asian women as the purveyors of social, moral, and physical decay dating back to nineteenth-century anti-Chinese movements. Daniel's own refusal and/or inability to give us the ending is the only mitigating factor. Her uncertainty opens up the possibility for multiple outcomes—including, possibly, happy ones.

Regardless of its ultimate ending, Joe's story provides clear evidence of the anxiety that attended gendered and sexualized relationships in this immigration pattern. Significantly, it was an anxiety not based solely on nurses' access to the U.S. labor market. It was also very much tied to their ability to access the family reunification provisions that are at the heart of Hart-Celler. It was precisely our anonymous nurse recruit's ability to access both that once again raised the specter of "women on the loose" and returned her through an anxiety over "women in the lead." "How am I going to get rid of this woman?" Indeed.

## The Kerala Conundrum

The anxiety over the female dominance characterizing nurse migration and settlement was not only expressed to me (however indirectly) through reference to male members of Indian nursing communities. It also came across in the words of Indian nurses themselves. Their stance on the stereotype of "women in the lead" was, overall, more ambivalent than castigating. This was understandable given the fact that they were, to one degree or another, talking about themselves and negotiating a negative stereotype at the same time. Given this, the most direct acknowledgment I heard from them regarding the stigmatization of Indian nurse immigrants proceeded through a process of "other"-ing. For instance, I heard comments such as these, offered to me by Ms. Dhas, a Tamilian Christian nurse immigrant: "See, actually, Tamils are very orthodox peoples. The husbands are very proud, and they don't allow their wives to work this job and that job and all this. . . . Among the Malayalees it's not that way. They say work two jobs and I'll look after the babies. Tamils don't want that. They'll beg and pray and say they'll work, you stay at home. They don't want some other men to look at their wife working and all. So they are very proud that way. For Malayalees, it's different. . . . They are rich also. They have money in Kerala. And Indians, Tamilians, have no money. Most of the time the men are educated and they do well, but still we want something more you know."[17]

With these remarks, Ms. Dhas simultaneously acknowledged and contributed to the discursive stigmatization of Indian nurses as both workers and wives. Indeed, she offered another context through which we can reread the story of Thankam and Tom Vellaringattu. In this interpretation, the night shift was not simply a solution to juggling a career and childcare. It also becomes the source of a stigmatization that attaches exclusively to Kerala nurses and Kerala nurse families/communities. These are the husbands who allow their wives to "work this job and that job and all this." And these are the families where the women are the primary earners, urged to take on more and more shifts by their husbands who stay at home and take care of the domestic duties. From her description, it would seem that this inversion of traditional gender roles is particular to this community, and therefore Kerala nurses are the ones who most accurately fit the stigmatization of "women in the lead." Tamilian Christians, however, are distinguished by their "orthodoxy," which here seems to translate most literally into their gender propriety. Tamilian Christian women are proper not only because they are married (a status that is assumed in her characterization) but also because their husbands would not allow them to engage in the publicly degrading work of nursing and/or earning the family's keep. They are thus primarily wives, not workers.

Ms. Dhas's comments were especially acute coming as they did from a woman who immigrated to the United States after she divorced her husband. She came to the United States as a single mother, and she was the one who sponsored her own two children as immigrants. There were signs in our interview that as a divorcé, she was marginalized within local Indian Christian churches, where conjugal families make up the dominant mode of belonging. She chose to mostly attend services in the Marble Hill neighborhood of New York City where she lived, the only Indian in an otherwise African American congregation. And yet, despite her own status as a successful independent single mother, Ms. Dhas spent a good portion of our conversation holding up marriage as something that should be done, at least once in a lifetime. In upholding the marital ideal for women, she echoed a sentiment I heard across my interviews, from all nurses, married, single, or divorced. At the same time, many of them made the message clear that they meant *this* kind of marriage, not *that*. "That" was laid onto Kerala nurses, who bore the brunt of the stigmatization of "women in the lead."

The fact that not all Indian nurses in the United States, or in my research sample, are from Kerala opened up a space for commentary among my interviewees. This was true primarily among nurses from different regions of India but also among nurses from Kerala who found other ways to distinguish themselves from the stereotype. References to "the" Kerala nurse migrant thus often functioned as a way for a particular participant to distance herself and/or her community from the stigmatization of Indian nurse immigrants. It allowed interviewees to say "not me/us, but them," while still somehow discussing Indian nurse migration in general. This was somewhat tricky terrain, for as I discerned through the details that emerged over the course of my interviews, nurse migration from all regions of India is female dominated. It was in this sense that I came to read Indian nurses' own characterizations of the gendered dynamics among Kerala nurse immigrant families and communities as, in part, a telescoping of a larger stigmatization. In this sense, it was as direct an address as I could hope to receive in light of this stereotype's ongoing effects.

The commentary I heard was not solely distancing and/or derogatory—but instead contradictory. Interviewees also found reasons to praise Kerala nurses, specifically. The following snippet of my conversation with Rajan, another Tamilian Christian nurse, enunciated this admiration explicitly:

RAJAN: Even though I come from Tamil Nadu, most of the nurses come from Kerala state. You didn't see a lot of Indians, I mean Tamilians, going into nursing. But now you see so many Tamilians going into nursing! The more they learn that education is more important, then they learn more about nursing. That's why it is, I think, that more people go to nursing now. Still Kerala is the one who gets lot of nurses but still. . . .

ME: Why do you think that so many nurses come from Kerala?

RAJAN: I think that if you go to the census you see that the most educated people live in Kerala. There I think there is a 90 percent literacy rate. Other states are not like that. I think that may be the reason, maybe. I don't know. That's what it seems to me.[18]

When Rajan listed education and near-total literacy, she referenced two of the key lynchpins that made Kerala a darling of development theorists during the very same decade when nurses began leaving the state. In 1975, the United Nations published "Poverty, Unemployment and Development Policy: A Case Study of Selected Issues with Reference to Kerala." The report had initially been issued by the Center for Development Studies in Trivandrum, Kerala, in 1970. It launched a series of investigations into what quickly came to be known as "the Kerala model." The model was characterized by the achievement of high indicators in key areas of social development: a low birth rate, low infant and maternal mortality rates, near-total adult literacy, and near-total access to adequate health care. Kerala outshone all of India, as well as most of the Third World, in all of these areas. What was most astonishing to observers was the fact that Kerala had achieved this without, depending on their angle of analysis, a red, green, or industrial revolution.[19] How had this happened, and what were its implications for other regions and countries of the Third World? Was this a model that could be replicated, or was it unique to the culture of Kerala?

My intention here is not a thorough investigation of the Kerala model as myth and/or reality. That is far beyond the scope of my present project. What I do want to focus on is how this discourse positioned nurses and nursing in particular and how this related to the ambivalent commentary surrounding what I have dubbed "women in the lead." There are several layers that need to at least be enumerated in order to do this. First was the way that the Kerala model appeared to turn the colonial "woman question" upside down. Material evidence for the high status of women manifested in terms of maternal and child welfare and birth rate and extended to observations that in Kerala, women outnumbered men, and female children had a lower mortality rate than male children. The contrast here was directly with parts of North India, characterized by the opposite in its most violent forms such as dowry deaths and female infanticide. The devaluation of "the" Indian woman in general contrasted with the evident elevation of "the" Kerala woman. Here explanations often lapse into a revisionist history, resorting to what Sharmila Sreekumar dubs a "nostalgic matriliny," one that conveniently forgets the arguments against a "degenerate matriliny," which won their final day in court in 1976.[20] Thus, at the very same time that matrilineal descent was legally abolished, Kerala's matrilineal past was invoked as a reason for women's higher status. The irony raises an eyebrow, at the very least.

"Degenerate matriliny" offers us one genealogy for the characterization of Kerala nurse immigrant families as "backwards," particularly in relation to uptake of the colonizing model of the heteropatriarchal nuclear family. In addition, and as outlined in chapter 5, the breakdown of matriliny was one reason that could compel some women into the world of waged work. Mrs. Iyengar of the Trivandrum School of Nursing seemed to be a case in point. Speculation that her status as a Nair woman might have made the public circulation inherent to paid nursing less of a taboo was undercut by what appeared to be a concomitant lack of respect, accompanied by the low pay that the state was notorious for.

Focusing on Mrs. Iyengar and matriliny could lead us astray, however, for nursing was still dominated by Kerala Christians, who were never matrilineal. Their family form, which was patriarchal, became what those arguing against matriliny (often professionalizing men from within the caste who were demanding a right to inheritance as well as a family form that fit with the colonial education they were receiving) aspired to. And here was where economics mattered. For part of what made Kerala so apparently miraculous was that high social indicators existed alongside high unemployment and low industrialization. These were the conditions under which the heteropatriarchal nuclear family could not fulfill the idealized roles of male breadwinner and unpaid female homemaker for the majority of Keralites.

If the need for income propelled some women to become nurses, nursing itself reminds us of the second lynchpin of Kerala's high social indicators: health. Some explanations of the widespread availability and accessibility of health care in Kerala may bring us back to Travancore's status as a "model princely state" positioned within a subcontinent dominated by British capitalist colonization. References to Kerala's enlightened royalty and their benevolent development of infrastructure for colonial medicine and vernacular education here became evidence for the region's "exceptional" entry into modernity.

There is much that is washed away if explanations are left here, including the politics of princely statehood and its relationship to both British rule and Christian missionary activity. Furthermore, when India gained independence from British rule in 1947, the princely state of Cochin joined the union immediately, but its neighbor Travancore did not. Instead, Dewan Iyengar declared Travancore independent on an "American model." His attempt at independence in a style that would invest the executive with power distinct from the British parliamentary system inherited by India came to naught. He was run out of the state, and in 1949, the state of Travancore-Cochin joined India. In the meantime, and not as a side note, the Communist Party of India (CPI) had made serious inroads into the Congress party, especially in Malabar but also in Travancore and Cochin. Their mobilization built upon the grassroots foundation established by the anticaste and caste-based organizations that had mobilized across Kerala since the late nineteenth century. Drawn, on one hand, from the ritually and economically dispossessed and, on the other, from those thrown into politics by the destabilization of matriliny, these organizations created a context for privileged and oppressed caste communists to work together. Elite communist leaders began in the Congress and Congress Socialist parties, while the working classes organized through industrial trade unions. By 1940, the Congress Socialist Party became the Communist Party of Kerala, whereupon it was illegalized for the next two years. During this time, it did not die so much as go underground.

Throughout the 1950s, Kerala was thus a model "problem state." The combination of ongoing radical mobilization and countervailing pressure from the central government of India created general political instability. One Congress-led state government after another collapsed, until finally in 1957, a Communist-led coalition won. It stayed in power only two years before the central government dismissed it, an act that helped to usher in an anti-Communist alliance. Notably, this was the same decade that the Rockefeller Foundation (RF) made its major investments in nursing in Kerala, especially in the years before the CPI took power. The political context is an added critical dimension for understanding the foundation's presence, and yet there is no explicit mention of the CPI or anti-Communist rhetoric in the archives that I have filed through. Instead, on the one side, there is the need for money and, on the other, the same characteristic elite focus and emphasis on expanding the RF's network.

The lack of an emphasis on Kerala's radical social movements in general, and communists in particular, was also characteristic of the broad strokes of the Kerala model, which tended to rely on notions of culture over and above political economy. Thus the proverbial elephant in the room was the political mobilization of vast numbers of Keralites through the anticaste and communist movements that dominated state politics throughout the twentieth century. Within the context of the Cold War, electoral communism crossed party lines, so to speak, and created the all too often unacknowledged question at the center of the Kerala model. In relation to health and education, as scholars have pointed out, evidence points to mass-based anticaste and communist mobilization as the key factor in spreading access to both health and adult education (the key producer of literacy statistics) across the state—not elite benevolence. In many ways, these were results achieved not because of, but in spite of, the state—even when Communist-led governments were in control (which they were, off and on, during the Cold War). This was for the simple reason that under colonization, the health and education systems were effectively for the elite and/or run by private institutions such as Christian missions. And after independence, the central government of India was utterly antagonistic to Communist rule in Kerala. The tenacity of people's movements is what emerges as reforms initiated under Communist-led governments were also passed under anti-Communist alliances, because the people continued to press for health care and education as their right.[21] The result was a relatively healthy and educated population—without enough jobs to go around.

Revisiting Susan George Arakal is also apropos here, for a key factor in Kerala's development was the role that outmigration in general, and Persian Gulf migration in particular, played in bringing up the bottom of an unstable economy. Nurses' prominence in Gulf migration was part of the background to how "the" Kerala nurse also became "the clinching figure" of the Kerala model.[22] Indeed, nurses could be seen to symbolize the emphases on women and health so central to the model and its modernity. At the same time, the contradictions at the model's core also serve as a dossier for the aura of ambivalence that surrounds "the" Kerala nurse. She is a model for the state, even as she increasingly lives outside of it. She stands for nostalgic *and* degenerate matriliny, elite-driven benevolence *and* mass-based demands for access to the indicators for social well-being, elected *and* suspected communism, a model "native state" *and* a problem postcolonial state, and what some may consider an oxymoron: "radical reform."

Cast in this light, "the" Kerala nurse embodies many of the contradictions at the heart of processes of decolonization as these took shape within an emerging Cold War global order. The fact that my interviews took place more than a decade after the fall of the Berlin Wall and the symbolic end of the Cold War added another layer to the ambivalences contained within my interviewee's comments. For by the dawn of the twenty-first century, emigration had become a preferred solution in many a nation, with remittances forming a major portion of the gross domestic product for large portions of the Global South. Returning to the comments of Ms. Dhas, when it came to wealth, it would seem that Kerala nurses and their families were in the more enviable positions. For while Tamilian Christians may keep their gender roles "straight," such orthodoxy apparently had limited cash value: "Most of the time the men are educated and they do well, but still we want something more you know." The statement served as part excuse and part explanation for the Tamilian Christian women who do work for wages—even if they are married and even if their husband is educated and has a respectable job. The assertion that Tamilian men are educated and "do well" distinguished them from the husbands of Kerala nurses, who continued to be haunted by shades of "degenerate matriliny" and/or "backwards conjugality" because of their presumed dependency on their wives' sponsorship and wages. The preservation of proper masculinity by Tamilian men was still not enough to secure their class status in sheer economic terms. They could not "protect" their wives from the world of wage work. The resulting crisis of the heteropatriarchal breadwinner was not unique to the men from Ms. Dhas's community. It was something they shared with the overwhelming majority of workers around the world, many of whom would also come to rely on women's access to the U.S. labor market as it restructured during the Cold War and under the aegis of American ascendancy.

Nursing exists on the high end of service sector employment, an area that expanded rapidly as the industrial jobs that had enabled the rise of a consolidated white American middle class left to take up shop in the decolonizing Third World. As the U.S. economy shifted toward the service sector, more and more of the jobs available consisted of often unregulated, and therefore highly exploitable, forms of "woman's work": domestic work, childcare, and the recurrence of supposedly outmoded and illegalized forms of sweatshop labor. This occurred alongside the continental shift within U.S. immigration. Thus, as immigration sources moved from Europe to the Third World, immigrant labor moved from primarily favoring men to increasingly seeking out women. Both of these shifts accompanied the retreat from the "golden years" of green cards and legal permanent residency and toward the proliferation of temporary work visas. The one area that remained open was family reunification. But this too began to be contested, leading up to passage of the Immigration Marriage Fraud Amendments (IMFA) of 1986. The IMFA provides me with a final focal point for examining the suspicion of "women in the lead" within the imperial nation.

## The Empire Strikes Back[23]

The IMFA passed within days of the Immigration Reform and Control Act of 1986 (IRCA). IRCA was the legislative response to an anti-immigrant surge that formed part of the post–civil rights rollback on the structural gains won during the 1960s. No longer cast explicitly in the language of race, anti-immigrant discourse shifted to framing the liberalization of immigration law as a source of illegality and illegitimacy. The most noted features of IRCA included its provision of amnesty and a pathway to citizenship for approximately two million unauthorized immigrants, the institution of sanctions on employers who were found to have hired unauthorized immigrants, and increased appropriations for border control and enforcement.[24] Among its efforts to stem the growth of an underground population of "illegal"[25] immigrants, IRCA extended public charge laws that had been on the books since 1882. The exclusion of immigrants "liable to become a public charge" had a long history of targeting single women, in particular. The assumption was that their lack of attachment to a male breadwinner positioned them as supplicants to the state. The fortification of this provision was but one step toward the IMFA, which expanded the focus of liability to include married women who immigrated, as well.

At stake in debates over the IMFA was the alleged abuse of spousal reunification's priority in post-1965 U.S. immigration law, a priority that had its origins in the attempt to rectify the nation-based quotas that had restricted southern and eastern European immigrants from 1924 to 1965. Lawmakers began by emphasizing the sanctity of the relationship between a man and his wife to the U.S. social and political order. It was this centrality that allowed family reunification in general, and spousal sponsorship in particular, such pride of place in immigration law.[26] What this meant in concrete terms was that alien spouses were not subject to the numerical limitations that curtailed the entry of labor immigrants. Before passage of the IMFA, spouses of U.S. citizens were granted the right of permanent legal residency (the green card) upon arrival and had to wait three years before applying for citizenship themselves. This distinguished them from other migrants in two key ways. One was that with the green card, they had no need for labor certification to find work once in the United States and could change employers at will. In addition, by the 1980s, the waits for other categories of immigrants were so long that the lack of a wait for a green card and the three-year wait for citizenship was far faster than other legal avenues. This combination raised fears that immigration via marriage was turning from a means for family reunification of Europe's unfairly excluded to a "cottage industry" channeling otherwise undesirable and excludable persons into the United States.[27]

The cure to the "underground economy" created by the abuse of this liberality in U.S. immigration law was not to eliminate spousal preferences but to distinguish between "good" and "bad" marriages. The former were recognized as a pillar of U.S. values and virtues; the latter were identified as threats to that same nation. As then Immigration and Naturalization Service (INS) Commissioner Alan C. Nelson made clear in his opening testimony, immigration marriage fraud was "not a victimless crime."[28] He argued instead that it was a crime that in all its incarnations placed U.S. citizens, not their alien spouses, at risk. This was the case when a "smooth talking alien"[29] convinced or conned a citizen into a marriage for immigration purposes *and* when a U.S. citizen knowingly sponsored a spouse for immigration purposes. In order to illustrate what pains such marriage fraud caused to U.S. citizens, Congress heard testimony from a panel of four individuals. While all of the panelists' testimony is rich with relevance, for my present purposes, the details of Ms. Amita Narielwala are the most immediately enlightening.

Senator Alan K. Simpson (R-WY) introduced Ms. Narielwala as a U.S. citizen of Indian origin. He noted that "in keeping with the common practice in India," her family arranged for her marriage to a young doctor who was still living in India.[30] The testimony then turned over to Ms. Narielwala, who described how she returned to her native Bombay in 1982 for her marriage. Two days later, the Indian consulate granted her new husband a U.S. visa. She continued:

Well, once we entered into the United States—he is a psychiatrist—his attitude, you know turned completely to be professional and he disregarded our personal life completely, went off to obtain a job in the United States. Then he left me in October, so we had been married 3 months. He left in October and in January, was the first time he called me, and let me know at that time that he had married me for a green card, and he had nothing—he did not want to have anything to do with me. After that, he has changed his address, and so I could not locate him, and we had to hire a sheriff who located him for us, and I delivered an annulment paper which was based on marriage fraud. The courts disregarded that, and I sent him divorce papers, which he disregarded.

And I have been to the INS, Senator Heinz, Senator—I have spoken to your committee. I have spoken to Congressmen Goodling. I have been to INS at least 50 times, putting in requests, asking them to look this matter over, and have had no results.[31]

Nothing in Ms. Narielwala's testimony indicated how she herself got her U.S. citizenship. We can, however, make several assumptions based on the available material. First, the fact that she is of Indian origin, that her parents remained in India, and that she appeared to have naturalized not through family reunification indicate that she was probably a labor immigrant herself. The arrangement of her marriage to an Indian doctor associates her story with the circuits of international and Indian medical migration and suggests that she too was possibly a medical immigrant herself. Given the time frame, the 1980s, the chances that she was either a female physician or nurse are high. In either case, she clearly fit the profile of a "woman in the lead." Indeed, the details of her postmarriage dilemma resonate strongly with those of the unnamed nurse in the tale that came to me via Vasantha Daniel and her friend the nurse recruiter, Joe. The primary difference is that in Joe's story, the nurse ostensibly knew what she was getting into while Ms. Narielwala did not.

At the end of her testimony, Senator Simpson asked Ms. Narielwala if there was anything else about her marriage that she would like to add, and the following exchange ensued:

MS. NARIELWALA: Sir, I did find a letter that he had written to his parents, and in the letter it basically stated—he had written it to his parents and was getting ready to mail it when I found it—and it stated that "I have married you to obtain a green card," or "I have married her to enter into this country, primarily as a doctor, and I am hoping to call all of my family here and build our empire." And so he will get his citizenship and bring his family here.

SENATOR SIMPSON: He said—those were the words he used in the letter, "to build the empire"?

MS. NARIELWALA: Yes, sir.

SENATOR SIMPSON: I think that sometimes American citizens also forget that a person using the legal immigration systems of the United States, and petitioning for relatives who are not in the United States, can bring in relatives as—I don't want to use the word remote but I will, because the American citizen, I think, thinks of a "cohesive family" or "nuclear family" as spouse and children, minor children; but to an Asian, it is the spouse, minor children, parents brothers, sisters, and we have a preference called the fifth preference, which is brothers and sisters of adult U.S. citizens. And I do think we have a recordholder in that area, one person who petitioned for 64 derivative relatives. That may be called building the empire I think, and indeed, it is real. But that is the essence of what he said?[32]

Somewhere during the course of Senator Simpson's speech at the end, it becomes clear that when he referred to "American citizens," he no longer included Ms. Narielwala, despite the fact that she was one. Instead, he made a clear distinction between "American" and "Asian" concepts of family and how the one was what the law was meant to uphold, and the other was how the law had been abused. When he stressed the word "empire," he invoked the long association within U.S. political culture of Asian immigration and fears of a "yellow peril," which in this case has been rendered a shade of brown by Ms. Narielwala's national origins. In yellow peril discourse, unattached Asian women were essentially prostitutes who morally and physically corrupted white men, and unattached Asian men were essentially out to morally and physically corrupt white women. Marriage altered, rather than eradicated, the threat. In the case of the Japanese families who were legally allowed to form in the early twentieth century, Japanese women's childbearing became an act of attempted colonization. And the rise of Chinese "paper sons" claiming birthright citizenship following the San Francisco earthquake of 1906 gave rise, concomitantly, to charges of fraudulent families. This set of associations reinforced the 1986 articulation of the danger of Asian family formation and its distinction from the "cohesive," "nuclear" family that lay at the core of both (white) American values and U.S. immigration law. Significantly, the "empire" was now channeled through Asian women who, being duped by their own husbands, became the channels through which their families propagated on U.S. soil as both workers and citizens. The former linked them to the charge of economic competition, the latter to the realm of the formerly excludable, which included not only those associated with illiteracy, mental retardation, tuberculosis, prostitution, and criminal convictions—but also Asians.

Senator Simpson's formulation turns on its head the work that South Asian community organizations have done to combat violence against women and sponsored spouses through family reunification law. As the work of Annanya Bhattacharjee outlines with utter clarity, the "private" space of the immigrant home (and indeed, the immigrant community) is actually constructed and constrained through state preferences. Bhattacharjee extends this analysis even further, noting that the bourgeois immigrant home is also a workplace for "other" immigrants: most often women performing undervalued and exploited forms of domestic work.[33] And yet, over the course of the exchange between Ms. Amita Narielwala and Senator Simpson, the question of victimhood shifted from the abandoned (and supplicating) Asian woman immigrant to the offended (and officiating) U.S. nation-state in a manner that resonated strongly with the history of racialized exclusion from the United States. In this sense, it was indicative of the tenor of the hearings. The testimony on record highlights, repeatedly, that individuals from Asia and/or the Middle East were the perpetrators of marriage fraud. According to the testimony, their marriages were not fueled by the love, devotion, and commitment at the core of the prototypical (white) American family but instead by the desire to settle in the United States. Aside from the motivation to take advantage of the resources and opportunities available in the United States, there was also the allegation that deviant marriage practices (such as bigamy) were actually constitutive of these "other" cultures. The charge of "bad marriages" as "un-American" thus came to be rather explicitly racialized over the course of the debates, with women (in the lead) being a particular vector for deviant social reproduction in the United States.

When the IMFA passed, it stipulated that immigrant spouses would receive a two-year conditional residence in the United States and that after that they could file for permanent residency (the green card), but that both the sponsoring and sponsored spouse had to apply. It thus strengthened the legacy of coverture outlined above to such a degree that it has had to be amended several times subsequently in order to prevent forms of domestic abuse that were, in effect, sanctioned by the law and suffered primarily by immigrant women. The IMFA also mandated the surprise investigation of applicant couples by immigration officials. Eithne Luibhéid writes, "The questions often include eliciting details about sexual practices; in this way, immigrant heterosexuality finds itself being inspected by the state."[34] Here, the demonization of primarily Third World immigrant sexuality took its place alongside "culture of poverty" arguments leveled against African Americans and Puerto Ricans, arguments that relied heavily on images of allegedly broken-because-female-dominated family forms—giving rise to images of black and brown "welfare queens" as a drain on U.S. society.

The IMFA helps us to reconsider the role played by the Asian American model minority stereotype within post–civil rights U.S. political culture. It was not simply a disciplinary tool of race and class, as scholars have so forcefully pointed out. It was also connected to both the making and remaking of anti-Asian discourse, understood as itself constitutive of normative U.S. culture and—even more specifically—as connected to the normalization of the white heteropatriarchal nuclear family as the central reproductive unit of the United States. It served this function at a time of renewed anxiety about the sanctity of that normative center. At this point, it's worth remembering that the Asian American model minority was not only a disciplinary tool against impoverished communities of color—it was also a disciplinary tool that worked against the mass entry of middle-class white women into the U.S. workforce, reminding them too of what a "good family" looked like. This was despite the fact that the Asian American model minority image also completely obscured the high workforce participation of Asian immigrant women themselves. The case of nursing is here especially relevant for the ways in which it straddles women's participation in the proliferation of skilled labor migration and the overall feminization of labor migration (especially, though not only, of the allegedly unskilled variety). The "problem" of Indian nurses as women in the lead thus offers us a window onto multiple, intersecting, and overlapping issues that lie at the core of social formation within the imperial nation.

# That Was the End of Marriage for Me

Subhashini was the last nurse I interviewed for this project. Born into the strictest of Marathi Brahmin families, she had been orphaned as a small baby and left in the care of her widowed grandmother. Orthodoxy had meant that her grandmother lived the life of a gendered ascetic. She shared space in her joint family with three other widows, all of whom maintained tonsured heads and only ever wore a simple maroon sari, without any additional adornments, not even a blouse. They were also without their own material means. As Subhashini explained it, her grandmother had once been wealthy, but her brother-in-law had denied her the bulk of her inheritance after her husband's death, leaving her with only a sack of silver vessels. Work outside the home was unthinkable. As a widow she practiced the strictest interdictions on contact within the family, let alone with outsiders. What was she to do with this small child?

As a solution, Subhashini's grandmother took up residence in the home of distant ("not even close") family in Pune. The head of their adopted household—"I will call him my uncle"—was a doctor. Subhashini grew up alongside his daughter, as a kind of elder sister. It was not an unhappy childhood. When the time came for college, Subhashini, like so many of my other interviewees, wanted to pursue medicine. Hers was a medical family, and it was a path her sister had also chosen. But being the dependent of a dependent and not wanting to inconvenience her uncle further, she made the radical move to become a nurse instead. Her choice was positively scandalous. The practice of nursing seemed to break every taboo that held her community together and kept them apart from others. It created a situation where she felt ex-communicated and accordingly kept her distance.

Within this context, the young Subhashini's entry into nursing could be read as a sign of the degree of her inherited dispossession, where loss of property could also be read as loss of propriety. However, Subhashini's story has another edge, and this was a "stubbornness" fueled by a fiercely independent streak. While still a student, she even found a way to get an allowance so that her grandmother could live with her in the nurses' quarters. Eventually, however, she had to leave that arrangement behind when and opportunity came up to work at the J. J. Hospital in Bombay. It was a big move to make on her own, into one of India's most prestigious medical institutions and one of its most massive metropolises. She took the risk, and before she knew it, she had become a head nurse in the pediatric ward there. Her success came with amorous attention. A doctor had fallen in love with her. Such a situation was, in her own description, fairly common. In fact, her suitor's mother and father had also met as doctor and nurse. He, in his turn, pursued Subhashini for three or four years, but when he eventually proposed, she said no. She described her refusal through an adherence to caste proscriptions, even after she had already crossed those lines with her career. First, this doctor was Gujarati, which meant, de facto, that he was of a different caste. Second, and more important to her, was her concern over what would happen to her grandmother if she got married. Her suitor had already made it clear to her that if she was his wife, she would no longer work for wages. He also promised that he would support her grandmother, but "somehow I thought he's saying it now but god forbid in case he stops. Then again she's [her grandmother] going to be a burden on these people, and I decided no this is not right. And one fine day I just took my decision that no matter what I cannot get married to this man because of these reasons and that was the end of my marriage part."[1]

This story, of how and why she never got married, was the first thing that Subhashini told me when we sat down to talk. The details came out in practiced succession, and the conclusion—"that was the end of my marriage part"—was declared with dramatic flair. No questions there. This contrasted with the slow and piecemeal way that her story of immigration unraveled. First, it was a trip to visit her sister who had already immigrated and was having her first child. Then, it was a rational decision made by a woman who was confirmed single and childless and who wanted to at least have the financial means to take care of herself as she grew older. Finally, it was a move she only felt comfortable making after her erstwhile suitor finally agreed to marry somebody else and start a family. Then, at long last, she could rest with a clean conscience that she hadn't ruined his life and could go on to make her own—abroad.

Subhashini's story takes us back to the beginning, when colonial nursing was first established on the Indian subcontinent. Then, orphans and widows were among colonial nursing's earliest recruits. Enforced widowhood was also a flashpoint for debates between Anglo-American colonists and the nascent Indian nationalist elite. These debates spilled over into the United States also, as Brahmin widows themselves became some of the earliest and most prominent Indians to migrate through the United States over the turn of the twentieth century. Parvati Athavale and Pandita Ramabai both toured the United States to publicize the plight of enforced widows, playing upon a theme that would be familiar to audiences attuned to the Anglo-American civilizing mission. Each of them, however, channeled this discourse to her own ends. Athavale called attention to the cause of Indian nationalism,[2] while Ramabai critiqued Hindu and male-dominated versions of middle-class nationalism through her own conversion to Christianity.[3] Ramabai's critique of brahmanical patriarchy also led to the publication of her book, *The High-Caste Hindu Woman*,[4] which inspired a movement on both sides of the Atlantic and included the formation of American Ramabai Societies across the United States. The funds raised allowed Ramabai to open schools and homes for gendered outcastes in India. During that same time period, her own relative, Anandibai Joshee, graduated from the Woman's Medical College in Pennsylvania. Joshee remains celebrated as the first Indian woman doctor (according to colonial qualifications) and one of the few who advanced through the medical circuits that otherwise privileged the colonial migration of white women. In addition, what distinguished Joshee was that she was married.

Moving almost a century forward, it is possible to read Subhashini's immigration as part of this lineage. Her story more closely finds a fit with the description of Dr. Rakhmabai as a "woman in the lead," whose refusal to get married to a man meant she remained a "woman on the loose." In this case, there was a way in which Subhashini specifically and purposefully inherited her grandmother's widowhood by remaining single so that she could continue to care for both of them. Her self-professedly "stubborn" independence has also affected her grandmother, who finally, in her last stages of life, broke with her caste orthodoxy. When her grandmother could no longer care for herself, Subhashini arranged for her to live in a small home with a Dalit woman as her caretaker. This supposedly "untouchable" woman, a single mother herself, became the orthodox widow's last refuge, and Subhashini has written it into her grandmother's will that the house will go to this caretaker when her grandmother passes. Thus it will be that her grandmother's inheritance of Subhashini's independent wealth will, in a sense, end by paying recompense to one who was cast aside by brahmanical patriarchy regardless of whether she was single, married, or a widow.

Subhashini's story after immigration takes us even further beyond the normative hold of patriarchal joint family structures and their caste, class, sexual, and gender norms. When she first moved to the United States, she lived with her sister but soon moved out by tapping into the network of Indian doctors and nurses from J. J. Hospital that had now relocated to the United States. She eventually ended up moving in with a Marathi doctor, also a single woman, and they lived together for over a decade. They soon became part of a group of five single Marathi medical women (Subhashini was the only nurse) who functioned as each other's chosen family. They got together regularly and even visited each other's biological families in India. Subhashini also spoke to me of how she and her roommate were constant hosts as their apartment became a refuge for many young medical interns first immigrating to the United States. With each one, she gained another addition to her family. When they left the apartment, she stayed involved in their lives. By the time of our interview her original roommate had since moved out of state, but they still visited regularly, and all five women have reunions with each other and their extended network regularly. Subhashini described to me how "all these kids were raised in front of me and they may not be my children but I have plenty of them. . . . They know everything about me and all my stories." They gather around her regularly and plead, "Tell me the story; tell me this story! But why didn't you get married—but tell me who dumped you?"[5]

The non-blood based homosocial network that Subhashini and her coterie of independent, "stubborn" women created speak to possibilities that lie outside of social reproduction viewed in strictly biological terms. It also lies largely outside of the archive as this was, in many ways, a matter of storytelling—and specifically which stories make it into the record. Here, in a reflection of my excavation of Salome, I am led back to the widowed, orphaned, divorced, oppressed, and dispossessed nurses who did not make it to the United States, or into the archives. With them in mind, Subhashini's name offers me an interesting ending. From the very beginning, and throughout our conversation, she described herself to me as a talker. Her stories were also clearly tried and true. And yet, she chose to opt for a pseudonym for the purposes of this project, for protection and in deference to the way in which pride and independence mix with a sense of shame of how her story departed from so many norms.

Many other nurses expressed to me the ways in which the interstices of immigration allowed them to renegotiate kinship and family ties, specifically around marriage. There were instances of divorce, delayed marriage, breaking with arranged marriages, pursuing love marriages, and choosing to remain single so that they could remain a resource to their natal families. These are stories that, in many cases, I cannot relate because they were specifically and explicitly "off the record." Thus, despite the fact that the archive can now more easily contain the voices of actual Indian nurses, it still houses silences that I learned to respect. Respect in this case means the recognition of silence as a chosen strategy, one not always reducible to the act of being silenced. Subhashini is a storyteller who, while in some critical ways constrained by dominant norms, also wanted to maintain a space for possibility—through a slippery kind of double-edged silence. While thinking of a name, she stopped, smiled, and said, "Why don't you call me Subhashini," which means, in Sanskrit, "well spoken."

# Notes

## Introduction

1. Melwani, "Clocking in Past Midnight," 28. "Im/migrant" is an inelegant but useful way of breaking up "immigrant" to represent the multiplicity of states that it encompasses. A seamless "immigrant" has a particular ideological narrative attached to it in a settler colony such as the United States. It implies permanent settlement, legality, and (a path to) citizenship. I use "immigrant" when it applies to the subject at hand either in fact or in aspiration as that aspiration is relevant to the point I'm discussing. "Im/migrant" is useful for capturing the boundaries between legality and nation-states that even those who eventually immigrate invariably navigate. When my usage is at its most capacious, I prefer "migrant."

2. The physician featured in the article is actually Sanjay Nigam, for whom the night shift was a step on the path to medical professionalization and the publication of his novel, *The Snake Charmer.*

3. Melwani, "Clocking in Past Midnight," 28.

4. In the United States, "middle class" is something of a catch-all phrase for the most valorized portion of the citizenry. In some sense, to be American is to be middle class, regardless of your actual income or financial net worth. In other words, there is a real degree of material imprecision as the term is the product of ideological overdetermination, and it is in relation to this that lifestyle, consumption patterns, kinship forms, and gender roles are so critical to one's identification as a member of the middle class.

5. "*Kuch kuch hota hai*" translates from Hindi, roughly, into "something happens," which commonly refers to the indescribable chemistry of attraction. It is also the title of a 1998 blockbuster Bollywood film and romantic comedy, so much so that to invoke the phrase is to invoke the movie and the kaleidoscopic visions of Bollywood-style love and romance. Vellaringattu clearly referenced the film and the Technicolor meaning of the phrase in our conversation. Author's interview with Thankam Vellaringattu, June 24, 2003.

6. Ibid.

7. Even as I invoke them, I am also wary of all the "firsts" here. In the sources I found, this is indeed how Dr. Swain appears, but this does not mean that there could not have been another who came before her but whose place in history has not been recorded in the same way. As I make clear in the pages that follow, so many of the categories of workers in these fields, particularly in the earliest years, do not appear in the archives.

8. The "first" here is in reference to the lineage of what we now know as biomedical nursing, not the forms of care work and care workers who have performed these and

related duties within the multiple and overlapping health care systems in use on the Indian subcontinent.

9. "Civilizing" is in quotes here because of its colonial assumptions about superiority and authority. I mark it off here as a sign of how I understand the term even as it remains without scare quotes throughout the rest of the book.

10. I conceived and began research for this book in the years just following September 11, 2001, when the United States launched a global "War on Terror" that included Great Britain as its staunchest ally. In this sense, the relationship of "junior partner" continued, albeit with the roles reversed.

11. I invoke "Third World" not to denote lesser but as a political formation pursuing decolonization. In other words, the Third World is the decolonizing world, and decolonization is understood as a task not yet accomplished but one imperiled also by processes of recolonization. Prashad, *The Darker Nations*.

12. There is a long lineage here, far too much for one citation. Some of the works influencing my own thought at present include Chakravarti, *Gendering Caste*; Davis, "Women and Capitalism"; Gibson-Graham, *The End of Capitalism (As We Knew It)*; Weeks, *The Problem with Work*; and Dalla Costa and James, *The Power of Women and the Subversion of the Community*.

13. My use of "brahmanical patriarchy" comes from Chakravarti, *Gendering Caste*. Chakravati coins the phrase to launch an intersectional analysis of caste, gender, and sexuality as they relate to the reproduction of brahmanical Hinduism.

14. My focus is on Protestant missions. For a related argument that focuses on government institutions, see the work of Madeleine Healey.

15. George, *When Women Come First*.

16. Under British-dominated colonization and prior to Indian independence/partition in 1947, "India" covered the present-day nation-states of India, Pakistan, and Bangladesh. So in this case, "India" is inclusive of migrants who were from regions of the subcontinent that are today Pakistan and Bangladesh, as many of them were.

17. Mazumdar, "What Happened to the Women?" Another article that helps us connect questions of gender between pre–World War II and post–World War II labor im/migration is Spivak, "Diasporas Old and New."

18. Sinha, *Specters of Mother India*; Nadkarni, *Eugenic Feminism*.

19. Williams, *The Tragedy of American Diplomacy*.

20. Brush, "The Rockefeller Agenda for American/Philippines Nursing Relations"; Ong and Azores, "The Migration and Incorporation of Filipino Nurses"; Choy, *Empire of Care*; Guevarra, *Marketing Dreams*.

21. Mohanty, *Feminism without Borders*. In particular, I draw on her definition of "Third World" that includes women from the geographical Third World as well as immigrant and indigenous women of color in the United States and Western Europe.

22. Omi and Winant, *Racial Formation in the United States*.

23. My argument is not dissimilar, in substance, from that made by Malcolm X when he outlines the relationship between segregation, integration, and separation: "The white man is more afraid of separation than he is of integration. Segregation means that he puts you away from him, but not far enough for you to be out of his ju-

risdiction; separation means you're gone. And the white man will integrate faster than he will let you separate." Malcolm X, "The Ballot or the Bullet," 42.

24. There is by now a fairly extensive literature on this transformation. Examples that influence my analysis include Jacobsen, *Whiteness of a Different Color*; Roediger, *Working toward Whiteness*; and Guglielmo, *Living the Revolution*.

25. Leonard-Spark and Saran, "The Indian Immigrant in America"; Liu, "The Contours of Asian Professional, Technical and Kindred Work Immigration"; and Daniels, "United States Policy towards Asian Immigrants."

26. Prashad, *Karma of Brown Folk*.

27. There are several possible reasons for this lack. First, the government of India did not keep records for nurse emigration during the period under investigation. Further complicating this is the fact that many Keralite nurses actually take part in a process of step-migration that might include several locations (such as the Persian Gulf, Australasia, the United Kingdom, and continental Europe) before the United States. And finally, the United States does not keep immigration records that would differentiate Indian nurses along the axes of religion or region in a clear or consistent manner. It is against this background that I proceed by stating that Kerala Christian nurses have come to overwhelmingly represent Indian nurses in the United States.

28. The literature here is vast. Some of the key pieces that produced this discourse include Glazer and Moynihan, *Beyond the Melting Pot*; Handlin, *The Newcomers*; Lewis, *La Vida*; and United States Department of Labor, Office of Policy and Planning and Research, *The Negro Family: The Case for National Action*. A work that expands our understanding of the relationship between U.S. Empire and culture of poverty discourse is Briggs, *Reproducing Empire*.

*Chapter One*

1. Abraham, *Religion, Caste and Gender*, 3.

2. I put "civilizing" in quotes to contest the assumption of cultural superiority.

3. Pathak, *American Missionaries and Hinduism*, 183. Unless otherwise noted, my references are to Protestant missions.

4. This was earlier than they arrived in either China (in the 1830s) or Japan (in the late 1850s).

5. Pathak, *American Missionaries and Hinduism*, 25.

6. Ibid., 241.

7. Singh, *Gender, Religion, and "Heathen Lands,"* 108.

8. Petty, *Laymen's Foreign Missions Inquiry*, as cited in Pathak, *American Missionaries and Hinduism*, 247.

9. In relation to India, the British ruling classes set up a three-tiered structure that included the imperial government in London, the central government in Calcutta, and then the provincial governments in the presidencies and provinces. When I say "British government" or "colonial government" without qualification, I am referring to this structure in total. When and where it is necessary, I will be more specific.

10. Pati, "Historians and Historiography"; Robb, "On the Rebellion of 1857"; Wagner, "The Marginal Mutiny."

11. Ramasubban, "Imperial Health Policy in British India"; and Arnold, *Coloniz-ing the Body.*

12. "Medical Side of Mission Work."

13. Heideman, *From Mission to Church.*

14. *Woman's Work for Woman* was a journal published by the Woman's Foreign Missionary Society of the Presbyterian Church from 1871–85. It eventually merged with another and continued publication under the name *Woman's Work* to 1905. "Woman's work for woman," however, was also a general descriptive for the missionary call among woman's foreign missionary societies during this period, and it is in this more general sense that I invoke the phrase. The fact that the woman's foreign mission society movement was motivated by such sentiments is made evident in the names of other journals of the period, including *Heathen Woman's Friend* (later *Woman's Missionary Friend*), Woman's Foreign Missionary Society of the Methodist Episcopal Church; and *Life and Light for Heathen Women* (later *Life and Light for Woman*), Woman's Board of Missions, Congregational.

15. In my research, I encountered two different sources for this request. Singh and Hoskins identify Mrs. D. W. Thomas's letter as the source of the appeal. However, Pathak cites Pandit Nandkishore, "an educated Brahmin of Nainital," as the source of the appeal. According to Pathak, Pandit Nandkishore had opened a school for train-ing nine Indian girls in midwifery. He then sent a request to the WMC for a female medical doctor, and this produced Dr. Swain. I have chosen to highlight Singh's ver-sion because she cites specific letters, whereas Pathak cites a missionary history writ-ten again by someone else. However, the possibility that an appeal also came from Pandit Nandkishore or that certain missionaries would reference such a figure as in-terested in medical education for Indian girls is suggestive, primarily, of the elite bias of the missionary mind. On the other hand, while it would have been a little pre-cocious, certainly by the late nineteenth century, many elite Indians also took up the cause of women's education and, to a lesser degree, medical training. However, their efforts were meant to offer alternatives to mission institutions, so it seems a bit odd that they would in this instance also appeal to them. In any case, historical anoma-lies/particularities do indeed exist and are always entirely plausible of their own ac-cord. In this sense, the matter requires further investigation.

16. Isabella Thoburn was a teacher. The arrival of both women together was a sign of the professionalization and feminization of mission work vis-à-vis the large-scale embrace of service work and institution building. Thoburn would go on to found what grew into the Isabella Thoburn College in Lucknow.

17. I have record of at least two more U.S.-based single female medical missionar-ies arriving in India before Dr. Butler: Dr. Sara Seward in 1871 and Dr. Sarah Norris in 1873. Balfour and Young, *The Work of Medical Women in India.*

18. Hill, *The World Their Household.*

19. For example, Pietzman, *A New and Untried Course.*

20. Pruitt, "*A Looking-Glass for Ladies.*"

21. Hill, *The World Their Household.*

22. Pruitt, "*A Looking Glass for Ladies.*"

23. Montgomery, *Western Women in Eastern Lands*. Montgomery's book was part of the educational curriculum launched by the United Study of Foreign Missions, which was an interdenominational women's group operating at the time. It sold 50,000 copies in its first six weeks of publication and 100,000 in its first year. It detailed the lives of Muslim women, Chinese women, and Hindu women. Publication statistics taken from Pruitt, *"A Looking Glass for Ladies."*

24. While my focus here is on the prominence of Protestant mission literature within U.S. public culture, we should not lose sight of its role in India. For instance, in 1842, U.S. missionaries launched the Anglo-Marathi publication *Dyanodaya* (the Rise of Knowledge), which went on to become one of the most successful publications in the nineteenth century. O'Hanlon, *Caste, Conflict and Ideology*.

25. This abbreviated name is not mine but is in fact the name used for this institution in India and among Indians in the diaspora. The fact that it subsumes the name of the whole town speaks to the dominance of the institution locally, as well as nationally and globally.

26. Jeffery, *Ida S. Scudder of Vellore*, 27.

27. Zenana evangelism began with a focus on North India but came to encompass the subcontinent in a way that spoke more to the currency of the term in the colonial/missionary imagination than an accurate description of a range of practices that varied by region and religion. It is certainly a valid question to what degree these practices existed in the Arcot district, a distinctly South Indian location. These details, while important, are not sufficient for understanding the impact of a story with such wide circulation. Its generalizations were critical to its role as a fundraising tool.

28. Viswanathan, *Outside the Fold*.

29. Pruitt, *"A Looking Glass for Ladies."*

30. Semple, *Missionary Women*. Furthermore, due to the nature of their work, missionaries most often lived among local Indian populations. This spatial proximity contrasted with the spatial segregation practiced by members of the colonial bureaucracy and army, who lived in separated cantonments/quarters. Missionaries thus had to find other ways to mark their boundaries/hierarchical difference from Indians.

31. Marriage was seen as a loss by sponsoring societies, as the women's work had to resume its unpaid status when the worker became a wife. In some cases, there were actually penalties imposed on single female missionaries who wanted to marry while working. In the rare instances where women's missionary societies considered paying mission wives, they agreed that they would cover only the amount of the supplement that male missionaries received when they were married, to provide for their families. For more on this in the United Kingdom, see Semple, *Missionary Women*, and for the United States, Singh, *Gender, Religion, and "Heathen Lands,"* and Hill, *The World Their Household*.

32. This move coincided with a period of "Hindu revivalism" and the growth of Hindu tract societies, as described by Jared Scudder of the Arcot mission. Heideman, *From Mission to Church*.

33. Ibid.

34. The London School of Medicine for Women opened in 1874. It too had strong ties to missionaries and medical missionary work.

35. The connection between women's medical and missionary work was made early in the career of the college. In 1851, Sarah Hale, editor of *Godey's Lady's Book* (one of the most popular women's magazines of its time), founded the Ladies Medical Missionary Society (LMMS) in conjunction with the WMC. The LMMS folded shortly after its formation; however, if Hale's efforts were premature, they were also prescient. In *A New and Untried Course*, Pietzman cites an interview he conducted with Marion Fay, former dean and president of the WMC, where she estimates that at least 230 graduates, among them Clara Swain, went abroad. Much of this occurred under the leadership of Rachel Bodley, who in particular encouraged medical missionary work. She was the host of Anandibai Joshee, the first Indian woman to study medicine in the United States. Joshee arrived at the WMC in 1883, graduating three years later. She died shortly after returning to India, so never got to take up her medical practice. For a contemporaneous account of her migration, see Dall, *The Life of Dr. Anandabai Joshee*. For analyses of her historical presence, see Chakravarti, *Rewriting History*, and Kosambi, "Anandibai Joshee."

36. Scudder, "Western Women in Exotic Countries," August 1931, p. 4, Scudder Papers, Radcliffe Archives, MC 205, Box 3, Folder 100, Schlesinger Library.

37. This went against the general principle that the mission had of renouncing caste as part of the process of conversion. It also proved difficult in that it was rooted in an understanding of conversion as a wholesale renunciation of not only religious beliefs but also of cultural practices that exceeded (or were not wholly contained) by the sphere of religion alone. For instance, at the end of the century, a controversy arose about whether or not converts had to cut off their *kudumi*, or top knot, which was a mark of caste. The missionaries held a full-scale debate about this, after which it was decided that the decision about whether or not one had to remove this during conversion was left open but that it had to be removed if the convert was to be employed by the mission. Heideman, *From Mission to Church*.

38. Scudder, "Picture the Home Life in India," Scudder Papers, Radcliffe Archives, MC 205, Box 3, Folder 100, Schlesinger Library.

39. Ibid.

40. Walsh, *Domesticity in Colonial India*.

41. Joshi, *The Middle Class in Colonial India* and *Fractured Modernity*.

42. It's necessary to mention both caste and class because of the way in which neither one is, on its own, fully descriptive of combined material and symbolic (status-based) privilege. For instance, many Brahmans were impoverished and worked for others in order to get by. In this case, their symbolic status compensated for their lack of material privilege in a way that it did not for the oppressed castes. Alternately, many of those who would have qualified as "middle class" were not necessarily from the most privileged castes (although, it should be noted, they were also not from the most oppressed) even as they accrued material and symbolic privilege.

43. Joshi, *The Middle Class in Colonial India*, xviii.

44. The marquis used numbers to a very different end than I am: "Consequently, it may be said that, out of a population of 200 millions, there are only a very few thou-

sands who may be considered to possess adequate qualifications, so far as education and an acquaintance with Western ideas or even Eastern learning are concerned, for taking an intelligent view of those intricate and complicated economic and political questions affecting the destinies of so many millions of men which are almost daily being presented for the consideration of the Government of India. (Applause.) I would as, then, how any reasonable man could imagine that the British Government would be content to allow this *microscopic minority* to control their administration of that majestic and multiform empire for whose safety and welfare they are responsible in the eyes of God and before the face of civilization? (Cheers.)" (emphasis added). "A Speech at St. Andrew's Dinner," as cited in Joshi, *The Middle Class in Colonial India*, 7.

45. Practices such as sati were also part of the "colonial phantasm" that produced the zenana. This is not to say that widow immolation did not exist but that colonial debates around it actually augmented the practice, giving it more life and reality than it had had beforehand, and publicizing it in a way that made it subsequently more central to "brahmanization" (the making and remaking of caste privilege).

46. Sreenivas, *Wives, Widows, Concubines*.

47. Chatterjee, "The Nationalist Resolution of the Woman Question," 233–53.

48. Here, Rosalind O'Hanlon reminds us, "Partha Chatterjee has seen these emerging divisions between public and private, politics and the purely 'social' domains of family, custom and religion, as an effective way of resisting colonial intervention. . . . On another reading, though, it may well have been that just the reverse was true. For what is striking is actually the broad degree of consensus between Indian politicians and the colonial state, established early in the nineteenth century, and reinforced in the years after the wars of 1857, that for all routine civil purposes domestic and family questions were outside the purview of the state, except in so far as it was necessary to 'administer' the appropriate community and religious law." O'Hanlon, *A Comparison between Women and Men*, 51.

This reminder is especially apt as I move on to compare the mobility of single female medical missionaries and middle-class Indian men. Protestant missions, while pursuing projects that were at times at odds with the colonial state, also were ultimately there because the state allowed them to be, legally.

49. Bannerjee, "Projects of Hegemony." Bannerjee also draws attention to the way in which Chatterjee evades a material (class) analysis for a solely discursive one.

50. Mani, *Contentious Traditions*.

51. Rozario and Samuels, *Daughters of Hariti*; Van Hollen, *Birth on the Threshold*; Forbes, "Managing Midwifery in India," in *Women in Colonial India*, 79–100; Lang, "Drop the Demon *Dai*," 357–78.

*Chapter Two*

1. *"A Pageant Depicting the History of the Christian Medical College Hospital and The School of Nursing" for the Golden Jubilee of Vellore's School of Nursing (1909–1959) and the Diamond Jubilee of Its Mission Hospital (1900–1960)*, Scudder Papers, Radcliffe Archives, MC 205, Box 3, Folder 140, Schlesinger Library.

2. The *Pageant* specifically instructs the announcer to acknowledge McGraw-Hill Book Company for permission to use material from Dorothy Clarke Wilson's book "DR IDA." This is a reference to Wilson, *Dr. Ida*. I also found similar scenes throughout the archival material produced by Dr. Ida Scudder and her colleagues in the institution's archives and other books from the time period.

3. So, for instance, the *Christian Medical College Vellore School of Nursing Announcement (1946–1947)* drops her from the institution's standard history. This was precisely the moment when Vellore opened a university-based nursing degree program. *The Christian Medical College Vellore School of Nursing Announcement (1946–1947)*, Scudder Papers, Radcliffe Archives, MC 205, Box 3, Folder 125, Schlesinger Library.

4. While this is largely undocumented or partially documented terrain, a clear boundary to my current effort is that I am limited to English-language source material. In my own research, I have found trails that lead to Indian-language sources that I could not read but that I do hope future research incorporates into our growing sense of the history of Indian nursing. Some of the sources I have found that allude to the presence of Indian nurses in the archive for the period when India was under British colonial domination include the mention of a Dalit nurse who spoke at the All India Women's Conference in 1920. The source is in Tamil (Moon and Pawar, "We Made History, Too"). Also, the Christian Medical Association of India's Nurses' Auxiliary started vernacular "Auxiliary News Sheets" for Indian nurses. In 1934, they began in six different Indian languages with the intention of publishing every two months. The issues of the *Journal of the Christian Medical Association of India* that I reviewed make clear that these vernacular sheets were sometimes more successful than the English-language news, especially those in Telugu and Tamil. By the 1930s, when these were published and circulated, there were enough Indians with some degree of hospital training who worked as nurses to sustain them. Salome and the proto-nurses/assistants/helpers that she stands in for do not seem to have had organizations like these.

5. *Pageant*, 51–52.

6. Whether or not she was a recent convert is, however, less clear. Roman Catholic Protestant missionaries had been in the area of the Arcot mission since the beginning of the sixteenth century. At the time, there were mass conversions to Roman Catholicism among the Paravas (a fishing community) in the deep south of present-day Tamil Nadu. Later in that same century, after these missionaries had left, Francis Xavier, a Jesuit, also came to work among them as he made his way from Goa, on India's west coast, to China. He started a chain of Jesuits in the area into the eighteenth century. The Portuguese presence in the area also created a population of mixed Portuguese-Indian descendants. The first Protestant missionary to India arrived in 1706 and settled at the Danish trading port of Tranquebar (present-day Tharandambadi). Other Protestant missionaries from Germany and Denmark followed. Heideman, *From Mission to Church*.

Nothing in the literature indicates Salome's background enough to know her relation to this history, although her proximity to the mission might suggest that she was a more recent convert.

7. Heideman states that 90 percent of Christians at the Arcot mission were Dalits. He has no citation for this, however, so it's unclear to me how he came up with this number. Heideman, *From Mission to Church*, 31.

In Dr. Clara Swain's letters, I found reference to a similar figure, Rebecca Gowen, more often described as "my faithful Rebecca." Similar to Salome, we know next to nothing about Rebecca except that she was Dr. Swain's primary and invaluable first assistant. When Dr. Swain had to temporarily leave her station for travel, she left Rebecca in charge, yet Rebecca does not seem to have been one of her students who was studying to become a medical practitioner herself. Swain, *A Glimpse of India*.

8. Roman Catholic missions had been providing education for Indians for two hundred years by the time of the Tranquebar mission, but their efforts were aimed at boys and men. Brockway, *A Larger Way for Women*.

9. The problem this posed for Christian converts was actually addressed within colonial law, through passage of the 1850 Caste Disabilities Removal Act. The act explicitly restored to converts property rights, but not the position they had formerly occupied in caste society. Viswanathan, *Outside the Fold*.

10. So, for example, the Church Missionary Society in Punjab created grades of schools for students according to societal rank in order to provide what it considered an appropriate education for each segment of society and to prevent "unseemly" upward mobility.

11. *Pageant*, 54.

12. Ibid.

13. This was also often the role of Indian Bible women. Kent, "Tamil Bible Women."

14. *Pageant*, 54.

15. Ambedkar, "Annihilation of Caste," 233.

16. Another relevant figure here was Pandita Ramabai, whose work I return to in the Epilogue.

17. Phule, "Memorial Addressed to the Education Commission 19 October 1882."

18. Dickens, *Martin Chuzzlewit*.

19. Roughly speaking, the Crimean War was fought between 1853 and 1856 and pit the Russian Empire against a combination of forces from the French Empire, the British Empire, the Ottoman Empire, and the Kingdom of Sardinia.

20. Nightingale, *Notes on Nursing*.

21. This division had origins in medieval Europe, during the centuries-long "witch craze" that demonized and decimated the population of female European lay healers and midwives. There is an expansive literature on the "witch hunts," which I do not cite here. I base my connections on Ehrenreich and English, *Witches, Midwives and Nurses*; Mies, *Patriarchy and Accumulation on a World Scale*; and Federici, *Caliban and the Witch*. Ehrenreich and English estimate that women made up 85 percent of those executed in the four-centuries-long witch hunts (8). The majority of these were women who used their knowledge to procure a living for themselves and their dependents. In this sense, their demonization was also, specifically, their dispossession in what scholars have characterized as a pogrom against poor women that went hand in hand with the rise of what has become biomedicine.

22. Nightingale, "Institution of Kaiserwerth" (1851), as cited in Gamarnikow, "Sexual Division of Labour," 112.

23. Gourlay, *Florence Nightingale and the Health of the Raj.*

24. Amott and Matthaei, *Race, Gender, and Work.*

25. Fitzgerald, "Making and Moulding the Nursing of the Indian Empire," 189.

26. An Anglo-Indian is someone of mixed British and Indian ancestry. It was a designation bequeathed paternally, so in order to be officially Anglo-Indian, one's father had to be British. Needless to say, at the time "British" equaled white.

27. Dr. Ida's mother, Sophia Weld Scudder, descended from an elite Southern U.S. family whose wealth was based on the enslavement of Africans and a plantation economy. Sophia Weld's father did legally free those enslaved on his plantation before the Emancipation Proclamation.

28. Fitzgerald, "Making and Moulding the Nursing of the Indian Empire," 188.

29. Nursing scholar Madeleine Healey argues that the wages and working conditions endured by Indian nurses were dirty and dangerous. She focuses on the failures of the colonial state to give any importance to Indian nursing and how this failure rubbed off on nurses, not the state. She emphasizes the ways in which colonial politicians evaded responsibility for their inattention by blaming Indian custom and caste. The majority of nurses working for government institutions were not, however, Indian. The Indians who worked as nurses generally worked at missions, where the pay was even worse if the working conditions were slightly better. Healey, "Regarded, Paid, and Housed as Menials."

30. First it was the American Society for the Superintendents of Training Schools for Nurses in the United States and Canada, which soon became the National League of Nursing Education (NLNE). In 1896, the NLNE gave birth to the Nurses Alumnae Association of the United States and Canada.

31. TNAI became the sole name of the joint organization in 1922.

32. Carnegie, *The Path We Tread.*

33. In 1885, Richards helped to establish Japan's first nurse training program at Doshisha Hospital in Kyoto. For more on Mahoney see Miller, *Mary Eliza Mahoney.*

34. Stockton, *Betsey Stockton's Journal*; Moffett, "Betsey Stockton"; Johnson, "Undaunted Courage and Faith."

35. Kinnlingray, "The Black Atlantic Missionary Movement and Africa."

36. Swain, *A Glimpse of India.*

37. Smith, *An Autobiography* (emphasis in the original).

38. The Colonial Nursing Association preceded both of these organizations. It was established in London in 1894, although it had no formal agreement with the India Office and therefore rarely sent nurses there.

39. Nutting and Dock, *A History of Nursing*, and Tooley, *The History of Nursing in the British Empire.*

40. For a long history of the ICN, see Brush et al., *Nurses of All Nations.*

41. Fitzgerald, "Making and Moulding the Nursing of the Indian Empire."

42. Significantly, this was after nurse registration had already begun in Britain's colonies. The first nursing registration act passed in the British Empire was in the Cape Colony, in 1891.

43. The minimum age decided upon was eighteen. Students were to be taught and take exams in the vernacular, with some instruction in English as well. The recommended training period was three years, with the first year consisting of basic nursing, bandaging, feeding of patients, and simple invalid cookery; the second year was for more advanced nursing and hygiene; and the third for midwifery and gynecology. Abraham, *Religion, Caste and Gender*.

44. *Pageant*, 58.

45. This is a reference to Dr. Ida's roadside clinics, which she conducted through the use of motor vehicles.

46. *Pageant*, 58–59 (emphasis in the original).

47. Hock, *The Infancy Gospels of James and Thomas*.

48. *Pageant*, 71.

49. Ibid.

50. In the Arcot district, birth attendants for caste Hindus were from the barber and/or washerwoman caste.

51. Forbes, *Women in Colonial India*, 95–96. Forbes gathered these responses from a scheme set up by the Dufferin Fund, a secular philanthropic alternative to missionary work that also emerged in the nineteenth century and that I will discuss in more detail in the next chapter.

52. Lang, "Drop the Demon *Dai*."

53. Abraham, *Religion, Caste and Gender*.

54. Abraham makes this point clearly in her work when she contrasts how hospital sick nursing in India grew out of the longstanding focus on maternal and infant health, as opposed to the way in which it developed in the United Kingdom and the United States, through the exigencies of war.

55. Healey elaborates that this was also sometimes grounded in truth as reported by missionaries. The pay scale for nurses was low enough that it made them vulnerable to being recruited into brothels to make ends meet. Healey, "Regarded, Paid, and Housed as Menials."

In India, there also developed a lower grade of nurses who only worked with women. This would have been the case in many female medical missions.

56. Bleakley, *Meet the Indian Nurse*.

57. Forbes, *Women in Colonial India*, 121–40.

58. Viswanathan, *Outside the Fold*.

59. Kumar, *History of Doing*; Chakravarti, *Rewriting History*.

60. Varde, *Dr. Rakhmabai*.

61. Chakravarti, *Gendering Caste*.


*Chapter Three*

1. Yergin, *The Prize*, 43. The basics in my summary of the evolution of Standard Oil are from Yergin's account.

2. This was in contrast to the other founding figure of American corporate philanthropy, Andrew Carnegie. Carnegie believed that his wealth should be distributed by the principles of social Darwinism.

3. Fosdick, *The Story of the Rockefeller Foundation*, 23–24. Fosdick's citation does not contain an exact date for the quote.

4. Regarding this, the Countess of Dufferin wrote in a letter to the mayor of London, "Numbers of English lady doctors will find employment in India, as I am in hopes that posts will multiply here very much more quickly than we can find native women ready to fill them, and in fact the most sanguine of us know that it will be many years before the medical schools here can be expected to supply candidates for the larger appointments." Countess of Dufferin's Fund, *First Annual Report*, 29, as quoted in Lal, "The Politics of Gender and Medicine," 50.

5. Lal, "The Politics of Gender and Medicine."

6. Van Hollen, *Birth on the Threshold*.

7. Significantly, in the late nineteenth century, it seems that members of this community, including Dadabai Naoroji, were in touch with Florence Nightingale with regards to establishing private nurse training in India. While Nightingale communicated with these business leaders, she ultimately advocated for the colonial government to take charge of this project. Gourlay, *Florence Nightingale and the Health of the Raj*.

8. Kittredge, *A Short History*; Balfour and Young, *The Work of Medical Women in India*; Ramana, "Women Physicians as Vital Intermediaries," 71–78.

9. Dr. Pechey-Phipson is a fascinating historical figure. She worked at Cama Hospital from 1886 to 1894, where she fought for a nurse training school. She was an officer for the Medical Women for India Fund while it remained in existence and was also the first woman to become part of the Senate at the University of Bombay. She led the fight for equal pay (for white women) at Cama Hospital. When she left the hospital, she ran a sanatorium with her husband just outside of Bombay and remained involved in social issues. The couple left India in 1905, after which she became a suffragist in England.

10. The appellation is from Brown, *Rockefeller Medicine Men*.

11. Starr, *The Social Transformation of American Medicine*, 121.

12. Ibid.; Pietzman, *A New and Untried Course*.

13. Yergin, *The Prize*, 113.

14. It is of note that the charter was from New York State because the federal government had denied the request.

15. This basic structure of corporate foundations and their relationship to formally registered nonprofit organizations has remained intact to the present day, with only minor modifications appearing at the mid-twentieth century. In 1969, as part of its Tax Reform Act, the U.S. Congress legislated that foundations had to pay a 4 percent excise tax on their net investment income and must spend 6 percent of that income annually. In addition, the act placed restrictions on foundations' ability to engage in business operations, restrictions borne out of the fact that some corporations were using the structure of a foundation to do business. The 6 percent expenditure was reduced to 5 percent in 1988. It can also include overhead (i.e., the cost of running the foundation, maintaining staff, etc.). Smith, "Introduction: The Revolution Will Not Be Funded," in INCITE! *The Revolution Will Not Be Funded*.

16. The first was the Russell-Sage Foundation in 1907, followed by the Carnegie Foundation in 1911. Andrew Carnegie, in particular, was, along with Rockefeller, at the forefront of the development of corporate philanthropy.

17. This same division was the International Health Commission from 1913–16, the International Health Board from 1916–27, and the International Health Division from 1927–51.

18. The Monroe Doctrine was issued by President James Monroe in 1923, at a moment when almost all of Latin America, excepting Cuba and Puerto Rico, was either independent or on the verge of independence from European territorial colonization. The doctrine positioned any act of aggression against any country in the Americas as an act of aggression that would require U.S. intervention. It was a founding document in establishing U.S. hegemony over both North and South America.

19. Sinha, *Specters of Mother India*, 4.

20. Williams, *The Tragedy of American Diplomacy*, 50, 52.

21. As quoted in Ettling, *The Germ of Laziness*, 35–36.

22. Ibid.

23. "Coolie" is often used as a derogatory term. For a history of its translation in relation to Asian exclusion in the United States, see Jung, *Coolies and Cane*.

24. *Hookworm Infection in Foreign Countries*, as cited in Farley, *To Cast Out Disease*, 4.

25. Kavadi, *The Rockefeller Foundation and Public Health*.

26. There is a large and largely neglected history here. For a beginning, see Tinker, *A New System of Slavery*, and Carter and Torabully, *Coolitude*. For histories of indentured women, in particular, see Shepherd, *Maharani's Misery*, and Bahadur, *Coolie Woman*.

27. Sarkar, *Modern India*, 167.

28. Farley, *To Cast Out Disease*; Kavadi, *The Rockefeller Foundation and Public Health*.

29. Farley, *To Cast Out Disease*.

30. Kavadi, *The Rockefeller Foundation and Public Health*.

31. For more on the Peking Union Medical College, see Brown, "Rockefeller Medicine in China: Professionalism and Imperialism"; Brown, "Public Health in Imperialism"; and Ma, "The Peking Union Medical College."

32. Kavadi, *The Rockefeller Foundation and Public Health*.

33. Lala Lajpat Rai was well known in the United States, too, where he traveled in 1907 and lived during World War I, helping to spread the cause of the Indian nationalist freedom struggle.

34. Colonial administrators expressed a willingness to forego RF funding if the institution devolved to provincial (i.e., Indian) control. Kavadi, *The Rockefeller Foundation and Public Health*.

35. Abrams, "Brilliance and Bureaucracy."

36. Hine, "The Ethel Johns Report," 214.

37. In her research, Hine uncovered a request by black social scientist Monroe N. Work of the Tuskegee Institute for further information about the report, and the

foundation denied him access. This points to an abandonment combined with an active suppression of its contents.

38. Hine, *Black Women in White.*

39. The nominal separation between the three major white philanthropies/philanthropists who came to support the NACGN should not blind us to their actually tight-knit relationship, a relationship that revolved around the Rockefellers. Frances Payne Bolton was the niece of Oliver Payne, who was the co-founder of Standard Oil. He established a trust for his niece, and this was the money she used to support the NACGN, among other causes, many of which involved nursing. (Bolton was soon to become Representative Bolton [Republican-Ohio], when she replaced her recently deceased husband in 1939. She went on to serve an additional fourteen terms in the House.) Also, when the Rosenwald Fund signed on to fund the NACGN, its director was Edwin R. Embree. Embree took on the post in 1929 after having served as an officer with the RF and directing the RF's nursing investments in particular. I highlight these facts not to mount some kind of facile conspiracy theory that amounts to saying that "the Rockefellers ruled the world." If it wasn't before, it should be manifestly clear by now that the Rockefellers were incredibly powerful players in the United States and globally by virtue of their enormous wealth and vast enterprises. What these philanthropic relationships point to are the way in which white philanthropists represented a network of elites who, while not entirely reducible to each other, did represent a constellation of coordinated class interests.

40. The ANA instituted a rule that membership to it would pass through state nursing organizations. The nursing associations in sixteen Southern states as well as the District of Columbia did not allow black nurses to be members, effectively barring them from the ANA. Massey-Riddle, "Training and Placement of Negro Nurses."

41. In relation to the hospital movement, I take my cue from Gamble, "Black Autonomy versus White Control" and *Making a Place for Ourselves.*

42. Lipstiz, *Possessive Investment in Whiteness,* and Harris, "Whiteness as Property," 276–91.

43. Gamble, "Black Autonomy versus White Control."

44. Johns, "A Study of the Present Status of the Negro Woman in Nursing," p. 6, Folder 1507, Series 200, Box 122, RC 1.1, Rockefeller Foundation Archives, Rockefeller Archive Center (hereafter, RAC).

45. Hine, "The Ethel Johns Report," 221.

46. Ibid., 213.


*Chapter Four*

1. Paranjape, *Sarojini Naidu,* 204.

2. The list is long and includes works in English and various Indian languages, written by both women and men and beginning as early as 1928. In 1929, K. L. Gauba published his wildly popular *Uncle Sham: The Strange Tale of a Civilization Run Amok,* which turned the tables to examine the United States.

3. Paranjape, *Sarojini Naidu,* 204.

4. Jha, *Katherine Mayo and India.*

5. Mayo, *Mother India.*

6. Rockefeller Archive Center, "Unhooking the Hookworm."

7. Nadkarni, "World-Menace."

8. Sinha, *Specters of Mother India.*

9. "Benevolent assimilation" was the phrase under which the U.S. civilizing mission in the Philippines was most famously known.

10. Farley, *To Cast Out Disease*, 12.

11. Sinha, *Specters of Mother India.*

12. John B. Grant, "Medical India—1933—Impressions and Comments," Folder 3779, Box 558, Series 464, Record Group 2GC, Rockefeller Foundation Archives, Rockefeller Archive Center (hereafter, RAC).

13. Mary Beard, "Report on India," 1935, p. 18, Folder 3793, Series 464C, Record Group 2CG, Rockefeller Foundation Archives, RAC.

14. The act shifted financial control from London to Delhi, but it remained the preserve of the viceroy in Delhi.

15. Sarkar, *Modern India*, 254.

16. Mayo, *Mother India*, 92.

17. Nadkarni, "World-Menace."

18. My access to the contents of the journal is via translation by Geetha and Rajadurai, *Revolt.*

19. Forbes, *Women in Colonial India*, 79–100.

20. Unfortunately, sources confirm that at present we have unearthed very little biographical information about Rajwade to help to fill in/complicate the picture presented to us by her work. Ahluwalia, *Reproductive Restraints.*

21. Ibid., 1.

22. There were others who followed in her footsteps, so to speak. For a sense of who they were, we can turn to Ramana, "Women Physicians as Vital Intermediaries in Colonial Bombay."

23. Brush et al., *Nurses of All Nations.*

24. Miss Mary Beard's earlier tour was sponsored by the foundation's Division of Medical Education (DME). At that time, the AIIHPH was under the control of the DME. In 1938, it shifted to the IHD, in part to enable the hiring of John Black Grant as director.

25. By the time of Stewart's resignation, the foundation's involvement with the running of the institute was meant to have ended. The agreement that it had hammered out with the government of India (GOI) was that it would provide the funds for construction and the hiring of an initial director and staff, but after the institute opened, maintenance and operation would shift to the central government of India.

My limited information on Dr. Lal comes from Kavadi, *The Rockefeller Foundation.* I could not track him down otherwise, to fill in more details even of his name.

26. Litsios, "John Black Grant."

27. Mary Elizabeth Tennant, "Summary of Impressions of Nursing in India," 1941, p. 4, Folder 3816, Box 561, Series 464C, Record Group 2, stacks, Rockefeller Foundation Archives, RAC.

28. I found one other reference to Mrs. Mitra later in the archives. She appears again in nursing advisor Elizabeth Warren Brackett's diary of her visit to India in 1952 as a nursing superintendent in West Bengal. Brackett also makes mention of Mrs. Mitra's previous name, Miss Naomi. She also refers to her as a Red Cross fellow who had studied in Toronto in 1946–47. From these details, Miss Naomi/Mrs. Mitra appears to be one of the nursing leaders promoted by the various international representatives at work in India during the transition to formal independence, a group of Indian women who I detail further below. Elizabeth W. Brackett, diary excerpt, January 25, 1952, Folder 403, Box 44, Series 2.1, Record Group 6.1, Rockefeller Foundation Archives, RAC.

29. Tennant, "Summary of Impressions."

30. Sir Joseph Bhore was an Indian civil servant who served many posts over his long career, including serving as secretary to the Simon Commission and, from 1914–19, Diwan of Cochin State, one of the princely states that eventually became Kerala.

31. "Proceedings of a Conference of representatives of Nursing in India held in New Delhi, Feb. 28–29 and March 1—1944," Record Collection 2, 1945, 464n, 306, Folder 2077, RAC.

32. Abrams, "Brilliance and Bureaucracy."

33. Schneider, "The Men Who Followed Flexner."

34. Berman, *The Influence of the Carnegie, Ford and Rockefeller Foundations.*

35. Parmar, *Foundations of the American Century,* 8 (emphasis in original).

36. Ibid., 11.

37. Tennant, "Summary of Impressions."

38. "India—Nursing—1st and 2nd Semi-Annual Reports," 1946, Folder 2494, Box 204, Series 464C, Record Group 5.3, Rockefeller Foundation Archives, RAC.

In addition, *The Rockefeller Foundation Directory of Fellowships and Scholarships 1917–1970* includes the following fellows in relation to the development of nursing education in Delhi:

K. Paulose Aleykutty, who graduated from the India School of Nursing Administration in 1949; was appointed an RF fellow from 1951–53; earned a BSc in nursing from Syracuse University in 1953; and was working as a Senior Tutor at the CON-D in 1964. (9)

Prema Sarathy, who was a BSc graduate from the CON-D in 1955; was an RF fellow who received her MSc from Columbia University in 1960; and who was also working as a Senior Tutor at the CON-D in 1960. (280)

Charlotte Isaac Abana, who earned a diploma from the "Missionary Medical College Hospital" in 1942; was an RF fellow who studied in the U.S. and Canada from 1946–47; and who was a Sister Tutor at the Silver Jubilee Hospital in Kingsway, Delhi in 1954. (3)

Edith Buchanan, who received a BSc from the University of Toronto in 1928; was an RF fellow in Canada from 1944–45; and was a nursing instructor at the CON-D. (45)

Daisy Charles, who was a diploma nurse from Rainey Hospital; who was an RF fellow from 1945–46 studying in Canada and the USA; and who in 1950 was working as the Superintendent of public health nursing at the CON-D. (58)

Mariam Korah, who also was a diploma nurse from Rainey Hospital; was an RF fellow studying in Canada from 1946–47; and was in 1964 the Superintendent of the Lady Reading Health School in Delhi. (166)

Melita Mascarenhas, who was a 1951 BSc gradate from the CON-D; was an RF fellow from 1955–56; receiving her MSc from Simmons College in the U.S.; and in 1958 was working as a teacher and supervisor of public health nursing at the CON-D. (198)

The information is taken from the guide, where it was compiled from recipients' correspondence. For this reason, it is somewhat scattered and incomplete, with references to hospitals and schools that are vague for the general reader. A couple of things are worth noting. One is that at least one of the nurses to receive an RF fellowship, Edith Buchanan, was not Indian. Buchanan was in fact a colonial nursing leader working with the TNAI. In addition, while early grants sent recipients to Canada and the United States, later ones were more U.S. focused, as was the general trend. And in general, compared to the fellowships that I will describe in relation to Vellore and Thiruvananthapuram (officially known by the colonial name Trivandrum during the period under investigation), the Delhi fellows were recipients during the earlier period of RF fellowships to Indian nurses and dwindled in numbers during the 1950s and 1960s.

39. Nielsen, *The Big Foundations*; Shaplen, *Toward the Well-Being of Mankind*; Jonas, *The Circuit Riders*; and Farley, *To Cast Out Disease*.

40. Abrams, "Brilliance and Bureaucracy."

41. Sood, "Nursing Services in India."

42. Jeffery, *Politics of Health in India*, 223.

43. Ibid.

44. In his own words, Anderson distinguishes between schools and colleges: "Two grades of medical education were developed; the so called medical *school* which gave a second rate type of training, required the equivalent of a high school education for entrance and gave a four year course; and the so called medical *college* which required the supposed equivalent of two years of college for entrance and gave a five year course, including more emphasis on laboratory subjects and in general a higher standard of accomplishment and teaching" (emphasis in original). He goes on to describe how, upon independence, India abolished all medical schools, upgraded them to colleges, and increased the number of colleges. He expresses the fear that, because of the sudden and rapid expansion, many of the new colleges are not able to sustain higher standards but are, in some cases, slipping even below those of the aforementioned schools. Richmond K. Anderson, "Medical Education in India," March 11, 1952, p. 1, Folder 79, Box 10, Subseries 464A: Medical Education, Series 464, Record Group 1.1, Rockefeller Foundation Archives, RAC.

45. Ibid., 2.

46. "India—Nursing—2nd Semi-Annual Report," 1946, Folder 2494, Box 204, Series 464C, Record Group 5.3, Rockefeller Foundation Archives, RAC.

47. "India—Nursing—Preliminary Report," 1947 (Jan.-Oct.), p. 7, Folder 2495, Box 204, Series 464C, Record Group 5.3, Rockefeller Foundation Archives, RAC.

48. "India—Nursing—Annual Report," 1949, p. 14, Folder 2497, Box 204, Series 464C, Record Group 5.3, Rockefeller Foundation Archives, RAC.

49. Healey, "Regarded, Paid, and Housed as Menials."

50. Article 25 of the Indian Constitution permits the right to propagate one's faith, and Article 30 permits minority groups to maintain their own institutions. *The Constitution of India* (as modified up to August 1, 1975) (New Delhi, 1975), 10, as cited in Abraham, *Religion, Caste and Gender.*

51. George E. Vincent, Diary Excerpt, October 6, 1927, Folder 78, Box 10, Series 464A, Record Group 1.1, Rockefeller Foundation Archives, RAC.

The diary entry was in reference to the "Conference on DME [Department of Medical Education] India proposals."

52. Both organizations still exist today, although in different incarnations: The Vellore Christian Medical College Board (United States), Inc. and the Friends of Vellore UK. The former is the larger and more powerful organization, which retains significant links to the CMC-Vellore. I attended three of its annual board meetings in New York City during the course of my research and interviewed three of the nursing alumnae who have served on the board as well as the director, the Reverend Lou Knowles.

53. Peabody to Richardson, September 27, 1920, Laura Spelman Rockefeller III, Box 7, Folder 85, RAC.

54. Gordon, "Wealth Equals Wisdom?," 115.

55. Abraham, *Religion, Caste and Gender*, 91–92.

56. It is of note, of course, that both institutions were long-time recipients of Rockefeller funding. Indeed, the University of Chicago was the first major institution of higher education to be overhauled through Rockefeller funds, at the very dawn of the Gates era.

57. Richmond K. Anderson to John C. Bugher, April 19, 1955, Folder 488, Box 51, Series 464A: India, Record Group 1.2, Rockefeller Foundation Archives, RAC.

The letter goes on to describe the purpose of the grant, pending progress on the noted RF reservations, as a "means for stimulating the development of Vellore into the type of institution which may warrant considerably larger support at a later date and for judging whether such developments can take place. If within the next few years it develops along the lines we and, I believe, Vellore authorities desire, it may well become an institution which we will want to back as a model for the rest of India."

In addition, and as a practical measure, in September of the same year, the RF received a request from John S. Carman, the director of the Medical College and hospital at Vellore, for a grant to fund an expedition of Vellore employees to the American University in Beirut. The visit originated as a suggestion of RF officers, because the American University was an example of a mission institution that had successfully made the transition to one of secular standing and importance. John S. Carman, September 7, 1955, Folder 486, Box 53, Series 464A, Record Group 1.2, Rockefeller Foundation Archives, RAC.

58. Vellore material sent to the RF, Folder 488, Box 51, Series 464A: India, Record Group 1.2, Rockefeller Foundation Archives, RAC.

59. A statement to this effect is in a letter from Richmond K. Anderson to John Weir, an RF associate director, dated August 30, 1955. The letter goes on to say that while 90 percent of Vellore's students were Christian, the institution had no religious

restrictions in graduate training and that it provided patient care for a population that was primarily non-Christian. Richmond K. Anderson to John Weir, August 30, 1955, Folder 486, Box 53, Series 464A, Record Group 1.2, Rockefeller Foundation Archives, RAC.

60. As far as nursing was concerned, the highest level Indian nurse was Anna Jacob, who was nursing superintendent at the time. She was the first Indian to hold the position. Jacob had not been a Rockefeller fellow but nevertheless had been funded through another channel to attain her bachelor's in nursing at McGill University in Montreal, Canada. In this sense, her posting as nursing superintendent reflected the institutional pattern linking upward mobility with higher education and international migration (and especially to North America). Jacob served in this post at Vellore from 1949/50 to 1974. She also served as president of the Madras state branch of the TNAI for four years in the 1950s and was a member of the Board of Directors of the Indian Council of Nurses (ICN) from 1963–67. She therefore occupied several key leadership positions during the first decades of Indian independence and through these continued to connect said leadership to international circuits.

My summary of her roles is from Abraham, *Religion, Caste and Gender*. At one point in her text, Abraham says that Jacob became nursing superintendent in 1950 and later dates it to 1949, which is why I include the slight ambiguity of start date as between those two.

61. Elizabeth W. Brackett, diary excerpt, January 25, 1952, Folder 403, Box 44, Series 2.1, Record Group 6.1, Rockefeller Foundation Archives, RAC.

62. This covers grants given up until 1968. It is actually not possible to give an entirely accurate number. The entries are based on fellows' responses, some of which are vague. Each contains information regarding their country of residence at time of award, date and place of birth, academic degree held (not including diplomas or certificates) at time of award, granting institution of this degree, foundation program and dates of fellowship, country of study, degree received, and field of study. In the context of Indian nursing, this leaves room for gaps. For example, Annamma Nattacheril Matthews Gupta received her BSc from Wayne State University in Detroit in 1952. She was appointed from the "Christian Medical College," to pursue her master's at Wayne State as well. She does not write "Vellore"; however, in this case it applies. For this is Annamma Matthews, who was the RF fellow originally slated to replace Florence Taylor but who, according to the fellowship directory, took a position instead as a professor in Windsor, Ontario, Canada. I later found in the archives that she spent eight years in Canada before returning to India to take up a position. Another possibility, for other entries, is that a nurse received a diploma from Vellore and then a BSc elsewhere, and so Vellore does not appear on the record. In terms of the available evidence, I counted thirteen graduates of Vellore and/or the University of Madras (with which the College of Nursing was affiliated and which thus amounts to the same thing). It is entirely possible that a couple more of the entries have a Vellore connection.

63. Abraham, *Religion, Caste and Gender*.

64. Author's interview with Rajan, July 9, 2003 (emphasis added).

*Chapter Five*

1. Kerala formed under the States Reorganisation Act of 1956. For purposes of ease, I will use the name "Kerala" when I am referring to the region in general (even if it predates the actual formation of the state) and be more specific when I am referring to items relating to the specificity of political units during the nineteenth and early twentieth centuries.

Also, in 1991, Trivandrum reverted to Thiruvananthapuram. For historical accuracy, I retain its Anglicized name in what follows.

2. Interestingly, in my research, I found reference to a particular role that Syrian Christians played in purifying—by their touch—items that had come into contact with the outcasted. This would have been a service for privileged Hindu castes, and while my information is limited, this does raise interesting possibilities when it comes to the eventual association between Kerala Christians, including Syrian Christians, and the ritual purification of colonial medicine. (Ayyar, *Anthropology of Syrian Christians*, as cited in Visvanathan, *The Christians of Kerala*, 3.)

In British-dominated India, ritual purification became something of a government strategy when medical schools began to court privileged caste and class Indians as medical students. Their efforts initially met with limited success, until they began to recruit poor Brahmans as students. The logic was that poverty would create adequate incentive for their entry into medical school and that their caste pedigree would consequently rub off on the profession. In the context of colonization, this recruitment had its racialized limits as well. For instance, Indians generally had access to government medical schools, not colleges. Students at the latter, which were of a higher grade, remained primarily European, including Anglo-Indians (in the Bombay Presidency), and Indian Christians in only some instances (Jeffery, *The Politics of Health in India*). Historian Anil Kumar argues that the tactic of government inducements helped to "ritually purify" the medical profession, first making it more acceptable to dominant caste Hindus and eventually turning it into their preserve (Kumar, *Medicine and the Raj*).

However, while Kumar does not mention this in his account, the practice of courting Brahmins had to have regional dimensions. For instance, there are no Brahmins in Punjab. It is also of note that of all the occupations associated with biomedicine, that of medical doctor is the only one that emerged out of the colonial period not entirely associated with Indian Christian communities.

3. Jeffrey, *Politics, Women and Well-Being*.

4. Mary Elizabeth Tennant, "Summary of Impressions of Nursing in India," 1941, Folder 3816, Box 561, Series 464C, Record Group 2, stack material, Rockefeller Foundation Archives, Rockefeller Archive Center (hereafter, RAC).

5. Rugmini S. Iyengar to Surgeon General, June, 15, 1945, Health, Labor and Education, Trivandrum, Bundle 637, File 8954, Kerala State Archives.

6. Dewan's Orders, May 10, 1945, Health, Labor and Education, Bundle 637, File 8954, Kerala State Archives.

7. Surgeon General to Chief Secretary, Government, May 18, 1945, Health, Labor and Education, Trivandrum, Bundle 637, File 8954, Kerala State Archives.

8. Healey, "Seeds."

9. Her entry in *The Rockefeller Foundation Directory of Fellowships and Scholarships 1917–1970* states that Shroff (listed as Narjidas Shroff Derasari) was appointed an IHD fellow from a position at Columbia University. In other words, she was already in the United States. It is not clear to me whether or not she was already at Columbia under the auspices of the RF or through another agency.

10. Robert Briggs Watson to E. W. Brackett, March 27, 1953, RF 6.1, 2.1, 44, 403, RAC.

11. A. Rugmini Amma to Chief Secretary, Government of Travancore-Cochin State, May 9, 1955, Confidential Bundle (1954–55) SL No. 2322, Bundle 740, File 12777 (Rugmini Amma), Kerala State Archives.

12. RBW to EWB, December 21, 1951, RF 1.2 464 C: India, 53, 492, RAC.

13. Elizabeth W. Brackett, diary excerpt, March 3, 1952, Folder 403, Box 44, Series 2.1, Record Group 6.1, Rockefeller Foundation Archives, RAC.

14. Lillian A. Johnson, January 23, 1953, Folder 492, Box 53, Series 464C, Record Group 1.2, Rockefeller Foundation Archives, RAC.

15. J. B. Cardoz to Minister for Health, Travancore-Cochin State, November 4, 1950, Education (1950), Bundle 522, Folder 4819, Kerala State Archives; G. Chandramathy to Minister for Health, Travancore-Cochin State, November 4, 1950, Education (1950), Bundle 522, Folder 4819, Kerala State Archives; A. G. Kunjamma to Minister for Health, Travancore-Cochin State, November 4, 1950, Education (1950), Bundle 522, Folder 4819, Kerala State Archives.

16. Surgeon General to Secretary of Education, Health, Local Self Government Department, Travancore-Cochin State, July, 29, 1952, Health Labor and Education, Bundle 640, File 10075, Kerala State Archives.

17. Rt. Reverend Mar Thomas Tarayil, Bishop of Kottayam to V. Madhavan, Minister of Health, Travancore-Cochin State, August 2, 1952, Confidential Bundle (1954–55), SL No. 2322, Bundle 740, File 12777 (Rugmini Amma), Kerala State Archives.

18. C. K. Leksmanan, Directorate General of Health Services Delhi to Surgeon General, Travancore-Cochin State, May 12, 1953, Health Labor and Education, Bundle 635, Folder 7954, Kerala State Archives.

19. Abraham, *Religion, Caste and Gender.*

20. Ibid., 106.

21. Trivandrum School of Nursing Scholarships 1963–67, Folder 495, Box 54, Series 464C, Record Group 1.2, Rockefeller Foundation Archives, RAC.

22. Author's interview with Susan George Arakal, July 17, 2003. "Cousin-sister" is a common appellation in Indian English. It refers to what in American English is a female first cousin. At times, it also refers to someone who is a close family friend or more distant relative.

23. Balsara, "The Role of Today's Nurse," 210.

24. Healey, "Regarded, Paid, and Housed as Menials" and "Seeds."

25. Mejia, Pizurki, and Royston, *Physician and Nurse Migration*, 284. When referencing this report and its findings, I will employ its terminology—that is to say, its categorization of countries like India as "developing" and the United States as "developed." I do not subscribe to such descriptions, which imply a particular trajectory and,

in that sense, distribute progress in a way that continues to disadvantage those who have been and/or continue to be subject to colonization. This is, however, the language that brain drain theory itself emerges out of. Thus, for purposes of expediency, I will retain this language in order to emphasize the flavor of the report and its findings.

26. Ibid., 277.

27. Ibid.

28. Ibid., 283.

29. Ibid., 284.

30. The following statistics are, like much of the information in this section, taken from the WHO report. In their "Methodology" section, the authors themselves comment on the nature of the data used. No original data were collected by them. They were instead based on a compilation of already available sources. On this they comment that "while the source of such data is given in each instance, no attempt has been made to assess their reliability except that data which seemed very improbable have not been included" (9). Consequently, "data had to be used in their original form with all their inherent weaknesses" (11).

With regard to data on nurses in particular, several obstacles presented themselves. First, most of the information on nurses available was licensing and immigration data, as opposed to annual stock data as in the case of physicians. However, licensing data were limited by the fact that individuals could obtain licenses without actually migrating (as a safety net); the nationality given on licenses refers to the country of basic training, which could have been different from the applicant's nationality; and, with regard to the United States, data were state based and thus for a particular year included nurses licensed for the first time as well as those previously licensed in another state or territory (and thus prone to double counting). Immigration data were also obscured by differences between migrants and immigrants and the way they are counted officially, a loose definition of "nurse" that allowed individuals to denote themselves as such upon entry but then prove unable to meet minimum standards and work as professional nurses within a particular country, and finally married professional nurses who entered as dependents and thus were not counted within occupational quotas. In the case of Indian nurses, all of this was complicated by the fact that India kept no records of emigration at the time. Thus, when it comes to the numbers cited for physician emigration, most of the information is taken from sources in the United Kingdom, the United States, and other receiving countries. In addition, chain migration makes nationality difficult to establish at times.

Thus, as the report itself flatly states, "The information as presented is as complete a picture as could be built up from known data but, inevitably, there are data gaps" (15).

31. Cherian, "Role of Nursing in India Today."

32. Harnar, "Social Forces and Factors," 56.

33. Nagpal, "From the Editor."

34. Mejia et al., *Physician and Nurse Migration*, 281.

35. Author's interview with Susan George Arakal, July 17, 2003.

36. Ibid.

37. Ibid.

38. Kurien, *Kaleidoscopic Ethnicity.*

39. Nayyar, *Migration, Remittances and Capital Flows.*

40. Mathew, "Indian Nurses Abroad," 69.

41. Author's interview with Annie Samuels, November 12, 2003.

42. Author's interview with Susan George Arakal, July 17, 2003.

43. Author's interview with Satwant Malhotra, July 28, 2003.

44. While the general pattern I discerned in my interviews was a movement from South to North India, this was not the only internal movement that manifested in my interviews. For instance, Mrs. Parmar, a nurse from the northwestern state of Gujarat, has a story that parallels Aleyamma Eapen's in several ways. She too was from a relatively provincial background and entered nursing by way of an advertisement. This time it was for the new BSc program in nursing at the University of Bombay. She applied, was accepted for an interview, and got into the school. She returned to Gujarat several years later as one of the only BSc nurses working in the state. Her story suggests that, with regard to nursing migration within India, it was not only south to north but also more generally rural to urban, with degree of industrialization being the key compass point.

45. The stipends were not much. However, Ms. Dhas, another one of my interviewees, explained to me her thrill at receiving it. She did not know what to do with the money at the time, since most of her expenses were already covered by the school. So she sent the money to her mother, who also did not know what to do with it, and hid it, untouched, under a mattress (author's interview with Ms. Dhas, July 22, 2003).

The practice of remitting some of the small nursing school stipend home was not uncommon among the nurses I interviewed for this project. It prefaced the larger contributions that nurses were able to make to their families upon graduation and, in these cases, migration.

46. Author's interview with Aleyamma Eapen, July 19, 2003.

47. Ibid.

48. Ibid.

49. Minocha, "South Asian Immigrants," 369.

50. Oomen, *Doctors and Nurses.*

51. Oomen's findings are largely corroborated by a smaller scale study conducted by G. Ramachandran Raj and published in the *Nursing Journal of India* in 1963. Raj surveyed nurses in a hospital in Kanpur, a city in the North Indian state of Uttar Pradesh. He too found that the majority of nurses employed were from lower middle-class backgrounds. However, Raj makes an interesting observation with regard to the relationship between gender and class in the case of nursing. He notes that nurses hold generally more progressive views regarding marriage. More nurses either remain single or have "love marriages" (nonarranged), both in much larger proportion than the general population. Part of this can be attributed to the fact that at the time and place of Raj's survey, entry into nursing was seen as a negative feature in the marriage market. Thus, through a combination of their economic and social positions, Raj concludes that nurses form "a class of their own." Raj, "The Indian Nurse," 285.

52. This was opposed to the "unclean castes," Scheduled Castes (SC). There were no SC nurses in Oomen's four-year sample. He attributes this to the fact that they lacked the basic socioeconomic level required for entry into the field. While this level

was not as high as that required for medical school, it still required a minimal base. For this reason, nurses were primarily lower middle class.

It should be noted also that conversion makes the question of caste potentially more complicated, as I detail in chapter 1. However, in Oomen's sample, he indicates that the majority of Christians are privileged caste (if not class) Syrian Christians from Kerala, which conforms to his observations.

We can also assume that the descendents of Salome (so to speak) at the time of Oomen's sample were not necessarily "higher grade" nurses but remained orderlies and ward ayahs working alongside their more credentialed counterparts. There was, in other words, also a division of Indian nursing labor that worked in conjunction with caste hierarchies. Indeed, many of the nurses I interviewed, who were among the more educated in the field, described how they did not do the "dirty work" of nursing after graduation.

53. Oomen cites a 1974 survey of nursing in India that reported nurses were 94 percent female at the time.

54. Oomen, *Doctors and Nurses*, 56 (emphasis in the original).

55. Ibid., viii (emphasis added).

56. Author's interview with Aleyamma James, October 15, 2003.

57. For mention of this within a broad analysis of caste, race, and culture, see Visweswaran, *Un/common Cultures*.

58. Phule, *Gulamgiri*, in *Selected Writings*, 25.


*Chapter Six*

1. Author's interview with Vasantha Daniel, August 21, 2004.

2. All of the Vellore graduates who I interviewed spoke to me of the way in which the institution, while enabling its graduates to study abroad, attached work bonds to these grants.

3. This seems to have been common among ANA-sponsored nurses who were subsequently sent to one or two hospitals for stays from six months to a year. It is not clear to me that the same would have been true if an exchange nurse was sponsored by an individual hospital, university, or foundation. Evidence for the ANA pattern can be found in articles from the ANA's written organ, the *American Journal of Nursing*. For an example of this, see "Nurses on the Two Way Street" and the three articles gathered under "Exchange for Education."

4. United States Information and Education Act of 1948.

5. As a minor means for mitigating this restriction, institutions could, on the behalf of individual nurses, petition the Exchange Visitor Waiver Board of the Department of Health, Education, and Welfare or, when all else failed, bring their case against the Immigration and Naturalization Service to a U.S. court of appeals.

6. Unless otherwise noted, this chapter refers to the position of exchange nurses in the white hospital system.

7. In addition, no sponsoring institution was required to provide travel expenses to and from the United States for exchange visitors.

With regard to stipends specifically, in 1958, the ANA estimated that this would normally amount to five-sixths of a staff nurse's salary. However, it is not quite clear to me how they came up with this figure and how it accounts for the wide variety of institutions and positions that exchange nurses might find themselves in. "Exchange for Education."

8. Brush, "Exchangees or Employees?," 173–74.

9. "*Protecting* Our Exchange Visitors," 698.

10. Reverby, *Ordered to Care*, 196.

11. As historian Rosemary Stevens details, Hill-Burton was both modeled on and in support of the foundation-supported model of research-oriented, university-based medicine. A committee that included philanthropies such as the Commonwealth Fund, the Kellogg Foundation, and the National Foundation for Infantile Paralysis conducted World War II planning for hospital expansion. The latter was funded in part by the Rockefeller Foundation, while the RF itself declined the invitation to join the team. The reports produced by this committee, particularly the one conducted by the Kellogg Foundation in Michigan, envisioned regional hospital systems that placed university-based research hospitals as the centers of each region. This was the basic plan that formed a crux of the bill that was passed by Congress. Because Hill-Burton was federally funded but state based, each state that applied for funds had to produce a report/survey that was modeled on the Kellogg survey in Michigan. As part of this, and in a classic philanthropic move, states had to prove that their plans would be able to elicit matching grants from nongovernment sources, thus fostering a corporate-state configuration (Stevens, *In Sickness and in Wealth*).

In addition, both the medical organizations and the foundations were at pains to ensure that Hill-Burton did *not* amount to public or socialized medicine. As Paul Starr details, the use of matching funds and other provisions allowed the legislation to primarily benefit middle-class communities while making "a powerful case that public aid to medicine should not bring public control" (Starr, *The Social Transformation of American Medicine*, 307).

12. Reverby, *Ordered to Care*, 60.

13. Ibid. and Melosh, "*The Physician's Hand.*"

14. There is scattered evidence that student nurses went on strike in the 1910s, but few details remain. Reverby, *Ordered to Care*.

15. Melosh, "*The Physician's Hand.*"

16. Reverby, *Ordered to Care*, 143–44.

17. Melosh, "*The Physician's Hand,*" 47.

18. Scherzer, "The Race and Class of Women's Work."

19. Ibid., 28.

20. Starr, *The Social Transformation of American Medicine*.

21. Brush, "Has Foreign Nurse Recruitment Impeded African American Access?"

22. Brush, "Exchangees or Employees?," 173. In my estimation, the actual composition of exchange nurses during these earliest years and beyond is not yet certain. This is because the sources I have found regarding the earliest years of the EVP are either produced by or rely primarily on estimates from the ANA. So, for instance, Brush's

statistics are compiled from data she researched in the ANA archives at Boston University's Mugar Library. The ANA, however, was only one (if a prominent one) of the sponsors of exchange nurses. Thus, while it is certain that the majority of ANA-sponsored exchangees were from Europe, it is not clear to me how far we can extend the claim or how comprehensive we can consider such statistics. In this sense, I agree with Catherine Ceniza Choy's assessment in *Empire of Care*.

23. *"Protecting* Our Exchange Visitors," 698.

24. Choy, *Empire of Care*, 63.

25. Ibid., 65.

26. Ong and Azores, "The Migration and Incorporation of Filipino Nurses," 165.

27. I have not yet found a source that definitively lists the numbers of Indian exchange nurses to the United States, nor have I been able to compile it yet myself. See footnote 22 for some of the limiting variables and add to these the fact that India did not record nurse emigration.

28. ANA Nursing Information Bureau, *Facts about Nursing*, 68.

29. Ibid. Australia tops the ANA's list for that year, with sixty-four exchange visitors listed.

30. In the first flush of post-1965 Asian nurse immigration to the United States, the Philippines, India, and Korea were routinely among the top sending countries, Asian or otherwise. According to Immigration and Naturalization Service statistics for the fiscal year of 1973–74, India was third after the Philippines and then Korea. Henning, "Nurses from Overseas," 21–28.

31. By this time, China was covered by extensions to the Chinese Exclusion Act of 1882. Japan, and Korea vis-à-vis its colonial status, were already covered by the Gentleman's Agreement of 1907, whereby the Japanese government agreed to restrict emigration to the United States rather than be subject to outright exclusion like the Chinese.

32. Ngai, *Impossible Subjects*.

33. Reimers, *Still the Golden Door*.

34. "Matter of Gutierrez."

35. Brannon, "Restructuring Hospital Nursing."

36. Brannon, *Intensifying Care*.

37. Brush and Berger, "Sending for Nurses."

38. Scherzer, "The Race and Class of Women's Work."

39. Kovner and Salsberg, "The Health Care Workforce."

40. Brannon, *Intensifying Care*.

41. Moore and Simendenger, *Managing the Nursing Shortage*.

42. Ong and Azores, "The Migration and Incorporation of Filipino Nurses." The 1980s were a high point for RN unionization.

43. U.S. Department of Health, Education, and Welfare, Division of Nursing, *Survey of Foreign Nurse Graduates*.

44. Brush and Berger, "Sending for Nurses."

45. Henning, "Nurses from Overseas," 21.

46. Ibid.; Arbeiter, "The Facts about Foreign Nurses"; Kalisch, Kalisch, and Clinton, "Minority Nurses in the News"; Dudas and Dzik, "Working with the Foreign

Nurse"; Sweeney, "Working with Nurses from Overseas"; and Davitz, Davitz, and Sameshima, "Foreign and American Nurses."The last article stands out in that it is the only one that relies on interviews with both FNGs and U.S. nurses to get different perspectives on the same situation/interaction.

47. Arbeiter, "The Facts about Foreign Nurses," 59. Contentions over language were interesting given the fact that the majority of FNGs worked in hospitals where they served primarily people of color. In U.S. nursing journals, when the issue of FNGs and language come up, there is an implicit assumption that English = Standard American English. In other words, it equals the idiom spoken by the majority of white, middle-to upper middle-class Americans. Such a complaint does not address difficulties that FNGs might have been communicating with the people of color whom they both worked alongside and served. In this case, the English spoken would certainly differ from that taught abroad or in FNG training programs in the United States, creating another sort of difficulty (Brush and Berger, "Sending for Nurses").

In addition, Gita Dhillon, an Indian nurse migrant who became a nurse educator in the United States in the 1970s, wrote an article detailing a workshop she ran. She differentiated between language and the ability to communicate in a way that highlighted the need to move beyond simple equations between the two and safe nursing practice (Dhillon, "Study Programs for Foreign Nurses").

Finally, a 1976 survey of foreign and American nurses reports on FNGs who worked in hospitals where English was not the only or dominant language spoken by patients (Davitz et al., "Foreign and American Nurses").

48. "Nursing Practice Acts."

49. This became true after passage of the 1970 amendment mentioned below.

50. Choy, *Empire of Care*.

51. Brush and Berger, "Sending for Nurses," 104. In addition, my own interviews with Indian nurses who immigrated during this early period confirm this practice.

52. Brush and Berger, "Sending for Nurses."

53. Choy, *Empire of Care*.

54. Brush and Berger, "Sending for Nurses."

55. Author's interview with Ms. Dhas, July 22, 2003.

56. Choy, *Empire of Care*.

57. In this sense, it followed the precedent set by the Educational Council for Foreign Medical Graduates (established in 1956), which had required a prescreening test for FMGs since 1958.

58. Herwitz and Michelmore, "The CGFNS Story," 75. Herwitz was the executive director of the CGFNS from 1977 to the date of publication. Michelmore was the research and credentials coordinator at the time of publication.

59. Ibid.

60. Choy, *Empire of Care*.

61. The campaign also targeted the CGFNS, the prescreening test that was in use by that time. However, the study referred to was in reference to the SBTPE, and it was this test that the state of California stopped using the next year.

62. Tamayo, "Foreign Nurses and the U.S. Nursing Crisis," as cited in Choy, *Empire of Care*.

63. The center officially opened on March 13, 2002. It was followed by CGFNS centers in Kochi (Kerala), New Delhi, and Mumbai. As of 2014, Bangalore is now called Bengalaru. Kochi was, prior to 1996, officially known as Cochin.

64. Williams, *Christian Pluralism in the United States*, 17.

65. Haniffa, "U.S. Body to Set Up Qualifying Exam Center."

*Chapter Seven*

1. Author's interview with Subhashini, August 11, 2004.

2. Ibid.

3. Ibid. She arrived in the late fall of 1975 and was required to appear for the next available exam, which was only a few short months later in February 1976.

4. All of the literature I read, regardless of viewpoint, cited these reasons. Psychiatry, in particular, was a common problem area in general and among the nurses whom I interviewed. Interestingly enough, as I describe below, many of the nurses I interviewed ended up working in psychiatric units and/or institutions for some portion of their work history, as these were often among the least desirable/chronically understaffed within the U.S. system.

Subhashini also elaborated on the difficulty of the multiple-choice format, a reason always cited without further explanation for why FNGs might find it difficult. She said that she had 120 minutes to complete 120 questions, and she needed to get at least 80 correct to pass. With one minute to read, comprehend, and answer each question, slight differences between Indian English and American English (in this case) become critical. So if by the end of the time she had only completed 80 questions, she needed to get all of them right.

5. One work that is very suggestive for this kind of recovery is *The Nun Runners* by Sonia Dougal. Dougal recounts her experiences working in an Italian convent that recruited Christian Indian women from Kerala in the late 1960s and early 1970s. Her investigation uncovers a system of trafficking nuns-in-training, with Indian priests cum recruiters as the main culprits. Her account suffers from certain blind spots; for example, her reluctance to acknowledge that European convents may also profit from the "nun trade." In addition, the reader cannot help but see the Indian girls as somewhat helpless victims throughout the process. Indeed, Dougal's whole investigation is sparked off by the illness of one of the new recruits. From the description, it sounds like a nervous breakdown, but we can read in between the lines and think about the possibilities of refusal and resistance encoded in "mental illness." The fact that several other recruits followed in the footsteps of the first one, who was eventually returned to India, suggests such a reading. For the purposes of the current work, *The Nun Runners'* revelation of an underground traffic in Indian Christian women to Europe begs further research. It occurs during the same time period and from the same Indian religious and regional community that provided the bulk of nurse emigrants. Furthermore, many nuns-in-training served simultaneously as nurses-in-training, and the two seem to coexist as options for women migrants in Kerala at the time. In my own research among Indian Christian communities in the greater New York metropolitan area, I found that religious institutions and leaders also play a primary role in

the social networks that enable nurse immigration. This is not to say that they are also involved in unauthorized immigration, simply that more work needs to be done on fleshing out these connections.

6. Author's interview with Susan George Arakal, July 17, 2003.

7. Brush, "Has Foreign Nurse Recruitment Impeded African American Access?," 176; on Cook County Hospital, see Ansell, *County*.

8. Author's interview with Thankam Vellaringattu, June 24, 2003.

9. Ibid.

10. Ibid.

11. Author's interview with Satwant Malhotra, July 28, 2003.

12. Author's interview with Suwersh Khanna, August 12, 2003.

13. Ibid.

14. Author's interview with Aleyamma Eapen, July 19, 2003.

15. Gonzalez, "Music Strikes Chord with Heart Patients"; Benjamin, "Knows about Patient Fear"; and "Keralites in U.S. Honoured."

16. Benjamin, "Knows about Patient Fear."

17. Author's interview with Aleyamma Eapen, July 19, 2003.

18. Author's interview with Mrs. Parmar, July 10, 2003.

19. Ibid.

20. Ibid.

21. In the section that follows, I use "African American" rather than "black" (the latter being the term most of the nurses I interviewed used) in order to specify what was clear in our conversations, which is that nurses were talking about African American coworkers, not coworkers from the Caribbean who would also fit under a generalized "blackness" but had a position in the nursing market closer to their own.

22. Author's interview with Rajan, July 9, 2003.

23. Brannon, *Intensifying Care*, 111–12.

24. "Pacific Hospital" is the pseudonym for the San Francisco Bay Area institution where Brannon conducted his ethnographic research from 1979–88.

25. Author's interview with Mrs. Parmar, July 10, 2003.

26. Author's interview with Vasantha Daniel, September 19, 2003.

27. Author's interview with Ms. Dhas, July 22, 2003.

28. Author's interview with Aleyamma Eapen, July 19, 2003. Eapen and her husband moved to Houston, where, interestingly enough, people reacted to her Brooklyn, not Indian, accent.

29. Author's interview with Aleyamma James, October 15, 2003.

30. Ibid.

31. Author's interview with Aleyamma James, January 7, 2003.

32. Ibid.

33. Author's interview with Aleyamma Eapen, July 19, 2003.


*Chapter Eight*

1. Author's interview with Ani Mathew, November 10, 2003.

2. Ibid.

3. Ibid.

4. Ibid.

5. The Chinese Exclusion Act of 1882 was aimed squarely at laborers. It contained an exception for Chinese merchants, and these merchants were also allowed to sponsor their wives. While some Chinese women did come this way, the overwhelming suspicion of Chinese women as, de facto, sex workers, affected their ability to legally enter nevertheless.

6. Lee, *Fictive Kinship*.

7. Ibid.

8. *Loving v. Virginia*, 13.

9. Author's interview with Mrs. Thannickal, November 3, 2003.

10. At the time of writing, Narendra Modi has moved on to become the prime minister of India.

11. Author's interview with Mrs. Parmar, July 10, 2003.

12. The University of Bombay opened a nursing college in 1959–60.

13. Author's interview with Mrs. Parmar, July 10, 2003.

14. Williams, *Christian Pluralism in the United States*.

15. George, *When Women Come First*.

16. Author's interview with Vasantha Daniel, April 11, 2003.

17. Author's interview with Ms. Dhas, July 22, 2003.

18. Author's interview with Rajan, July 9, 2003.

19. The literature on this is larger than one footnote. I draw my summary from historical works that investigate the social and political history of Kerala from multiple perspectives, such as Jeffrey, *Politics, Women and Well-Being*; Namboodiripad, *Kerala*; Menon, *Caste, Nationalism and Communalism*; and Sreekumar, *Scripting Lives*. I also draw from Franke and Chasin, *Kerala: Radical Reform as Development*; Heller, *The Labor of Development*; and Oomen, *Rethinking Development*, vols. 1 and 2.

20. Sreekumar, *Scripting Lives*.

21. Jeffrey, *Politics, Women and Well Being*; Franke and Chasin, *Kerala*.

22. Sreekumar, *Scripting Lives*.

23. There are of course many references for "The Empire Strikes Back." Mine is meant to purposefully recall a collection about the impact of postcolonial migration on race and racism in Great Britain during the 1970s in an evocation of what, from a South Asian worldview, is the Brown Atlantic Centre for Contemporary Cultural Studies, *The Empire Strikes Back: Race and Racism in 70s Britain*.

24. Opposition to employer sanctions, in particular, has become a key demand of immigrant rights movements, as these have limited consequences for those found guilty and have instead been employed by employers as a strike-breaking tool.

25. "Illegal" is a technical term and accurate within the realm of immigration law even though it is, as immigrant and human rights advocates point out, dehumanizing (Race Forward, "Drop the I-Word Campaign"). Here, I employ it in relation to both the law and the movements that employ it, explicitly. The most common replacement term for "illegal" is "undocumented." While I understand the shift, I follow the lead of other historians and opt instead for "unauthorized" as more accurate. Many immigrants in the United States without legal status are still, technically speaking, docu-

mented by virtue of lapsed papers and/or false documents (often employer produced, especially after passage of IRCA's employer sanctions provision).

26. The first page of congressional hearings opens with this quote by Senator Alan K. Simpson (R-WY): "Our present immigration laws reserve our very most favored top-drawer status for spouses of American citizens, and the U.S. system, based to a large degree on the principle of family reunification, certainly there can be no more important reunification than spouses, husband and wife." *"Immigration Marriage Fraud,"* 1 (U.S. Congressional hearing).

27. Ibid., 7.

28. Ibid., 4.

29. Ibid., 14.

30. Ibid., 42.

31. Ibid., 42–43.

32. Ibid., 43–44.

33. Bhattacharjee, "The Habit of Ex-Nomination" and "The Public/Private Mirage."

34. Luibheid, *Entry Denied*, 25.

*Epilogue*

1. Author's interview with Subhashini, August 11, 2004.

2. Athavale, *My Story*.

3. Chakravarti, *Rewriting History*.

4. Ramabai, *The High-Caste Hindu Woman*. See also Ramabai, *Pandita Ramabai's American Encounter*.

5. Author's interview with Subhashini, August 11, 2004.

# Bibliography

## Archival Sources

Kerala State Archives, Thiruvanathapuram, Kerala.
Rockefeller Foundation Archives, Rockefeller Archive Center, Sleepy Hollow, N.Y.
Schlesinger Library, Radcliffe Institute, Harvard University, Cambridge, Mass.
    Ida Sophia Scudder Papers

## Author Interviews

RECORDINGS AND TRANSCRIPTIONS OF THE FOLLOWING INTERVIEWS
ARE IN THE AUTHOR'S POSSESSION.

Susan George Arakal, July 17, 2003.
Vasantha Daniel, April 11, 2003.
Vasantha Daniel, September 19, 2003.
Vasantha Daniel, July 11, 2004.
Vasantha Daniel, August 21, 2004.
Ms. Dhas, July 22, 2003.
Suganthi J. Edwin, August 13, 2003.
Aleyamma Eapen, July 19, 2003.
Aleyamma James, October 15, 2003.
Aleyamma James, January 7, 2004.
Suwersh Khanna, August 12, 2003.
Satwant Malhotra, July 28, 2003.
Ani Mathew (pseudonym), November 10, 2003.
Mrs. Parmar, July 10, 2003.
Rajan (pseudonym), July 9, 2003.
Annie Samuels, November 12, 2003.
Subhashini (pseudonym), August 11, 2004.
Mrs. Thannickal, November 3, 2003.
Thankam Vellaringattu, June 24, 2003.

## Government Documents

"Hearings on HR 7700 to Amend the Immigration and Nationality Act, Part 1." *House Subcommittee No. 1 of the Committee on the Judiciary*, 88th Congress, 2nd Session.
"Immigration Marriage Fraud: Hearing before the Subcommittee on Immigration and Refugee Policy of the Committee on the Judiciary, United States Senate, Ninety-Ninth Congress, First Session, on Fraudulent Marriage and Finance

Arrangements to Obtain Permanent Resident Immigration Status."
Washington, D.C.: Government Printing Office, 1985.

*Loving v. Virginia*, 388 U.S. 1, 87 S. Ct. 1817, 18 L.Ed. 2d 1010, 1967 U.S.

Matter of Gutierrez in Visa Petition Proceedings a-17653997, 1967.

*Projected Supply, Demand, and Shortages of Registered Nurses: 2000–2020*.
Washington, D.C.: U.S. Department of Health and Human Services, 2002.

United States Department of Health, Education, and Welfare, Division of Nursing.
*Survey of Foreign Nurse Graduates*. Bethesda, Md.: Government Printing Office,
1976.

United States Department of Labor, Office of Policy and Planning and Research.
*The Negro Family: The Case for National Action*, by Daniel Patrick Moynihan.
Washington, D.C.: Government Printing Office, 1965.

*United States Information and Education Act of 1948*. January 27, 1948.

Varghese, Lillykutty K. *The Nursing Profession in India: A Manpower Study*.
Trivandrum, India: Bureau of Economics and Statistics, 1977.


*Books and Articles*

Abraham, Margaret. *Speaking the Unspeakable: Marital Violence among South
Asian Immigrants in the United States*. New Brunswick, N.J.: Rutgers University
Press, 2000.

Abraham, Meera. *Religion, Caste and Gender: Missionaries and Nursing History
in South India*. Bangalore, India: B I Publications, Pvt. Ltd., 1996.

Abramovitz, Mimi. *Regulating the Lives of Women: Social Welfare Policy from
Colonial Times to the Present*. Boston: South End Press, 1988.

Abrams, Sarah E. "Brilliance and Bureaucracy: Nursing and Changes in the
Rockefeller Foundation, 1915–1930." *Nursing History Review* 1 (1993): 119–37.

———. "Seeking Jurisdiction: A Sociological Perspective on Rockefeller Foundation
Activities in the 1920s." In *Nursing and the Politics of Welfare*, edited by Anne
Marie Rafferty, Jane Robinson, and Ruth Elkan. London: Routledge, 1997.

Abu-Lughod, Lila. *Veiled Sentiments: Honor and Poetry in a Bedouin Society*.
Berkeley: University of California Press, 1986.

Ahluwalia, Sanjam. *Reproductive Restraints: Birth Control in India, 1877–1947*.
Urbana: University of Illinois Press, 2008.

Alexander, M. Jacqui, and Chandra Talpade Mohanty. *Feminist Genealogies,
Colonial Legacies, Democratic Futures*. New York: Routledge, 1997.

Ambedkar, B. R. "Annihilation of Caste" (An Undelivered Speech, 1936).
In *Annihilation of Caste: The Annotated Critical Edition*, edited by S. Ananad,
with an introduction, "The Doctor and the Saint," by Arundhati Roy. New Delhi,
India: Navayana Publishing Pvt Ltd, 2014.

Amott, Teresa, and Julie Matthaei. *Race, Gender, and Work: A Multicultural
Economic History of Women in the United States*. Boston: South End Press, 1991.

ANA Nursing Information Bureau. *Facts about Nursing*. New York: American
Nurses Association, 1960.

Ansell, David A. *County: Life, Death, and Politics at Chicago's Public Hospital.* Chicago: Academy Chicago Publishers, 2011.

Arbeiter, Jean S. "The Facts about Foreign Nurses." *RN* 51, no. 9 (1988): 57–73.

Arnold, David. *Colonizing the Body: State Medicine and Epidemic Disease in Colonial India.* Berkeley: University of California Press, 1993.

Arnove, Robert F., ed. *Philanthropy and Cultural Imperialism: The Foundations at Home and Abroad.* Boston: G. K. Hall & Co., 1980.

Arora, Varun. "Nurses: India's Hot New Export." *India-West,* February 21, 2003.

Athavale, Parvati. *My Story: Autobiography of a Hindu Widow.* New Delhi, India: Reliance Publishing House, 1996.

Ayyar, L. K. Ananta Krishna. *Anthropology of Syrian Christians.* Ernakulam, India: Cochin Government Press, 1926.

Bachu, A. "Indian Nurses in the United States." *International Nursing Review* 20, no. 4 (1973): 114–16.

Bahadur, Gaiutra. *Coolie Woman: The Odyssey of Indenture.* Chicago: University of Chicago Press, 2014.

Balfour, Margaret, and Ruth Young. *The Work of Medical Women in India.* London: Oxford University Press, 1929.

Balsara, Moti. "The Role of Today's Nurse in Society." *Nursing Journal of India* 51, no. 8 (1960): 210–11.

Baly, Monica. *Florence Nightingale and the Nursing Legacy.* London: Croom Helm, 1986.

Bannerjee, Himani. "Projects of Hegemony: Towards a Critique of Subaltern Studies' 'Resolution of the Women's Question.'" *Economic and Political Weekly* 35, no. 11 (March 11–17, 2000): 902–20.

Bayley, Susan. *Saints, Goddesses, and Kings: Muslims and Christians in South Indian Society.* Cambridge: Cambridge University Press, 1989.

Behar, Ruth. *Translated Woman: Crossing the Border with Esperanza's Story.* Boston: Beacon, 1993.

Benjamin, Peter. "Knows about Patient Fear." *New York Times,* December 16, 1997.

Berman, Edward H. *The Influence of the Carnegie, Ford and Rockefeller Foundations on American Foreign Policy: The Ideology of Philanthropy.* Albany: State University of New York Press, 1983.

Bhattacharjee, Anannya. "The Habit of Ex-Nomination." In *Emerging Voices: South Asian American Women Redefine Self, Family, and Community,* edited by Sangeeta Gupta. Walnut Creek, CA: AltaMira Press, 1999.

———. "The Public/Private Mirage: Mapping Homes and Undomesticating Violence Work in the South Asian Immigrant Community." In *Feminist Genealogies, Colonial Legacies, Democratic Futures,* edited by M. Jacqui and Chandra Talpade Mohanty Alexander. New York: Routledge, 1997.

Bleakley, Ethel. *Meet the Indian Nurse.* London: Zenith Press, 1949.

Brannon, Robert L. *Intensifying Care: The Hospital Industry, Professionalization, and the Reorganization of the Nursing Labor Process.* Amityville, N.Y.: Baywood Publishing Company, Inc., 1994.

———. "Restructuring Hospital Nursing: Reversing the Trend toward a Professional Workforce." *International Journal of Health Services* 26, no. 4 (1996): 643–54.

Briggs, Laura. *Reproducing Empire: Race, Sex, Science and U.S. Imperialism in Puerto Rico.* Berkeley: University of California Press, 2002.

Broadhurst, Martha Jeanne. *Nurses from Abroad: Values in International Exchange of Persons.* New York: The American Nurses' Foundation, Inc., 1962.

Brockway, Nora. *A Larger Way for Women: Aspects of Christian Education for Girls in South India, 1712–1948.* Oxford: Oxford University Press, 1949.

Brown, E. Richard. "Public Health in Imperialism." *American Journal of Public Health* 66 (1976): 897–903.

———. "Rockefeller Medicine in China: Professionalism and Imperialism." In *Philanthropy and Cultural Imperialism: The Foundations at Home and Abroad,* edited by Robert F. Arnove. Boston: G. K. Hall & Co., 1980.

———. *Rockefeller Medicine Men: Medicine and Capitalism in America.* Berkeley: University of California Press, 1979.

Brown, Esther Lucile. *Nursing for the Future.* New York: Russell Sage Foundation, 1948.

Brush, Barbara L. "Exchangees or Employees? The Exchange Visitor Program and Foreign Nurse Immigration to the United States, 1945–1990." *Nursing History Review* 1 (1993): 171–80.

———. "Has Foreign Nurse Recruitment Impeded African American Access to Nursing Education and Practice?" *Nursing Outlook* 4 (1999): 175–80.

———. "The Rockefeller Agenda for American/Philippines Nursing Relations." *Western Journal of Nursing Research* 17, no. 5 (1995): 540–55.

Brush, Barbara L., and Anne E. Berger. "Sending for Nurses: Foreign Nurse Migration, 1965–2002." *Nursing and Health Policy Review* 1, no. 3 (2002): 103–15.

Brush, Barbara L., Joan E. Lynaugh, Geertje Boschma, Anne Marie Rafferty, Meryn Stuart, and Nancy J. Tomes. *Nurses of All Nations: A History of the International Council of Nurses, 1899–1999.* Philadelphia: Lippincott Williams & Wilkins, 1999.

Burton, Antoinette. *Burdens of History: British Feminists, Indian Women, and Imperial Culture, 1865–1915.* Chapel Hill: University of North Carolina Press, 1994.

Butalia, Urvashi. *The Other Side of Silence: Voices from the Partition of India.* Durham, N.C.: Duke University Press, 2000.

Carnegie, M. Elizabeth. *The Path We Tread: Blacks in Nursing Worldwide, 1854–1994.* 3rd ed. New York: National League for Nursing Press, 1995.

Carter, Marina, and Khal Torabully. *Coolitude: An Anthology of the Indian Labour Diaspora.* London: Anthem, 2002.

Centre for Contemporary Cultural Studies. *The Empire Strikes Back: Race and Racism in 70s Britain.* London: Hutchinson in association with the Centre for Contemporary Cultural Studies, University of Birmingham, 1982.

Chakravarti, Uma. *Gendering Caste through a Feminist Lens.* Calcutta, India: Stree, 2003.

———. *Rewriting History: The Life and Times of Pandita Ramabai.* Delhi, India: Kali for Women, 1998.

Chatterjee, Partha. *The Nation and Its Fragments: Colonial and Postcolonial Histories*. Princeton, N.J.: Princeton University Press, 1993.

——. "The Nationalist Resolution of the Woman Question." In *Recasting Women: Essays in Colonial History*, edited by Kumkum Sangari and Sudesh Vaid. New Delhi, India: Kali for Women, 1989.

Chaudhuri, Nupur, and Margaret Strobel, eds. *Western Women and Imperialism: Complicity and Resistance*. Bloomington: Indiana University Press, 1992.

Chen, Kaiyi. "Missionaries and the Early Development of Nursing in China." *Nursing History Review* 4 (1996): 129–49.

Cheng, Lucie. "Free, Indentured, Enslaved: Chinese Prostitutes in Nineteenth-Century America." In *Labor Immigration under Capitalism: Asian Workers in the United States before World War II*, edited by Lucie and Edna Bonacich Cheng. Berkeley: University of California Press, 1984.

Cherian, A. "Role of Nursing in India Today." *Nursing Journal of India* 67, no. 11 (1976): 258–59.

Choy, Catherine Ceniza. *Empire of Care: Nursing and Migration in Filipino American History*. Durham, N.C.: Duke University Press, 2003.

Clymer, Kenton J. *Protestant Missionaries in the Philippines, 1898–1916: An Inquiry into the American Colonial Mentality*. Urbana: University of Illinois Press, 1986.

Collins, Patricia Hill. *Black Feminist Thought: Knowledge, Consciousness and the Politics of Empowerment*. New York: Routledge, 1991.

Comaroff, Jean, and John Comaroff. *Of Revelation and Revolution: Christianity, Colonialism and Consciousness in South Africa*. Vol. 1. Chicago: University of Chicago Press, 1991.

Cox, Jeffrey. *Imperial Fault Lines: Christianity and Colonial Power in India, 1818–1940*. Stanford, Calif.: Stanford University Press, 2002.

Dall, Mrs. Caroline Healey. *The Life of Dr. Anandabai Joshee: A Kinswoman of the Pundita Ramabai*. Boston: Roberts Brothers, 1888.

Dalla Costa, Mariarosa, and Selma James. *The Power of Women and the Subversion of the Community*. London: Falling Wall Press, 1972.

Daniels, Roger. "United States Policy towards Asian Immigrants: Contemporary Developments in Historical Perspective." In *New American Destinies: A Reader in Contemporary Asian and Latino Immigration*, edited by Darrell Y. Hamamoto and Rodolfo D. Torres. New York: Routledge, 1997.

Dasgupta, Shamita Das. *Body Evidence: Intimate Violence against South Asian Women in America*. New Brunswick, N.J.: Rutgers University Press, 2007.

——. *A Patchwork Shawl: Chronicles of South Asian Women in America*. New Brunswick, N.J.: Rutgers University Press, 1998.

Dasgupta, Shamita Das, and Sayantani. "Women in Exile: Gender Relations in the Asian Indian Community in the U.S." In *Contours of the Heart: South Asians Map North America*, edited by Sunaina Maira and Rajini Srikanth. New York: Asian American Writers Workshop, 1996.

Davis, Angela. "Women and Capitalism: Dialectics of Oppression and Liberation." In *Marxism, Revolution, and Peace*, edited by Howard Parsons and John Sommerville. Amsterdam: B. R. Grüner, 1977.

———. *Women, Race & Class*. New York: Vintage, 1981.

Davitz, Lois J., Joel R. Davitz, and Yasuko Sameshima. "Foreign and American Nurses: Restrictions and Interactions." *Nursing Outlook* 24, no. 4 (1976): 237–42.

Dhillon, Gita L. "Study Programs for Foreign Nurses . . . Special Needs of Foreign Nurses." *Nursing Outlook* 24, no. 1 (1976): 43–44.

DiCiccio-Bloom, Barbara. "The Racial and Gendered Experiences of Immigrant Nurses from Kerala, India." *Journal of Transcultural Nursing* 15, no. 1 (2004): 26–33.

Dickens, Charles. *The Life and Adventures of Martin Chuzzlewit*. London: Chapman & Hall, 1844.

Dougal, Sonia. *The Nun Runners*. London: Hodder and Stoughton, 1971.

Dowling, Harry Filmore. *City Hospitals: The Undercare of the Underprivileged*. Cambridge, Mass.: Harvard University Press, 1982.

Dudas, Susan, and Mary Ann Dzik. "Working with the Foreign Nurse in the United States." *Journal of Nursing Education* 10, no. 1 (1971): 27–31.

Dvorak, Eileen McQuaid, and Mark H. Waymack. "Is It Ethical to Recruit Foreign Nurses?" *Nursing Outlook* 39, no. 3 (1991): 126–23.

Ehrenreich, Barbara. *Fear of Falling: The Inner Life of the Middle Class*. New York: Pantheon, 1989.

Ehrenreich, Barbara, and Deidre English. *Witches, Midwives and Nurses: A History of Women Healers*. New York: The Feminist Press of the City University of New York, 1973.

Espiritu, Yen Le. *Asian American Women and Men: Labor, Laws and Love*. Walnut Creek, CA: AltaMira Press, 2000.

Ettling, John. *The Germ of Laziness: Rockefeller Philanthropy and Public Health in the New South*. Cambridge, Mass.: Harvard University Press, 1981.

"Exchange for Education." *American Journal of Nursing* 58, no. 12 (1958): 1666–71.

Fanon, Frantz. *A Dying Colonialism*. New York: Grove Press, 1967, c1965.

Farley, John. *To Cast Out Disease: A History of the International Health Division of the Rockefeller Foundation (1913–1951)*. Oxford: Oxford University Press, 2004.

Federici, Silvia. *Caliban and the Witch: Women, the Body and Primitive Accumulation*. Brooklyn, N.Y.: Autonomedia, 2004.

Fitzgerald, Rosemary. "Making and Moulding the Nursing of the Indian Empire." In *Rhetoric and Reality: Gender and the Colonial Experience in South Asia*, edited by Avril A. Powell and Siobhan Lambert-Hurley. New Delhi, India: Oxford University Press, 2006.

———. "Rescue and Redemption: The Rise of Female Medical Missions in Colonial India During the Late Nineteenth and Early Twentieth Centuries." In *Nursing History and the Politics of Welfare*, edited by Anne Marie Rafferty, Jane Robinson, and Ruth Elkan. London: Routledge, 1997.

Flemming, Leslie A. "A New Humanity: American Missionaries' Ideals for Women in North India, 1870–1930." In *Western Women and Imperialism: Complicity and Resistance*, edited by Nupur and Margaret Strobel Chaudhuri. Bloomington: Indiana University Press, 1992.

Forbes, Geraldine. *Women in Colonial India: Essays on Politics, Medicine, and Historiography*. New Delhi, India: Chronicle Books, 2005.

Fosdick, Raymond B. *The Story of the Rockefeller Foundation*. New York: Harper & Brothers, 1952.

Franke, Richard W., and Barbara H. Chasin. *Kerala: Radical Reform as Development in an Indian State*. Oakland, Calif.: The Institute for Food Development and Policy, 1994.

Gamarnikow, Eva. "Sexual Division of Labour: The Case of Nursing." In *Feminism and Materialism: Women and Modes of Production*, edited by Annette Kuhn and AnnMarie Wolpe Kuhn. London: Routledge & Kegan Paul, 1978.

Gamble, Vanessa Northington. "Black Autonomy versus White Control: Black Hospitals and the Dilemmas of White Philanthropy, 1920–1940." *Minerva* 35 (1997): 247–67.

———. *Making a Place for Ourselves: The Black Hospital Movement 1920–1945*. Oxford: Oxford University Press, 1995.

Gauba, K. L. *Uncle Sham: The Strange Tale of a Civilization Run Amok*. Lahore, Pakistan: Time Publishing Co., Ltd., 1929.

George, Sheba Mariam. *When Women Come First: Gender and Class in Transnational Migration*. Berkeley: University of California Press, 2005.

Gibson-Graham, J. K. *The End of Capitalism (As We Knew It): A Feminist Critique of Political Economy; with a New Introduction*. Minneapolis: University of Minnesota Press, 2006.

Glazer, Nathan, and Daniel Patrick Moynihan. *Beyond the Melting Pot: The Negroes, Puerto Ricans, Jews, Italians and Irish of New York City*. Cambridge, Mass.: MIT Press, 1963.

Glenn, Evelyn Nakano. *Forced to Care: Coercion and Caregiving in America*. Cambridge, Mass.: Harvard University Press, 2010.

———. *Issei, Nisei, War Bride: Three Generations of Japanese American Women in Domestic Service*. Philadelphia: Temple University Press, 1986.

———. *Unequal Freedom: How Race and Gender Shaped American Citizenship and Labor*. Cambridge, Mass.: Harvard University Press, 2002.

Gluck, Sherna Berger, and Daphne Patai, eds. *Women's Words: The Feminist Practice of Oral History*. New York: Routledge, 1991.

Goldstein, Michael S., and Peter J. Donaldson. "Exporting Professionalism: A Case Study of Medical Education." *Journal of Health and Social Behaviour* 20 (1979): 322–37.

Gonzalez, Carolina. "Music Strikes Chord with Heart Patients." *New York Daily News*, December 10, 1997.

Gordon, Leonard A. "Wealth Equals Wisdom?" *Annals of the American Academy of Political and Social Science* 554 (1997): 104–16.

Gourlay, Jharna. *Florence Nightingale and the Health of the Raj*. Aldershot, UK: Ashgate, 2003.

Grele, Ronald J., ed. *Envelopes of Sound: Six Practitioners Discuss the Method, Theory and Practice of Oral Testimony*. Chicago: Precedent Publishing, Inc., 1975.

Grewal, Inderpal. *Home and Harem: Nation, Gender, Empire and the Cultures of Travel*. Durham, N.C.: Duke University Press, 1996.

Guevarra, Anna. *Marketing Dreams, Manufacturing Heroes: The Transnational Labor Brokering of Filipino Workers.* New Brunswick, NJ: Rutgers University Press, 2010.

Guglielmo, Jennifer. *Living the Revolution: Italian Women's Resistance and Radicalism in New York City, 1880–1945.* Chapel Hill: University of North Carolina Press, 2010.

Hall, D. C. "WHO's Contribution to Nursing Education in India." *Nursing Journal of India* 57, no. 1 (1966): 21–22.

Handlin, Oscar. *The Newcomers: Negroes and Puerto Ricans in a Changing Metropolis.* Cambridge, Mass.: Harvard University Press, 1959.

Haney-Lopez, Ian. *White by Law: The Legal Construction of Race.* New York: New York University Press, 1995.

Haniffa, Aziz. "U.S. Body to Set Up Qualifying Exam Center." *India Abroad* 32, no. 40 (July 5, 2002): 8.

Harnar, Ruth M. "Social Forces and Factors Influencing Nursing Education in India." *Nursing Journal of India* 67, no. 5 (1976): 54–56.

Harris, Cheryl. "Whiteness as Property." In *Critical Race Theory: The Key Writings that Formed the Movement*, edited by Kimberlé Crenshaw, Neil Gotanda, Gary Peller, and Kendall Thomas, 276–91. New York: The New Press, 1995.

Healey, Madeleine. "Regarded, Paid, and Housed as Menials: Nursing in Colonial India, 1900–1948." *South Asian History and Culture* 2, no. 1 (2011): 55–75.

———. "Seeds That May Have Been Planted May Take Root: International Aid Nurses and Projects of Professionalism in Postindependence India, 1947–65." *Nursing History Review* 16 (2008): 58–90.

Heideman, Eugene P. *From Mission to Church: The Reformed Church in America Mission to India.* Grand Rapids, Mich.: Wm. B. Eerdmans Publishing Co., 2001.

Heller, Patrick. *The Labor of Development: Workers and the Transformation of Capitalism in Kerala, India.* Ithaca, N.Y.: Cornell University Press, 1999.

Helweg, Arthur Wesley. *An Immigrant Success Story: East Indians in America.* Philadelphia: University of Pennsylvania Press, 1990.

Henning, Janet. "Nurses from Overseas." *Modern Healthcare* 3, no. 5 (1975): 21–28.

Herwitz, Adele, and Ellen Michelmore. "The CGFNS Story." *Nursing Outlook* 31, no. 2 (1983): 75.

Hill, Patricia R. *The World Their Household: The American Woman's Foreign Mission Movement and Cultural Transformation, 1870–1920.* Ann Arbor: University of Michigan Press, 1985.

Hine, Darlene Clark. *Black Women in White: Racial Conflict and Cooperation in the Nursing Profession, 1890–1950.* Bloomington: Indiana University Press, 1989.

———. "The Ethel Johns Report: Black Women in the Nursing Profession, 1925." *Journal of Negro History* 67, no. 3 (1982): 212–28.

———. "From Hospital to College: Black Nurse Leaders and the Rise of Collegiate Nursing Schools." *Journal of Negro Education* 51, no. 3 (1982): 222–37.

Hock, Ronald F., ed. *The Infancy Gospels of James and Thomas.* Santa Rosa, CA: Polebridge Press, 1995.

Hondagneu-Sotelo, Pierrette. *Gender and U.S. Immigration: Contemporary Trends.* Berkeley: University of California Press, 2003.

*Hookworm Infection in Foreign Countries.* Washington, D.C.: Rockefeller Sanitary Commission, 1911.

Hoskins, Mrs. Robert. *Clara A. Swain, M.D. First Medical Missionary to the Women of the Orient.* Boston: Woman's Foreign Missionary Society Methodist Episcopal Church, 1912.

INCITE! Women of Color Against Violence, ed. *The Revolution Will Not Be Funded: Beyond the Non-Profit Industrial Complex.* Cambridge, Mass.: South End Press, 2007.

Jacobsen, Mathew Frye. *Whiteness of a Different Color: European Immigrants and the Alchemy of Race.* Cambridge, Mass.: Harvard University Press, 1998.

Jaggi, O. P. *Medicine in India: Modern Period.* New Delhi, India: Oxford University Press, 2000.

James, P. J. *Global Funding and NGO Network: The True Mission.* Thrissur, India: New Spring Publication, 2004.

James, Selma. *Sex, Race and Class: The Perspective of Winning: A Selection of Writings 1952-2012.* Oakland, Calif.: PM Press, 2012.

Janssens, Angelique, ed. *The Rise and Decline of the Male Breadwinner Family?* Cambridge: Press Syndicate of the University of Cambridge, 1998.

Jayawardena, Kumari, *The White Woman's Other Burden: Western Women and South Asia during British Rule.* New York: Routledge, 1995.

Jeffery, Mary Pauline. *Ida S. Scudder of Vellore: The Life Story of Ida Sophia Scudder.* Mysore, India: Welsey Press, 1951.

Jeffery, Roger. *The Politics of Health in India.* Berkeley: University of California Press, 1988.

Jeffrey, Robin. *Politics, Women and Well-Being: How Kerala Became 'a Model.'* London: The Macmillan Press LTD, 1992.

Jha, Manoranjan. *Katherine Mayo and India.* New Delhi, India: People's Publishing House, 1971.

Johnson, Karen A. "Undaunted Courage and Faith: The Lives of Three Black Women in the West and Hawaii in the Early Nineteenth Century." *Journal of African American History* 91, no. 1 (2006): 4–22.

Jonas, Gerald. *The Circuit Riders: Rockefeller Money and the Rise of Modern Science.* New York: W. W. Norton, 1989.

Joshi, Sanjay. *Fractured Modernity: The Making of a Middle Class in Colonial North India.* Delhi, India: Oxford University Press, 2001.

———, ed. *The Middle Class in Colonial India.* New Delhi, India: Oxford University Press, 2010.

Jung, Moon-Ho. *Coolies and Cane: Race, Labor and Sugar in the Age of Emancipation.* Baltimore: Johns Hopkins University Press, 2006.

Kalisch, Beatrice J., Philip A. Kalisch, and Jacqueline Clinton. "Minority Nurses in the News." *Nursing Outlook* 21, no. 1 (1981): 49–54.

Kaplan, Amy. "Manifest Domesticity." *American Literature* 70, no. 3 (1998): 581–606.

Kaplan, Amy, and Donald E. Pease, eds. *Cultures of United States Imperialism.* Durham, N.C.: Duke University Press, 1993.

Kaur, Rajkumari Amrit. "Rajkumari Amrit Kaur: Address to the Skidmore Nursing College, New York." *Nursing Journal of India* 52, no. 6 (1961): 150–51, 166.

Kavadi, Shirish N. *The Rockefeller Foundation and Public Health in Colonial India, 1916–1945: A Narrative History.* Pune/Mumbai, India: Foundation for Research in Community Health, 1999.

Kent, Eliza F. "Tamil Bible Women and the Zenana Missions of Colonial South India." *History of Religions* 39, no.2 (November 1999): 117–49.

"Keralites in U.S. Honoured." *Times of India*, November 16, 2000.

Kessler-Harris, Alice. *Out to Work: A History of Wage-Earning Women in the United States.* New York: Oxford University Press, 1982.

Khanna, Suwersh K. *The History of Nursing in India from 1947–1989.* Cape Girardeau, Mo.: Nursing Honor Society of India: St. Francis Medical Center, Distributors, KMG Publications, 1991.

Kingma, Mireille. *Nurses on the Move: Migration and the Global Health Care Economy.* Ithaca, N.Y.: IRL Press, 2006.

Kinnlingray, David. "The Black Atlantic Missionary Movement and Africa, 1780s–1920s." *Journal of Religion in Africa* 33, no. 1 (2003): 1–30.

Kittredge, George A. *A Short History of the "Medical Women for India" Fund of Bombay.* Bombay, India: Education Society's Press, Byculla, 1889.

Kosambi, Meera. "Anandibai Joshee: Retrieving a Fragmented Feminist Image." *Economic and Political Weekly* 31, no. 49 (1996): 3189–97.

Koshy, Ninan. *Caste in the Kerala Churches.* Bangalore, India: The Christian Institute for the Study of Religion and Society, 1968.

Kovner, Christine, and Edward S. Salsberg. "The Health Care Workforce." In *Jonas and Kovner's Health Care Delivery in the United States*, edited by Anthony R. and Steven Jonas Kovner. New York: Springer Publishing Company, 1999.

Kumar, Anil. *Medicine and the Raj: British Medical Policy in India, 1835–1911.* Walnut Creek, Calif.: AltaMira Press, 1998.

Kumar, Radha. *The History of Doing: An Illustrated Account of Movements for Women's Rights and Feminism in India 1800–1990.* New Delhi, India: Kali for Women, 1993.

Kurien, Prema A. *Kaleidoscopic Ethnicity: International Migration and the Reconstruction of Community Identities in India.* New Brunswick, N.J.: Rutgers University Press, 2002.

Lal, Maneesha. "The Politics of Gender and Medicine in Colonial India: The Countess of Dufferin's Fund, 1885–1888." *Bulletin of the History of Medicine* 68 (1994): 26–66.

Lang, Seán. "Drop the Demon *Dai*: Maternal Mortality and the State in Colonial Madras, 1840–1875." *Social History of Medicine* 18, no. 3 (2005): 357–78.

Lee, Catherine. *Fictive Kinship: Family Reunification and the Meaning of Race and Nation in the American Imagination.* New York: Russell Sage Foundation, 2013.

Leonard-Spark, Philip, and Paramatma Saran. "The Indian Immigrant in America: A Demographic Profile." In *The New Ethnics: Asian Indians in the United States*, edited by Paramatma and Edwin Eames Saran. New York: Praeger, 1980.

Lewis, Oscar. *La Vida: A Puerto Rican Family in the Culture of Poverty: San Juan and New York*. New York: Random House, 1966.

Lipstiz, George. *Possessive Investment in Whiteness: How White People Profit from Identity Politics*. Philadelphia: Temple University Press, 1998.

Litsios, Socrates. "John Black Grant: A Public Health Giant." *Perspectives in Biology and Medicine* 54, no. 4 (2011): 532–49.

Liu, John. "The Contours of Asian Professional, Technical and Kindred Work Immigration, 1965–1988." *Sociological Perspectives* 35, no. 4 (1992): 673–704.

Lowe, J. *Medical Missions: Their Place and Power*. Edinburgh: Oliphant, Anderson & Ferrier, 1886.

Luibheid, Eithne. *Entry Denied: Controlling Sexuality at the Border*. Minneapolis: University of Minnesota Press, 2002.

Ma, Quisha. "The Peking Union Medical College and the Rockefeller Foundation's Medical Programs in China." In *Rockefeller Philanthropy and Modern Biomedicine: International Initiatives from World War I to the Cold War*, edited by William H. Schneider. Bloomington: Indian University Press, 2002.

Malcolm X. "The Ballot or the Bullet." In *Malcolm X Speaks: Selected Speeches and Statements*, edited by George Breitman. New York: Grove Press, 1990.

Mani, Lata. *Contentious Traditions: The Debate on Sati in Colonial India*. Berkeley: University of California Press, 1998.

Marks, Shula. *Divided Sisterhood: Race, Class and Gender in the South African Nursing Profession*. New York: St. Martin's Press, 1994.

Massey-Riddle, Estelle. "The Training and Placement of Negro Nurses." *Journal of Negro Education* 4, no. 1 (1935): 42–48.

Mathew, George. "Indian Nurses Abroad." *Nursing Journal of India* 65, no. 3 (1974): 69.

Mayo, Katherine. *The Isles of Fear: The Truth about the Philippines*. New York: Harcourt, Brace and Co., 1925.

———. *Mother India*. New York: Harcourt, Brace and Co., 1927.

Mazumdar, Sucheta. "What Happened to the Women? Chinese and Indian Male Migration to the United States in Global Perspective." In *Asian/Pacific Islander American Women: A Historical Anthology*, edited by Shirley Hune and Gail M. Nomura. New York: New York University Press, 2003.

McClintock, Anne. *Imperial Leather: Race, Gender, and Sexuality in the Colonial Conquest*. New York: Routledge, 1995.

"Medical Side of Mission Work." *New York Times*, May 1, 1900, 6.

Mejia, Alfonso, Helena Pizurki, and Erica Royston. *Physician and Nurse Migration: Analysis and Policy Implications: Report of a WHO Study*. Geneva, Switzerland: World Health Organization, 1979.

Melosh, Barbara. *"The Physician's Hand": Work Culture and Conflict in American Nursing*. Philadelphia: Temple University Press, 1982.

Melwani, Lavina. "Clocking in Past Midnight." *Little India*, July 31, 1998, 28.

Menon, Dilip M. *Caste, Nationalism and Communism in South India: Malabar, 1900-1948*. Cambridge: Cambridge University Press, 1994.

Metcalf, Thomas R. *Ideologies of the Raj*. Cambridge: Cambridge University Press, 1998.

Mies, Maria. *Patriarchy and Accumulation on a World Scale: Women in the International Division of Labour*. New Edition ed. London: Zed Books, 1998.

Miller, Helen S. *Mary Eliza Mahoney 1845-1926, America's First Black Professional Nurse: A Historical Perspective*. Atlanta, Ga.: Wright Publishing Co., Inc., 1986.

Minocha, Urmil. "South Asian Immigrants: Trends and Impacts on the Sending and Receiving Societies." In *Pacific Bridges: The New Immigration from Asia and the Pacific Islands*, edited by James T. and Benjamin V. Cariño Fawcett. Staten Island, N.Y.: Center for Migration Studies, 1987.

Misra, B. B. *The Indian Middle Classes: Their Growth in Modern Times*. London: Oxford University Press, 1961.

Mohanty, Chandra Talpade. *Feminism without Borders: Decolonizing Theory, Practicing Solidarity*. Durham, N.C.: Duke University Press, 2003.

Montgomery, Helen Barrett. *Western Women in Eastern Lands: An Outline Study of Fifty Years of Woman's Work in Foreign Missions*. New York: MacMillan Co., 1910.

*Monthly Labor Review* 128, no. 11 (November 2005).

Moon, Meenakshi, and Urmila Pawar. "We Made History, Too: Women in the Early Untouchable Liberation Movement." In *Gender and Caste: Issues in Indian Feminism*, edited by Rao Anupama. New Delhi, India: Kali for Women, 2003.

Moore, Terence F., and Earl A. Simendenger. *Managing the Nursing Shortage: A Guide to Recruitment and Retention*. Rockville, Md.: Aspen Publishers, 1989.

Nadkarni, Asha. *Eugenic Feminism: Reproductive Nationalism in the United States and India*. Minneapolis: University of Minnesota Press, 2014.

——. "World Menace: National Reproduction and Public Health in Katherine Mayo's Mother India." *American Quarterly* 60, no. 30 (2008): 805–27.

Nagpal, Narender. "From the Editor." *Nursing Journal of India* 79, no. 8 (1988): 1.

Nair, Sreelekha, and Madeleine Healey. *A Profession on the Margins: Status Issues in Indian Nursing*. Occasional Paper. New Delhi, India: Center for Women's Development Studies, 2006.

Namboodiripad, E. M. S. *Kerala: Yesterday, Today and Tomorrow*. Calcutta, India: National Book Agency Private Limited, 1967.

Nandy, Ashis, and Shiv Visvanathan. "Modern Medicine and Its Non-Modern Critics: A Study in Discourse." In *Dominating Knowledge: Development, Culture, and Resistance*, edited by Frederique Apffell and Stephen A. Marglin. Oxford: Clarendon Press, 1990.

Narula, Smita. *Broken People: Caste Violence against India's "Untouchables."* New York: Human Rights Watch, 1999.

Nayyar, Deepak. *Migration, Remittances and Capital Flows: The Indian Experience*. Delhi, India: Oxford University Press, 1994.

Ngai, Mae. *Impossible Subjects: Illegal Aliens and the Making of Modern America*. Princeton, N.J.: Princeton University Press, 2004.

Nielsen, Waldemar A. *The Big Foundations*. New York: Columbia University Press, 1972.

Nigam, Sanjay. *The Snake Charmer*. New York: William Morrow & Co., 1998.

Nightingale, Florence. *Notes on Nursing: What It Is and What It Is Not*. London: Harrison, 1860.

"Nurses on the Two Way Street." *American Journal of Nursing* 53, no. 6 (1953): 683–86.

"Nursing Practice Acts." *American Journal of Nursing* 74, no. 7 (1974): 1310–19.

Nutting, M. Adeladie, and Lavinia L. Dock. *A History of Nursing*. Bristol, UK: Thoemmes Press, 2000.

O'Hanlon, Rosalind. *Caste, Conflict and Ideology: Mahatma Jotirao Phule and Low Caste Protest in Nineteenth-Century Western India*. Cambridge: Cambridge University Press, 1985.

———. *A Comparison between Women and Men: Tarabai Shinde and the Critique of Gender Relations in Colonial India*. New Delhi, India: Oxford University Press, 1994.

Omi, Michael, and Howard Winant. *Racial Formation in the United States from the 1960s to the 1990s*. New York: Routledge, 1994.

Omvedt, Gail. *Understanding Caste: From Buddha to Ambedkar and Beyond*. 2nd ed. New Delhi, India: Orient BlackSwan Private Limited, 2012.

Ong, Paul, and Tania Azores. "The Migration and Incorporation of Filipino Nurses." In *The New Asian Immigration in Los Angeles and Global Restructuring*, edited by Paul Ong, Edna Bonacich, and Lucie Cheng. Philadelphia: Temple University Press, 1994.

Ong, Paul M., Edna Bonacich, and Lucie Cheng, eds. *The New Asian Immigration in Los Angeles and Global Restructuring*. Philadelphia: Temple University Press, 1994.

Oomen, M. A. *Rethinking Development: Kerala's Development Experience*. 2 vols. New Delhi: Concept Publishing, 1999.

Oomen, T. K. *Doctors and Nurses: A Study in Occupational Role Structures*. Delhi, India: MacMillan Company of India, Ltd., 1978.

Palumbo-Liu, David. *Asian/American: Historical Crossings of a Racial Frontier*. Palo Alto, Calif.: Stanford University Press, 1999.

Paranjape, Makarand, ed. *Sarojini Naidu: Selected Letters 1890s to 1940s*. New Delhi, India: Kali for Woman, 1996.

Parmar, Inderjeet. *Foundations of the American Century: The Ford, Carnegie and Rockefeller Foundations in the Rise of American Power*. New York: Columbia University Press, 2012.

Parrenas, Rhacel Salazar. *The Force of Domesticity: Filipina Migrants and Globalization*. New York: New York University Press, 2008.

———. *Servants of Globalization: Women, Migration and Domestic Work*. Stanford, Calif.: Stanford University Press, 2001.

Pathak, Sunil Madhava. *American Missionaries and Hinduism (A Study of Their Contacts from 1813 to 1910).* Delhi, India: Munshiram Manorhalal, 1967.

Pati, Biswamoy. "Historians and Historiography: Situating 1857." *Economic and Political Weekly* 42, no. 19 (2007): 1686–91.

Paul, Mr. Kurian. "Nursing in India and Its Possible Future Development." *Nursing Journal of India* 37, no. 3 (1945): 49–51.

Phule, Jotirao. "Memorial Addressed to the Education Commission 19 October 1882." In *Selected Writings of Jotirao Phule*, edited by G. P. Deshpande. Delhi, India: Leftword Books, 2002.

———. *Selected Writings of Jotirao Phule.* Edited by G. P. Deshpande. Delhi, India: Leftword Books, 2002.

Pietzman, Steven J. *A New and Untried Course: Women's Medical College and Medical College of Pennsylvania, 1850–1998.* New Brunswick, N.J.: Rutgers University Press, 2000.

Piper, Nicola, and Mina Roces, eds. *Wife or Worker? Asian Women and Migration.* Lanham, Md.: Rowman & Littlefield Publishers, Inc., 2003.

Portelli, Alessandro. *The Battle of Valle Giulia: Oral History and the Art of Dialogue.* Madison: University of Wisconsin Press, 1997.

———. *The Death of Luigi Trastulli, and Other Stories: Form and Meaning in Oral History.* Albany: State University of New York Press, 1991.

Portes, Alejandro. "Determinants of the Brain Drain." *International Migration Review* 10, no. 4 (1976): 489–508.

Portes, Alejandro, Luis E. Guarnizo, and Patricia Landolt. "The Study of Transnationalism: Pitfalls and Promises of an Emergent Research Field." *Ethnic and Racial Studies* 22, no. 2 (1999): 217–37.

Prakash, Gyan. *Another Reason: Science and the Imagination of Modern India.* Princeton, N.J.: Princeton University Press, 1999.

Prashad, Vijay. *The Darker Nations: A People's History of the Third World.* New York: The New Press, 2007.

———. *The Karma of Brown Folk.* Minneapolis: University of Minnesota Press, 2000.

"President's Address." *Nursing Journal of India* 37 (1946): 13–14, 27.

"Protecting Our Exchange Visitors and Nursing Practice." *American Journal of Nursing* 60, no. 5 (1960): 698.

Pruitt, Lisa Joy. *"A Looking-Glass for Ladies": American Protestant Women and the Orient in the Nineteenth Century.* Macon, Ga.: Mercer University Press, 2005.

Rafferty, Anne Marie, Jane Robinson, and Ruth Elkan, eds. *Nursing History and the Politics of Welfare.* London: Routledge, 1997.

Ragavachari, Ranjana. *Conflicts and Adjustments: Indian Nurses in an Urban Milieu.* Delhi, India: Academic Foundation, 1990.

Raghuram, Parvati. "Gendering Skilled Migratory Streams: Implications for Conceptualizations of Migration." *Asian Pacific Migration Journal* 9, no. 4 (2000): 429–57.

Raj, G. Ramachandran. "The Indian Nurse: A Socio-Economic Study." *Nursing Journal of India* 54, no. 2 (1963): 284–86.

Ramabai, Pandita. *The High-Caste Hindu Woman*. Philadelphia: Press of the
J. B. Rodgers Print Co., 1888.
———. *Pandita Ramabai's American Encounter: The Peoples of the United States*.
Trans. Meera Kosambi. Bloomington: Indiana University Press, 2003.
Ramana, Mridula. "Women Physicians as Vital Intermediaries in Colonial Bombay."
*Economic and Political Weekly* 43, no. 12–13 (2008): 71–78.
Ramasubban, Radhika. "Imperial Health Policy in British India, 1857–1900." In
*Disease, Medicine, and Empire*, edited by Roy and Milton Lewis MacLeod.
London: Routledge, 1988.
Rao, Anupama, ed. *Gender and Caste: Issues in Indian Feminism*. New Delhi,
India: Kali for Women, 2003.
Rayaprol, Aparna. *Negotiating Identities: Women in the Indian Diaspora*. Delhi,
India: Oxford University Press, 1997.
Reeves-Ellington, Barbara, Kathryn Kish Sklar, and Connie A. Shemo, eds.
*Competing Kingdoms: Women, Mission, Nation, and the American Protestant
Empire, 1812–1960*. Durham, N.C.: Duke University Press, 2010.
Reimers, David. *Still the Golden Door: The Third World Comes to America*. New
York: Columbia University Press, 1985.
Reverby, Susan. *Ordered to Care: The Dilemma of American Nursing, 1850–1945*.
Cambridge: Cambridge University Press, 1987.
Robb, Peter. "On the Rebellion of 1857: A Brief History of an Idea." *Economic and
Political Weekly* 42, no. 19 (2007): 1696–702.
*The Rockefeller Foundation Annual Report, 1912–1914*. New York: The Rockefeller
Foundation, 1915.
*Rockefeller Foundation Directory of Fellowships and Scholarships 1917–1970*. New
York: The Rockefeller Foundation, 1972.
Roediger, David. *Working toward Whiteness: How America's Immigrants Became
White: The Strange Journey from Ellis Island to the Suburbs*. New York: Basic
Books, 2005.
Rozario, Santi, and Geoffrey Samuels, eds. *Daughters of Hariti: Childbirth and
Female Healers in South and Southeast Asia*. London: Routledge, 2002.
Sangari, Kumkum, and Sudesh Vaid. *Recasting Women: Essays in Colonial History*.
New Delhi, India: Kali for Women, 1989.
Saran, Paramatma. *The Asian Indian Experience in the United States*. Cambridge,
Mass.: Schenkman, 1985.
Saran, Paramatma, and Edwin Eames, eds. *The New Ethnics: Asian Indians in the
United States*. New York: Praeger, 1980.
Sarkar, Sumit. *Modern India 1885–1947*. Delhi, India: MacMillan, 1983.
Sassen, Saskia. *The Mobility of Labor and Capital: A Study in International
Investment and Labor Flow*. Cambridge: Cambridge University Press, 1988.
Scherzer, Teresa. "The Race and Class of Women's Work." *Race, Gender & Class* 10,
no. 3 (2003): 23–41.
Schneider, William H. "The Men Who Followed Flexner: Richard Pearce, Alan
Gregg, and the Rockefeller Foundation Medical Divisions, 1919–1951." In

*Rockefeller Philanthropy and Modern Biomedicine: International Initiatives from World War I to the Cold War*, edited by William H. Schneider. Bloomington: Indiana University Press, 2002.

Scott, James C. *Domination and the Arts of Resistance: Hidden Transcripts*. New Haven, Conn.: Yale University Press, 1990.

Scott, Joan W. "Experience." In *Feminists Theorize the Political*, edited by Judith Butler and Joan Wallach Scott. New York: Routledge, 1992.

Semple, Rhoda Anne. *Missionary Women: Gender, Professionalism and the Victorian Idea of Christian Mission*. Suffolk, UK: The Boydell Press, 2003.

Shah, Nayan. *Contagious Divides: Epidemics and Race in San Francisco's Chinatown*. Berkeley: University of California Press, 2001.

Shanta, Mohan N. *Status of Nurses in India*. New Delhi, India: Uppal Publishing House, 1985.

Shaplen, Robert. *Toward the Well-Being of Mankind: Fifty Years of the Rockefeller Foundation*. Garden City, N.Y.: Doubleday & Company, Inc., 1964.

Shepherd, Verene. *Maharani's Misery: Narratives of Passage from India to the Caribbean*. Kingston, Jamaica: University of West Indies Press, 2002.

Singh, Maina Chawla. *Gender, Religion, and "Heathen Lands": American Missionary Women in South Asia (1860s–1940s)*. New York: Garland Publishing, Inc., 2000.

Sinha, Mrinalini. *Specters of Mother India: The Global Restructuring of an Empire*. Durham, N.C.: Duke University Press, 2006.

Snow, Jennifer C. *Protestant Missionaries, Asian Immigrants, and Ideologies of Race in America, 1850–1924*. New York: Routledge, 2007.

Sood, Mrs. Raj Kumari. "Nursing Services in India: An Urgent Need for Reorganisation in View of the Goal Health for All by 2000 A.D." *Nursing Journal of India* 79, no. 11 (1988): 288–91.

Sorrel, Lorraine. "Nurses Face Deportation." *off our backs* 11, no. 2 (1981): 7.

Spivak, Gayatri Chakravarti. "Diasporas Old and New: Women in the Transnational World." *Textual Practice* 10, no. 2 (1996): 245–69.

Sreekumar, Sharmila. *Scripting Lives: Narratives of 'Dominant Women' in Kerala*. Hyderabad, India: Orient BlackSwan, 2009.

Sreenivas, Mytheli. *Wives, Widows, Concubines: The Conjugal Family Ideal in Colonial India*. Bloomington: Indiana University Press, 2008.

Starr, Paul. *The Social Transformation of American Medicine: The Rise of a Sovereign Profession and the Making of a Vast Industry*. New York: Basic Books, 1982.

Stevens, Jacqueline. *Reproducing the State*. Princeton, N.J.: Princeton University Press, 1999.

Stevens, Rosemary. *In Sickness and in Wealth: American Hospitals in the Twentieth Century*. New York: Basic Books, 1989.

Stevens, Rosemary, Louis Wolf Goodman, and Stephen S. Mick. *The Alien Doctors: Foreign Medical Graduates in American Hospitals*. New York: John Wiley & Sons, 1978.

Swain, Clara A. *A Glimpse of India being a collection of extracts from the letters of Dr. Clara A. Swain, first medical missionary to India of the Woman's Foreign*

*Missionary Society of the Methodist Episcopal Church in America*. New York: J. Potts & Co., 1909.

Sweeney, Virginia K. "Working with Nurses from Overseas." *American Journal of Nursing* 73, no. 10 (1973): 1768–70.

Tarbell, Ida M. *The History of the Standard Oil Company Two Volumes in One*. New York: The Macmillan Company, 1933.

Thomas, Annamma, and T. M. *Kerala Immigrants in America: A Sociological Study of the St. Thomas Christians*. Cochin, India: Simon Printers and Publishers, 1984.

Tinker, Hugh. *A New System of Slavery: The Export of Indian Labour Overseas 1830–1920*. London: Hansib Publishing Limited, 1993.

Tooley, Sarah A. *The History of Nursing in the British Empire*. London: S. H. Bousfield, 1906.

Van Hollen, Cecilia. *Birth on the Threshold: Childbirth and Modernity in South India*. Berkeley: University of California Press, 2003.

Varde, Mohini, *Dr. Rakhmabai: An Odyssey*. New Delhi, India: Minerva Press, 2000.

Visvanathan, Susan. *The Christians of Kerala: History, Belief and Ritual among the Yakoba*. Madras, India: Oxford University Press, 1993.

Viswanathan, Gauri. *Masks of Conquest: Literary Study and British Rule in India*. New York: Columbia University Press, 1989.

———. *Outside the Fold: Conversion, Modernity, and Belief.* Princeton, N.J.: Princeton University Press, 1998.

Visweswaran, Kamala. *Fictions of Feminist Ethnography*. Minneapolis: University of Minnesota Press, 1994.

———. *Un/common Cultures: Racism and the Rearticulation of Cultural Difference.* Durham, N.C.: Duke University Press, 2010.

Wagner, Kim A. "The Marginal Mutiny: the New Historiography of the Indian Uprising of 1857." *History Compass* 9, no. 10 (2011): 760–66.

Walby, Sylvia. *Theorizing Patriarchy*. Oxford: Basil Blackwell, Inc., 1990.

Walsh, Judith E. *Domesticity in Colonial India: What Women Learned When Men Gave Them Advice*. Lanham, Md.: Rowman & Littlefield Publishers, Inc., 2004.

Webster, John C. B., and Ellen Low, eds. *The Church and Women in the Third World*. Philadelphia: The Westminster Press, 1985.

Weeks, Kathi. *The Problem with Work: Feminism, Marxism, Antiwork Politics, and Postwork Imaginaries*. Durham, N.C.: Duke University Press, 2011.

Whittaker, Elvi, and Virginia Olesen. "The Faces of Florence Nightingale: Functions of the Heroine Legend in an Occupational Sub-Culture." In *Anthropology and American Life*, edited by Joseph G. and Marcello Truzzi Jorgenson. Englewood Cliffs, N.J.: Prentice-Hall, Inc., 1974.

Wilkinson, A. *A Brief History of Nursing in India and Pakistan*. Delhi: Trained Nurses Association of India, 1958.

Williams, Raymond Brady. *Christian Pluralism in the United States: The Indian Immigrant Experience*. Cambridge: Cambridge University Press, 1996.

Williams, William Appleman. *The Tragedy of American Diplomacy.* 2nd revised and enlarged edition. New York: Dell Publishing Co, Inc., 1972.

Wilson, Dorothy Clarke. *Dr. Ida: The Story of Dr. Ida Scudder of Vellore.* New York: McGraw-Hill Book Company, Inc., 1959.

"Woman's Task to Uplift Woman." *New York Times,* April, 27, 1900.

Women of South Asian Descent Collective, ed. *Our Feet Walk the Sky: Women in the South Asian Diaspora.* San Francisco: Aunt Lute Books, 1993.

Xenos, Peter S., Robert W. Gardner, Herbert R. Berringer, and Michael J. Levin. "Asian Americans: Growth and Change in the 1970s." In *Pacific Bridges,* edited by James T. and Benjamin V. Cariño Fawcett. Staten Island, N.Y.: Center for Migration Studies, 1987.

Yergin, Daniel. *The Prize: The Epic Quest for Oil, Money and Power.* New York: Simon & Schuster, 1991.

Zinn, Howard. *A People's History of the United States 1492–Present.* New York: HarperCollins, 1999.


*Websites*

Geetha, V., and S. V. Rajadurai, eds. *Revolt: A Radical Weekly in Colonial Madras.* Chennai: Periyar Dravidar Kazhagam. http://www.thamizhagam.net /thamizhagam/elibrary/Kudiyarasu/Revolt.pdf (accessed April 27, 2014).

Moffett, Eileen F. 1995. "Betsey Stockton: Pioneer American Missionary." The Free Library (April 1). http://www.thefreelibrary.com/Betsey Stockton: pioneer American missionary.-a016921617 (accessed June 28, 2013).

Race Forward. "Drop the I-Word Campaign." https://www.raceforward.org/practice /tools/drop-i-word-campaign (accessed June 30, 2014).

Rockefeller Archive Center. "Featured Film: Unhooking the Hookworm." 1920. http://www.rockarch.org/feature/hookworm.php (accessed July 31, 2013).

Smith, Amanda. *An Autobiography.* http://docsouth.unc.edu/neh/smitham/smith .html (accessed June 28, 2013).

Stockton, Betsey. *Betsey Stockton's Journal (November 20, 1822–July 4, 1823).* http://www3.amherst.edu/~aardoc/Betsey_Stockton_Journal_1.html (accessed June 28, 2013).

U.S. Department of Health and Human Services, Health Resources and Service Administration, Bureau of Health Professions, National Center for Health Workforce Analysis. *Projected Supply, Demand, and Shortages of Registered Nurses: 2000–2020.* July 2002. http://www.ahcancal.org/research_data/staffing /documents/registered_nurse_supply_demand.pdf (accessed May 25, 2015).

# Index

Commission on Graduates of Foreign Nursing Schools (CGFNS), 162–64

CON-D. *See* College of Nursing at New Delhi

Corporate civilizing mission, 78–80

Corporate philanthropy, 108, 223 (n. 2), 225 (n. 16); as hidden hand, 78; imperatives, 146; in India, 15; public health and, 97; recipients, 74; RF pioneering, 9; secularized, 87; U.S., 108, 118; white, 89, 90

Corwin, Janet, 109, 123, 124

Countess of Dufferin's Fund, 70–71

Craig, Margaretta, 109

Crimean War, 50–52

CSTM (Calcutta School of Tropical Medicine), 82–84

Culture of poverty, 16, 206

Da Gama, Vasco, 120

*Dai* (birth attendant): as demon, 60–61; grandmothers and, 61; as oppressed class, 42–43

Dalits, 141, 209

Daniel, Vasantha, 18, 143, 178–80, 192–93

Degenerate matriliny, 122, 197, 199, 200

Desegregation, 11, 14, 141, 175

Devaprasad, Sunder, 19, 190

Diaspora of decolonization, 11

Dickens, Charles, 49

Dillard University nursing program, 111–12

Dirty work: of health care, 47; manual labor, 48; of nurses and nursing, 4, 63, 92, 149, 156, 165–66, 179, 236 (n. 52); stigmatization of, 52–53, 129

Dix, Dorothea, 55

Dock, Lavinia, 57

Domestic evangelism, 32

Dougal, Sonia, 240 (n. 5)

Eapen, Aleyamma, 19, 135–37, 140, 142; on African Americans, 179; on ER experiences, 181–82; pioneering techniques, 172–73

Education: GEB, 74, 89, 111; Indian nurse im/migrants, 147–50; JHU model, 74; Mutual Educational and Cultural Exchange Act, 145–46; RF and, 14–15; upward mobility and, 65, 134, 231 (n. 60). *See also* College of Nursing at New Delhi; Johns Hopkins University; Spelman Seminary; Vellore Christian Medical College; Women's Medical College, Philadelphia

*Empire of Care* (Choy), 9

Employer sanctions, 242 (n. 24)

*An Essay on Health* (Rama Varma), 120–21

Ettling, John, 79

Evangelism: in Christian civilizing mission, 23–24; domestic, 32; family and, 31; in feminizing Christian medical mission, 25; J. D. Rockefeller Sr. and, 69. *See also* Zenana evangelism

EVP. *See* Exchange visitor period

Exceptionalism: American, 6; model minority, 13–17

Exchange visitor period (EVP), 237 (n. 22); ANA and, 144–46, 149, 151, 154; Filipino nurses and, 151–54; Indian nurse im/migrants and, 144–47; racializing of in U.S., 150–54

Expatriation Act, 185

Family: bad, 16, 17; community and, 21, 63; division of labor, 7; evangelism and, 31; good, 106–7, 109, 206; income earners, 1; joint models of, 38–39, 122–23, 207, 209; maintaining, 2; marriage and ties to, 210; middle-class, 41; nuclear, 7, 16, 17, 185, 204; nurse, 5; reunification, 164, 185, 187, 193, 201–3. *See also* Brahmanical patriarchy; Heteropatriarchal family; Marriage

Farley, John, 97

Farrar, Cynthia, 48

Feminization: of Christian civilizing mission, 7–9; colonial medicine and, 47, 71; of missionary work, 29, 216 (n. 16); of wage labor, 17, 206

ICN. *See* International Council of Nurses

IHB. *See* International Health Board, in India

IHC. *See* International Health Commission

IHD. *See* International Health Division

IMFA. *See* Immigration Marriage Fraud Amendments

Im/migrant, 213 (n. 1); Asian, 7; Cold War, 14; Filipino, 9; occupational exchange, 160, 167; politics, 167; struggles of, 3. *See also* Indian nurse im/migrants

Immigration and immigrants: American success, 138; bourgeois, 17; Chinese nonquota, 156; Chinese quotas, 153; EVP and, 144–47; FGN, 155, 181; foreign nurse migrant, 20–21, 154; hookworm and, 79–80; Immigration Act of 1917, 152; Immigration Act of 1924, 151, 153, 185; Indian nurses, 5, 18, 172, 175, 177, 195, 197; male, 193; model minority exceptionalism and, 13–17; opening of, 183; outmigration, 199; post–World War II, 2; sponsoring, 187; successful India and, 2, 5–6, 13; third preference, 164; Third World, 17, 134, 144; upward mobility and, 31

Immigration and Nationality Act of 1965, 6, 152, 186. *See also* Hart-Celler Act of 1965

Immigration Marriage Fraud Amendments (IMFA), 201, 205–6

Immigration Reform and Control Act of 1986 (IRCA), 201

Imperialism, 2; Anglo-American capitalist, 3, 7, 9, 11, 14, 152; exclusions and hierarchies, 52; open door, 9, 77, 134. *See also* Anglo-American capitalist imperialism

IMS. *See* Indian Medical Service

India: Brahmanical patriarchy, 4–5; brain drain, 3, 14, 129–31; British colonization, 81–82; Christian civilizing mission in, 22–23; coloniza-tion and subordination, 47; corporate philanthropy in, 15; diaspora of decolonization, 11; first female doctor missionaries, 2; Hinduization of, 38; labor migration, 7; middle class, 15, 20, 36–40, 191; RF in, 83–85; rise of colonial nursing leadership, 53–58; social order, 45; successful immi-grants, 2, 5–6, 13. *See also* Kerala

Indian Medical Service (IMS), 80–81

Indian National Congress Party, 98–99

Indian nurse im/migrants, 12, 21, 137; after-dark economy and, 1; education of, and division of nursing labor, 147–50; EVP, 144–47; Kerala and, 119; politics and, 147; post-1965, 154–59; professionalization and, 148; racializing of, in United States, 150–54; settlement patterns, 15–16, 20; standardizing FGN, 160–64; study of, 190. *See also* Foreign nurse graduate

Indian nurses: acknowledgment and appreciation of, 179; African Americans and, 174–75, 178; as Christian converts, 63–64; Cold War and, 10; colonial nursing and, 4, 16, 43, 49, 64; commitment, 171; desegregation and, 11; diploma-based training, 107; good girl associated with, 58–66; immigra-tion, 5, 18, 172, 175, 177, 195, 197; Kerala nursing network, 15–16, 20–21, 119–28; mass transfer of, 3; open door nursing, 7–13, 109; professionalization, 11–12; promi-nence and promotion, 109, 171–72; prostitution associated with, 4; Protestant missionaries and, 4–5; racialization, 173–76; RF and, 124–26; stigmatization, 5–6, 47–48, 53; upward mobility, 2, 5, 11, 17, 171; from "women on the loose" to "women in the lead," 4–7, 66, 194, 206; workplace experiences, 174–75

Indian Rebellion of 1857, 23

Madras Presidency, 22, 25–26, 61, 81–82, 119, 123
Magnuson Act, 153
Mahoney, Mary Eliza, 55
Malcolm X, 214 (n. 23)
Male-out migration, 7
Malhotra, Satwant, 135, 170
Mandal Commission, 141
Mandeville, Martha, 32
Mani, Lata, 41
Manifest Destiny, 138
Marriage, 217 (n. 31); arranged, 184–85, 187; banned, 186; child, 27, 64, 94; family ties and, 210; fraud, 202–3, 205; good and bad, 202; green-card, 192; IMFA and, 201, 205–6; love, 184, 235 (n. 51); marriageability and, 4, 19, 63, 66; post–World War II boom, 146; professionalization and, 19; restrictions, 120; role of wife, 38; socially sanctioned, 183; social networks, 190
Mary Taber Schell Memorial Center for Women and Children, 43, 53–54; establishment, 34–35; nursing school, 58; recruiting for, 57
Matriliny, 121–22, 197–200
"Matter of Gutierrez," 154, 157
Mayo, Katherine, 8–9, 94, 100, 117; RF and, 95–98; on self-rule, 97
Mazumdar, Sucheta, 7
McCarran-Walter Act, 186–87
McKinley, William, 22, 23
Medicalization: of Christian civilizing mission, 7–9; of woman's work for woman, 35
Medical Women for India Fund, 72
Medicine: colonial, 47, 71; scientific, 73–78
*Meet the Indian Nurse* (Bleakley), 63
Megaw, J. W. D., 83
Meharry Medical College, 174–77
Middle class, 213 (n. 4), 218 (n. 42); colonization and, 36–39; family, 41; India, 15, 20, 36–40, 191; RF and, 99; woman question and, 42

Midwives, 60, 61, 62
Miller, Rita, 111
Minocha, Urmil, 138
Missionaries: ABCFM polices, 31; American Medical Missionary Society, 26; corporate civilizing mission, 78–80; feminization of missionary work, 29, 216 (n. 16); India first female doctor, 2; Nurses Missionary League, 57; Protestant, 4–5, 120; SIMMA, 57; upward mobility, 40; Woman's Foreign Missionary Society of the Methodist Episcopal Church, 2; Woman's Union Foreign Missionary Society, 26–27. *See also* Arcot Mission; Christian civilizing mission; Protestant medical missions; Women missionaries
Model minority, 3; exceptionalism, 13–17
*Modern Healthcare*, 157
Modi, Narendra, 188–89
Monopoly capitalism, 68–69
Montgomery, Helen Barrett, 27, 114
*Mother India* (Mayo), 8, 94–96, 98, 100
Multiculturalism, 15, 180
Mutual Educational and Cultural Exchange Act, 145–46

NACGN. *See* National Association of Colored Graduate Nurses
Nadkarni, Asha, 9, 96, 100
Nagpal, Narender, 131
Naicker, E. V. Ramaswami, 100
Naidu, Sarojini, 94–95, 117–18
Nairs, 121–23
Narielwala, Amita, 202–5
National Association for Supplying Female Medical Aid to the Women of India, 70
National Association of Colored Graduate Nurses (NACGN), 226 (n. 39); ANA and, 150, 155; headquarters, 89–90
National Council Licensure Exam (NCLEX), 163

National Nursing Council, 148

NCLEX. *See* National Council Licensure Exam

Nehru, Jawaharlal, 98, 117

Nelson, Alan C., 202

Neocolonialism, 11

*New York Sun*, 78

*New York Times*, 172

Nightingale, Florence, 6, 55, 65, 191, 224 (n. 7); Christian civilizing mission and, 101; colonial nursing and, 79; emphasis on training and sanitation, 50–51, 52, 79; Hospital nursing and, 62; nursing style, 62; with Sisters of Charity, 49

"Night of Three Knocks" story, 29–35, 60, 63–64

Noll, Anna Mary, 113

Nostalgic matriliny, 197

*Notes on Nursing* (Nightingale), 50

Nuclear family, 7, 16, 17, 185, 204

*The Nun Runners* (Dougal), 240 (n. 5)

Nun trade, 240 (n. 5)

Nurses and nursing: African American, 55–56, 88; during Civil War, 55, 79; colonization and training of, 49–53; dirty work of, 4, 63, 92, 149, 156, 165–66, 179, 236 (n. 52); family, 5; Filipino, 133, 151–52, 162; impoverished white women as, 52; Jane Crow, 87–93; mass transfer of, from India, 3; Nurses Missionary League, 57; Primary Nursing, 156–57; professionalization, 6; prototypes, 49; racialization and, 49–53; Red Cross, 103; registration, 57; in remaking Mother India, 100–117; RF and, 86; rise of India colonial leadership, 53–58; sanitary mission, 50; stigmatization, 4; Team Nursing, 155–56, 186; Third World, 158, 187; World War II shortage, 146, 149. *See also* Colonial nursing; Hospital nursing; Indian nurse im/migrants; Indian nurses; Licensed practical

nurses; Open door nursing; Registered nurses

*Nurses from Abroad; Values in International Exchange of Persons* (Broadhurst), 145–46

*Nursing Journal of India*, 55, 131

OBCs. *See* Other backward castes

Omi, Michael, 11

Ong, Paul, 152

Oomen, T. K., 138–39

Open door imperialism, 9, 77, 134

"Open Door Notes" (Hay), 77

Open door nursing, 7–13; colonial nursing and, 109; CON-D, 141; professionalization, 134; RF, 126

Open door philanthropy, 20

Orientalism, 7

Other backward castes (OBCs), 141

Other-ing, 194

Out-casting, 21

Outmigration, 199

*Outside the Fold* (Viswanathan), 63

Ozawa, Takao, 153

Packard, Sophia, 67, 69

Parmar, Inderjeet, 109

Patel, Sardar Vallabhai, 98

Peabody, Lucy, 114

Pechey-Phipson, Edith, 72, 224 (n. 9)

Peters, Lucy, 127

Philanthropy: as investment, 77–78; open door, 20, 77; of J. D. Rockefeller Sr., 9. *See also* Corporate philanthropy

Phule, Jotirao, 48–49, 142

Phule, Savithribai, 48–49

Picture brides, 184, 187

"Picture of Home Life in India" (I. S. Scudder), 35

Pitman, Vera K., 114–15, 123

Politics: im/migrant, 167; Indian nurse im/migrants and, 147

Poona Pact of 1932, 101

Poverty, 4, 16, 45, 70, 138, 206

"Poverty, Unemployment and Development Policy: A Case Study of Selected Issues with Reference to Kerala," 196

Primary Nursing, 156–57

Professionalization: Indian nurse im/migrants and, 148; Indian nurses and, 11–12; marriage and, 19; nurses and, 6; open door nursing and, 134; RF and, 14–15

Prostitution, 4, 185, 204

Protestant medical missions, 10, 20, 69, 70–71, 113–14; groundwork, 9; height of, 114; Indian nurses and, 4–5; secularization and, 70. *See also* Christian civilizing mission

Public health: AIIHPH, 83–85, 104–5, 107; corporate civilizing mission and, 78–80; corporate philanthropy and, 97; IHD and, 110; JHU program, 79; nursing, 129; shifting imperial formations and, 80–87; Vellore Christian Medical College, 115

Racialization: FNG, 177; of Indian nurse im/migrants, 150–54; of Indian nurses, 173–76; Jim Crow segregation, 68; nurses and nursing and, 49–53

Rai, Lala Lajpat, 84

Rajagopalachari, C., 98

Rajwade, Rani Laxmibai, 102–4

Rakhmabai, 64, 72, 103

Ramabai, Pandita, 209

Rama Varma, Ayilyam Thirunal, 120–21, 123

Ranipet Hospital, 25, 34, 53

Rao, Kasturi Sunder, 117

Rao, Tanjore Madhava, 121

Red Cross nursing, 103

Registered nurses (RNs), 1, 57, 160; certification of, 188; distinguishing from LPNs, 154–57; FGN, 157; rank of, 167; rise of, 148–49

Revenue Act of 1913, 75

Reverby, Susan, 146

RF. *See* Rockefeller Foundation

Richards, Linda, 55

RNs. *See* Registered nurses

Rockefeller, John D., Jr., 75, 76

Rockefeller, John D., Sr.: funding JHU, 73; funding Spelman Seminary, 67; monopoly capitalism and protestant evangelism, 69; philanthropic work, 9; scientific medicine and medicine men, 73–78; seeds of secularization and, 68–73; wealth, 12, 20, 68, 72, 79

Rockefeller Foundation (RF), 9, 143, 175; Christian civilizing mission and, 9–10; corporate philanthropy pioneered by, 9, 20, 77; expanding network, 198; fellowships, 108–9, 112, 116–17, 119, 125, 228 (n. 38); founding, 75–76; global biomedical system, 10, 110; IHD and, 110, 129; in India, 83–85; Indian nurses and, 124–26; Kerala investments, 128; mandate, 87; Mayo and, 95–98; medicine men on board, 74; middle-class nationalists and, 99; NACGN and, 89–90; nursing and, 86; open door nursing, 126; philanthropy as investment, 77–78; professionalization and ideologies of higher education and, 14–15; J. D. Rockefeller Jr. as president of, 75; standards, 105; Vellore Christian Medical College and, 113–16. *See also* International Health Division

Rockefeller Sanitary Commission for the Eradiation of Hookworm Disease (RSC), 78–80

"The Role of Today's Nurse in Society" (Balsara), 129

Rosenwald Fund, 89, 111, 226 (n. 39)

Rowlatt Act, 81

Roy, Rammohan, 37

RSC. *See* Rockefeller Sanitary Commission for the Eradiation of Hookworm Disease

Thoburn, Isabella, 26, 28, 32
Thoburn, James Mills, 56
Thomas, Mrs. D. W., 26, 32
Tilak, Bal Gangadhar, 98
TNAI. *See* Trained Nurses Association
  of India
*The Tragedy of American Diplomacy*
  (Williams), 9
Trained Nurses Association of India
  (TNAI), 19, 55, 117, 130; breaking race
  barriers, 57–58; conferences, 106
Tubman, Harriet, 55
Turner, Frederick Jackson, 77
Tydings-McDuffie Act of 1934, 152

Unclean caste, 47–48, 53, 235 (n. 52)
Underground economy, 202
UNICEF. *See* United Nations Children's
  Fund
United Nations, 181, 196
United Nations Children's Fund
  (UNICEF), 128
United States (U.S.): colonies, 22;
  corporate philanthropy, 108, 118; as
  imperial nation, 3; Kerala migration,
  135–42; Open Door policy, 77;
  racializing Indian nurse im/
  migrants, 150–54; university-based
  nursing, 107–8. *See also* Civil
  War, U.S.; Supreme Court, U.S.
United States Agency for International
  Development (USAID), 15, 110, 128
Upward mobility, 64, 88, 176, 221 (n.10);
  achieving, 131; availability, 140;
  colonial nursing, 8, 53, 65, 118;
  degrees of, 167; education and, 65,
  134, 231 (n. 60); immigration and, 31;
  Indian nurses, 2, 5, 11, 17, 171; limits,
  174; missionaries, 40; opportunities,
  33, 56; questions of, 19

Vellaringattu, Thankam, 5, 168–70, 192,
  194; career visibility, 3; maintaining
  family, 2; working as FNG, 1–2, 12
Vellaringattu, Tom, 1–2, 5, 194

Vellore Christian Medical College, 18,
  20, 143, 175; celebration pageant,
  43–48, 53, 58–60, 62–65, 92;
  development and public health, 115;
  education level, 128; graduates, 119,
  127, 231 (n.62); Masters program,
  117; "Night of Three Knocks" story,
  29–35, 60, 63–64; RF and, 113–16;
  Syrian Christian students, 123; at
  vanguard, 57; woman's work for
  woman and, 115
Victimhood, 205
Vidyaben, 64, 103
Vincent, George E., 97, 113
Viswanathan, Gauri, 63
*A Voice from the East to the Young*
  (Scudder, J.), 27
Voting Rights Act of 1965, 150

War Brides Act of 1945 (WBA), 185–86
Wealth: health and, 69–70; of J. D.
  Rockefeller Sr., 12, 20, 68, 72, 79
Welch, William, 74
Welfare queens, 16
*Western Women in Eastern Lands*
  (Montgomery), 27
White women in white, 51
WHO. *See* World Health Organization
Widow immolation (*sati*), 27–28, 37–38,
  41, 219 (n. 45)
Williams, Raymond Brady, 164, 190
Williams, William Appleman, 9, 77
Wilson, Woodrow, 76
Winant, Howard, 11
Witch craze, 221 (n. 21)
WMC. *See* Women's Medical College,
  Philadelphia
Woman question: civilizing mission in,
  28; for female medical missionaries,
  35, 37; Hinduization of India and,
  38; infant health and, 62; Kerala
  and, 121; meets woman's work for
  woman, 8, 20, 26–29; middle-class
  resolution, 42; nationalist resolution,
  41; public health and, 9